WATER GOVERNANCE AS CONNECTIVE CAPACITY

Water governance is becoming one of the most significant challenges of this century and our current technocratic and fragmented approaches are ill prepared to respond. This superbly organized book draws on a rich array of theory and applied research from Europe, North America and Australia. For anyone involved in the policy, management and governance of water, this book not only explains the most important challenges, but also provides valuable guidance on the effectiveness of water governance approaches.

Richard D. Margerum, University of Oregon, USA and author of *Beyond Consensus: Improving Collaborative Planning and Management*

Water Governance as
Connective Capacity

JURIAN EDELENBOS, NANNY BRESSERS and PETER SCHOLTEN
Erasmus University Rotterdam, The Netherlands

ASHGATE

Published by
Ashgate Publishing Limited
Wey Court East
Union Road
Farnham
Surrey, GU9 7PT
England

Ashgate Publishing Company
110 Cherry Street
Suite 3-1
Burlington, VT 05401-3818
USA

www.ashgate.com

British Library Cataloguing in Publication Data
Water governance as connective capacity.
  1. Water-supply--Management. 2. Flood control--Planning.
  3. Communication in water resources development.
  4. Public-private sector cooperation. 5. Interprofessional
  relations.
  I. Edelenbos, Jurian. II. Bressers, N. III. Scholten,
  Peter.
  711.8-dc23

The Library of Congress has cataloged the printed edition as follows:
Edelenbos, Jurian.
  Water governance as connective capacity / by J. Edelenbos, N. Bressers, and P. Scholten.
    p. cm.
  Includes bibliographical references and index.
  ISBN 978-1-4094-4746-7 (hardback) -- ISBN 978-1-4094-4747-4 (ebook) 1. Water-supply--Management. 2. Water resources development. 3. Communication in water resources development. 4. Flood control--Planning. I. Bressers, N. II. Scholten, Peter. III. Title.
  TD345.E34 2013
  333.91--dc23

2012030431

ISBN 9781409447467 (hbk)
ISBN 9781409447474 (ebk – PDF)
ISBN 9781409484806 (ebk – ePUB)

Printed and bound in Great Britain
by MPG PRINTGROUP

Contents

List of Figures

List of Tables

List of Contributors

Jacko van Ast joined the Centre for Environmental Studies (ESM) at Erasmus University Rotterdam, the Netherlands, after his graduating in Law at Erasmus University Rotterdam. He currently teaches "Administrative Law" at Public Administration and "Environmental science" at the same university. He is responsible for the pre-master for Public Administration and the Infrastructure Specialization of the Master on Urban Development. His research focuses on institutional and legal aspects of international water management and sustainable development.

Denie Augustijn is Associate Professor at the Department of Water Engineering and Management of the University of Twente, the Netherlands. He has an interest in topics related to water management varying from a better understanding of physical, chemical and ecological processes in water systems to application of this knowledge in policy processes.

Mansee Bal is pursuing her PhD research on 'Sustainability of Urban Lake Systems in India: Towards a Governance Approach' at Public Administration, Erasmus University, the Netherlands, with funding from the Institute for Housing and Urban Development Studies. Her research takes a diagnostic approach towards understanding the social-ecological values and dynamics of urban lake systems management and applies the social-ecological systems framework developed by Professor Elinor Ostrom.

Geertje Bekebrede is Assistant Professor at the Faculty of Technology, Policy and Management of Delft University of Technology, the Netherlands. In 2010, she finished her PhD research about the use of serious gaming in the understanding of complex infrastructure projects. Her research topic is the use of gaming in education and policy making, especially related to complex decision making processes. In addition to her position at the university, she works part-time at Tygron Serious Gaming as game designer. She is Chair of the board of the Dutch Simulation and Gaming Association (SAGANET).

Yvette Bettini is a PhD Candidate at Monash University, Australia. Her background in resource management, planning and experience in community engagement and policy making has led to her interest in the interface between western society's sustainable use and management of natural resources. Her PhD research is examining how adaptive capacity in urban water institutions can help decision-makers to map and strategize routes toward a more sustainable urban water management.

Cheryl de Boer is Coordinator of the Twente Water Centre at the University of Twente, the Netherlands. She has a Master's Degree in Engineering and Public Policy from McMaster University, Canada and is currently undertaking her PhD in Governance and Sustainability. She has worked in academia, industry and the public sector. She has recently co-authored a book on the implementation of stream restoration projects in the Netherlands.

Jan Jaap Bouma is Professor at the Social Sciences Faculty of Erasmus University Rotterdam and Associate Professor at the section Economics and Infrastructure at the Faculty Technology, Policy and Management of the Technical University Delft, the Netherlands. He publishes on the area of environmental valuation in relation to sustainability and corporate social responsibility. His main attention goes to valuation and the management of natural resources in relation to spatial development.

Nanny Bressers is Post-doctoral Researcher at the Department of Public Administration at Erasmus University Rotterdam, the Netherlands. She completed her PhD on the evaluation of complex knowledge and innovation programmes in 2011. Research topics she works on include learning and systemic evaluation, water governance, and knowledge and innovations developing multi-actor programmes and projects.

Rebekah Brown is Director of the Urban Water Governance Programme and Centre for Water Sensitive Cities at Monash University, Melbourne. As a social scientist and civil engineer, Rebekah's research has developed frameworks for benchmarking sustainable urban water management and future trajectories for policy-makers and strategists. She has been awarded national industry and government awards in recognition of her contribution to advancing sustainable futures.

Marcela Brugnach is Assistant Professor at the University of Twente, the Netherlands. She has an interdisciplinary background that combines social sciences, ecology, engineering and modelling. She specializes in collective decision-making processes and has written extensively on the themes of uncertainty, ambiguity and decision making in water management.

Arwin van Buuren is Associate Professor at the Department of Public Administration, Erasmus University Rotterdam, the Netherlands. His research deals with the topic of water governance in general and more specifically with the governance of knowledge and innovation in complex water governance processes, synchronization issues between water governance, climate adaptation and spatial planning, and implementation issues with regard to adaptive and integrated management approaches in the field of water governance.

Miriam Cuppen was born in 1982 in Eindhoven, the Netherlands. After a year studying civil Engineering at the Technical University Delft, the Netherlands she switched to studying Political Science at the University of Leiden, the Netherlands, receiving her MA in June 2006. Between December 2006 and December 2011, she worked as a PhD researcher at the Technical University Delft, the Netherlands.

Ytsen Deelstra is Management Consultant at DHV since 2001 and has wide experience as a process manager and policy analyst within the areas of infrastructure and water management. He is currently working part-time on his PhD-thesis about complexity leadership in the Deltaprogram. He is currently associated with the Dutch Water Governance Centre as secretary of a working group chaired by Professor Geert Teisman that develops an assessment method for governance capacity regarding water management.

Art Dewulf received his PhD in 2006 from the University of Leuven, Belgium, with a dissertation on *issue framing* in multi-actor contexts. After a year of post-doctoral research at Leuven, he started working as Assistant Professor at the Public Administration and Policy Group (Wageningen University, the Netherlands). Art is, or has been, involved in research projects on river basin management, adaptive water management and climate adaptation governance. He has published various articles on topics like framing theory, collaborative governance, dealing with uncertainties and cross-disciplinary research.

Jurian Edelenbos is Professor of Public Administration, in the field of Water Governance, at the Department of Public Administration (Faculty of Social Sciences) of Erasmus University Rotterdam, the Netherlands. He focuses on processes of water governance through the lens of complexity (self-organization, coevolution, and complexity management). In his research he pays special attention to citizen participation (self-governance), the role and meaning of trust and control in inter-organizational cooperation, boundary spanning leadership, and institutional evolution in democracy.

Josee van Eijndhoven is Emeritus Professor in Sustainability Management at Erasmus University Rotterdam. From 1991-2001, she was Director of the Rathenau Institute for Technology Assessment. She is a member of the Dutch National UNESCO Committee. In this capacity, she organizes meetings to broaden the perspectives of water professionals and connect them to policy makers. Topics include: law, governance, disaster management, economics and ground water governance.

Megan Farrelly is Senior Research Fellow with the Centre for Water Sensitive Cities based at Monash University. She is currently involved in a large number of research projects within the Centre that focus on exploring complex governance mechanisms to support a transition towards sustainable urban water management.

Niki Frantzeskaki completed her PhD in 2011 at Delft University of Technology, the Netherlands, on the subject of "Dynamics of societal transitions: Driving forces and feedback loops". Since April 2010, she has been working with the Dutch Research Institute for Transitions (DRIFT), Erasmus University Rotterdam. From November 2011 until June 2012 Niki worked as visiting scholar with Monash University Melbourne at the Center of Water Sensitive Cities, Australia. Her research interests include policy dynamics, social-ecological systems governance, and sustainability transitions.

Helen Ingram is Research Fellow at the Southwest Center at the University of Arizona and is Professor Emeritus at the University of California, Irvine and the University of Arizona. She is a member of the Executive Committee of the Rosenberg International Forum on Water Policy. She has written widely on public policy, the environment and water resources, particularly emphasizing the processes of knowledge creation.

Sirkku Juhola has a PhD in Development Studies from the University of East Anglia, UK. Her most recent projects have focused on adaptation to climate change in both the developed and developing countries. She is the deputy chief scientist of the Nordic Centre for Excellence for Nordic Strategic Adaptation Research (NORD-STAR), and she is also a member of the Finnish Climate Science Panel that advises the Finnish Government on climate policy.

Carina Keskitalo is Professor of Political Science at Department of Geography and Economic History, Umeå University, Sweden. She has published widely on multi-level governance and adaptation to climate change in amongst other forest and water systems, within national and international projects. She led the Swedish Research Agency-funded project "Organising Adaptation to Climate Change in Europe" (EUR-ADAPT), within which the chapter published in this book was produced.

Erik-Hans Klijn is Professor at the Department of Public Administration at Erasmus University Rotterdam and Visiting Professor at the University of Birmingham (School of Government and Society), UK. His research and teaching activities focus on complex decision-making, network management, branding and the impact of media on complex decision-making. He has published extensively in international journals and is author together with Joop Koppenjan of the book *Managing Uncertainties in Networks* (2004, Routledge).

Maxim Knepflé is Co-founder and Director of R&D at Tygron Serious Gaming (www.tygron.nl) in The Hague, the Netherlands. He studied Computer Sciences at The Delft University of Technology (TUD) and in 2005 he was one of the co-founders of the TUD start-up Tygron. At the moment the company focuses on the water sector, where it has delivered several (international) serious games, ranging from urban development issues to big regional challenges with multiple parties.

Gail Krantzberg is Professor and Director of the Arcelor Mittal Dofasco Centre for Engineering and Public Policy at McMaster University. She completed her PhD at the University of Toronto, Canada, on contaminants in freshwaters. She was previously Senior Policy Advisor on Great Lakes at the Ontario Ministry of Environment and Director of the Great Lakes Office of the International Joint Commission, She has authored more than 100 scientific and policy articles on ecosystem quality and sustainability.

Stefan Kuks is Professor of Water Policy Implementation and Innovation at the University of Twente (School of Management and Governance). He specializes in water governance and institutional change. Stefan Kuks is also 'watergraaf' (chairman) at the 'Waterschap Regge en Dinkel', one of the 25 regional water authorities in the Netherlands. In addition to this, he is executive committee member at the Unie van Waterschappen (Association of Regional Water Authorities) in The Hague, the Netherlands.

Corniel van Leeuwen is junior researcher and PhD researcher at the Department of Public Administration (Faculty of Social Sciences) at the Erasmus University Rotterdam, The Netherlands. In his research he focuses on the effectiveness of methods, instruments and strategies used by practitioners to connect time spans in complex decision making processes related to climate adaptation and the field of water governance. His specialties are related to subjects such as the learning evaluation, project, process and programme management all related to the field of water governance.

Derk Loorbach is Associate Professor and Director of the Dutch Research Institute for Transitions (DRIFT), Erasmus University Rotterdam, the Netherlands. He pioneered the transition management approach for which he received his PhD in 2007. He works on developing theory and practice of transitions in various areas such as social sustainability, energy transition, area-based transitions and new business strategies.

Igor Mayer is Senior Associate Professor in the faculty of Technology, Policy and Management (TPM) at Delft University of Technology, the Netherlands. He is also the director of CPS, the TU-Delft Centre for Serious Gaming (www. seriousgaming.tudelft.nl). His main subjects of interest are concerned with the development, use and evaluation of interactive and participatory methods for policy analysis and policy development in general, and gaming-simulation/serious games/virtual worlds in particular.

Ingmar van Meerkerk graduated cum laude and is now a PhD student, Department of Public Administration, Erasmus University Rotterdam, the Netherlands. His PhD research is actualized in cooperation with TNO Innovation and Environment. His research interests include complexity management, boundary spanning, legitimacy of governance networks, citizen participation and institutional innovations. Besides his research activities, he provides lectures in the Master course Complexity Management at the Erasmus University Rotterdam.

Joanna Pardoe is Researcher at the Flood Hazard Research Centre, Middlesex University (UK). Her work focuses on the social and economic aspects of flood risk management, with a particular interest in the role of spatial planning and participatory approaches to flood risk management. Most recently, Joanna has been involved in projects that assess the social justice implications of economic instruments and policy shifts. She is also involved in update the FHRC 'Multi-coloured Manual' of appraisal techniques.

Jeroen Rijke is a joint PhD candidate at TU Delft, the Netherlands/Monash University, Australia. With a background in civil/environmental engineering and policy science, his work focuses primarily on the interface between technology and governance. His research studies how multi-level governance arrangements enable adaptive and integrated approaches to water management.

Peter Scholten has worked as a researcher in water governance at the Department for Sustainable Management of Resources, Radboud University Nijmegen and at the Department of Public Administration, Erasmus University Rotterdam. In 2011, he worked as a post-doctoral researcher at the Department of Social & Economic Geography, University of Umeå, Sweden, on the role of water related industry in climate adaptation policy. He is a member of the Earth System Governance research fellow network.

Katrien Termeer is Chair of the Public Administration and Policy Group at Wageningen University, the Netherlands. Her research focuses on processes of societal innovation, public leadership, new modes of governance and reflective action research. Her main fields of interests are adaptation to climate change, sustainable agriculture, food security and rural areas.

Simon Verduijn has a background in Public Administration and Organizational Science. In 2009 he received his Master of Science degree with honours, and since January 2010 he has been working on his doctorate research at the Radboud University Nijmegen, Institute for Management Research. His research is financed by Nieuw Land museum+archive+study centre in Lelystad. Verduijn's research focuses on gaining insight into strategies for policy change from an agency perspective, while taking into account the institutional, political and societal context as well.

Joanne Vinke-De Kruijf is PhD candidate at the Department of Water Engineering and Management and at the Twente Centre for Studies in Technology and Sustainable Development, at the University of Twente. She is especially interested in the human aspects of water management. For her PhD research on the effectiveness of Dutch-funded water projects she resided three years in Romania. Central in her research is the dynamic interaction between actors and contextual factors including governance structures.

Jeroen Warmerdam is co-founder and currently Director at Tygron Serious Gaming (www.tygron.nl), The Hague, The Netherlands. He studied Computer Sciences at Delft University of Technology (TUD) and in 2005 he was one of the co-founders of the TUD start-up Tygron. After starting with a very diverse set of domains, the company currently focuses on the Water sector, where it has delivered several (international) serious games, ranging from urban development issues to big regional challenges with multiple parties.

Jeroen Warner has an MSc in International Relations and a PhD in Disaster Studies. He teaches, trains and publishes on domestic and transboundary water governance, politics, conflict and participation, especially on floods. He has published five books and some 30 peer-reviewed articles. In 2010 he worked with Erasmus University's Public Administration Group to prepare an international book publication, 'Making Space for the River' (co-editors Arwin van Buuren and Jurian Edelenbos, which has been published in 2012 with IWA Press). Currently he is Assistant Professor with Wageningen University's Disaster Studies group.

Lisa Westerhoff is engaged in a doctorate degree programme at the Institute for Resources, Environment and Sustainability at the University of British Columbia, Canada. Prior to her current position, Lisa contributed to the EUR-ADAPT project on multi-level governance in climate change adaptation out of Umeå University in Sweden. Lisa has published on climate change adaptation both in developed and developing nations.

Qiqi Zhou finished her MSc in Environmental Management at Wageningen University. Now she is working as a PhD researcher at Technology University of Delft, faculty TPM. In her PhD research the main subject is concerned with the development and use interactive and participatory methods for policy analysis and decision making in different political cultures, such as in China and the Netherlands. The research interest is particularly on using advanced communication tool such as gaming-simulation and visualization to facilitate the interactive process.

Acknowledgements

This book is one of the results of the colloquium Water Governance of the Netherlands Institute of Government (NIG). The editors would like to thank the NIG for both the opportunity of starting the colloquium and the (financial) support in writing this volume.

Chapter 1

Introduction: Conceptualizing Connective Capacity in Water Governance

Jurian Edelenbos, Nanny Bressers and Peter Scholten

Water Issues and the Need for Water Governance

Water is an important source for living. It is expected that due to interplay of climate change, population growth and industrialization, fresh water will become one of the scarcest resources for humans, societies, and ecosystems. In several areas of the world, for example, the state of California in the US and southern parts of Australia, this is already visible. Water shortage affects not only social human conditions, but also has an economic impact, for example in the agricultural domain. Water has social, economic, and environmental aspects. A country is said to experience 'water stress' when annual water supplies drop below 1,700 cubic meters per person. It is argued that a third of the world's population nowadays lives in water-stressed countries. By 2025, this is expected to rise to two-thirds (Edelenbos and Teisman 2011, IPCC-WGII 2007).

However, not only water shortage is a problem. In almost all delta areas in the world also the surplus of water causes problems. Three-quarters of the world population lives in deltas and runs the risk of severe flooding due to climate change. This will occur by, for example, heavy peak rainfalls and extreme weather conditions (IPCC-WGII 2007), such as in Louisiana (2005), Great Britain (2007), Romania in 2010, and recently the Queensland flood in Australia (2010-2011) and the floods in Thailand (2011). In numerous countries all over the world, defense strategies, such as constructing dams, dykes and levees, are employed. At the same time many countries develop adaptive approaches in trying to face water surplus by providing more room for the rivers. These room for the river programs are being developed to provide space for the rivers that are often been enclosed by urban areas (Warner et al. 2012). In practice a combination of resistance (defensive) and resilience (adaptive) strategies are employed in water governance processes.

At the same time countries all over the world, especially the developing countries, face problems of poor water quality, for example, due to water pollution by industries. But also in developed countries these issues remain high on the political agenda. The Water Framework Directive of the European Union

(Directive 2000/60/EC[1]), for instance, urges the countries of the European Union to come up with policies to (further) improve the quality of drinking water by explicitly providing guidelines on how to involve stakeholders in this process.

It is argued that governments should take drastic action to address the problems of water pollution, water shortage/supply and water surplus (for instance, Edelenbos and Teisman 2011). Numerous methods and technologies for solving water problems seem to be at hand, but at the same time the capacity (for example: skills, experience, financial resources, etc.) to implement these methods and technologies seems to be lacking. Some argue that the current 'water crisis' is not caused by a lack of water technology, but rather by a failure in water governance (UNESCO 2006). The explanation for this is that water issues cannot be solved by new water technologies in a top-down, hierarchical manner, but need to be addressed and approached through a bottom up, horizontal and multi-stakeholder way of working. This is what is meant by the shift from a government approach to a governance approach (Kooiman 1993, 2003). Water can be considered a complex and interconnected system, which touches upon other domains and fields like agriculture, economic development, social development, ecology, health, etc. Water is of interest to many stakeholders, industries, municipalities, farmers, recreational sector, environmental organizations and others, who all approach the problem and the possible solutions differently (Leach and Pelkey 2001, Kuks 2004). Consistent with the global rise of (formal and informal) networks (Castells 2000), water is a governance challenge, which requires certain capacities to solve water problems in an effective, efficient and legitimate way (Edelenbos et al. 2010).

Due to the complex nature of water systems, a water governance approach is needed in which different values, interests and uses of water are interconnected so that water policy and measurements are developed and implemented with the support of different stakeholder groups. However, effective and legitimate water governance approaches are not easy to develop because of the wicked nature of the problem due to conflicting values and interests. This means that the solution can only be found beyond the boundaries of one layer and segment of government and even often beyond the boundaries of government as a whole. It requires delicate ways of governing multi-actor processes, which we call *water governance* in this book. As in the case with governance in general (Kickert et al. 1997) and also in the case of water governance, there has been a general shift from an emphasis on state provision to private provision based on market principles and more recently a multi-stakeholder approach in water governance. We will come back to this core concept in this introduction and the book itself.

Oftentimes the water governance capacity to solve water problems is insufficient due to the existing institutional fragmentation of responsibilities in this field. Water has many aspects, which are often handled by different organizations and institutions and these themselves are often bound by geographical and

---

1   See http://ec.europa.eu/environment/water/water-framework/index_en.html for more information and the document.

functional jurisdictions (Sabatier et al. 2005). In many cases there are different institutions with different and conflicting interests concerning water, like water safety, water quality or water shortage (Leach and Pelkey 2001, Lubell and Lippert 2011, Sabatier et al. 2005). But water also touches the issues of climate change, spatial planning and development. In this perspective spatial quality and integrated planning are often-mentioned goals and ambitions (Edelenbos 2010, Van Schie 2010). Achieving cooperation, joint responsibility and integration in such fragmented water governance systems is a core problem (Edelenbos and Teisman 2011). The water system is complex and interconnected of nature, but at the same time the governmental institutions and processes are fragmented and not capable of developing and implementing integrated and interconnected visions, plans, projects and programs. Therefore, dealing with water systems seems to become more and more a compounded problem. If a problem becomes more compounded, the interdependency with adjoining policy fields will grow, the amount of actors (uses and users) involved often tends to increase and the amount of frames, goals and ways of working easily multiplies. Within this kaleidoscopic environment the *capacity* to *connect* to other domains, levels, scales, organizations and actors becomes a very important aspect of water governance. The importance of connective capacity is also stressed in holistic approaches of water issues (Margerum 1999, Borin and Sonzogni 1995). In this holistic approach the interconnective dimension is emphasized, addressing interrelationship and linkages among multiple, cross-cutting, and often conflicting resource uses. This holistic approach is gaining popularity. However, it is not yet (fully) implemented in practice: "This is not surprising, since most water professionals consider, at least implicitly, water to be very important, if not the most important resource" (Biswas 2004: 253).

This interconnecitivity aspect of water governance, and its struggle with it, is the main topic of this book. Connective capacity revolves around connecting arrangements (such as institutions), actors (for instance individuals) and approaches (such as instruments). Water governance in this book will be approached as a way of *connecting* organizations, actors and institutions from different sectors and domains (agriculture, environment, economy, social welfare, nature, regional, landscape and spatial planning) to jointly face water problems and cooperate in developing effective, integrative and legitimate solutions for those water problems. This connecting aspect is often touched upon in water policy and management literature by literature on co-management and adaptive management (Pahl-Wostl 2007, Tortajada 2010), Integrated Water Resource Management (IWRM, for example, Margerum 1995) and Integrated Regional Water Management (IRWM, for example, Lubell and Lippert 2011), but has not yet been an exclusive point of view in literature on water policy and management. This book is devoted to this view. Therefore the following main research question is leading in this book: *which connective capacities in water governance are to be developed in order to face water problems in an integrative, effective and legitimate way?*

The water sector is a perfect field of research for the exploration of this question. Water systems are complex and compounded and often go beyond the boundaries of municipalities, regions and states. The issue of scarcity, pollution and flooding is furthermore complicated by the fact that they are heavily interrelated with other systems, like land-use and climate. In all there is much institutional and organizational complexity and fragmentation around water issues.

This book is primarily aimed at researchers working on (water) governance. However, due to our focus on concrete cases and tangible projects we believe this book is valuable for practitioners in the water field as well.

Fragmentation and Integration Regarding Water Issues

Society has become increasingly specialized and, as a consequence, fragmented. Specialization has for decades been the driving force for economic prosperity and wealth (Edelenbos and Teisman 2011). The division of labor and specialization was seen as an inevitable feature of modern society and modern organizations. Specialized organizations were able to do their specific task by internal coordination, often in hierarchical terms. The external coordination was assumed to be managed by the hidden hand of the market or formal rules. Organizations were perceived as a machine, composed of different parts that were managed and coordinated in a mechanical way (Morgan 1986: 27). Coordination is in itself a specialty and the coordinators will ensure that activities fit together in a coherent and beneficial way (Kanter 1983: 58-61).

Although this specialization brought increasing wealth, there are also negative side effects. Weber already discovered that bureaucracies undermined the capacity of spontaneous action (Kanter 1983: 60). Furthermore, increased emphasis on control and reduction of transaction costs by increasing specialization can lead to a simplification of reality and a limitation of connections with other actors and domains. "Organizations seek to transform confusing, interactive environments into less confusing, less interactive ones by decomposing domains and incline to treat their own subdomains as more or less autonomous. Organizations even tend to create buffers with surrounding subdomains" (March 1999: 197). Organizations often strive for autonomous space and maintaining, defending or enlarging that space. Each subunit of an organization strives for more autonomy and optimization of its self-interest. The unit does this by breaking down a complex problem into separate parts in which its own part is analyzed and solved separately without much attention for the combination or aggregate level of the subparts.

The problem of collective action is also present in water management (Sabatier et al. 2002). Fragmented and uncoordinated action guided by sub-goals and individual time frames and action schemes, may become rather dysfunctional on a larger system level leading for solving societal problems (March 1999). Functional specialization creates a structure that is supposed to be a system of cooperation but often turns out as a system of competition (Morgan 1986). Due to this, the envisaged benefits of specialization may hamper progress and development of the public system. Regarding water, we see specialization on water safety, water quality, droughts, etc. that each has its quality, but hampers a more integrated view on water because each discipline has its own background, way of working and substantial focus.

The Need for Connective Capacity: From Water Management toward Water Governance

Water governance takes place in circumstances of high complexity. This complexity is characterized by the involvement of many organizations, institutions and actors in solving water issues. In literature on governance networks (see Koppenjan and Klijn 2004) and network society (see Castells 2000) the issues of interdependencies and interconnectivity are seen as the main cause of complexity. Responsibilities for water (such as water quality, water safety and water supply) are dispersed among different organizations and sectors, leading on the one hand to institutional fragmentation but on the other to interdependent relationships creating balanced and legitimate solutions (Lubell and Lippert 2011, Edelenbos and Teisman 2011).

The field of water management, in which different organizations and institutions take up water supply and water resource management, specifically constitutes a case of fragmentation. Although the stakes are high, in classic water management actors often maintain their working on specific subsystems instead of connecting to the broader picture (Lubell and Lippert 2011). Fragmentation is often not effectively countered by integration and synchronization efforts, because every pillar, turf and sector is defending its own interest and responsibility. This has resulted in smaller problem solving capacity, problem displacement and conflicts in decision-making (Lubell and Lippert 2011). Finding a solution in the one sector (for example: intrusion of salt water for nature development), could lead to negative consequences in the other sector (for example: fresh water use for agricultural purposes). This multi-issue character of water makes the problem situation highly complex. As a way to deal with this fragmentation, the concept of water governance has developed. In contrast to traditional water management, this approach strongly underlines the need for coordination, integration and synchronization of values, interests, responsibilities and tasks within water management (Teisman and Edelenbos 2011).

Water governance is an upcoming theme in public administration (Edelenbos and Teisman 2011, Teisman and Edelenbos 2011, Pahl-Wostl 2007, Huitema et al. 2009, Kuks 2004). Some explicitly speak of *adaptive* water governance in order to stress the need for using adaptive management approaches to deal with complex water issues. These approaches can be characterized as flexible, inclusive, participative, bottom-up, learning and reflexive and are needed to taking into account the true complexity of water systems (Folke et al. 2007, Pahl-Wostl 2007, Brunner and Steelman 2005). Our use of the concept water governance in this book touches upon the adaptive nature of water governance by explicitly stressing the inclusive nature of it. Water governance encompasses more than preventing the people from being struck by floods. Water governance has become an integral part of spatial planning and regional development. Water governance requires the combination of different functions and values (nature, recreation, agriculture, housing, economy and infrastructure) with measures to increase water retention capacity and safety against floods, to restore estuarine dynamics and to anticipate droughts. Aside from measures for water quantity issues, it also addresses issues of quality, supply and distribution of water.

Modes of Government and Governance

From prior research (Kickert et al. 1997, Koppenjan and Klijn 2004, Van Buuren et al. 2010) we know that monocentric government models and approaches are incapable of handling persistent uncertain and complex situations. Multi or polycentric governance models are better equipped for this, because these modes give more room for a variety of actors, ideas and frames. These governance modes are more capable of handling fundamental environmental uncertainties (Folke et al. 2007). Climate change and adaptation, after all, do not occur in a vacuum (Edelenbos 2010). It will lead, for example, to water problems on quality (fresh water) and quantity (drought, flooding, water retention). However, the contents of those water policies are subject to intense discussion and negotiation. The conflict between values is played out here, especially between safety, spatial development, environmental and ecological qualities. The issue of water safety touches the possibilities for the development of agriculture, nature, urban areas, infrastructure, and recreation areas.

A system-wide governance perspective is thus required, especially in the case of water issues (Edelenbos 2010). This system-wide approach should provide space for all the values actors may attribute to water. Water, after all, fulfills various functions for very different audiences and interest groups. Sometimes it is a difficult condition for housing and economic development. It can also be a desired quality for recreation and nature. Sometimes it is a threat that should be banned. Then again, it is vital for agriculture and horticulture. In other words, water is valued differently by various groups of stakeholders. These stakeholders and their values and ideas have to be integrated into the decision-making processes about water. The resulting shift in governing has been generally called the shift from government to governance (Loorbach 2007, Kickert et al. 1997, Kooiman 1993). This shift involves the recognition that modes of governing are multiple and include processes and institutions that transverse scales as well as networks of actors which cannot easily be characterized by the state/non-state dichotomy (Betsill and Bulkeley 2006). Water governance is then about the ability to connect different frames, values and ambitions. It is for example about finding balanced solutions in which (conflicting) interests are combined and integrated. The connective capacity also relates to the ability to connect the local (city) with the regional, the metropolitan area. Moreover, it is about the capacity to connect different processes from society, market and government (Van Buuren, Edelenbos and Klijn 2010).

The water governance approach emphasizes horizontality and reciprocity. Water governance is the set of interplay of processes of coordination and cooperation and the set of interfaces between various actors (Edelenbos 2010). It is multi-level, multi-scale, multi-process and multi-actor. "... the speed of interactions and the multiplication of linkages among elements in the biophysical, technical, and human systems at a number of spatial scales seems to be increasing, creating a global "time-space compression" (Duit and Galaz 2008: 311). Crossovers between frames, scales and levels do not add up in a linear, predictable manner. Negative and positive feedback loops between (temporal and spatial) levels and scales result in unexpected consequences that need adaptive and above all connective capacity (Edelenbos 2010, Teisman and Edelenbos 2011).

Connective Capacity in Water Governance

This book focuses on how to deal with the various sources of fragmentation in water governance by organizing meaningful connections and developing 'connective capacity'. What 'ticks connective capacity'? What are its determinants, how is it manifested in practice and how can we mobilize, use, and consolidate the capacity to connect different scales, domains, levels, actors, agendas, processes and more? Connective capacity does have many components: personal, relational, organizational, and institutional (Innes and Booher 2002, Sabatier et al. 2005, Foster-Fishman et al. 2001, Leach and Pelkey 2001, Weber et al. 2007, Williams 2002). In this book we define connective capacity as the capabilities of individuals, instruments and institutions to counter fragmentation in water governance processes by crossing boundaries (structure, organization, language and so on) and establishing linkages between different actors (on different levels, at various scales and in numerous domains) in the light of solving water issues.

Following these definitions, we approach and investigate connective capacity in a two-fold way, by looking at (1) carriers of connective capacity and (2) focal points of connective capacity. Carriers of connectedness can be distinguished as an attribute or capacity of (a) individuals or groups, (b) instruments or approaches, and (c) institutions or (governmental) arrangements. This connectedness can be applied on different focal points (the objects of fragmentation and integration). We distinguish five different focal points:

1. government layers and levels.
2. sectors and domains.
3. time orientation of the long and the short term.
4. perceptions and actor frames.
5. public and private spheres.

Carriers of Connective Capacity

The concept "connective capacity" is an attribute of someone or something. It is empty without a subject owning a certain extent of connective capacity. Therefore, in this study we distinguish different carriers (or owners) of connective capacity. First, this capacity can be carried by *individuals*, by certain specific persons like water managers, but also by other stakeholders involved in the water governance process. Second, connective capacity can be considered an aspect of *instruments* used in the water governance process. For example, a modeling instrument in which flooding is forecasted. Third, *institutions* can be 'owners' of connective capacity. In this respect, scholars speak of institutional capacity building (Healy 1997), by developing rules and structures which have the capacity to bind and interrelate fragmented action and behavior. These three carriers will be explored below.

Individuals

Personal aspects are considered crucial in developing governance capacity (Foster-Fishman 2001). Human conditions in governance processes are of importance because they deliver important resources, that is, knowledge, skills, capabilities, motivation, attitude, and etcetera, which feed collaboration in watershed partnerships (Leach and Pelkey 2001). In the field of water management we can see a development from a technocratic approach in which water experts dominate, to a more democratic approach in which there is space and opportunity for stakeholders to bring in and develop their knowledge, interests and demands together with the regular experts. As of yet, there have been few encounters with this latter form, and many experiences so far have been disappointing because the process requires for each participant to leave his own turf and boundaries and dare to engage in interconnections (Edelenbos et al. 2010). Looking at things from a new perspective and stepping out of your comfort zone of the home organization into informal spheres and onto crossroads of different organizations requires new skills like, for example, relational capacities (Foster-Fishman et al. 2001) that are not easily developed or learned.

These activities of constantly connecting scales, organizations, levels, and actors are called boundary-spanning activities (Leifer and Delbecq 1978, Williams 2002). Boundary persons are always acting in an in-between space. Innovation literature (cf. Bekkers et al. 2011, Loorbach 2007) has shown that innovative solutions are developed in these border areas, so-called niches, in-between areas, and gray zones (Bekkers et al. 2011). These areas embody the organizational crossroads on which innovative solutions and daily practice can be brought together. Looking beyond organizational boundaries is an effort that specifically requires individuals. The literature on boundary spanning is focused on organizational members who are able to link organizations with their environment (Leifer and Delbecq 1978, Williams 2002). "Boundary spanners are characterized by their ability to engage with others and deploy effective relational and interpersonal competencies. This is motivated by a need to acquire an understanding of people and organizations outside their own circles ..." (Williams 2002: 110). Boundary spanners are able to deploy effective relational competencies and are important for building trust within partnerships and coordinating activities and policy making in separate organizations (Williams 2002).

In this volume we will focus on activities that connect new ways of working with established ways of working. Williams (2002: 115) mentions different key factors which influence collaborative working: the use of particular skills, abilities, experience and personal characteristics. We argue that individuals play an important role in this connective capacity and that these collaborative activities are important within processes of adaptation with regard to the interaction between emerging governance arrangements and established institutions of representative democracy.

Instruments

In water resource management all kinds of instruments are used in order to analyze water issues and to develop and implement water solutions and scenarios such as risk analyses, hydraulic modeling, scenario techniques, etc. (Lintsen 2002). These techniques, approaches, and instruments are often technocratic of nature and based on scientific knowledge (Van Buuren and Edelenbos 2004). The validity of this type of knowledge is based on scientific models and methods and on the rigorous quality checks of peer review (Van der Brugge et al. 2009). This scientific approach and use of instruments makes water management in many countries all over the world very technocratic of nature.

However, we see a general transition from technocratic towards open and more inclusive approaches in which new instruments and approaches are developed, such as water gaming, scenario building, strategies, techniques and joined up approaches, which aim for connecting actors, frames, ambitions, time horizon, spatial scales, and etcetera (Van der Brugge et al. 2009). For example, in the Netherlands in the Room for the River program, a special tool, the building box, was developed. This instrument was designed for interactive use by all interested parties in developing and measuring the effects of solutions confronting the problem of high river discharge of the main rivers in the Netherlands (Van Buuren et al. 2010).

In general, we see approaches and instruments develop which are oriented on improving collaboration between professionals from multiple domains (climate change, spatial planning, water management), but also between water professionals on the one hand and stakeholders (for instance citizens, farmers, NGOs) on the other hand (Van der Brugge et al. 2009, Kuks 2004). All kinds of new techniques are developed, such as water gaming. Water gaming can be described as computer assisted collaboration between all kinds of actors in the water governance network. These gaming techniques aim at visualization of problems and possible solutions in order to stimulate coordination and cooperation between different organizations and sectors. One can argue that these instruments and approaches deliberately try to enhance connections in a fragmented water governance process (Edelenbos 2010). Instruments therefore include all possible approaches that might be employed to influence connective capacity in water governance, ranging from techniques to strategies, to models, to games, to scenarios and many more. The effect on connective capacity of this influence through instruments is undefined: it can lead to enhanced connective capacity but equally to decreasing or stabilizing connective capacity.

Institutions

Many scholars stress the importance of institutional capacity in realizing connections across organizations, sectors and domains (Healy 1997, Putnam 1993, Amin and Thrift 1996). Institutions as a concept are much discussed but at the same time interpreted in various ways. In studying the functioning of public administration over the last years, the institutional approach received a lot of attention (Goodin 1996). The institutional theory has a versatile 'body of knowledge'. This theory involves roughly three streams: an economic, a political and a sociological stream. Some interpret institutions as organizations or organizational structures (see Lubell and Lippert 2011), others approach it as rules in use or roles actors play in policy processes (Goodin 1996). Healy (1997) argues that governance capacity of institutions lies in the quality of local policy cultures and practices. Some are well integrated, well connected and well informed to capture opportunities. Others are fragmented, and lack the connections to sources of power and knowledge.

When relating water governance with institutional perspectives, the discussion on river basin management and organization is interesting (see Huitema et al. 2009). For some, the river basin is the ideal scale to approach river and watershed management. It is about a regional scale in which various local issues and challenges can come together and can be integrated or coordinated. At the same time we see the river basin organization develop as a single centralized organization structure functioning as one team and integration of that one single organization into a broader community or network of organizations (Edelenbos and Teisman 2011). Some question the reality of grasping all dispersed layers of water management into one single organization structure (Huitema et al. 2009). There are endless local initiatives, more or less embedded in several regional and provincial plans and actions schemes, more or less embedded in a variety of national economic, spatial, infrastructural and water plans and programs. Nobody is in charge of the whole but rather many of a part of a collective (Edelenbos and Teisman 2011).

In this view institutional capacity is not built through robust structures but through resilient, lively and rich social networks as research of institutional capital through which coordination and integration can be organized rapidly and legitimately (Healy 1997). It is then about building relational resources (Williams 2002), about developing a context within which is sufficient mutual trust and discourse. A communication arena is developed in which a discourse is developed by which stakeholders can understand each other and take joint action (Healy 1997). The quality of this arena is reflected by the range and density of informal network relations between stakeholders and the degree of trust (Edelenbos and Klijn 2007) and translatability identified as 'social capital' (Putnam 1993) or institutional capacity (Amin and Thrift 1996). Institutions, in this sense, therefore also include informal networks and other temporary arrangements. Institutions are all structures, whether formal or informal, whether permanent or temporary, which influence connective capacity in water governance.

Focal Points of Connective Capacity

Water problems transcend jurisdictional, organizational, regional, and even country boundaries. In this volume we address the three above described carriers of connective capacity with regard to five focal points for connective capacity:

1. government layers and levels.
2. sectors and domains.
3. time orientation of the long and the short term.
4. perceptions and actor frames.
5. public and private spheres.

We will discuss each focal point with some conceptualization and examples in the following sections.

Water Governance Crosses Governmental Layers and Levels

Water management is closely related to processes of climate change and climate adaptation. These matters are multi-level issues. They cross local, regional and national borders and jurisdictions. Rivers do not restrict themselves to borders, and effects of climate change may be induced from developments elsewhere in the world. To address these multi-level issues, the various layers of government within and between states need to be coordinated. This is called multi-level governance (Hooghe and Marks 2003). Networks resulting from this multi-level governance are simultaneously global and local, state and non-state. Multilevel governance, which emphasizes the connections between vertical tiers of government on the one hand and horizontally organized forms of interactions on the other hand, helps us to understand water and climate governance within and across scales (Betsill and Bulkeley 2006: 149). Processes, programs and institutions are developed between levels and create new spheres of authority, which require new analytical perspectives on governing. Many authors stress the importance of cross-scale and multi-level interactions (Adger, Brown, and Tompkins 2005). Interconnectivity between levels and scales focuses on how to interrelate actions, events and processes in surrounding subsystems.

We can illustrate the challenges of multi-level governance and the role of individual interactions in water and climate issues with two cases. The first case concerns an urban development project (Stadshavens) in the floodplain area of the city of Rotterdam. Specific questions concerning adaptation issues of this development on the local scale coincided with questions about developments on regional and national level, such as the regional decision about a main waterway close to the city (Nieuwe Waterweg). If this waterway would be closed, effects on sea level rise would be different than if the waterway remained open and thus would have different consequences on the local project scale. On the national level a program was developed to counter long-term changes in water and climate change: the Delta Program. One of its nine subprograms concerned the region in which Rotterdam can be found. This subprogram was especially developed to address the boundless issue of climate change and regional development. All these developments on the local, regional and national level had to be taken into account to decide on the plans for the Stadshavens project.

Second is the case on the Fraser Basin Council (FBC), in British Columbia, Canada (see Watson 2004). The Basin is highly important for the provincial area, both in terms of drainage as in terms of Gross Provincial Product. In the last 200 years, activities such as mining, timber production, fishing, agricultural settlement, port development and urban expansion have produced a complex mix of land and water-related problems together with climate challenges (Watson 2004). To address these problems the Fraser Basin Management Program was established. The program was based on a five-year agreement to pursue sustainability signed by representatives from the federal, provincial, and local tiers of government. It was developed through a multi-stakeholder board, which included representatives for the four levels of government – federal, provincial, municipal, and First Nations – and economic, social and environmental interests from different parts of the Fraser Basin. Watson concludes that the success of this program was not the installation of a new institutional structure but the people who worked in the program: '... it is people and not institutional structures ... that determine the outcomes of collaboration. There are no substitutes for mutual respect, patience, dedication, trust, negotiation, skills, and endurance' (Watson 2004: 251). This case demonstrates that multi-level governance is an important step in handling water and climate challenges.

Water Governance Transcends Sectors and Domains

Water governance is multi-issue. The interconnected nature of many water and climate issues means that a sector-transcending, or holistic, approach is needed in dealing with cross-sector challenges. Examples of these holistic approaches are the Integrated Regional Water Management (IRWM) or Integrated Water Resources Management (IWRM) approaches. An example of this cross-sector water and climate governance can be found in the relation between climate change and urban area development. Global warming and related climate changes are likely to significantly increase the weather-related risks facing human settlements, including floods, water and power supply failures and associated economic collapse. This means that both urban area development and climate and water adaptation have to take the interests and prospects of the other sectors like water, agriculture, nature, environment, building, infrastructure, and etcetera into account (Edelenbos and Teisman: 2011).

Domains are interdependent and need constant coordination and fine-tuning. Water policy needs to be embedded in other policy fields as water, infrastructure, urban development and agriculture. A study from Van Buuren, Edelenbos and Klijn (2010), which researched eight Dutch water related regional development projects, indicates that regional development is a multi-functions issue. All the researched cases show to a certain extent the interconnected nature of regional governance.

To provide an example, we briefly discuss the case of the Bay Area Integrated Regional Water Management program (Bay Area IRWM) in California USA to illustrate the challenge of meeting climate change and domain and function integration. Several studies have indicated that California's climate is variable over history and in the present is experiencing sea level rise and may experience significant effects of climate warming (cf. Lubell and Lippert 2011). For the Bay Area IRWM we see fragmentation and interrelation on the following functional areas: water quality, water supply, waste water, urban development, flood protection, storm water management, and habitat protection/restoration (Lubell and Lippert 2011). In the Bay Area the IRWM approach is started especially to try to integrate the different abovementioned function areas, functions or domains.

Lubell and Lippert (2011) found that IRWM approaches in California largely fail to integrate different functional domains/functions. Participants considered the IRWM administration as confusing and inflexible, the process too complex, time consuming and unfair. However, participation in IRWM was associated with a higher level of collaboration on implementation activities. The integrated approach had a small but positive influence on levels of collaboration and probably increased the breadth and density of policy networks in the Bay Area. However, this increased collaboration did not yet result in the integration of functional areas and different interests stakeholders want to realize in developing the region in order to face climate change. This means more research about effective cross-sector cooperation is required to improve its application.

Water Governance Transcends Time Orientations

Time orientations make water governance even more challenging. Connecting the present to possible futures is necessary before good choices can be made (Loorbach 2007, Rotmans 2006, Peterson et al. 1997). Climate change brings new challenges, concerning for instance the rate (and magnitude) of change of climate, the potential for non-linear changes and the long time horizons. All these issues are plagued with substantial uncertainties, which make implementing adaptation strategies difficult.

Burton et al. (2002: 154) argue that 'the essential starting point is the present'. However, the future is uncertain. Overall, it is argued that realizing system change and system innovation requires generations. It is, in other words, a long term process (Rogers 2003, Rotmans 2006). The effects of actions will take a long time to become visible.

Another cross-time problem in complex governance processes is that different actors hold different time frames and agendas (Bressers, Avelino and Geerlings 2012, Rotmans 2006: 56). Attempts to clarify these agendas might be flawed when actors still discuss their objectives in terms of long term or short term. What one considers to fall under which category differs per actor (Bressers, Avelino and Geerlings 2012). Private actors, such as investors in real estate (for example, developing business areas), hold time frames of 15 years or longer, whereas politicians and governments hold time frames of four years ('election cycles'). "Time horizons of a century, and over continental scales, are not compelling to most policymakers" (Someshwar 2008). Primary temporal planning and policy horizons are from one season to at the most a decade ahead. This makes it difficult to set goals and develop and implement strategies for the long run. Adaptation policies and programs need to be contextualized in place and time. Governments find it difficult to bring this place and time contextualization into practice because it is not common practice.

For example, we see in The Netherlands that different municipalities, such as Dordrecht and Rotterdam, are developing outer dyke urban development and taking safety measures. But these processes of local self-governance are being frustrated by the fact that national government has not yet set the norms for water safety for the future. This will probably not be realized before 2017. In The Netherlands it is important that national government facilitates the local and regional initiatives that counter climate challenges and water management issues. If national governments don't make steps in making policy for the long run, for example, policy with the necessary safety criteria and norms, local initiatives come to a standstill. It is important that proactive and adaptive local policymaking and implementation is stimulated in time. Challenges in water and climate governance across time are therefore the third focal point of this book.

Water Governance Crosses Actor Frames

Water governance processes can be approached as complex actor networks (Edelenbos et al. 2010, Dewulf et al. 2011). Competing claims of actors from different organizations, domains and sectors make it inherently difficult to manage the divergent claims on water (Edelenbos 2010). All sorts of actors ask for attention in water governance processes: farmers, industry, inhabitants of higher and lower areas, water power plants, municipal, regional and national governments. The involved actors are using different frames to make sense of the issues that they face. Integration cannot be imposed or defined beforehand but will depend on connecting the fragmented frames and actors that populate a specific problem domain (Dewulf et al. 2011). Every actor brings his or her own scripts and routines to the multi-actor setting and these can diverge substantially, especially when actors from different sectors are involved.

Water governance can be characterized as a multi-actor setting in which various stakeholders often voice divergent opinions about what the issue is exactly or what the whole situation is about (Adger et al. 2005). From their different backgrounds they pay attention to different aspects of the situation and tell a different story about what the problem is and what should be done to solve this problem. Confusion, misunderstanding, disagreement or even intractable controversy are likely when participants frame the issues in divergent ways (Koppenjan and Klijn 2004). Framing is a three-fold process of selection, focusing and embedding (Dewulf et al. 2011). People frame issues by bringing certain aspects of a complex problem domain into the picture (a process of selection), by putting certain aspects on the foreground and others on the background (a process of focusing) and by using certain aspects as the overarching elements within which the rest fits (a process of embedding).

Dewulf et al. (2011) demonstrate the importance of framing in their study of the Tabacay project in the Paute catchment in Ecuador, Southern America. They show that different actors frame the problem differently (erosion, sedimentation, insufficient drinking water, etc.) resulting in a fragmented problem domain. In this case, formulating the issue in terms of 'erosion', for example, bring actors into the picture who suffer from the loss of 'fertile soil' (for example, farmers at the Tabacay level), while a formulation in terms of 'sediment' directs the attention towards actors who suffer from the 'dirt' carried by the river (for example, water power plant at the Paute level). Dewulf et al. (2005) show that attempts to interconnect this variety of frames was productive in generating a joint sense making of the problem situation. The importance of connecting technical and scientific frames to frames of other actors emerged as a crucial aspect in this case. Through a translation of technical language to language that is closer to the language other actors use, frame interconnection was realized.

When people frame problem situations differently, ambiguity arises (Dewulf et al. 2011). This is a specific kind of uncertainty that cannot be solved by simply generating more information, because actors frame usable and relevant information and knowledge in different ways (Van Buuren and Edelenbos 2004, Dewulf et al. 2005). In other words: they interpret and value (process of selection) data and information differently. This results from the simultaneous presence of two or more ways of framing the situation. Information providing doesn't solve this. Instead a coordination or interconnection of frames is needed to realize mutual understanding. This is called the interaction dimension of framing (Dewulf et al. 2011). Interaction and framing are prominent in complex systems such as water and climate. Water governance across actor frames is therefore our fourth focal point.

Water Governance Exceeds Public, Private and Societal Spheres

Water governance issues and processes do not stop at the borders of public spheres and governmental institutions. It concerns also other actors in the playing field, such as NGOs and (organized) citizens. The transition in modern water management from technocratic towards more adaptive and democratic approaches is widely acknowledged (Sabatier et al. 2005, Van der Brugge et al. 2009). There are all kinds of initiatives that illustrate this development: citizen participation, public private partnerships, civic environmentalism and community based initiatives (Brunner and Steelman 2005).

Public participation and interactive policy-making is spread all over the world. Stakeholder involvement goes around under a lot of labels such as citizens panels, citizens charters, interactive decision-making, governance, and so on (Edelenbos et al. 2010). Main motives to involve stakeholders in decision-making are diminishing the veto power of various societal actors by involving them in decision making, improving the quality of decision making by using information and solutions of various actors and bridging the perceived growing cleavage between citizens and elected politicians. These arguments can also be found in literature about governance (Sørensen and Torfing 2007). Environmental issues are so-called 'wicked problems' which – according to theories of governance – require the involvement of various stakeholders (Koppenjan and Klijn 2004). Citizens and social groups show their self-organizing ability to develop and implement well-founded plans through citizens' initiatives (Edelenbos 2010, Edelenbos et al. 2010). These people are often retired, highly educated and – very important – are equipped with local knowledge of the specific locations.

A Dutch case illustrates this focal point. In the east of the Netherlands the river Waal runs through the cities Nijmegen and Lent, which means that in cases of high water discharge, a bottleneck may be formed in the populated areas so close to the river banks. To address this matter the area became one of the 39 measures in the Dutch Program Space for the Rivers (Warner et al. 2012). In this program it was decided by local, regional and national government that the river Waal had to be broadened by dike reallocation. However, the area was also allocated for the creation of new housing. This meant existing building plans had to be altered. Although the private housing corporation and the city council of Nijmegen were not happy with this change of plans, a new plan was developed. As harmony between the stakeholders developed, they decided that the dike would be reallocated (Van Buuren, Edelenbos and Klijn 2010).

Inhabitants of Lent, however, were less happy with the new ambitions for city development. Approximately 50 houses would be demolished to realize the reallocation. The inhabitants developed a plan of their own, the 'Lents Warande' plan. However, this plan did not meet national objectives in discharge amounts, and national governmental actors therefore did not consider it a feasible alternative. Local stakeholders were still not convinced of the long term prognoses and plans, but had to give up in the end as the national government (House of Representatives) decided in favor of dyke reallocation. This example demonstrates that many stakeholders participate in water governance and that even when public-private partnerships reach agreement, they still might encounter resistance from, for instance, inhabitants. Arranging connections does not occur without tensions. Therefore, public/society interaction will be the fifth focal point.

Closing and Prospect to Contributions to this Volume

This chapter has discussed the development of fragmentation, its role in water governance and the need for connective capacity in water governance to overcome fragmentation and integrate approaches, actors, frames and many more. This connectivity will be analyzed based on two analytical dividing lines. First, we have discussed three carriers of connective capacity: individuals, instruments and institutions. Second, we have discussed five focal points for our analysis: government layers and levels, sectors and domains, time orientation of the long and the short term, perceptions and actor frames and public and private spheres. With this point of departure we will be able to gain insights of the nature and the strengths and weaknesses of connective capacity in water governance in various countries and in various cases.

There are limits to connective capacity. Not everything has to be connected at the same time with the same level of intensity (Edelenbos 2010). Energy and time effort put in one connection cannot be invested in another connection at the same time. It is about a delicate balance between exploring and exploiting relations and connections (March 1999, Duit and Galaz 2008). If this balance is found, integration will lead to adaptive water governance systems with a high capacity for exploration with an equally high level of capacity for exploitation (for example, Duit and Galaz 2008: 321). In the chapters of this book an inquiry is made into connective capacity, its failures, its successes, its effects and its development. The next section will discuss the structure/grid of the book and introduce the individual chapters of this book.

Book Structure and Outlook to the Book Chapters

In this book we will discuss the notion of connective capacity by the combination of two perspectives: carriers and focal points of connective capacity. The three carriers and five focal points result in a grid in which the chapters of the book are positioned. The contributors to this book will discuss theory and empirics of water governance, with an emphasis on a combination of one carrier and one focal point. Table 1.1 outlines this book's structure.

Table 1.1   Book structure and the position of the contributions in it

Connector carriers/focal points	Individuals (agency)	Instruments (approaches)	Institutions (arrangements)
Layers/levels	Chapter 2 – Scholten and Edelenbos: Complexity Leaders. Cases from The Netherlands	Chapter 3 – Vinke-de Kruijf et al.: cases from Romania	Chapter 4 – Keskitalo et al.: Adaptation policies cases from Sweden, Finland, UK and Italy
Sectors/ domains	Chapter 5 – Warner: Boundary spanners cases from The Netherlands	Chapter 6 – Zhou et al.: Serious Gaming: cases from The Netherlands	Chapter 7 – Bettini et al.: Governing the future cases from Australia
Time orientations/ long-short term	Chapter 8 – Bressers and Deelstra: Complexity leadership roles. Cases from The Netherlands	Chapter 9 – Van Eijndhoven et al.: Transition arena. Cases from The Netherlands	Chapter 10 – Van Leeuwen and Van Buuren: cases from The Netherlands
Frames/ perceptions	Chapter 11 – Verduijn: Delta committee. Cases from The Netherlands	Chapter 12 – Dewulf et al.: bridging climate frames. Various international cases	Chapter 13 – Van Ast et al.: actors and value chains. Cases from India and The Netherlands
Spheres: government-society	Chapter 14 – Edelenbos et al.: Boundary spanners and legitimacy. Cases from The Netherlands	Chapter 15 – Cuppen and Pardoe: Stakeholder involvement and legitimacy. Cases from United Kingdom	Chapter 16 – De Boer and Krantzberg: cross national water programs. Cases from Canada and United States

Outlook to the Chapters

First, the book deals with the layer fragmentation within water governance and the connective capacities of individuals, instruments and institutions in trying to overcome this fragmentation. Scholten and Edelenbos (Chapter 2) argue that individuals, in this case political public leaders, are of essential importance in connective capacity, due to their pivotal position in which they are able to connect new and innovative proposals that encompass various stakes and stakeholders in integrated solution strategies to the existing context of policy making (Scholten 2011). Using a typology of leadership behavior, they show that Dutch leaders use various strategies for creating interconnections between layers and levels of the policy process.

Vinke-de Kruijf, Kuks and Augustijn (Chapter 3) investigate how to create and consolidate connective capacity under changing circumstances in Romanian case studies where water governance has been undergoing strong reforms in the process of aligning with EU standards. They focus on the identification of ways and approaches (roles, responsibilities and cooperation structures) to overcome incoherence between the various layers and levels of the governance structure.

Keskitalo, Juhola and Westerhoff (Chapter 4) show that water governance is a multi-level governance phenomenon. Drawing upon cases in the UK, Finland, Sweden and Italy, the study shows that an exclusive focus on national adaptation policy obscures the complexity of emergence of adaptation across layers and levels of governance. They argue that a coherent application of a multi-level framework that takes interactions between levels and how these are shaped by the political system into account, is a prerequisite for understanding the development and implementation of adaptation policies.

Secondly, the book addresses the domain fragmentation of water governance processes. In three different chapters, the connective capacities of individuals, instruments and institutions are discussed and analyzed. Warner (Chapter 5) discusses the concept of boundary spanning to discuss domain tensions in the Grensmaas case in The Netherlands and Belgium. His discussion demonstrates tensions in water governance between greening and extracting natural resources (gravel). He shows how the individual boundary spanners employ proactive and reactive linkage and framing to deal with specific moments of tensions in the Grensmaas process.

Zhou, Bekebrede, Mayer, Warmerdam and Knepflé (Chapter 6) approach gaming as an instrument to develop a learning process among stakeholders in the water governance process to gain better understanding of the coordination and cooperation needs of stakeholders representing various policy sectors which might result in the enhancement of integrated planning in real life policy making. They show results from their research experiences with the Climate Game, a realistic, computer-supported, multiplayer policy game about a water governance issue in Delft (The Netherlands).

Bettini, Rijke, Farrelly and Brown (Chapter 7) describe how institutions enable and bound connective capacity across different domains and disciplines of the urban water sector in a context of Australian water scarcity. In their contribution, they point out that actors and institutions set the magnitude and potential impact of connective capacity through interaction and leadership processes and as such acknowledge the linkages between policy sectors and domains.

Thirdly, the book discusses the time aspect of water governance. Three different chapters pay attention to how individuals, instruments and institutions are trying to develop connective capacity in order to relate the short with the long term horizon. Bressers and Deelstra (Chapter 8) use a complexity leadership approach to explore tensions between the short-term and long-term orientations. From the complexity leadership perspective they describe strategies that were employed by individuals to deal with these tensions as well as their possible reducing effects on existing tensions in two water programs in The Netherlands. They argue that strong relations exist between the type of leadership and a specific time orientation.

Van Eijndhoven, Frantzeskaki and Loorbach (Chapter 9) investigate the possibilities of envisioning as a tool for enhancing connectivity between long term directions and the short term actions. In these dynamics, the authors identify a specific misfit due to the problem that so-called 'front runners' in water management operate largely within their water context and as such neglect that these issues also relate to other policy domains.

Van Leeuwen and Van Buuren (Chapter 10) discuss connecting time spans in the case of the Program Southwest Delta (The Netherlands). Project and program management is in their view a device to organize decision-making on complex spatial issues. They use their discussion to come to building blocks for connective capacity in institutionally connecting time spans.

Fourthly, the book focusses on frame fragmentation and interconnection among actors in water governance processes from an individual, instrumental and institutional perspective.

Verduijn (Chapter 11) reviews the efforts of the Second Delta Committee which formulated recommendations for strategies for long-term flood protection and freshwater management in The Netherlands. He argues that creating connectivity between frames and perceptions can in some cases be done through a strong coherent one-dimensional policy frame that overarches the various existing frames and perceptions.

Dewulf, Brugnach, Termeer and Ingram (Chapter 12) focus on the climate debate and argue that mechanisms are needed that enable debate, clarification, and enactment in order to create meaning through discussion and joint interpretation. Important bridging conditions are found in institutions and arrangements such as boundary organizations, but also in instruments such as boundary objects and by the agency of individuals or groups through boundary experiences.

Van Ast, Bouma and Bal (Chapter 13) explore linkages between values of water, the shaping of an institutional context through these values and consequently, and the way actors behave in their management practices of water systems. They argue that water systems such as rivers and lakes have always had different social, ecological and economical values at different spatial and temporal scales of societal developments. In an international comparison they look at the expected and realized values of lake systems in the Netherlands and India.

Finally, the book addresses the relation between societal, private and governmental spheres in water governance. Edelenbos, Van Meerkerk en Klijn (Chapter 14) elaborate on the relation between societal and governmental spheres from a perspective of network managers. They investigate the relationship between a certain management style that they coin as complexity sensitive management and the legitimacy issues involved in these processes. They use survey research on water governance projects in The Netherlands.

Cuppen and Pardoe (Chapter 15) also take up the issue of legitimacy in the light of specific instruments and strategies that can be employed to connect different societal and governmental spheres. In their chapter they aim to discover in what way connective strategies such as stakeholder engagement enhance the legitimacy in an urban flood risk management project in the UK.

De Boer and Krantzberg (Chapter 16) emphasize the nature of the relationship between society and institutions in the context of the Great Lakes governance regime in the USA and Canada. In overcoming the differences that evolved through traditionally separated mechanisms for improving water quality and quantity concerns, connective capacity to bring various spheres together and therewith reduce conflicting uses and policies is a prerequisite for achieving a more coherent and sustainable governance regime. They argue that the discussed inter-regime is inadequately formed in practice.

The book concludes with Chapter 17, which is written by the editors Edelenbos, Bressers and Scholten, in which they discuss the insights from the different contributions and draw conclusions on the three distinguished carriers of connective capacity. They develop a perspective of synchronicity as a potential perspective for enhancing connective capacity in water governance.

Bibliography

Adger, W.N., Brown, K. and Tompkins, E.L. 2005. The political economy of cross-scale networks in resource co-management. *Ecology and Society*, 10(2), 9-20 [online], http://www.ecologyandsociety.org/vol10/iss2/art9/.

Amin, A. and Thrift, N. 1996. Globalisation, institutional thickness and the local economy, in *Managing Cities*, edited by P. Healy, S. Cameron, S. Davoudi, S. Graham and A. Madaripour. Chichester: John Wiley, 91-108.

Bekkers, V.J.J.M., Edelenbos, J. and Steijn, B. 2011. Linking innovation to the public sector: Contexts, concepts and challenges, in *Innovation in the Public Sector. Linking Capacity and Leadership* (Governance and Public Management, 6), edited by V.J.J.M. Bekkers, J. Edelenbos and B. Steijn. Houndmills: Palgrave Macmillan, 3-34.

Betsill, M.M. and Bulkeley, H. 2006. Cities and the multilevel governance of global climate change. *Global Governance*, 12(2), 141-59.

Biswas, A.K. 2004. Integrated water resources management: A reassessment. *Water International*, 29(2), 248-56.

Born, S.M. and Sonzogni, W.C. 1995. Integrated environmental management: Strengthening the conceptualization. *Environmental Management*, 19(2), 167-81.

Bressers, N., Avelino, F. and Geerlings, H. 2012. Short- versus long-term and other dichotomies: Applying transition management in the A15-project, in *Transition towards Sustainable Mobility: The Role of Instruments, Individuals and Institutions*, edited by H. Geerlings, Y. Shiftan and D. Stead. Farnham: Ashgate.

Brunner, R.D. and Steelman, T.A. 2005. Towards adaptive governance, in *Adaptive Governance: Integrating Science, Policy and Decision Making*, edited by R.D. Brunner, T.A. Steelman, L. Coe-Juell, C.M. Cromley, C.M. Edwards and D.W. Tucker. New York: Columbia University Press, 1-21.

Burton, I., Huq, S., Lim, B., Pilifosova, O. and Schipper, E.L. 2002. From impacts assessment to adaptation priorities: The shaping of adaptation policy. *Climate Policy*, 6(2), 145-59.

Brugge, R. van der, Rotmans, J. and Loorbach, D. 2009. The transition in Dutch water management. *Regional Environmental Change*, 5(4), 164-76.

Castells, M. 2000. Toward a sociology of the network society. *Contemporary Sociology*, 29(5), 693-99.

Dewulf, A., Craps, M., Bouwen, R., Taillieu, T. and Pahl-Wostl, C. 2005. Integrated management of natural resources: Dealing with ambiguous issues, multiple actors and diverging frames. *Water Science & Technology*, 52(2), 115-24.

Dewulf, A., Mancero, M., Cárdenas, G. and Sucozhañay, D. 2011. Fragmentation and connection of frames in collaborative water governance: A case study of river catchment management in Southern Ecuador. *International Review of Administrative Sciences*, 77(1), 50-75.

Duit, A. and Galaz, F. 2008. Governance and Complexity: Emerging Issues for Governance Theory, *Governance*, 21(3), 311-35.

Edelenbos, J. 2010. *Water as Connective Current/water als spanningsvolle verbinding*, inaugurele rede. Den Haag: Boom/Lemma.

Edelenbos, J. and Teisman, G.R. 2011. Symposium on water governance. Prologue: Water governance as a government's actions between the reality of fragmentation and the need for integration. *International Review of Administrative Sciences*, 77(1), 5-30.

Edelenbos, J., Steijn, A.J. and Klijn, E.H. 2010. Does Democratic Anchorage Matter? An Inquiry into the Relation between Democratic Anchorage and Outcome of Dutch Environmental Projects. *American Review of Public Administration*, 40(1), 46-63.

Folke, C., Pritchard L., Berkes, F., Colding J. and Svedin, U. 2007. The problem of fit between ecosystems and institutions: Ten years later. *Ecology & Society*, 12(4), 201-20.

Foster-Fishman, P.G., Berkowitz, S.L., Lounsbury, D.W., Jacobsen, S. and Allen, N.A. 2001. Building Collaborative Capacity in Community Coalitions: A review and integrative framework. *American Journal of Community Psychology*, 29(2), 180-201.

Goodin, R.E. 1996. *The Theory of Institutional Design*. Cambridge: Cambridge University Press.

Healy, P. 1997. *Collaborative Planning: Shaping Places in Fragmented Societies*. London: Macmillan.

Huitema, D., Mostert, E., Egas, W., Moellenkamp, S. and Pahl-Wostl, C. 2009. Adaptive Water Governance: Assessing the Institutional Prescriptions of

Adaptive (Co-) Management from a Governance Perspective and Defining a Research Agenda, *Ecology and Society*, 14(1), 1-19.

Innes, J.E. and Booher, D.E. 2002. The Impact of Collaborative Planning on Governance Capacity, working paper 2003-3, prepared for the presentation at the Annual Conference of the Association of Collegiate Schools of Planning, Baltimore, November 21-24.

IPCC-WGII 2007. Climate change 2007: Impacts, adaptation and vulnerability. Contribution of the Working Group II to the Fourth Assessment report of the Intergovernmental Panel on Climate Change Summary for Policy Making.

Kickert, W.J.M., Klijn, E-H. and Koppenjan, J.F.M. (eds) 1997. *Managing Complex Networks: Strategies for the Public Sector*. London: SAGE Publications.

Kooiman, J. 2003. *Governing as Governance: Part III*. London: SAGE Publications.

Kooiman, J. (ed.). 1993. *Modern Governance: New Government–Society Interactions*. London: SAGE Publications.

Koppenjan, J. and Klijn, E-H. 2004. *Managing Uncertainties in Networks: A Network Approach to Problem Solving and Decision Making*. London: Routledge.

Kuks, S.M.M. 2004. *Water Governance and Institutional Change*. PhD Thesis. Enschede: University of Twente.

Leach, W.D., Pelkey, N. and Twente, W. 2001. Making Watershed Partnerships Work: A Review of the Empirical Literature. *Journal of Water Resource Planning and Management*, 127(6), 378-85.

Leifer, R. and Delbecq, A. 1978. Organizational/environmental interchange: A model of boundary spanning activity, *The Academy of Management Review*, 3(1), 40-50.

Lintsen, H. 2002. Two centuries of Central Water Management in the Netherlands. *Technology and Culture*, 43(2), 549-68.

Loorbach, D. 2007. *Transition Management: New Mode of Governance for Sustainable Development.* Utrecht: International Books.

Lubell, M. and Lippert, L. 2011. Integrated regional water management: A study of collaboration or water politics-as-usual in California, USA. *International Review of Administrative Sciences*, 77(1), 76-100.

March, J.G. 1999. *The Pursuit of Organizational Intelligence*. New York: Blackwell.

Margerum, R.D. 1999. Integrated environmental management: The foundations for successful practice. *Environmental Management*, 24(2), 151-66.

Margerum, R.D. and Born, S.M. 1995. Integrated environmental management: Moving from theory to practice, *Journal of Environmental Planning and Management*, 38(3), 371-91.

Hooghe, L. and Marks, G. 2003. Unraveling the Central State, but How? Types of Multi-level Governance, *American Political Science Review*, 97(2), 233-43.

Morgan, G. 1989. *Images of Organizations*. London: Sage.

Pahl-Wostl, C. 2007. Transitions towards adaptive management of water facing climate and global change. *Water Resource Management*, 21(1), 49-62.

Peterson, G., De Leo, G.A., Hellmann, J.J., Janssen, M.A., Kinzig, A., Malcolm, J.R., O'Brien, K.L., Pope, S.E., Rothman, D.S., Shevliakova, E. and Tinch, R.R.T. 1997. Uncertainty, Climate Change, and Adaptive Management. *Conservation Ecology*, 1(2), 4-23.

Putnam, R. 1993. *Making Democracy Work: Civil Traditions in Modern Italy.* Princeton, NJ: University of Princeton Press.

Rogers, E. 2003. *Diffusion of Innovations.* New York: Free Press.

Rotmans, J. 2006. *Transitiemanagement. Sleutel voor een duurzame samenleving.* 2nd edition. Assen: Van Gorcum.

Sabatier, P.A., Focht, W., Lubell, M., Trachtenberg, Z., Vedlitz, A. and Matlock, M. 2005. *Swimming Upstream: Collaborative Approaches to Watershed Management, American and Comparative Environmental Policy Series.* Cambridge, MA: MIT Press.

Schie, N. van. 2010. *Co-Valuation of Water. An Institutional Perspective on Valuation in Spatial Water Management.* PhD Thesis. Rotterdam: Erasmus University Rotterdam.

Scholten, P.H.T. 2011. *Daring Leadership. A Study of Water Governance on the Edge of Innovation and Democracy.* PhD thesis. Nijmegen: Radboud University Nijmegen.

Someshwar, S. 2008. Adaptation as "Climate-Smart" Development, Development 01/2008, 51(3), 366-74.

Sørensen, E. and Torfing, J. 2007. *Theories of Democratic Network Governance.* Basingstoke: Palgrave Macmillan.

Teisman, G.R. and Edelenbos, J. 2011. Towards a perspective of system synchronization in water governance: A synthesis of empirical lessons and complexity theories, *International Review of Administrative Sciences*, 77(1), 101-18.

Tortajada, C. 2010. Water Governance: A research agenda, *International Journal on Water Resources Development*, 26(3), 309-16.

UNESCO. 2006. *Water, a Shared Responsibility.* Barcelona: UNESCO/Berghahn Books.

Van Buuren, M.W. and Edelenbos, J. 2004. Conflicting Knowledge: Why is Knowledge Production Such a Problem? *Science and Public Policy*, 31(4), 289-99.

Van Buuren, A., Edelenbos, J. and Klijn, E.H. 2010. *Gebiedsontwikkeling in Woelig Water. Over water governance bewegend tussen adaptief waterbeheer en ruimtelijke besluitvorming.* Den Haag: Boom Lemma uitgevers.

Warner, J., van Buuren, M.W. and Edelenbos, J. 2012. *Space for the River.* London: IWApress.

Watson, N. 2004. Integrated river basin management: A case for collaboration. *International Journal River Basin Management*, 2(4), 243-57.

Weber, E., Lovrich, N.P. and Gaffney, M.J. 2007. Assessing Collaborative Capacity in a Multidimensional World. *Administration and Society*, 39(2), 89-116.

Williams, P. 2002. The competent boundary spanner. *Public Administration*, 80(1), 103-24.

Chapter 2

The Role of Political-public Leadership for Connective Capacity in Water Governance

Peter Scholten and Jurian Edelenbos

Introduction

As stressed in the previous chapter, an approach to water governance is needed in which different values, interests and uses of water are interconnected so that water policy and measures are developed and implemented with the support of different stakeholder groups. In the Netherlands, where over sixteen-million inhabitants lay their diverse claims on one of Europe's smallest countries, this is especially relevant. As a result, water governance in the Netherlands can be characterized as a multidimensional governance issue that combines spatial management, economic functionality, ecological values and infrastructural problems and that involves many actors with different opinions and interests. This multi-leveled and kaleidoscopic characterization of water governance implies a complex and unpredictable policy process (van Buuren et al. 2010).

Within this kaleidoscopic environment the capacity to connect the various domains, levels, scales, organizations and actors becomes highly important. Hence, the water governance approach of this book strongly underlines the need for coordination, integration and synchronization of values, interests, responsibilities and tasks within water management (Teisman and Edelenbos 2011).

Because of the complex network character of society, water governance capacity is realized in cooperation between organizations and actors from governmental, private and societal institutions, which makes governance inter-organizational and multi-actor of nature. Connective capacity is therefore a prerequisite for realizing water governance capacity in coping with uncertain developments and complex challenges (Edelenbos 2010).

Especially in a situation of such complexity the specific position of public political leadership is considered of great importance with regard to connective capacity. In its inter-organizational position, public leadership has the possibility to detach from specific organization interests, to see the bigger picture and develop long-term planning, to reach beyond traditional domains and combine stakes and stakeholders in order to arrive at innovative solutions to existing problems (Scholten 2011).

In this chapter we focus on individuals as carriers for connective capacity. We will specifically focus on the role of *political public leadership* ('t Hart and Uhr

2008) and elaborate on its essential importance in connective capacity of water governance processes. Political public leaders, because of their specific inter-organizational position, have the ability to connect networks, levels and domains. In the complex context of water governance where integrated solutions are needed, political public leadership has the pivotal position to connect new and innovative proposals that encompass various stakes and stakeholders in integrated solution strategies, to the existing context of policy making (Scholten 2011). In that sense, political public leadership is considered of great significance in the establishment of connective capacity. Due to its specific position and inter-organizational character, public political leadership can play an important role in connecting and synchronizing governmental layers and levels. In this chapter we will elaborate more specifically on that role of political public leadership.

In our case study, concerning the management problems of a large fresh water basin in the Dutch southwestern delta region, a situation characterized by high complexity and fragmentation exists. This fragmentation is found in the divergent societal functionalities such as safety, ecological values and interests of economic sectors such as agriculture and industry. These different interests and their corresponding stakeholders are also further reflected in the involvement of various governmental organizations on different levels and divided in different political administrations. We will examine the leadership styles of three provincial delegates involved in the case and assess in how far their specific styles and actions create connections between the various layers and levels of policy making in which they operate.

Connective capacity is therewith regarded from a leadership point of view. In this description we will use a conceptual framework of leadership ideal types; the TDT-typology (Scholten 2011), to assess the nature and extent of connective capacity of the individual political-public leaders.

We will make clear, through the three empirical examples of leadership in a multi-level context that the approaches toward developing connectivity and interconnections between the various parties on different levels of the policy process are specifically dependent on the individual leader, resulting in different exercises of leadership behavior. In the following section we will elaborate on the conceptual framework. Then we will describe and analyze the three cases of leadership and finally draw conclusions in the light of the connective capacities of specific leadership behavior.

Framework: Transactional, Transformational and Daring Leadership in the TDT-typology

Conceptualizing Three Forms of Leadership

In the description of the exercise of public leadership as it occurs in practice, we make use of an ideal-type classification of leadership behavior, the TDT typology.

Based on the existing typology used in descriptions of intra-organizational leadership (Bass 1985, Bass and Avolio 1994), this typology describes public leadership behavior in an inter-organizational context.

The TDT-typology uses the original dichotomy of transactional and transformational leadership to which a third type, daring leadership, is added. We will conceptually distinguish the three ideal-types of leadership based on several specific leadership elements. First a short description of the main characteristics of each type is given.

Transactional leadership is focused on marginal improvements, maintaining the quantity and quality of performance, how to substitute one goal for another, how to reduce resistance and how to implement decisions (Bass 1985, Avolio and Bass 1995), This type of leadership is essentially focused on the maintenance of the process of policy making. Activities are aimed at accommodating the current system and maintaining the existing status quo.

Transformational leadership is specifically focused on raising awareness about certain issues and convincing or motivating others to share the ideas on these issues. This requires a leader with vision, self-confidence and inner strength to argue successfully for what he or she thinks is right or good, not for what is popular or acceptable (Bass 1985: 17). In terms of end and means, transformational leadership is generally more concerned about the ends in contrast to transactional leadership which is mostly concerned with the means.

Public leadership can play an important role in the process of pushing innovative proposals forward (Termeer 2007). Although a transformational style seems a convincing strategy to do this, in the context of public policy making, which is largely based on transactional processes, leadership styles that have a sole focus on the outcome have the risk of losing the connections with the processes through which decisions can be made. The transactional leadership style is focused on existing decision-making procedures and structures. This style approaches an issue from the logic of appropriateness (March and Olsen 2006). The logic of appropriateness is a perspective that sees human action as driven by rules of appropriate or exemplary behavior, organized into institutions. Rules are followed because they are seen as natural, rightful, expected and legitimate.

Especially in the case of inter-organizational leadership connections with the processes of decision making, the various actors in the process and the context within which policy proposals are to be embedded, need to be maintained (Edelenbos 2005). Connective capacities are therefore highly important in the public leadership role that is focused on combining existing processes of transaction with bringing in alternative issues that require adjustment of these processes.

Capacities to create the stimulating environment in which connections can be made require a certain daring from the leadership position. This daring is needed to allow complexity and uncertainty into the policy system in order to enable possibilities for the development of creative and innovative solutions. Such an uncertain situation in the policy system is not without risk and can often be considered a bet on the public and political backing of the proposed plan. Uhl-

Bien et al. (2007: 311) refer to this as: 'risking catastrophe to enable creativity and fitness.' This leads us to the alternative ideal type of daring leadership. In its focus on the connecting of alternative issues to the existing context the daring leadership ideal type forms a new combination of partly intermediary, partly crossed-over and partly unique aspects with regard to the ideal types of transactional and transformational leadership.

In the act of coupling an innovative proposal to an existing context, daring leadership is primarily recognizable in its bet on support. Without losing focus on the issue at hand, daring leadership aims to create new connections and to bargain with other parties, thereby connecting stakeholders on different layers and levels, not just with each other but ultimately also with the issue. As such daring leadership actively deals with the complexities of a multi layered governance process.

Throughout this process it remains unclear whether public and political support can ultimately be expected. This leadership can therefore be characterized as daring. The three types are distinguished and described in the TDT-typology based on specific elements of leadership (see Table 2.1).

Table 2.1   Exercise of leadership in the TDT-typology

	Transactional	**Daring**	**Transformational**
Focus of Action	Process	Connecting Content with Process	Content
Main repertoire of activities	Accommodating brokerage	Issue Management & Multi-actor connectivity	Advocacy
Interaction form	Cooperation	Coopetition	Competition
Strategies	Dialogue, Decide and Deliver	Announce, Dialogue and Adjust	Decide, Announce and Defend
Betting on support	No	Yes	No
Interest in the content of the decision	Low	High	High

Focus of Action

In this category of leadership exercise we distinguish between actions that are primarily focused on either process (transactional) or content (transformational) or, in case of daring leadership, on a combination of both. Transactional leadership is primarily focused on the maintenance of the decision-making process, the reduction of conflict and the following of procedures. Process is leading, and substance follows from process (Edelenbos et al. 2009). Contrary, transformational leadership is strongly content oriented and focuses primarily on the pushing of a proposal and the convincing of others. This approach is comparable with what is labeled in literature as project management (Mantel. 2005).

In daring leadership the focus of action is on connecting the efforts to promote the preferred content with existing processes and deliberative routines. Actions are focused on influencing and directing toward certain policy content whilst simultaneously an openness and adaptability in the process of decision-making is created. New process rules may be negotiated along the way if the content of the plan so requires. In other words, the focus of daring leadership lies on the issue that is under consideration as well as on connecting of innovative proposals that address this issue to the existing context of policy making. With this focus the daring leader actively embraces complexity.

Main Repertoire

The main repertoire of leadership activities in transactional leadership consists of accommodating brokerage. This type of brokerage has a solely facilitative role in the processes of decision-making. It is focused on maintenance of the policy process and keeping conflict levels low. In transformational leadership the repertoire exists mainly of advocacy activities. Here, the leader is constantly trying to convince others that this is the most preferable option to address a specific issue of consequence (Scholten 2010).

The repertoire in the daring leadership ideal-type is built on what can be identified as *issue management* and *multi stakeholder connectivity*. With an eye on the issue that is under consideration as well as on the connection of innovative proposals that address this issue to the existing context of policy making, brokerage activities in the daring ideal-type are not focused solely on process accommodation, as is the case in transactional leadership, but are deployed in the light of the specific issue at hand. This issue is the focal point or the 'umbrella' under which different parties in the process can bring in their adjustments and dimensions that represent their own interests and viewpoints in a dynamic and open process in which the leader aims to create new connections across existing coalitions and bargains with other parties in the light of bringing the issue further. Such a focusing on the issue while creating new connections and bargaining with other parties can be identified as issue management.

This approach to the management of decision-making processes transcends the boundaries of traditional process accommodation based on existing rules, procedures and codes of conduct and aims to arrive at new interpretations of multi-level and multi-stakeholder governance and participatory processes in which a variety of actors are invited to engage in the decision-making process. In such processes however, the issue remains the focal point, with the connection of various stakeholders, levels and layers with each other and with the issue as a primary activity. This connective capacity of such a multi-stakeholder orientation can be identified as multi-actor connectivity. Multi- actor connectivity is thus directly linked with issue management; they are two sides of the same coin.

Interaction Form

Transactional leadership structures the process of decision-making on cooperation and continuous interaction with the different stakeholders in which conflictive decisions are avoided by merging all interests in an attempt to strike an average. This interaction form often results in a compromise that addresses the various different opinions but risks a reinterpretation of the initial policy goals (Scholten 2010). The transformational form of interaction is characterized as competitive. A preferred proposal is pushed forward and put to compete with possible other ideas or interests. The manager operates based on exclusion and avoids cooperation because this makes things too (needlessly) complex (Edelenbos et al. 2009).

Daring leadership refers to the attempt to create a balanced process of competition and cooperation in multiple interactions between stakeholders in processes that are aimed to transcend boundaries of different stakes, levels and domains. In these processes the policy direction is fixed beforehand but the various different aspects and ideas get room to compete in order to generate creativity and mutual understanding in a cooperative as well as a slightly competitive search for solutions that concur with the policy direction. This combined interaction form is characterized as 'coopetition' (Teisman 2001).

Strategies of Decision-making

A transactional communication strategy is strongly focused on dialogue between the different stakeholders in the project. Decisions result only from the process of communication and need to encompass the views of all participants. This strategy can be characterized as a DDD strategy: Dialogue, Decide and Deliver (Edelenbos et al. 2009).

Transactional leaders focus on controlling the policy process and therefore apply regulated openness for the environment to their project. The process is open to all parties but the involvement of stakeholders is organized through strict procedures and rules of conduct. Decision-making in a transactional style is directed toward a compromise. The leadership role is focused on accommodating the discussion and debate between stakeholders which will eventually leads to a decision that is supported by the majority of involved actors. Yet this might be hardly effective in addressing the problem at hand.

A transformational communication strategy is characterized by the relative absence of dialogue. The desired solution is decided upon in a more or less autocratic fashion, without consultation and deliberation. This decision is then announced to the environment and defended against opposing arguments or misgivings (Beierle and Cayford 2002, Quah and Tan 2002). This strategy can be characterized as a Decide, Announce and Defend (DAD) strategy. As a result the decision-making process in transformational leadership is closed for the whole range of stakeholders. Only those actors that have sympathy for the proposed policy or can be convinced to share the vision are actively involved. Although this can be convincing, a transformational orientation might push for a proposed solution too hard, and risk ending up with a lack of public and political support.

Combining both strategies in a daring leadership style leads to an advertising strategy that announces an issue of consequence in the form of an explorative proposal and invites to a dialogue between all stakeholders. This can lead to an adjustment within the fixed boundaries of the proposed policy direction. Such a style can be characterized as an Announce, Dialogue and Adjust (ADA) strategy (Scholten 2011). In the combining of both repertoires daring leadership expresses a clear policy goal and accompanying direction and attempts to combine this with a joint effort of exploration with stakeholders to determine how the proposed concept can be brought further. In the decision-making process the leader alternates between moments of exploration and fixation. In such a combination of fixating achieved consensus on partial results and further exploration of the following steps, the decision-making is being shaped.

Betting on Support and Dealing with Complexity

The public domain is characterized by a specific complexity. In processes of policy-making, various parties interact on various levels with different goals and different backgrounds, using different rules and perceptions, in an ever-changing world (Scholten 2011). Within this complexity, public leaders have to operate based on the support of the majority of parties. When focusing on an issue of consequence and promoting a specific innovative proposal that combines the issue with the existing context of policy making, a step beyond daily routine is taken. In an attempt to push such a proposal further and connect the innovative ideas to the existing policy arena, public and political support are ultimately essential. Initially it is unclear whether the necessary support will ultimately be found. The aspect of betting on support in the TDT-typology represents the specific way that the three ideal types relate to this issue as well as how they deal with the uncertainties that it provokes in the complex context of decision-making (Teisman 2001).

The ideal typical transactional leader would, in the case of such uncertainty, remain focused on the process and as a result this approach leaves little room for pushing an innovative proposal. The process oriented transactional style can only function within the boundaries of existing commitment to a certain issue. Without the commitment of stakeholders the transactional leader cannot initiate a process. In other words, the transactional type does not display a bet on support.

Leadership that goes beyond transactional behavior and focuses attention on a specific issue in the form of a proposal without the assurance of support for such ideas can be regarded as betting on public and political support. Such leadership exercise requires daring. Yet, there is an important difference between the ideal types of transformational and daring leadership. The typical transformational leader strongly believes in the content of the proposal and is convinced that others will become followers as soon as they are confronted with compelling arguments that show that the proposed solution is indeed the best solution. This typical way of dealing with support can seem like a bet for outsiders but the individual leader has no doubt in this case. Therefore, from the leadership point of view, it can be concluded that there is no actual bet on support.

Daring leadership considers the existence of ultimate support as uncertain and therefore is actively betting on support. In this case the bet is accompanied with an active involvement in the process of exchanging viewpoints with other stakeholders. The daring leader is attempting to merge views and incorporate different interests into a policy trajectory that still aims for the goals that were set in the initial proposal.

As such a daring style actively engages the complexities of the policy process[1] instead of attempting to reduce complexity. Such a complexity reducing behavior can be witnessed in the strong focus on the rules and regulations of the process as it is done in transactional leadership. Transformational leadership attempts to reduce complexity by a sole focus on the content and the pushing of this proposal, regardless of the specific circumstances.

Interest in the Content of the Decision

Generally the transformational leadership type is accompanied with a high interest in the content of the specific outcome of the decision-making process. Contrarily, the transactional type is mainly occupied with process maintenance. In this style the process denominates content. A daring type of leadership is also accompanied by a high interest in the content of the proposed decision and specifically tries to connect this content with the existing context.

Methods Used in the Research

In this study we selected three 'cases' of individual political-public leaders in their role of provincial delegates in the project Volkerak Zoommeer (abbreviated 'VZ'). The three individuals were delegates of the three provinces Zeeland, Zuid-Holland and Noord-Brabant. The three provinces are connected in the project VZ due to their location, adjoining the Volkerak-Zoommeer.

In the description and analysis of the three individual leaders and their specific contexts, a qualitative multiple case study design was used. To capture the richness

---

1　The characteristics of such a complexity embracing style of leadership can be related to styles of management, on a project level, described as complexity sensitive management by Edelenbos, van Meerkerk and Klijn in Chapter 14 of this book.

of individual settings and understand how actors act and think within their specific contexts, a case study approach is highly appropriate (Yin 1994).

The empirical material in this study has been obtained from two sources. Firstly, the main part of the data has been obtained through semi-structured interviewing[2]. This type of interviewing allows for openness and dynamics and is considered the most appropriate tool in explorative research designs (Corbin and Strauss 2008). These interviews have been conducted in two rounds. The first round focused on the direct circle of public servants, process facilitators and other colleagues in the VZ project surrounding the individual leaders that were the focus of this study. One on one semi-structured interviews that took 30 minutes were undertaken. If necessary for additional data certainty or precision, a follow up by telephone, e-mail and even additional interviews has been carried out. Respondents were selected based on the following criteria: 1) long tenure in the organization in order to provide an historical overview that stretches beyond the position of the current leaders, 2) direct involvement with the three individual leaders, to provide deeper and first-hand knowledge and 3) functional variety to obtain a more colorful range of perspectives on the leadership position. The second round consisted of interviews with the three public leaders themselves. The use of multiple respondents provides the opportunity to mitigate biases or socially desirable answering by allowing the information to be confirmed across several sources. A total of 14 qualitative in-depth interviews were carried out. In addition to this, observations during public meetings concerning the decision-making process of the VZ project have been made.

Furthermore, a document analysis was undertaken. This included documents such as policy papers, technical reports and notes of meetings. This document analysis was used to reconstruct the various events in the process and forms the basis for the case description in this article. The combining of this archival data with the information obtained in the interviews provided opportunities for data triangulation.

Based on the TDT-typology and the methods used, we can now describe and analyze the various actions of political leaders in the case study. Through this

---

2   The interviews were recorded, transcribed and subsequently processed with the software package MAXQDA. The transcripts were analyzed through selective coding (Corbin and Strauss 2008). The process of coding was based on the conceptual model of leadership exercise described in Table 2.1. The various components of the leadership exercise have been further developed into codes and sub codes. These codes were used to group and structure the statements from respondents. Text segments that gave the most expressive, colorful or pronounced description of the component behind the code are also used in the empirical description that follows in the next section. In addition to the codes that were derived from the conceptual model, alternative codes were created to capture other factors that emerged from the empirical research but were not conceptualized beforehand. One example is found in the exercise table in which the element 'Interest in the content of the decision' was added during the process of data analysis.

description we can also asses what the characteristics of these leadership activities are in terms of connective capacity.

Case Study: Leadership Activities in the Case of the Volkerak Zoommeer

In this section we will describe the political-public leadership activities of three provincial delegates, working on innovative proposals for the management of a large water body in the Netherlands. Before we describe the three cases of leadership we will first provide background information on the project.

Background Information on the VZ Case

The south-western part of the Netherlands consists of a large estuary in which some of Europe's largest rivers find their way into the North Sea. In this area safety against floods has always been an important issue. The constant building and improving of storm and flood barriers proved to be difficult and expensive. A solution was found in the closing of the main river estuaries. This solution is widely known as the 'delta works'. A hazardous flood in 1953 created a sense of urgency that lead to the adoption of the delta works solution and implementation of the plans started in 1954.

The delta works were intended to protect large areas that had been prone to frequent flooding and soil salinization. All but one of the estuaries was sealed off by storm barriers, sluices and dams which created a highly compartmentalized, and highly controllable, estuarine area.

Besides the safety measures, the dams in the delta were functional in the controlling of the water levels in the Rhine-Scheldt connection, that formed a direct route between the ports of Rotterdam and Antwerp. They further functioned as means to stabilize the environment for agriculture in the provinces of Zeeland and Noord-Brabant. Due to the dam structure a number of fresh water basins were formed. These basins provided possibilities for the development of intensive agriculture in an area that had been historically unfit for cropping. The Volkerak-Zoommeer (VZ) consists of two of these basins which are connected through the Rhine-Scheldt canal.

Although the delta works have been regarded as a wonderful piece of engineering, it appears that it is not the solution it once seemed to be. Over the past years a steady decline in ecological diversity and water quality have been identified in almost all parts of the delta region. Even the once so innovative sluice construction in the eastern Scheldt has resulted in an unforeseen decline of marine sedimentation. Apart from ecological degradation due to this decline, the process is also counterproductive regarding flood prevention since the natural accretion of land in a natural situation is now reversed into sand decretion due to the technical measures that have been implemented.

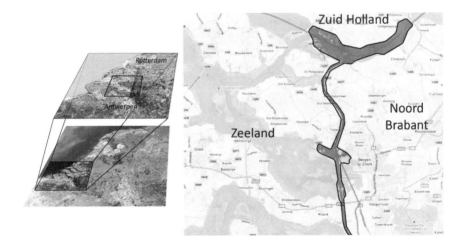

Figure 2.1   The Volkerak Zoommeer

In order to create a more ecologically sound environment in the delta and enhance adaptive capacity to rising water levels due to climatic changes, a change in the management strategy is needed. The former perspective of extreme control needs to be changed toward a management style that allows the return of estuarine dynamics in the delta area.

As a result of the deployment of storm barriers and dykes in the eastern Scheldt, two large fresh water basins connected by the Rhine-Scheldt corridor formed the Volkerak- Zoommeer. The basin receives fresh water from several rivers and canals. Due to the high concentration of nutrients in the water as well as the marginal outflow due to the dams, the basin is highly eutrophicated. As a former estuary the bottom soil is rich in phosphates which flow into the water during the summer season.

These circumstances culminate in a severe algae bloom during the summer period which severely destabilizes the ecosystem and creates a major impediment to the local communities. The decay of algae results in a toxic residue that leads to a high mortality of fish and bird species and results in skin and stomach problems for humans. The water is very low on oxygen and emits an awful smell.

From 2002 onward, the administrative council for the VZ together with the national water authority have investigated possible solution strategies with the ambition to have found and implemented a solution by the year 2015. After intense research it appeared that a re-salinization of the basin in combination with a reintroduction of some of the original tidal flows would be the only viable solution. Such a solution strategy would be much more costly and intensive than what was initially hoped for. However, the proposed solution fits very well with the changing paradigm in Dutch water management based on the idea that less human control and more space for water dynamics in riverine and maritime areas can provide more safety as well as a growth in ecological and landscape quality (Van Buuren et al. 2010).

Local agriculture is very dependent on the availability of fresh water in the region and uses the VZ as a source for fresh water. The re-salinization of the region could pose a threat to the agricultural industry on the islands. An alternative supply of fresh water is necessary to continue agricultural production in its current form. In the period of 2005-2009 a decision-making process that involved a large group of stakeholders led to a proposal for re-salinization on the condition that alternative supplies of fresh water would be established (Stuurgroep Zuidwestelijke Delta 2009).

The Role of Individual Political-public Leadership in the VZ Project

In this section we will describe the leadership behavior of the three provincial delegates that have a key role in the VZ project. These are the delegates from the provinces of Zuid-Holland, Brabant and Zeeland. A case description is given of every individual delegate based on the delegate's actions and behaviors within the context of decision-making concerning the VZ project. This so-called exercise of leadership is described and then further clarified through the conceptual lens provided in Table 2.2.

The Case of Zuid-Holland

The leadership exercise of the delegate of Zuid-Holland has been undergoing a radical change in recent years from a rather uninterested and inactive position toward a highly committed and decisive role in the process of the southwestern Delta and specifically the VZ project.

In this moment of change the delegate has put in many efforts to gain the chair position of the committee that is responsible for the South Western Delta. The VZ project is one of the key projects in the proposed plans for this area. This resulted in the fact that she is now a leading figure in the policy process. A bureaucratic staff member from the neighboring provincial government of Brabant remembers:

> In that specific week she has been calling our delegate almost every day to make sure that she would be getting the chair position.

The delegate shows an intention to couple the plans for the VZ project with the interests of the larger delta area and specifically with the interests of the involved stakeholders in her province. As such the focus of her actions is on connecting the content of the VZ proposal with the existing processes, which is consistent with daring leadership behavior. Generally her leadership style can be described as trying to convince others with an energetic and dash leadership exercise.

She wants inspiring results and when she believes she knows the ins and outs, she starts to convince others. She has a lot of energy and inner drive.

Consequently, advocacy is a dominant factor in her attempts to bring various parties together in light of the proposal. The content of the VZ proposal is a leading element in the establishing of connections between parties on various levels of the policy process. This tendency toward advocacy behavior sometimes has negative effects in the case of the VZ project where so many different opinions and interests collide. The delegate herself is aware of this and refers to this in the context of the VZ project as follows:

My personal weakness is that if I personally believe in a proposal I want others to believe in it too! But oftentimes they don't. This makes it very difficult to deal with.

The difficulties of such a style were also experienced in the general interaction with other parties which is initially characterized by a competitive form. One of the informants points out that:

The power in her style is more articulated through conflict than through connectivity.

It is important to note that, although in practice the delegate often has the tendency toward a competitive interaction, the overall aim and strategy in the VZ project can be characterized as a daring leadership style in which the announced and initially defended idea is eventually subject to dialogue and can as such be adjusted to the various different opinions within the parameters of the proposed policy direction, following the ADA-strategy. The delegate describes this as follows:

Communication in this process is in two directions. And those that object the proposed policy must eventually be able to find that their objections have had an influence on the process and are as such embedded in the eventual decision.

Furthermore, the delegate shows an intention to couple the plans for the VZ project with the interests of the larger delta area and specifically with the interests of the involved stakeholders in her province. In this process the delegate attempts to combine openness toward stakeholders with decisiveness.

You need to always stay open minded to the ideas and input of others and to the fact that these might change the initial viewpoint or proposal, but this should not prevent the necessity of reaching a decision in a timely fashion.

In Table 2.2, the visualization of the exercise of leadership describes a leadership behavior which has a daring orientation but simultaneously involves a specific transformational element.

Table 2.2   The leadership exercise of leader 1

	Transactional	**Daring**	**Transformational**
Focus of Action	Process	Connecting Content with Process	Content
Main repertoire of activities	Accommodating brokerage	Issue Management & Multi-actor connectivity	Advocacy
Interaction form	Cooperation	Coopetition	Competition
Strategies	Dialogue, Decide and Deliver	Announce, Dialogue and Adjust	Decide, Announce and Defend
Betting on support	No	Yes	No
Interest in the content of the decision	Low	High	High

With the sudden change in interest for the VZ project and the assuming of a leading role in the policy process, the delegate displays a daring attitude and takes a bet on support in the pursuit of success in this difficult project which is faced with a lot of opposition. Although her direct political environment is not at all convinced of the plans for the VZ project, she continues to push forward and states that:

> The mobilizing of power to convince them is needed.

She also shows a high interest in the content of the proposed plan and uses this knowledge of the ins and outs of the plan to ensure the interests of the stakeholders in Zuid-Holland are being looked after and as such create connections between the level of the VZ project and the level of the province of Zuid-Holland.

Analyzing the Nature of Connective Capacity

This leader shows a style of leadership that uses the content of the proposed plans, largely as a driving force for developing interconnections. Although she propagates a specific direction in which the VZ project should develop, she is also very much oriented on connecting certain content to the process in which this content needs further development and support. She shows receptivity to other interests, values and perspectives and is prepared to adjust the visions or solution in a way that meets the values and interests of other stakeholders in the project. Especially on local levels in interactions with stakeholders such as local farmers and water boards. In the process of coupling the generated proposals to the provincial level she tends to rely strongly on an advocacy of the proposed content, emphasizing its importance in the relation to other provincial interests. So far, this strategy of pushing the content has not yet resulted in convincing other parties at the provincial level.

The Case of Noord-Brabant

The exercise of leadership in the project VZ of this delegate has been far less intense compared to his colleagues in the project. Initially he put some effort in the project but later on his role has been characterized by absence.

His initial effort is characterized by a transformational style of leadership. During this phase a public meeting was held to discuss the problem of fresh water supply to the region of the VZ project. The delegate's repertoire of activities consisted mainly out of advocacy behavior in which a proposed solution was pushed forward. With the display of a decisive and convincing decision-making strategy it was hoped followers could be found and as such the meetings would give birth to immediate results. He started the process of deliberation with stakeholders by announcing the results of research reports about the possible solution strategies concerning the alternative fresh water supply and attempted to push the proposal that was provided by his department based on these reports. One of the process facilitators during this period describes it as follows:

> We wanted to start with an orientation of stakeholder opinions but the delegate had different ideas on that. He believed everything was sorted out and solution strategies could be presented and put into action. He wanted actions that lead to results. If there is no immediate result to focus on, he won't act.

A transformational leadership style could also be found in the strategies of communication and the interaction with other parties in the policy process.

> In this case I think the delegate is not so interested in listening, he will be more apt to send out his message.

This message contained the proposed solution strategy and was communicated in a style that can be characterized as a Decide Announce and Defend strategy. The proposal was treated as the preferable decision and as such announced and defended. In that specific exercise of leadership the involvement of stakeholders was closed for those that had possible other opinions.

Although it was hoped to establish connections between the various stakeholders on different levels through the pushing of a convincing proposal, this competitive interaction form did not result in the emergence of followers. The groups of stakeholders that were present at the meeting didn't agree with the delegate and demanded a process of deliberation about the possible solutions. With this outcome the delegate reoriented his focus and attention and decided to put little further effort in the project. Consequently, this led to a period of absence of the delegate in the decision making process.

> He thought it could be arranged in two meetings, but when it appeared to take longer, he sent his subordinate to attend the meetings. We haven't seen him since.

Summarizing the exercise of leadership using the exercise table we can clearly observe a transformational leadership exercise in this specific case.

Table 2.3   The leadership exercise delegate 2

	Transactional	**Daring**	**Transformational**
Focus of Action	Process	Connecting Content with Process	Content
Main repertoire of activities	Accommodating brokerage	Issue Management & Multi-actor connectivity	Advocacy
Interaction form	Cooperation	Coopetition	Competition
Strategies	Dialogue, Decide and Deliver	Announce, Dialogue and Adjust	Decide, Announce and Defend
Betting on support	No	Yes	No
Interest in the content of the decision	Low	High	High

The element 'focus of action' remains empty. Due to the decision to refrain from an active involvement in the policy process it is concluded that the delegate's actions were not convincingly focused on either facilitating the process or pushing for specific content. Efforts to connect process and content were also not undertaken.

> I am more interested in the main issue. And others tend to focus on the problems
> and side issues. Well, that probably all needs to be solved but I leave that to
> others. I am holding on to the main issue.

The delegate's interest in the specific content of the decision is considered low. In the project VZ his attention has been focused on the possibilities for achieving direct results and making possible decisive moves.

> He seems only committed to direct results with which he can show his decisive
> skills.

When results were not directly available the delegate left the process in the hands of his subordinates and the process facilitators while concentrating his efforts on other things. A bet on support for the initially proposed content is therefore also not made.

Analyzing the Nature of Connective Capacity

In this case we see that the leader relies strongly on specific content in attempting to establish connections of the proposal with the various parties on different levels of the policy process. The specific content of his proposal is largely created at the provincial level and as such, without possibilities to adjust the content, advocated as the preferable option. This strategy leaves no room for adjustment in relation to other parties on other levels, such as for instance the local community or the farmer organizations. This results in a very low connectivity. The connections that exist are fragile and the required longer term commitment in order to adapt and develop the proposal in congruence to the various stakes and viewpoints of participants is not generated through the delegate's strategy of competition and mutual exclusion.

The Case of Zeeland

The delegate of Zeeland is considered an important figure in the process of the VZ project due to his commitment to the content of the plans.

> The delegate is important because he strives for realization of this project. He
> sees an intrinsic need for salinization.

With his instatement as delegate, this leader took up the chair position of the dormant regional board concerning the affairs connected to the VZ. He initiated the revival of this assembly in order to bring the VZ project further in a regional cooperation. His focus of action can be described as daring since he is focused on connecting the content of the proposal to the existing context and the mechanisms that are involved in the decision-making process. In a personal interview the delegate states:

> Personally I would say that content should be primarily important, yet support
> for this content is indispensable. Therefore, the process is of great importance.
> So it is my goal to create a good balance between them.

In this act of balancing content and process a tendency toward accommodating
brokerage behavior is recognized by several respondents in the interviews.

> The delegate has a very careful and conscientious role in the process of decision-
> making.
> He's a man who tends to seek the middle of the road.
> He is more conserving than an innovator.
> He wants to keep everyone in the process on board.

Another example of this process accommodating style can be found in the
interaction form. Here, this leader uses a non-competitive style, which is mostly
focused on stimulating and preserving cooperation between the various parties in
the process. Brokerage activities are not entrepreneurial but aimed at facilitating
the process, through which he seeks to establish connections between stakeholders
and levels. In the interactions with the neighboring province, he has already in a
premature stadium declared that he will not push the proposal and strive for the
chosen policy direction in case the experimental measures to retain the salt leak
into the Hollands Diep would fail. It can be expected that re-salinization of the
VZ would then meet lots of opposition from the neighboring province of Zuid-
Holland. Here an emphasis on the content of the plan is considered less important
than the process of decision-making and the preservation of a low conflict level in
order to keep all parties involved in the interaction.

In his overall strategies this leader displays an openness and flexibility in
the communication which is congruent with a daring leadership style. He does
not push his own position at the costs of other arguments yet at the same time
remains focused on a distinct policy direction. He puts in a lot of effort to engage
stakeholders in the decision-making process.

> He took the initiative to ask the involved farmers what would be the best next
> step in their opinion.

> It was his idea to form alliances of stakeholders that can operate together and
> find possibilities to cover the costs for the planned innovations.

However, it seems questionable whether a distinctively daring leadership moment
of decisiveness in which a fixation of partial results is established, is reached as
well.

He has been a very good leader when it comes to the decision-making process and hearing all the stakes and opinions, yet I think it would be good if he would sometimes be a little more decisive.

Generally this delegate performs an important role in the process of the VZ project. He puts in lots of energy to bring the process further. Characteristically this is not done with an advocating and energizing style but rather in an explanatory fashion, highlighting the substantive elements of the project and their necessity. As such he can sustain long in the processes of decision-making without taking the lead and displaying strong directive actions. With this process oriented and non-advocating style he has been able to modestly influence the process.

Table 2.4   The leadership exercise of delegate 3

	Transactional	Daring	Transformational
Focus of Action	Process	Connecting Content with Process	Content
Main repertoire of activities	Accommodating brokerage	Issue Management & Multi-actor connectivity	Advocacy
Interaction form	Cooperation	Coopetition	Competition
Strategies	Dialogue, Decide and Deliver	Announce, Dialogue and Adjust	Decide, Announce and Defend
Betting on support	No	Yes	No
Interest in the content of the decision	Low	High	High

When summarized in Table 2.4, again a hybrid description of the leadership exercise emerges. With a high interest in the content of the VZ proposal and a clear focus on combining this content with the existing context of policy-making, this leadership can be initially described as daring. Yet, simultaneously in the day to day practice of decision-making the delegate shows a strong tendency toward transactional activities and interactions. The process accommodating fashion with which the leader operates in combination with the existing political and public support for the plans of the VZ project indicate that this exercise of leadership is hardly a bet on support.

Analyzing the Nature of Connective Capacity

In this case, the nature of the leadership exercise is that of a combined daring and transactional style. The leader is generally focused on accommodating brokerage. He leaves room for stakeholders to bring in their interests and viewpoints on the project VZ. For him a carefully designed and implemented process is of high importance.

Connective capacity is thus sought mainly via process in which content is a product. This contrary to the other two cases in which content was more a driving force for developing interconnections among the other two provincial levels. This is especially seen in the interactions with other provincial governments. The delegate depends strongly on process as a means to connect the different provincial agendas.

The result of this process orientation shows decision-making in which various parties on different levels can voice their opinions, however an active involvement of the leader to develop the process toward an incorporation of the various stakes and viewpoints is not shown. The possibility to forge strong connections between the for instance the provincial governments is therewith not fully achieved.

Conclusion

In our case descriptions and analyses we discovered that the three political-public leader all used different combinations of leadership styles. One conclusion is that leadership styles pay attention to connective capacity in specific ways. Transactional leadership is approaching connectivity in a process oriented way, through focusing on interactions and cooperative relationships among stakeholders in different layers and governmental levels. The transformational leadership style is more focused on creating and developing connections in competition with other involved stakeholders. Through convincing and persuasion strategies the leader tries to realize that other stakeholders adapt to his or her preferred solution. Finally, the daring leadership style is also departing from a preferred vision, but the connective activities are more focused on mobilizing other actors through an appealing first idea or solution and then to further develop and adapt this idea in interaction with other stakeholders.

Secondly we found that, although in theory one can distinguish three general types of leadership, in practice the three modes of political leadership merge. So the different aspects from the three different perspectives are exchangeable. These mixtures of leadership types resulted in different approaches and effects on the establishing of multi-level interconnections. In the first leadership example we have witnessed a daring leadership exercise in which also a strong advocacy style played a role. In an attempt to connect various stakeholders, layers and levels with each other and with the issue, the advocating of a specific characterization of this issue was used as a connective strategy. However, apart from the advocacy, the delegate also found ways to adjust the initially defended content to the interests of the various stakeholders in the process. As such, she could establish connections between stakeholders on both the local and the provincial level.

In the second example an even stronger case of content driven connectivity behavior was witnessed. Here connectivity was hoped to be achieved through convincing other parties of the better proposal and out-competing other content. Instead of creating multi-level connections, this strategy resulted in a lack of functional interrelations and stalemate. In the third example the leader attempted to establish connectivity by focusing on the process. Although the process created possibilities for the various stakeholders to interact, the connections lack specific mutually defined content. Existing process dynamics might create interrelationships but are hardly expected to emanate new interpretations of multi-level and multi-stakeholder governance in which parties adjust their proposals in order to adapt to each other's interests. Such a focus on process will therefore not actively create the necessary connections across layers and levels that are based on a mutually shared content, which can encompass the diverse interests of the various parties in the process.

From the experiences with leadership in the case study we can conclude that connective capacity, needed to bring together various parties on different levels of the policy process, is best developed through a leadership effort that combines both a focus on the process dynamics of decision-making and a focus on the specific content of the proposal, whereby the content can be shaped through continuous processes of mutual adjustment of the different parties on different levels. Therefore, we argue that the leadership exercise in the light of connecting layers and levels could be enhanced if leaders are able to shape their leadership activities more in congruence with the specific elements of issue management and multi-stakeholder connectivity, as they are found in the daring leadership repertoire.

Bibliography

Bass, B.M. 1985. *Leadership and Performance beyond Expectations*. New York: Free Press.

Bass, B.M and Avolio, B.J. 1994. *Improving Organizational Effectiveness through Transformational Leadership*. Thousand Oaks, CA: Sage Publications.

Beierle, T.C. and Cayford, J. 2002. *Democracy in Practice: Public Participation in Environmental Decisions*. Washington, DC: RFF Press Books.

Corbin, J. and Strauss, A. 2008. *Basics of Qualitative Research* (3rd edition). Thousand Oaks, CA: Sage Publications.

Edelenbos, J. 2005. Institutional implications of interactive governance: Insights from Dutch practice. *Governance*, 18(1), 111-34.

Edelenbos, J., Klijn, E.H. and Kort, M. 2009. Managing complex process systems: Surviving at the edge of chaos, in *Managing Complex Governance Systems*, edited by G.R. Teisman, M.W. van Buuren and L. Gerrits. London: Routledge, 172-92.

Edelenbos, J. 2010. *Water as Connective Current/water als spanningsvolle verbinding*, inaugurele rede. Den Haag: Boom/Lemma.

Hart, P.'t and Uhr, J. 2008. *Public Leadership: Perspectives and Practices*. Canberra: ANU E Press.

Mantel, S. 2005. *Core Concepts of Project Management*. Hoboken, NJ: Wiley.

March, J. and Olsen, P. 2006. The logic of appropriateness, *The Oxford Handbook of Public Policy*, edited by M. Moran, M. Rein and R.E. Goodin. Oxford: Oxford University Press Inc., 221-42.

Quah, E. and Tan, K.C. 2002. *Siting Environmentally Unwanted Facilities*. Cheltenham: Edward Edgar.

Scholten, P. 2010. Daring decisions and representative municipal democracy: An exploration within new river management in The Netherlands. *The Innovation Journal*, 14(1), 28-42.

Scholten, P.H.T. 2011. *Daring Leadership: A Study of Water Governance on the Edge of Innovation and Democracy*. PhD Thesis. Nijmegen: Radboud University Nijmegen.

Stuurgroep Zuidwestelijke Delta. 2009. Zoet water Zuidwestelijke Delta. Middelburg.

Teisman, G.R. 2001. *Creating Space for Cooperative Government*. Rotterdam: Erasmus University Rotterdam.

Teisman, G.R. and Edelenbos, J. 2011. Towards a perspective of system synchronization in water governance: A synthesis of empirical lessons and complexity theories. *International Review of Administrative Sciences*, 77(1), 101-18.

Termeer, C.J.A.M. 2007. Betekenissen van publiek leiderschap voor maatschappelijke innovatie. *Bestuurskunde*, 12(2), 104-13.

Uhl-Bien, M., Marion, R. and McKelvey, B. 2007. Complexity Leadership Theory: Shifting leadership from the industrial age to the knowledge age. *The Leadership Quarterly*, 18(3), 298-318.

Van Buuren, A., Edelenbos, J. and Klijn, E.H. 2010. *Gebiedsontwikkeling in Woelig Water. Over water governance bewegend tussen adaptief waterbeheer en ruimtelijke besluitvorming*. Den Haag: Boom Lemma uitgevers.

Yin, R. 1994. *Case Study Research: Design and Methods* (2nd edition). Beverly Hills, CA: Sage Publishing.

Chapter 3

Connective Capacity in a Dynamic Context: Changing Water Governance Structures in Romania

Joanne Vinke-de Kruijf, Stefan Kuks and Denie Augustijn

Introduction

It is widely acknowledged that many of the world's pressing water problems are not resource or technology problems. They are rather issues of governance (Pahl-Wostl 2008). This means that they are rooted in the manner in which water resources are allocated and regulated. More specifically, they often relate to a lack of connective capacity, which is understood in this chapter as a lack of coherence or meaningful connections between various objects of water governance (Bressers and Kuks 2004, see also Chapter 1 of this book).

This chapter contributes to the overall theme of the book by discussing connective capacity in relation to change. It concentrates on questions like: how do governance structures (and its coherence) change over time and how to 'govern change' – this is, how to create or consolidate connective capacity under changing circumstances? To answer these questions, this chapter builds upon an analysis of recent changes in the water sector of Romania, a transition country that recently accessed the European Union (EU). In terms of carriers of connectedness and focal points of connective capacity, this chapter concentrates on: (1) reforms as *instruments* that are employed by governmental actors to improve water governance; and (2) the role and implications of the integration of an additional (EU) level as a change in government *layers and levels* (see Chapter 1 of this book). Reforms refer here to deliberate changes in governance structures for the purpose of making them function better (Pollitt and Bouckaert 2011). We especially focus on reforms in water governance, which we define as the "range of political, social, economic and administrative systems that are in place to develop and manage water resources, and the delivery of water services, at different levels of a society" (Rogers and Hall 2003: 7). Water governance is thus about the structures that are in place for water resources (that is, the quality and quantity of surface water and ground water) and/or water services (that is, drinking water supply and treatment and wastewater collection and treatment). As activities in these sectors are shaped by various actors at different levels with different objectives and strategies, water governance can only be effective when these elements are connected in a meaningful way. This is referred to as *connective capacity*, which we define as the ability to overcome incoherence (inconsistencies) between and within various structural elements that comprise a governance structure (Bressers and Kuks 2004, Young 1982). We recognize that other qualities – such as extent, intensity and flexibility – also influence the effectiveness of a water governance structure (De Boer and Krantzberg in Chapter 16 of this book). However, we focus here on the coherence of a governance structure as this has the strongest correlation with the status and use of water resources (Kuks 2004). The reason for analyzing coherence is not that we see it as a 'must' or a pre-requisite for 'good governance'. We rather aim to draw attention to those inconsistencies that have or are expected to have practical implications (Young 1982).

Empirically, this chapter builds upon the qualitative analysis of two recent reforms in the Romanian water sector: (1) the regionalization process in the water services sector; and (2) the implementation of a strategy in the flood risk sector. The analysis concentrates on the changes between 2005 and 2010 but also pays attention to the developments that preceded these reforms. To create some understanding of these developments, we will first shortly introduce the transition that Romania is currently going through. In the period between World War II and 1989, Romania was ruled by a communist regime, which imposed a centralized economy, collective ownership and a dictatorial form of government. During this regime, water management largely focused on the construction of irrigation and drainage facilities, large-scale hydrotechnical works and regulation of the river flow (Vadineanu and Preda 2008).

Following the collapse of this regime, a gradual transition towards a pluralistic political and economic system began. This transition was and is strongly influenced by external forces that seek to integrate Romania into a mainstream, international system. Romania's adherence to the European Union (EU)[1] plays a key role in this transition process (Gallagher 2005). In order to become a member state, the country first had to feature stable political and legal institutions, a functioning market economy and to accept the *acquis communautaire* (that is, rules and legislations that were adopted by the EU member states in various policy fields, including the ones related to the environment) (Tews 2009). Like in most new EU member states, the implementation of the environmental *acquis* is challenging. As the environment has never been high on the agenda, major investments are needed to bring environmental infrastructure in line with EU standards. This challenges the financial and administrative capacity of these countries. In addition, there is often limited experience with the implementation of more participatory and integrated approaches that are promoted in various EU guidelines (Kremlis and Dusik 2005, Teodosiu et al. 2003, Tews 2009). This chapter further elaborates on these challenges with a focus on the changes in the governance of water services and flood risks.

---

1   Romania applied for EU membership in 1995 and accessed the EU – following a negotiation period between 2000 and 2004 – on the 1st of January 2007.

The remainder of this chapter is structured as follows. The next section presents the theoretical concepts that support our empirical analysis. The following sections describe and analyze recent changes in, respectively, the Romanian water services sector and the flood risk sector. The chapter then goes on to discuss and compares the change in the governance structures in both sectors. The last section presents our main conclusions regarding connective capacity in relation to these changes.

The Coherence and Dynamics of a Governance Structure

In recent years, there has been a growing recognition that society is not shaped by just one central actor but through the interaction between many actors, both public and private. This change is generally referred to as a shift from 'government' to 'governance' (Bressers and Kuks 2003). This shift is, first and foremost, associated with the declining ability of central governments to steer society. Control is increasingly shared with supranational actors, local and regional actors and also non-governmental or private actors (Jordan et al. 2005). This does not mean that the role of traditional public administrations in water management has been diminishing. The majority of actors involved in water projects still represent a public organization. What has been changing is that most contemporary policy interventions require collaborative efforts between various organizations (Bressers 2009). This especially applies to issues that cross local, regional and national jurisdictions, including water issues. The interrelatedness between varies layers and levels of government is also referred to as multi-level governance (see Chapter 1 in this book). This chapter addresses several questions related to the emergence of multi-level governance within the context of EU integration. How does it affect existing governance structures? And to what extent does it enhance or impede connective capacity? To support our analysis, we adopt a model that was developed by Bressers and Kuks (2003) and that describes a governance structure in terms of five dimensions:

1. Problem perceptions and policy objectives. What is seen as the problem? What are the causes and potential solutions? What are the objectives or standards?
2. Levels and scales of governance. Which levels are dominant? How is the interaction between various levels?
3. Actors in the policy network. Who is involved? What is their position? Who is having property and use rights? How do actors cooperate, are there any structures?
4. Strategies and instruments. Which instruments are used? How flexible are they? How are costs and benefits distributed? Which resources do they require?

5. Responsibilities and resources for implementation. Which organizations are responsible for implementation? What authority and resources are made to these organizations? What are the restrictions?

The above presented model has been used, among others, to describe and analyze transboundary regimes (see De Boer and Krantzberg in this book) and the development of water management regimes in Europe (Bressers and Kuks 2004). In this chapter, the model is used to describe a governance structure at various points in time in order to understand how it has been changing over time. Research on institutional change highlights that structures for water governance have the tendency to become more complex due to the inclusion of more dimensions. The reason for this is that with the growing number of water uses and users, the need for regulation and thus the scope of a regime also needs to increase. This contributes to the multiplication of governance dimensions: more levels, more actors, more perceptions, more instruments, more organizations with responsibilities and so on. Once regimes are becoming more complex, *coherence* becomes a relevant concept. Coherent governance implies, among others, that actors involved are aware of their mutual dependencies and interact with each other, that the existence of multiple perceptions is taken into account in strategies and objectives and that responsibilities are accompanied by resources for implementation. Coherence does not develop spontaneously: it requires deliberate interaction efforts. Such efforts are often lacking, which means that complex regimes are often examples of fragmented regimes, instead of integrated regimes. In other words: complex regimes often lack coherence as various dimensions are not connected with each other in a meaningful way (Bressers and Kuks 2004, Kuks 2004). Within the context of this book, the ability to overcome this fragmentation is called 'connective capacity'.

The above already suggests that governance structures are likely to change over time. Such changes take place within the context of two types of triggers (external sources of change): (1) the gradual or sudden increase of problem pressures; and (2) institutional changes, such as, the introduction of new guidelines. The actual impact of these triggers depends not only on the trigger itself but also on existing conditions. In other words, changes in a governance structure result from a trigger that affects one of multiple governance dimensions, which may lead to adjustment of other dimensions.

Whether such 'mutual adjustment' takes place depends on three causal mechanisms: (1) actors tend to act from a set of constant values; (2) actors tend to use a common cognitive reference frame; and (3) actors are dependent on each other's resources. The dominant set of values, the dominant cognitive reference frame and the traditional power configurations thus explain the overall impact of a trigger. If these conditions are already in line with the direction of the trigger, they can become a generator of change. If they are not in line, they can also explain stability. These conditions thus explain why a similar trigger evokes no change in one country and an incremental or radical change in another country (Bressers and Kuks 2004, Kuks 2004).

The basic analytical framework that will be used to analyze coherent governance in relation to change is schematized in Figure 3.1. The right side of the figure illustrates that a governance structure can be described in terms of five dimensions. Within this context, connective capacity refers to those instruments that are used to create or maintain coherence (represented by the two-sided arrows) within and between each of these dimensions. The left side of the figure illustrates that the overall impact of triggers for change (that is, the extent to which a trigger also evokes changes in other dimensions) depends on existing conditions.

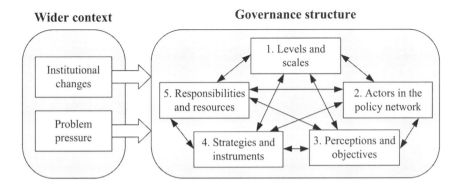

Figure 3.1   **Analytical model of a governance structure (coherence is determined by the consistency between its five dimensions) and its context (with triggers and conditions for change)**

Case Study: Regionalization of Water Services

This section describes and analyses recent changes in the governance structure of the water services sector with a focus on the regionalization process. The case study description is based on an analysis of the governance of water services in Teleorman County (before regionalization) and in Tulcea County (after regionalization). Data about Teleorman County were collected by Dinica and includes document analysis, in-depth interviews and a stakeholder survey in the period 2006-2007 (Dinica 2007). For Tulcea County, data were collected through document analysis and in-depth interviews (Vinke-de Kruijf et al. 2009).

Problems and Reforms in the Water Services Sector

Under the communist regime, water services were operated as public services at county level. After 1990, Romania returned to the local autonomy principle, which involved the transfer of major responsibilities to the local level. Local authorities became responsible for the delivery of water services. They owned water infrastructure and delegated the operation of water services to public companies (direct management) or to specialized commercial companies (delegated management). In the case of Teleorman County, two towns adopted the first model and three towns the latter. Financing was a major issue in both cases. Water companies could extract funds from seven sources of which two were used in Teleorman: water charges and local taxes. For political reasons, local councils preferred to keep both as low as possible. They were legally obliged to obtain tariff advice from a regulating authority. However, they could easily ignore this advice (and often did) as it was not binding. As a result, water tariffs were sometimes not even covering production costs. All companies in Teleorman County were having serious problems related to the quality and costs of water services. These problems are closely related to a lack of coherence within and between several governance dimensions. There was no coherence within 'responsibilities and resources for implementation' as actors responsible for the delivery of water services did not have access to sufficient resources to execute their tasks. An underlying problem was that there was no counterbalancing of the strong influence of local authorities by any higher level or independent authorities (incoherence between 'responsibilities' and 'governance level'). Local operators had no instruments to change this situation (incoherence between 'responsibilities' and 'strategies'). In addition, there was also no productive interaction between local operators on the one hand and local councils and river basin management authorities on the other hand (incoherence within 'actors in the policy network'). Actors involved mentioned the payment of fines, high fees for obtaining information and a lack of cooperation and involvement regarding the implementation of EU directives (Dinica 2007, Vinke-de Kruijf et al. 2009).

The situation in Teleorman County was not unique. In the majority of the towns, operators were unable to attract sufficient funds to maintain and develop their infrastructure. In the period between 1990 and 2005, very little investments were made. As a result, the condition of water infrastructure was generally poor when Romania started to negotiate its EU membership. In 2004, only 52 per cent of the population was connected to drinking water and sewage systems and 71 per cent of the wastewater was not or insufficiently treated (GoR 2007). Since 2001, national authorities already started to support local authorities to access international funds and to create viable operators.

However, despite several pre-accession programs, it was impossible to bring water services already in line with EU standards before accession. Hence, a transition period was negotiated for drinking water (98/93/EC) and wastewater (91/271/EC) until the end of 2015 and the end of 2018, respectively (GoR 2007). The first priority of Romania's operational program for environment (which describes how the country plans to meet de EU environmental *acquis*) is therefore to "improve the quality and access to water and wastewater infrastructure" (GoR 2007: 7). On the basis of the experiences that were gained during the pre-accession period, it was decided to reform the water services through a regionalization process. This basically involved that national authorities encouraged local authorities (owners of infrastructure) to organize themselves at regional level and to delegate their water services to a certified regional operator (service providers).

This process is still ongoing and supported by capacity building programs (GoR 2007). The case of Tulcea County (one of the forerunners in the regionalization process) illustrates that the regionalization is a challenging process that involves considerable changes in governance. One of the main changes was the redistribution of roles and responsibilities. Most investments that used to be done by local authorities are now done by the regional operator. The shares of the regional operator are distributed among local and regional authorities who have to team up in a regional association. The process also involved that the most viable operator overtook the services of smaller, less-performing operators. Viable operators participated in this process as only regional operators were eligible for EU funds. Operators urgently need these funds as they have no finances to pay for the rehabilitation and extension of infrastructure, which are both needed to comply with EU directives.

Changes in the Governance Structure

When analyzing recent developments, we observe that all dimensions of the governance structure have been changing (see Table 3.1). These changes were initiated by an institutional change (Romania's EU accession). This trigger affected several governance dimensions, including levels, objectives (EU standards) and resources (EU funds). This does, however, not yet explain why other dimensions changed as well. For this, we take a closer look at the values, cognitions and power configurations.

After communism, a high value was placed in Romania on local autonomy (decentralization). Changes in this direction were rather difficult as there was no tradition of effective co-governance by central and local authorities. Due to its lack of coherence the structure was not functioning well. In the meanwhile, EU integration was highly valued (all government parties unanimously wanted Romania to become EU member) and seen as the only way forward. From an EU perspective, water services in Romania were far too fragmented (hard to monitor) and lagging behind. To bring the situation in line with EU standards, it made a large amount of EU funds available. These funds last at least until 2018 and are an important source of motivation to bring governance in line with the structure that is promoted by the EU. The dependency on EU resources (power configuration) thus also created a tendency to adjust to EU values and cognitions. What made the changes in this direction relatively easy is that the development of a more centralized structure also fitted well with Romania's tradition. It is within this context that the external trigger evoked changes in all other dimensions as well.

Table 3.1   Recent changes in the governance of water services

Governance dimension	Main recent changes
Perceptions and objectives	Local, short-term objectives replaced by regional, long-term objectives to comply with EU standards; cost-recovery introduced.
Levels and scales of governance	Introduction of the EU level; from local-focused to regional-focused scale of governance.
Actors in the policy network	Associations introduced for local authorities; operators become regional operating (commercial) companies.
Strategies and instruments	New methods and rules for tariff setting and approval; introduction of instruments for improved management (for example, strategic planning and asset management).
Responsibilities and resources for implementation	Redefinition of roles of operator and authorities (delegation contract); operators can apply for EU funds and make investments.

The newly created structure is not yet functioning optimal. The operator in Tulcea mentioned, for example, that past power configurations still affect the functioning of the regional operator (that is, the influence of local politics is still a problem). The performance of the new regional operators is also not yet convincing. As well-performing operators are overtaking services from poor-performing operators, the performance of the former is initially going down. This is because investments are needed to bring the equipment of poor operators in line with the standards for a certified operator. The dominant cognitive reference frame will probably only become in favor of the new structure once water services improve. This is expected, as the reforms created a much more coherent structure. By creating regional associations and regional operating companies, the regionalization contributed to the interaction between and thus coherence within, 'actors in the policy network'. In the new structure, shareholders can only approve tariffs that are in line with the binding advice of the national regulating authority. This implies that local authorities (and politics) have less influence on tariff setting, which improves coherence between 'level' and 'resources and responsibilities'.

To become eligible for EU funds, operators also have to prepare a long-term strategic plan based on principles of cost-recovery. In this way, operators are forced to bring their 'objectives', 'resources' and 'strategies' in line with each other. To deal with their new role and responsibilities, operators receive training and assistance in various fields, such as human resources management, asset management and financial planning. This also enhances coherence as it provides regional operators with the 'strategies and instruments' needed to deal with their new 'responsibilities' (Sannen et al. 2008, Vinke-de Kruijf et al. 2009).

Case Study: Implementation of a Flood Risk Management Strategy

This section describes and analyses recent developments in the governance structure for flood risk management in Romania. For this case study, data were collected through document analysis, observations, in-depth interviews and a questionnaire. Most observations and interviews were related to projects in the field of flood risk management that involved Dutch and Romanian actors (September 2008 – July 2011). The questionnaire was developed and executed in cooperation with researchers from the "Gh. Asachi" Technical University of Iasi (May – September 2010). It was distributed among the monitoring departments of all eleven branches of the Romanian water management authority.

Problems and Reforms in the Flood Risk Sector

In Romania, floods have always been a recurring issue, especially in mountainous areas during spring and summer, when snow starts to melt and heavy rainfalls occur regularly (Serban and Galie 2006). Floods usually result from high waters on the Danube (the country is almost fully located in the Danube river basin, see Figure 3.2), high waters on one of the larger interior rivers or from a sudden rise of the water level in small rivers or streams (flash floods caused by torrential rain). However, during the last decades the frequency and intensity of floods increased noticeably. In recent years, floods have become yearly recurring issues causing major damage to all kind of economic objects (for example, roads, dikes, houses, bridges or dams). They resulted in many deathly casualties; in the period 1969 – 2006, there were on average 13 deathly casualties per year (MEF 2010). One of the worst recent floods took place in 2005, when high water levels throughout the country affected 1734 communities, resulted in 76 deathly casualties and caused about 1.5 billion euro of damage (GoR 2007). The increase of floods is caused by a complex set of factors including intensified land use, deforestation, increased vulnerability of buildings, (unauthorized) construction in flood-prone areas, poor design and construction of flood defense infrastructure, low safety levels, poor maintenance of water courses (obstruction) and infrastructure, and the increase of extreme meteorological events (climate variability that might be the result of climate change) (GoR 2005, 2007). A further analysis reveals that this increase also relates to a lack of information and financial resources and to poor cooperation with other stakeholders. Many of these problems are somehow related to the incoherent governance structure that emerged during the last two decades.

Figure 3.2   The location of Romania in the Danube river basin

Under the communist regime, flood prevention was a relatively orderly activity as all water courses, land and infrastructure were owned by the state. After the revolution, in 1991, legislation was introduced that allowed former owners to apply for the restitution of confiscated agricultural land and forests. In 2005, almost 96 per cent of the agricultural land and 35 per cent of the forests was restituted. It is expected that eventually about 65 per cent of the forests will be restituted to private parties or to local authorities. In terms of governance, the restitution involved a redistribution of property rights (resources) and introduced many new 'actors in the policy network'.

Due to excessive fragmentation of land, new owners have difficulties to manage their forests in a sustainable manner. In addition, they often lack the knowledge on sustainable land management and are more interested in quick economic benefits. Many of the new forest owners decided to log it, whether this was legal or not. Infrastructure, including small water courses and drainage systems with a role in flood protection, was often restituted together with the land. In many cases, this infrastructure was not maintained, abandoned or destroyed (GoR 2009). One of the underlying problems was that responsible actors were not having resources or instruments to achieve their objectives regarding the mitigation of flood risks. The governance structure was thus lacking coherence within and between 'resources and responsibilities', 'instruments' and 'objectives'.

Recently, this incoherence was (at least partly) addressed in a rural development program through which landowners can access EU funds. This program aims to contribute to flood risk reduction by means of preventing further soil degradation, preventing soil erosion and landslides through afforestation and improving and developing infrastructure. This means that land owners are now also having an incentive to contribute to flood risk mitigation. The coherence within 'actors in the policy network' also improved as private owners are obliged to organize themselves in districts and to hire a forest ranger since 2005 (GoR 2009).

Another issue is the fragmented ownership of flood defense infrastructure. The main rivers and the majority of the dikes (about 7100 km) are owned by the national water authority. This authority is organized as a national administration under the authority of the Ministry of Environment (and Forests) and operates through eleven branches at river basin level. Another important owner is the national land improvement authority of the Ministry of Agriculture, which owns 1200 km of dikes along the Danube and about 1100 km of dikes along interior rivers (ANAR 2010, ANIF 2010). In addition to this infrastructure, about 2000 dams have a role in flood protection (at permanent and non-permanent water retention reservoirs). Most of the rather large and important dams with a highly important role in flood protection (circa 10 per cent) are owned by the water authority or by the hydropower company (related to the Ministry of Economy). About 87 per cent of the smaller dams are owned by other parties: the land improvement authority, local authorities, fishery associations and private agents or individuals. In 2006, over 50 per cent of the important dams had to be repaired and circa 12 per cent of the small dams had safety problems (Abdulamit and Tanasescu 2009).

One of the main causes used to be that dam owners were not legally obliged to preserve safety levels. This changed with the introduction of new legislation (G.O. 138/2005) but dam owners are still often not preserving safety levels as they have no access to specific resources for this. Due to the fragmentation of property rights, there is thus still incoherence within and between 'resources and responsibilities' and other governance dimensions. Incoherence within the dimensions 'actors in the policy network' and 'responsibilities and resources' and between 'objectives', 'responsibilities' and 'instruments' also form the underlying cause of other flood related problems. Obstruction of the river flow at bridges or with waste (for example, from logging activities or households) is one of the issues that can only be solved in cooperation with other actors (for example, local authorities and actors in the forest sector and transport sector). However, these actors have other priorities and water authorities have no instruments to enforce or enhance such cooperation.

The construction of buildings in flood-prone areas also contributes to an increase of flood risks. The procedure for new buildings is that the advice of water authorities is used as one of the bases for the environmental permit. However, other authorities are not obliged to follow this advice. As adequate or recent hazard or risk maps are often not available, authorities also lack the information to give an adequate advice. Water authorities also reported that another more general problem is a lack of financial resources.

The above illustrates that external developments, such as land restitution and decentralization, contributed to the growing complexity of flood risk governance since communism. As these developments were not accompanied, for example, by intensified cooperation, accurate information, and new instruments, flood risk governance gradually became less coherent which contributed to an increase of flood risks. Floods currently represent the most important natural risk and the "reduction of the incidence of natural disasters affecting the population" (GoR 2007: 7) is one of the priorities of the operational program for environment. The program reads that although various actions were already taken, major investments are still needed to protect inhabitants from floods. The government therefore decided to elaborate, in collaboration with relevant stakeholders, a strategic document for flood protection (GoR 2007). This resulted in a National Strategy for Flood Risk Management (GO No. 1854/2005) for the short term (2005-2010) that was later extended with another strategy (GO No. 846/2010) for the medium and long term (2010-2035). The short term strategy marks two major changes: (1) a shift in perception and measures, that is, from passive flood defense to proactive management and from structural protection measures to a strong emphasis on non-structural measures and prevention and evaluation of flood events; and (2) cooperation with stakeholders from various sectors (for example, environment, transport, agriculture, finance, health and education), including the definition of their roles and responsibilities at various levels (national, county, local and individual citizens) (GoR 2005). The strategy thus acknowledges that besides water management authorities, other actors also have a role in flood risk management.

The medium and long term strategy complements these changes with several proposals for institutional change: (1) to extend the existing inter-ministerial council for water with a secretary for flood prevention and a technical secretariat for the evaluation of major investments; (2) to give the river basin management committees, which were established for the EU Water Framework Directive, also a role in the approval of flood prevention measures; and (3) to establish local flood agencies, consisting of volunteers who are trained by experts of the water authorities and land improvement authorities (GoR 2010). In addition, the government is currently undertaking other actions, such as: (4) the transfer of dikes owned by the land improvement authorities to the water authorities (GoR 2010); and (5) the establishment of a new Authority of Water Management and Floods at the Ministry of Environment (headed by the former, abolished State Secretary of Water). The latter is meant to improve the coordination between various authorities and probably also to diminish the influence of politics on water management. The medium and long term strategy also introduces new safety objectives, especially regarding the vulnerability to floods. The flood probability in rural areas, for example, is currently 1/20 years and should become 1/100 years. The strategy will be implemented with funds from various ministries and EU funds (MEF 2010).

Changes in the Governance Structure

Analysis of the recent developments in the flood risk sector shows that all governance dimensions have been changing (see Table 3.2). The main trigger of these changes was the increasing intensity and frequency of floods (problem pressure). A representative of the Ministry of Environment mentioned that especially the floods of 2005 and 2010 were important events that also created necessary support among other Ministries to implement such strategy.

Another (institutional) trigger for change was Romania's integration into the EU. For the implementation of the EU Floods Directive, all countries currently need to develop hazard and risk maps (2007/60/EC) (MEF 2010). There are also EU funds available for the reduction of flood risks. However, water authorities only became eligible for these funds after the government adopted a coherent strategy and could ensure that the benefiting water authorities are institutionally and financially viable organizations. Also in this sector, the power configuration between Romania and the EU is thus in favor of changes in the direction of EU best practices. What also plays a role in this sector is Romania's location in the Danube river basin. Recent floods in this basin forced countries to rethink their planning tradition and to put a stronger value on joint action.

When analyzing national conditions, we observe that developments since communism reflect a strong value on private property and economic development. This changed existing power configurations: water managers became increasingly dependent on the resources of other actors. This change and the increase of flood risks forced water managers to also rethink their traditional flood risk approach. Given the dependency of Romania on neighboring countries and the EU, the only way forward is to bring governance in line with EU practices. The recently adopted strategies are a reflection of changes that occur throughout Europe: a stronger emphasis on collaboration and prevention and preparedness.

Table 3.2   Recent changes in the governance of flood risks

Governance dimension	Main recent changes
Perceptions and objectives	From passive defence to pro-active flood risk management, proposal to reduce vulnerability; increase of safety levels.
Levels and scales of governance	Introduction of the EU level; proposal to increase cooperation across national, regional and local level.
Actors in the policy network	Proposal to give river basin committees and the inter-ministerial committee for water a role in flood risk management and to establish local flood agencies; establishment of a new Authority at the Ministry.
Strategies and instruments	Emphasis on non-structural measures and on cooperation; new instruments, such as automatic monitoring stations.
Responsibilities and resources for implementation	Ownership of dikes transferred to water authorities; funds available at various ministries and at the EU; increase of data and information (for example, maps and monitoring stations).

The recently adopted strategies involve, among others, a new 'perspective' on flood risk management and introduces new objectives (that is, an increase of safety levels objectives) and new 'strategies and instruments'. The implementation of these strategies also involves the redefinition of roles and responsibilities of various 'actors in the policy network' and promotes several new structures for cooperation. The strategy hereby aims to improve coherence within and between 'actors in the policy network' and 'resources and responsibilities'. What remains to be seen is whether responsible actors also have the capacity to coordinate and implement the suggested reforms. This is questionable as there has been very little attention for capacity-building in this sector.

Reflection on the Case Study Results

This section reflects on the developments and reforms in the water services sector (first case) and the flood risk sector (second case). An analysis of the changes in both sectors reveals that problem-related as well as institutional triggers changed several dimensions of existing governance structures, which led to adjustment of other dimensions (see Table 3.1 and Table 3.2). To understand these changes, we introduced three mechanisms for mutual adjustment. After communism, we observe a radical change in the dominant set of values towards local autonomy and free market economy. Decentralization and land restitution led to considerable changes and weakened power configurations.

One of the issues was that there was no tradition of co-governance, which meant that the changes brought about an incoherent governance structure. This created a problem-related trigger in both sectors as water services were deteriorating and flood risks increasing. This trigger especially brought about change in the flood risk sector: actors realized that there was a need to change the approach to flood risk management and to increase collaboration (in response to the irreversible changes in property rights). In the water services sector, Romania's integration into the EU (institutional trigger) was relatively more important. This trigger brought about several changes: it introduced another governance level and also created the need to comply with EU standards (change of objectives) and the possibility to access EU funds (change of resources). These changes also created a dependency on the EU (only for environment the EU already allocated 4.5 billion euro). In the environmental domain, about 60 per cent of the funds are allocated to water services (highest priority) and about 6 per cent is allocated to the reduction of natural risks (of which half for flood risk reduction) (GoR 2007).

Dependency on the EU funds is relatively less important in the flood risk sector. Within this sector, international dependency relations still exist via Romania's position in the Danube river basin. This probably explains why adjustments in both sectors mainly reflect mainstream EU values and cognitions. In the water services sector, a strong value is now placed on larger, autonomous operators instead of on local autonomy. In the flood risk sector, a strong value is now placed on collaboration and non-structural measures instead of on structural defense. The changes thus reflect changes in the dominant set of values and cognitive reference frames in the direction of mainstream EU values and frames.

Both cases confirm the assumption that governance structures have the tendency to become more complex and less coherent. Sources of incoherence were especially responsible actors who had no access to resources or instruments to execute their tasks and limited interaction between a growing number of actors in the policy network. In both cases, the Ministry of Environment initiated reforms to reduce these sources of incoherence. In the water services case, fragmentation was dealt with by regionalization. Various instruments were employed to improve the connections within and between various governance dimensions. This included legislative changes that strengthened the position of operators and of the national regulating authority, the development of a new cooperation structure for operators and local authorities and the implementation of assistance programs to strengthen the capacity of operators to handle their new responsibilities. Within the context of long-term sustainability, worth mentioning is the crucial importance of strengthening the position of the regulating authority so that it can enforce cost recovery.

While these instruments contributed to a more coherent governance structure, it was also a means to bring Romania's situation in line with EU standards and best practices. The case also highlights that existing power configurations can complicate adjustment, that is, local politics still complicate collaboration and tariff setting.

In the flood risk case, slightly different instruments were employed to reduce incoherence and to bring flood risk governance in line with EU directives. Efforts were in this sector focusing more on property rights. One of the instruments is transferring the ownership of flood protection infrastructure. As this only partly solves the fragmentation problem, the government also employed instruments that enhance collaboration between actors involved. The flood risk management strategy (developed in collaboration with various actors) suggests the establishment of new cooperation structures at the national level, the river basin level and the local level and also defines the roles of other relevant actors. Besides this, the Ministry established a new authority that will coordinate the actions of various actors. In this sector, connections were thus also created through the better definition of roles and responsibilities and the establishment of new collaboration structures. Whether these instruments indeed created more connections between various actors is yet unknown. Another point of attention in this sector is whether water management authorities also have the experience and capacity to realize new safety levels, non-structural measures and flood risk maps. Unlike in the water services sector, there has not been special attention for capacity building in the flood risk sector.

Conclusion

This chapter elaborated connective capacity in water governance in relation to change. Central in our analysis was a model that describes a governance structure in terms of five dimensions. As governance structures tend to be more complex over time, deliberate efforts are needed to create and maintain the coherence between these dimensions (Bressers and Kuks 2004, Kuks 2004). Within the context of this book, the ability to overcome this fragmentation is also referred to as 'connective capacity'. This chapter especially concentrated on reforms (instruments) as carriers of connectedness and layers and levels as focal points of connective capacity. We applied these concepts to the water services sector and the flood risk sector in Romania.

Both sectors were strongly affected by an additional level of governance that emerged following Romania's adherence to the European Union. As a result, the governance structures for both sectors have been changing considerably: changes were observed in all governance dimensions. One of the triggers for change was an increasing problem pressure (especially in the flood risk sector). The direction for change was, however, determined by Romania's accession to the EU that resulted in changed objectives and resources. To understand the overall impact of these external triggers, we took up the idea of 'mutual adjustment'. This concept suggests that the impact of triggers depends on existing values, cognitive reference frames and power configurations.

An important conclusion within this context is that the changes in both Romanian sectors are characterized by adjustments that bring the governance structure more in line with mainstream EU values and cognitive reference frames. This is understandable given the high dependency of Romania on the EU (or other countries in the Danube basin). At the same time, these adjustments do not always reflect conditions within the country (that is, there is no tradition of collaboration or co-governance) and can therefore be difficult to implement.

The above explains how governance structures in Romania have been changing in recent years. In addition, we also questioned how connective capacity can be created or consolidated under such changing circumstances. What appeared to be a major issue in both sectors was the incoherence between actors that were operating at various levels. More specific, responsible actors were lacking resources/instruments and there was insufficient interaction between actors in the policy network. In the water services sector, this incoherence was dealt with by changing its overall administrative structure and introducing principles of cost recovery. In the flood risk management sector, interventions rather focused on more coordination and improved policy and planning. The consolidation of connective capacity will be especially challenging in the flood risk sector. Besides that no attention was given to capacity-building, flood risk authorities are also much more dependent on the resources of other actors. Whether the employed instruments indeed contribute to improved connections between actors at various levels especially depends on the functioning of the new structures that were put in place.

On the basis of the presented case studies, we conclude that the following three instruments may especially contribute to the creation and maintenance of connective capacity in a dynamic multi-level governance context. Firstly, cooperation structures help actors at various levels in tuning their actions. Secondly, an adequate definition of roles of responsibilities of actors at various levels is needed, so that responsible actors have the resources to implement their tasks. Thirdly, the raising of objectives by a higher governance level should be accompanied by capacity-building so that ambitions can be realized. These instruments are complementary and additional instruments may be needed to overcome fragmentation in other contexts. The main lesson here is that connective capacity needs to be created and maintained. This is especially the case as multi-level governance structures have the tendency to become fragmented. In other words, connective capacity in water governance requires continuous and deliberate efforts.

Bibliography

Abdulamit, A. and Tanasescu, M. 2009. Consideraţii privind Registrul Naţional al Barajelor din România – REBAR (Considerations regarding the National Dam Register of Romania – REBAR). *Hidrotehnica*, 54(4-5).

ANAR: Administratia Nationale Apele Romane. 2010a. *Consideratii generale (General Considerations)* [Online]. Available at: http://www.rowater.ro/default.aspx [accessed: 25 August 2010].

ANIF: Administratia Nationale a Imbunatatirilor Funciare. 2010b. *Administrare patrimoniu (Asset Management)* [Online]. Available at: http://www.anif.ro/patrimoniu/ [accessed: 25 August 2010].

Bressers, H. and Kuks, S. 2003. What does "governance" mean? From conception to elaboration, in *Achieving Sustainable Development: The Challenge of Governance across Social Scales*, edited by H. Bressers and W.A. Rosenbaum. Westport, CA: Praeger Publishers, 65-88.

Bressers, H. and Kuks, S. 2004. *Integrated Governance and Water Basin Management: Conditions for Regime Change towards Sustainability*. Dordrecht, Boston, MA and London: Kluwer Academic Publishers.

Bressers, H.T.A. 2009. From public administration to policy networks: Contextual interaction analysis, in *Rediscovering Public Law and Public Administration in Comparative Policy Analysis: Tribute to Peter Knoepfel*, edited by S. Nahrath and F. Varone. Lausanne: Presses Polytechniques et Universitaires Romandes, 123-42.

Dinica, V. 2007. *An Institutional Analysis of Water Management Issues in the Teleorman County, Romania.* Enschede: CSTM, University of Twente.

Gallagher, T. 2005. *Theft of a Nation: Romania since Communism.* London: C. Hurst & Co.

GoR: Government of Romania 2005. Strategia Nationala de Management al riscului la inundatii: Prevenirea, protectia si diminuarea efectelor inundatiilor (National Strategy for Flood Risk Management: Prevention, protection and mitigation of flood effects) – Annex 1 to Governmental Ordinance No. 1854/2005. *Monitorul Oficial*, 72 (26 January 2006).

GoR: Government of Romania 2007. *Sectoral Operational Programme Environment 2007-2013, Final Version.* Ministry of Environment and Sustainable Development.

GoR: Government of Romania 2009. *National Rural Development Programme 2007-2013, Consolidated Version December 2009.* Ministry of Agriculture, Forests and Rural Development.

GoR: Government of Romania – press agency 2010a. Declaraţii de presă susţinute de ministrul Mediului şi Pădurilor, Laszlo Borbely la finalul şedinţei de Guvern (Press statement supported by the Minister of Environment and Forests, Laszlo Borbely at the end of the Government meeting).

GoR: Government of Romania 2010b. Strategia Nationala de Management al riscului la inundatii pe termen mediu si lung (National Strategy for Flood Risk Management for the medium and long term) – Annex to Governmental Decision No. 846/2010 *Monitorul Oficial*, 626 (6 September 2010).

Jordan, A., Wurzel, R.K.W. and Zito, A. 2005. The rise of 'new' policy instruments in comparative perspective: Has governance eclipsed government? *Political Studies*, 53(3), 477-96.

Kremlis, G. and Dusik, J. 2005. The Challenge of the Implementation of the Environmental Acquis Communautaire in the New Member States. *Seventh International Conference on Environmental Compliance and Enforcement.* Marrakech, Morocco.

Kuks, S.M.M. 2004. *Water Governance and Institutional Change.* Enschede: University of Twente.

Pahl-Wostl, C. 2008. Requirements for adaptive water management, in *Adaptive and Integrated Water Management: Coping with Complexity and Uncertainty*, edited by C. Pahl-Wostl, P. Kabat and J. Möltgen. Berlin: Springer-Verlag, 1-22.

Pollitt, C. and Bouckaert, G. 2011. *Public Management Reform; A Comparative Analysis: New Public Management, Governance, and the Neo-weberian State.* Oxford: Oxford University Press.

Rogers, P. and Hall, A.W. 2003. *Effective Water Governance* (TEC Background papers no. 7). Sweden: Global Water Partnership Technical Committee. Available at: www.gwpforum.org/gwp/library/TEC%207.pdf.

Sannen, A., Caian, S., Huet, L., Marcu, C., Fryer, A., Bowden, A., Boomsma, J., Baron, M. and Bancu, R. 2008. *National Water and Wastewater Utility Manual.* Bucharest: Royal Haskoning, Louis Berger, BDO Conti Audit.

Serban, P. and Galie, A. 2006. *Managementul apelor. Principii si reglementari europene (Water Management: European Principles and Regulations).* Bucharest: Editura Tipored.

Teodosiu, C., Barjoveanu, G. and Teleman, D. 2003. Sustainable Water Resources Management 1. River Basin Management and the EC Water Framework Directive. *Environmental Engineering and Management Journal*, 2(4), 377-94.

Tews, K. 2009. From law taking to policy making: The environmental dimension of the EU accession process – challenges, risks and chances for the SEE countries. *Environmental Policy and Governance*, 19(2), 130-39.

Vadineanu, A. and Preda, E. 2008. Watersheds Management in Romania: Challenges and Opportunities, in *Sustainable Use and Development of Watersheds*, edited by I.E. Gönenç, A. Vadineanu, J.P. Wolflin and R.S. Russo. Dordrecht: Springer.

Vinke-de Kruijf, J., Dinica, V. and Augustijn, D.C.M. 2009. Reorganization of water and wastewater management in Romania: From local to regional water governance. *Journal of Environmental Engineering and Management*, 8(5), 1061-71.

Wong, C.M., Williams, C.E., Pittock, J., Collier, U. and Schelle, P. 2007. *World's Top 10 Rivers at Risk*. Gland, Switzerland: WWF International. http://assets. panda.org/downloads/worldstop10riversatriskfinalmarch13.pdf.

Young, O.R. 1982. *Resource Regimes: Natural Resources and Social Institutions*. Berkeley, CA: University of California Press.

Chapter 4

Connecting Multiple Levels of Governance for Adaptation to Climate Change in Advanced Industrial States

Carina Keskitalo, Sirkku Juhola and Lisa Westerhoff

Introduction

The need to adapt to the impacts of climate change (IPCC 2007) has resulted in the proliferation of adaptation strategies among advanced industrial states. The majority of countries in the European Union (EU) now have or are in the process of producing guidelines for action on adaptation (EEA 2010), joined by many industrial countries in other parts of the world, that is, Canada and Australia. Many of these initiatives are contained within national adaptation policies, which range from broad statements on the need to adapt, to detailed assessments of sectoral vulnerabilities and possible measures for adaptation.

In addition to developments at the national level, adaptation initiatives have also emerged at regional and local levels across Europe (Ribeiro et al. 2009) and elsewhere in the industrialized North (Westerhoff et al. 2010). These regional and local adaptation strategies have predominantly emerged in larger cities, or regions, and often address specific local vulnerabilities.

Studies on the development of planned adaptation in Europe and other highly industrialized states have begun to emerge, although their numbers are so far limited (Gagnon-Lebrun and Agarwala 2007, Massey and Bergsma 2008, Swart et al. 2009). Early studies on the emergence of adaptation policy focused on the National Communications of the United Nations Framework Convention on Climate Change (UNFCCC) in order to compare the developments between countries (Gagnon-Lebrun and Agarwala 2006, Gagnon-Lebrun and Agarwala 2007, Massey and Bergma 2008).

In general, explorations of specific adaptation policies have mainly focused on the national scale in the discussion of national adaptation strategies (cf. Swartz et al. 2009, Biesbroek et al. 2010). Arguing that until then these developments had 'only been assessed in a superficial manner' (Biesbroek et al. 2010: 441), one recent set of studies has analysed the development and content of national adaptation strategies to draw lessons on the emergence of adaptation (Swart et al. 2009; Biesbroek et al. 2010). These authors briefly discuss national adaptation strategies through the lenses of science and policy, information dissemination, policy integration and multi-level governance. In an analysis that focuses particularly on the national level, the authors conclude that due to their recent development, most national adaptation policies do not explicitly specify the roles and responsibilities for adaptation at lower levels of governance (Biesbroek et al. 2010).

This issue of limited integration between levels – limited connectivity – constitutes an impediment to effective interaction on adaptation. In cases where divisions of responsibility and authority between different levels are not clear, effective multi-level governance is impeded as lower levels may not gain sufficient guidance as to what their responsibilities are or, indeed, funding to cover any implicit or explicit responsibilities (cf. Keskitalo 2008). Such problems may be particularly grave with regard to adaptation, as this constitutes a new policy issue for which actors at different levels may be unwilling to take on responsibility – and cost – unless determined through national decision-making processes. In local and regional cases where vulnerabilities and needs for adaptation are identified, the lack of clear divisions of responsibility, authority and funding may also limit the possibilities for lower levels to act on the issues or to claim support from the state. This is despite that identification of needs for adaptation may often emerge at local or regional levels (Naess et al. 2005). Studies of adaptation policy development at the regional level have so far been less prominent within the field, though studies of regional adaptation policy are currently under development (Ribeiro et al. 2009). Instead, the local level is often seen as the level at which impacts of climate change will fundamentally manifest, and that will ultimately need to respond to them (cf. Næss et al. 2005). As a result, a large number of case studies have targeted the local level and community adaptation specifically (see, for example, Hovelsrud and Smit 2010).

Though the need to view local adaptation in the context of other levels has often been highlighted as a general requirement for adaptation studies, few studies have yet to focus on these interlinkages and connectivities across levels (see Keskitalo 2008 for a discussion on how adaptation at the local level is dependent on regional, national and even international governance). This study asks *how national adaptation policy or attempts to develop national adaptation policy have evolved across scales.* The study thus assumes that national policy may not only be a result of national level developments, but must be seen in context and possibly as a result of interaction at different scales. To do this, the chapter advances a coherent framework for the functions and abilities at different levels, and targets its research at local, regional and national level actors in four countries: the United Kingdom (UK), Finland, Sweden and Italy. The chapter reviews four industrialized countries with varying degrees of national engagement in adaptation policy and draws on a multilevel case study using policy and interview data at national, regional and local levels. As water-related hazards were in particular focused within these developments on adaptation, the study has a particular relevance for the water governance field.

Theoretical Framework

A coherent application of a multi-level framework that takes the interaction between levels and how these may be shaped by the political system into account is a prerequisite for understanding the development and implementation of adaptation. Climate change adaptation is an issue that requires coordination across levels and sectors, and highlights the need for legislation and regulation that may support the varying impacts and circumstances experienced by different localities. The concept of multi-level governance helps to highlight this interrelation between levels by demonstrating that the steering of decision-making is no longer a function of government only, but of a broader array of actors and levels (Boland 1999, Hooghe and Marks 2003). The multi-level governance concept has been developed out of literature that shows that decentralization to other levels may make regional/local and supranational (international and EU) steering more important.

While this shift does not supplant the state, it both adds to and changes decision-making processes. Initiatives that manifest on the state level may therefore originate at other levels and be "lifted" to the level of the state and formal decision-making processes through such processes as lobbying from influential regional or local actors (Rhodes 2000). Initiatives may also manifest at the national level as a result of state commitments under international conventions that bind states to decision-making that originates elsewhere. Within the EU context, states have also agreed to be bound by EU legislation, so that directives taken on the EU level directly become law in EU states (Princen 2007).

The potential for more informal processes on local and regional levels or in connection with other actors, such as the private or third sectors, has resulted in the prevalence of less easily distinguished processes for decision-making over hierarchical, state-steered decision-making. Governance may take place by more or less fluid networks or pressure groups, while decentralization may further result in a larger role for city networks or voluntary local level declarations in decision-making (Rhodes 2000). Given that some processes have moved up to the international level (or in Europe, to the EU level), network governance may also allow some actors to "jump scale" (Gupta 2008, Princen 2007) by drawing on or even lobbying processes at such levels, thereby superseding the level of the state.

The way in which such processes take place and the extent to which national, regional, and local levels are able to gain influence largely depend on the characteristics of a given national system and the power it attributes to different levels and actors. These factors have been developed more generally in the political science and, to some extent, planning literatures, but have not been examined specifically in relation to the development of adaptation. National systems can be said to differ along formal structural lines, such as the unitary-federal organization of the state or along a spectrum of centralization-decentralization, as well as along informal characteristics, such as the general decision-making culture.

On the *national level*, a differentiation can be made between unitary states that are in some ways less attuned to acting on multiple levels, and federal states characterized by the relationship between self-governing states and the national (or federal) level (cf. Lijphart 1999). However, these distinctions obscure the great variety among both federal and unitary states, where levels of decentralization may differ significantly between states (Lijphart 1999, Newman and Thornley 2002).

For adaptation, one important aspect regarding the decentralization of power concerns the planning system and the responsibility for physical planning. Here, for instance, Sweden and Finland have a very decentralized structure with 'planning monopolies' at the local level (cf. Peters and Pierre 2005), whereas the UK is instead strongly centralized with limited power allocated to local and regional levels (Sandford 2005). Informal characteristics of each country framework may also impact national functioning. For instance, Newman and Thornley (2002) note that northern Europe follows a structure of conformity to legal and formal requirements, whereas countries in southern Europe may exhibit some differentiation between formal law and implementation requirements. States also differ in the extent to which they rely on more traditional bureaucratic means of steering (such as regulation), or have included so-called New Public Management methods, including economically based incentives or partnerships with the private sector (Rhodes 2000).

This context defines the ability of different levels and actors to act within each system. Differences in the extent to which responsibilities are decentralized create differences in the role of the *regional level*, ranging from fully-fledged regional governments (in federal and some unitary states) to purely administrative levels that constitute the regional arm of the state (Keating and Loughlin 1997). Different regions within a country may also reflect diverging capacities, where larger, economically richer and politically more powerful regions may be able to create networks and lobby the EU or other regional or international power centres, thereby affecting regulation and accessing resources in a way that smaller, poorer and politically weaker regions cannot. This argument, which to some extent formalizes aspects of adaptive capacity, is captured in 'new regionalism' literature (for example, Veggeland 2000) in the political science field.

At the *local level*, differences between states range from those that provide the local level power of 'general competence' to take local actions permitted by law and perceived as in the interest of the local citizenry, to those that only give local level the right to fulfil explicitly given statutory aims (Wilson and Game 2006). Like regional actors, local actors may be able to access levels beyond those immediately relevant to them by 'jumping scale' (Princen 2007, Gupta 2008). As Princen (2007: 26-27) notes for the EU, 'subnational and private actors will turn to the EU in order to bypass their national governments'. This may take place through the use of EU funding mechanisms or by developing coordinated actions together with actors other than national level (cf. Bulkeley 2005). Local actors may also act through coordinated local government or city networks on national or international levels (cf. Bulkeley and Betsil 2005), or through dedicated local government interest organizations that exist in many European countries, thereby contributing to network governance (Rhodes 2000).

Methods

Case Study Selection and Data Collection

The selection of the UK, Finland, Sweden and Italy as the focus of this study was based on the need to explore a range of advanced industrial states with varying engagement with adaptation policy and has been identified for inclusion in this study.

Firstly, the United Kingdom has been noted as one of the few developed countries that has begun to implement a "comprehensive approach to implementing adaptation and the 'mainstreaming' of such measures within sectoral policies and projects" (Gagnon-Lebrun and Agrawala 2007: 401).

The UK has instituted measures to integrate adaptation into the activities of national, regional and local governments and stakeholders, taking a multi-level approach that explicitly links levels to each other. Finland is also noted as an early actor on adaptation, but has chosen to mainstream adaptation across sectors at the national level, as outlined in its 2005 National Adaptation Strategy. Though structurally similar to Finland, Sweden began to develop adaptation measures later on in its 2007 Commission on Climate and Vulnerability, out of which recommendations for the allocation of responsibility to different scales and sectors were included in a 2009 Bill on climate change. Finally, Italy represents a slow mover on adaptation policy, though attempts to form a comprehensive adaptation policy at the national level have been made.

The countries above also reflect a range of systems of governance, and include a spectrum of varying degrees of decentralization within formal unitary states. Both Finland and Sweden represent Nordic governance systems in which local governments retain considerable authority in planning and other measures, guided by administrative regional bodies. Conversely, the UK is a clear example of a centralized state in which actions and funding are attributed in a top-down fashion from the national level. Though Italy is technically considered a unitary state, it shares several characteristics with federal states, particularly with regards to the increasing authority and autonomy conferred to the regions.

For each country, nested cases at regional and local levels were selected in order to assess the relationship between scales with regard to the development of adaptation policy. Cases that demonstrated an active interest or engagement in adaptation policies were selected, as evidenced through the development of adaptation strategies, the publication of relevant reports, and/or the participation in networks that sought to address adaptation needs. A biased selection towards localities that have been proactive in adaptation policy was thus sought in order to determine the existence of constraining or enabling factors for adaptation development in these cases. Where adaptation policy remained underdeveloped at local or regional levels, cases were instead selected for a demonstrated engagement or interest in climate-related policy in general (comprising either mitigation or climate-relevant risk management). Finally, as policies on water-related hazards were those most developed in the cases, the study has focused on these issues. Flood risk (and to some extent drought) thus represent issues that have so far been among those most focused in practical adaptation policy development in these cases.

Primary data were collected for this study from two principal sources. Firstly, comprehensive literature reviews undertaken during 2008 and 2009 allowed for the identification of adaptation policies and other measures at each scale. Documents reviewed included policies and legislation, climate impact reports, studies, and project documents, published by either government or non-governmental (for example, research and advocacy groups) organizations. Secondly, interviews were conducted with adaptation policy-relevant actors at each level, targeting those actors who are involved in policy development or administration, resulting in a total of 94 interviews across the four European countries. Each interview was conducted in the language of the interviewee, transcribed and translated (Table 4.1, see next page).

Applying the Multi-level Governance Framework

To determine the ways in which adaptation policy has emerged or is emerging within a multi-level governance framework, it is necessary to assess the ways in which adaptation policies and other actions have been developed at each level. Such an assessment was conducted by applying a set of three broad questions to the empirical data:

1. What policies or initiatives have been developed on each level?
2. How have such policies been formed and through what influence by other levels?
3. How do such policies affect other levels?

Responses to these broad lines of inquiry were situated within the respective system of governance of each country in order to determine the influence of the governance system in enabling or constraining adaptation action on and between different levels. In the following sections, adaptation policies and initiatives, the processes and actors involved in their formation, and their impacts at various levels are described for each of the four case study countries.

Table 4.1   Case study selection on national to local levels

Characteristics States	Adaptation policy development	Political system	Sub-national case study areas (specific nested local authorities or municipalities in brackets)	Semi-structured interviews
UK	Often seen as leader with multi-level perspective, regional organizations from early 2000s, Act 2008	Centralized state	South East region (Hampshire and Surrey counties, selected lower-level local authorities Woking, Winchester, Portsmouth)	n=22
Finland	First formal adaptation strategy (2005)	Nordic small-state with municipal planning monopoly	Uusimaa Region (Espoo, Tuusula, Kerava, Mäntsälä, Pornainen)	n=22
Sweden	Later and less focused adaptation development, Commission on vulnerability (2007), Bill 2009	Nordic small state with municipal planning monopoly	Västra Götaland (municipalities Gothenburg, Mölndal, Trollhättan, Munkedal).	n=25
Italy	No formally established national adaptation structure although attempts have been made	Large regional self-determination	Emilia Romagna (Province and City of Ferrara)	n=25

Results

Adaptation in the UK: England and South-East England

As a relatively centralized state, the UK's early action on adaptation has resulted in a multi-level, national to local framework with associated funding and funding criteria. Adaptation has been addressed at the national scale most importantly by the 2007 Climate Act (and an earlier Bill), and through the Adapting to Climate Change strategy for England in 2008 (UK Government 2008). Together, these have permitted the state to require any body that provides services to the state to report on their climate change adaptation activities, as well as to set up a framework for risk assessment. These actions were joined by state commissions for awareness and acceptance of the adaptation issue, such as the 2007 Pitt Review in response to flooding in 2006 (building upon long-term established concerns on vulnerability to flooding, Cabinet Office 2007), and the widely acknowledged Stern Report (2006) on the economic impacts of climate change.

At the regional level, regional climate change partnerships (RCCP) were developed on central initiative from the late 1990s to support regional studies under the government's UK Climate Impacts Programme (UKCIP), a body that continues to support adaptation in English regions. Though the role of the region is limited, the RCCP act as a liaison between local authorities, existing regional agencies, industry and NGOs in each English region. As a result, the region has taken on a partnership-based role initiated by the state, while the UKCIP acts as a largely distinctive organization that supports multi-level adaptation and integration. As one actor within the largely informal coordination group for RCCP noted, "without UKCIP (. .) it would have been difficult, if not impossible, for regions to really take [adaptation] forward" (UK Interregional Climate Change Group, interview). In 2011, this role for the UKCIP was transferred to the Environment Agency, with consequences yet too early to determine.

The local level was also strongly steered from the central state during the time period of this study. In 2008/2009, the State institutionalized a new local performance assessment framework that comprises 198 National Indicators (NI), including one on adaptation (DEFRA 2009). Progress under this framework has implications for national funding attributed to individual local authorities, and thus constitutes an economic incentive. Of the UK's 450 authorities, roughly 100 have selected the adaptation indicator as one of the 35 indicators on which they are assessed. The legislative and regulative framework therefore includes a well-integrated adaptation component to be undertaken within local authority partnerships with local stakeholders. The adaptation indicator has been particularly well received as a result of its more procedural approach and, in the words of a representative of an interest organization for local government, has "encourage[d] people to … actually own the process a bit more" (Local Government Association, interview). In the UK, then, strong national steering on adaptation was during this period supported by local interests.[1]

In one notable case, local process have also been expanded by national level organizations and used to develop stronger actions on adaptation. The Nottingham Declaration on local council mitigation and adaptation is a document that was voluntarily developed by local authorities and that binds signatories to certain

---

1   The new UK government from 2010 has removed the indicator system, making it less clear how this national-local linkage will be developed in the future.

commitments. Developed in Nottingham in the mid-1990s, the document gained in popularity following its re-launch in 2005 in cooperation with the UKCIP and other bodies. Noting the importance of this document for developing support for the local performance assessment (including the new adaptation indicator), one interviewee noted: "Government could never have set up something like that unless a bottom-up process had pre-prepared the regions and local authorities to accept it'" (UKCIP, interview). Voluntary local action was thus extended through the involvement of the UKCIP, and used as a basis for developing local priorities on adaptation, underlined by the Local Government Association's lobbying on adaptation. As such, the UK illustrates some level of network governance on adaptation despite its centralised nature, where initiatives at the local level have influenced national activities.

In the South East England region, growth areas such as the upper-tier local authority Hampshire County Council have also played important roles in the development of early adaptation commitments, something that has been formalized for instance in an accord with central level on Hampshire developing good practice examples on adaptation. Due to its established position with regard to environmental policy it has also been lobbying the EU on adaptation. As a result, Hampshire may be seen as the type of actor able to benefit from mechanisms described in terms of "new regionalism", jumping scale to influence the EU level directly. However, significant discrepancies between areas do exist; for instance, both Hampshire and its neighbour Portsmouth have been concerned with climate-related impacts in the water management sector, but differ in terms of economic strength and leadership on environmental issues. In the lower-tier local authority of Woking, a novel funding arrangement and aspirations to leadership in environmental policy over the long term have instead supported the local authority's agency on adaptation. However, adaptation action in Woking has largely occurred as a result of the state performance assessment framework, again indicating the role that central state measures play at the local level. Following its development of adaptation actions in 2008, Woking was appointed one of the national "Climate Change Beacons" to serve as an inspiration to other local authorities.

Adaptation in Finland

In Finland, adaptation policy development has taken place mainly through the preparation process for the Finnish NAS in 2003, published in 2005 out of the recognition that adaptation will be required irrespective of the success of mitigation measures (Marttila, Granholm et al. 2005). The preparation of the NAS was led by the Ministry of Agriculture and Forestry and developed through horizontal interlinkages at government departments in Finland, with the aim to mainstream adaptation as an issue across administrative sectors. This method of preparation followed the same method for governmental strategies for other cross-cutting issues used in the past: 'there was enough practice of co-operation between the Ministries to do this' (Ministry of Agriculture and Forestry, interview). Implementation of the NAS has advanced fastest within the environment administration, within which the publication of an action plan in 2008 has outlined ways to mainstream adaptation across existing planning, implementation and monitoring measures (Ympäristöministeriön työryhmä 2008). The importance for the Ministry of the Environment to proceed from a strategy document to implementation was noted by one interviewee: 'it is natural for this Ministry to pick it up as a topic' (Ministry of the Environment, interview).

The first evaluation of the implementation of the NAS outlines the use of an indicator to evaluate the extent to which adaptation has been mainstreamed within the different sectors of the government (Ministry of Agriculture and Forestry 2009). The evaluation concluded that some understanding of the impacts of climate change exists in most sectors of the government, and that the need for adaptation measures has been recognized by some decision-makers within a select few sectors. However, this recognition varies greatly between sectors, and has advanced the least within the economic and health sectors. One area in which adaptation has been taken into account in legislation is the revision of the 2000 Land Use Act to include adaptation in 2008.

Overall, well functioning horizontal linkages at the national level have aided the preparation of the NAS, during which each Ministry identified the needs for adaptation within their own administrative sector, and have contributed to its early publication. Explicit linkages to lower levels of government have, however, remained weak within the NAS, through which measures generally only trickle down through revisions in legislation. This is due to the fact that from the beginning, the NAS does not outline any specific measures for either the regional or local levels. This is partially due to the reason that it never meant to address lower levels of governance and also due to the fact that the national level is unable to steer the lower levels due to the devolvement of power to municipalities. This issue is currently discussed in the revision of the NAS that began in 2010 (Ministry of Agriculture and Forestry, interview). This may, however, be hampered by the fact that the state has no mandate due to the fairly extensive autonomy of the local level.

Although there has been no direct steering towards adaptation from the national level, regional and local initiatives have emerged in Finland. The regional level in Finland is characterized by non-elected regional councils that serve as co-operative bodies for municipalities, which in turn have autonomy over their territory. In the Uusimaa region, the Regional Council is pursuing a climate strategy that includes an adaptation alongside mitigation, and which has benefitted from a participation in project funded by the EU Regional Development Fund. Similarly, the Helsinki Environment Services Authority is currently pursuing an adaptation strategy in two different EU funded projects within the context of the Baltic Sea region in the absence of any government direction (Helsinki Environment Services Authority, interview). The only city to currently have an adaptation strategy, the City of Espoo published its climate change preparedness strategy with measures for adaptation in 2007 (Soini 2007). Preliminary flood mappings in the preparation phase were conducted as part of EU funded projects. Municipalities have also accessed national funding to begin work on adaptation in cases where they have not been part of EU projects. By using existing municipality co-operation networks and pooling funding, the KUUMA municipalities have been able to begin a preparation of a climate strategy that otherwise would have been beyond the means of small, single municipalities (Municipality of Mäntsälä, interview).

Adaptation in Sweden

Issues of vulnerability and adaptation in Sweden have been addressed mainly through the Commission on Climate and Vulnerability (2005; Commission on Climate and Vulnerability 2007), from which main suggestions were adopted into the 2009 Climate Bill (Government Offices of Sweden 2009) and enforced through decisions later in 2009. Principal measures in the Bill pertaining to adaptation included the provision of funding for three major areas: to the regional arm of the state (the county administrative boards) to coordinate adaptation; to specific governmental bodies and agencies to develop a common elevation data basis; and for the assessment of flood risk and erosion defense measures around Lake Vänern. Risks considered by the Bill include the flooding of central Gothenburg, the second largest city of Sweden (a risk increasing with rising sea level). The Bill recommends an assessment of possible adaptation actions, including a tunnel for diverting water from Lake Vänern to the sea for which the distribution of funding between municipal and state levels is to be decided at a later point. The decentralized Swedish system thus manifests in issues such as the sharing of responsibility and funding for planned adaptations between national and local levels.

   The development of the Commission on Climate and Vulnerability was at least in part attributed to lobbying by representatives at the regional (county) level around lake Vänern (including Västra Götaland, the case study region) to request special attention to flood risk following major floods in 2000. As one interviewee at the Commission on Climate and Vulnerability noted, "the counties had written to the Government, to the Department of Defense. They [the government] had to reply and do something about this" (Commission on Climate and Vulnerability, interview). The subsequent emphasis of the state on the need to address future flooding in the two lakes is highlighted by the Commission on Climate and Vulnerability's release of two separate reports: the final report in 2007, and an interim report developed in 2006 focused specifically on flooding requested by the government (Commission on Climate and Vulnerability 2006). Despite the limited power attributed to regional level within the Swedish state, it was nevertheless in this case able to voice concerns for constituent municipalities and influence the direction of adaptation policy development.

   At the local level, projects relevant to adaptation have been underway in the city of Gothenburg (*Extreme Weather* Phases 1 and 2) since about 2003, and have resulted in concrete changes in minimum building elevations in light of sea level rise. These projects have also fostered general awareness of adaptation at the local level, and particularly as a result of comparative work on flooding completed within an EU project. However, the national Bill has attributed greater general responsibility to municipalities to adapt to climate change, with the exception of 'extraordinary' requirements such as the Göta Älv/Lake Vänern flood risk. During the review process, many municipalities contested this attribution and instead requested an increase in state grants to assist in the funding of preparedness at the local level. However, adaptation was determined to fall under the municipal responsibility for local planning, thereby decentralizing responsibility to the local level in line with the Swedish regulative system. According to some local authorities, this decision may render greater difficulty for smaller municipalities to develop policy and planning on adaptation issues (Munkedal municipality, interview). While Gothenburg and the neighbouring municipalities of Mölndal have the funding and administrative resources of larger municipalities, the case study areas of Munkedal and Trollhättan have not yet developed measures or policy in the area of climate change adaptation.

Adaptation in Italy

Italian national activities with regard to climate change adaptation have been limited in both their extent and impact. A national conference in 2007 held by agencies under the Ministry of Environment, Land and Sea (MATTM) served to pool existing research and broaden understanding of sectoral and regional impacts and vulnerability, and produced two short documents. The first of these outlined the need to coordinate and integrate adaptation into existing policy and legislation within a national adaptation strategy to be produced by 2008 and implemented over the following three years (MATTM 2007c), while the second outlined priority areas of intervention (MATTM 2007b).

However, a national strategy has not yet been produced. Conflict between research institutions, the change in administration, and the failure of the preceding Prodi government to organize or earmark funds for a national adaptation strategy are all cited as possible reasons behind the apparent stalemate. Select interviewees at the national scale also indicated that work on such a strategy would be resumed in the near future through an interministerial committee headed by the Directorate for Environmental Research and Development (under MATTM) and made up of representatives of relevant technical bodies (including the CMCC) and other ministries. In the interim, several existing plans and legislative frameworks that address various facets of adaptation, including the National Action Plan to Combat Drought and Desertification and the National Plan for the Prevention of the Effects of Heat on Human Health, are considered means to address adaptation. Though neither of these specifically target climate change impacts, they are recognized as having implications for implementation of measures at regional and local levels.

The absence of a national strategy on climate change adaptation and the existing measures that address vulnerabilities have certain implications for both Italy's regions and municipalities. Though State legislation guides the regions and allocates funds towards the implementation of certain policies, regions in Italy enjoy considerable autonomy in several sectors. In the case of the region of Emilia-Romagna, this freedom has translated into the pursuit of climate change impact research through the Regional Environmental Protection Agency (ARPA). Policy action with regards to adaptation remains limited to brief consideration of climate change impacts in regional water and agricultural plans. For instance, the Water Protection Plan (2005) describes a need to address potential changes in water availability and recommends updates of the plan's strategies as new climate impact information developed by the ARPA becomes available. This reflects the general attitude towards climate adaptation at the regional level, as captured by one actor: "We do not have an adaptation plan to climate change. We try to adapt public policies to the climate change that is in action; so, climate change for us is a compass, an obligatory reference point" (Regional Ministry of Agriculture, interview).

Below the level of the region, provinces and municipalities make up the local scale in Italy, with differing responsibilities. In Emilia-Romagna, provinces represent the administrative arm of the region and carry out policies determined at the regional (and national) level. As such, many of their activities are guided by the region, but provinces may also choose to engage in other activities provided they are in line with the mandates set by the region. With regards to adaptation, the participation of the Province of Ferrara in a partly EU-funded project, the Climate Alliance's *Adaptation and Mitigation – an Integrated Climate Policy Approach* (AMICA), has allowed the province to access information and best practice networks on adaptation. Beyond this engagement, the Province of Ferrara and is responsible for implementing the region's water and other plans, including those aspects relevant to climate change adaptation.

The municipalities in Italy constitute a somewhat different scale of administration, in that they are obliged to follow regional and national guidelines (with associated funding) but have relative freedom in local planning. In the municipality of Ferrara, very little has been done in the way of adaptation. Interviewees highlighted the limited focus on adaptation at the national scale (and absence of allocated funds), few local human and financial resources, and limited observation of or information on climate impacts as reasons behind the lack of activity. As noted by one local actor, "We live in a phase in which an increase in our responsibilities corresponds to a reduction in resources. Now we are also in a moment of economic crisis and so the State is reducing, little by little, the resources that are transferred to the periphery" (Provincial Ministry of Environment, interview). Like the province, however, the municipality benefits from networks with other cities and has been able to engage in mitigative actions beyond state or regional requirements, indicating that any future interest in adaptation may yield comparable results.

Discussion and Case Comparison

The comparison of each of the above case studies yields interesting insights into the nature of multi-level governance of climate change adaptation. First, the study shows that an exclusive focus on national adaptation policy obscures the complexity of emergence of adaptation across multiple scales. In the UK, Finland

and Sweden all, formal adaptation policies were developed at the national level, while such attempts at the national level in Italy failed. However, the UK, Finland and Sweden utilize largely different processes through which national actions were made possible. In the UK, the prioritization of adaptation at the national level was supported by bottom-up, local government movements towards adaptation in the Nottingham Declaration. In Sweden, the investigation into adaptation at national level was given urgency and motivated at least in part by regional initiatives that asserted the state's responsibility to act on climate change to protect its regions as long as no other measures were in place. In Sweden, local adaptation initiatives also existed but were not linked to developments at the national level. Only in Finland were local-national linkages difficult to discern, despite the fact that some local level actors were independently working on local adaptation policies.

Table 4.2   Case study comparison

Country case	The UK	Finland	Sweden	Italy
Steering measures developed at different levels				
National	Climate Change Act, UK Climate Impacts Programme, National Indicator system	National Adaptation Strategy	Commission and Bill	National conference and informal adaptation measures prioritarization documents
Regional	Regional Climate Change Partnerships (initially developed as state initiative, some are now self-managing)	Project-based work in some cases	Incentive towards national Bill	Integration of adaptation on regional incentive in some cases
Local	Nottingham Declaration	Municipal or municipal cooperation strategies in some cases, mainly on own incentive	Municipal adaptation projects in some cases, mainly on own incentive	Project-based work on own incentive

The study's findings thus indicate significant variability with regard to the involvement and impact of local governments in national level adaptation decisions. Firstly, as others have also concluded, national action on adaptation does not always contribute to the emergence of adaptation on lower levels of governance (Swart et al. 2009, Biesbroek et al. 2010). This means that while national policy may exist, it may not coherently or deliberately attribute roles to other levels. In Sweden, general adaptation actions at the local level are deemed the responsibility of the municipality under the municipal planning monopoly. In Finland, the national adaptation strategy requires action only from national level bodies, and so has little impact on local adaptation policies that have developed principally in response to locally identified needs and funded through channels such as EU frameworks. Interviewees did themselves not comment on this fact, other than that this was seen as a normal practice and "the way things were done" in Finland. The research thus underlines the role not only of the formal structure of national governmental systems at large, but the importance of informal norms and administrative practice that may differ between states and impact how and on what levels certain issues are handled. Further investigation into adaptation policy development and interlinkages in Finland are needed to review how such norms and implicit divisions of responsibility impact steering on adaptation. While it may be that local levels would integrate with national demands were these to exist formally – thus supporting integration on adaptation – the Finnish case may also evidence some disconnect between levels on adaptation. The limited connectivity between local and national levels on this issue may thus constitute an important impediment to adaptation policy integration in the future.

Secondly, local and regional initiatives may in some cases support or provide initiative for national actions, or help form the shape that national actions take. This illustrates the fact that though a national policy may be the most visible, it may have been motivated or informed by lower levels in a way that is not apparent from an examination of the NAS alone. Examples include the influence of the regional level in Sweden in placing adaptation to flood risk on the national agenda, fundamentally contributing to the development of a Commission on Climate and Vulnerability through which a Swedish adaptation framework was developed. In the centralized UK, the Nottingham Declaration government network still played a significant role in garnering local acceptance on adaptation (and mitigation), and which to some rendered the state inclusion of adaptation in the local performance assessment framework possible. While it is difficult to pinpoint conditions beyond differences in state systems under which local or regional initiatives may develop to support national action and policy development, local and regional action in these cases seem to have related to experiences of extreme events (in Sweden) and to developed priorities on the issue (in the UK, potentially related to experiences with flooding). Issues such as media reporting and awareness on climate change, which may support local development, could also play a role (Kingdon 1995).

Thirdly, the study also indicates that adaptation action may occur at lower levels even in the absence of a national adaptation framework. This study thereby supports findings of local level policy development for adaptation as previously examined by Bulkeley and Betsill (2005) in relation to mitigation. This has taken place in particular in Italy, where local and regional levels have begun to include adaptation-relevant measures for flooding and drought within regional and local plans; however, these are yet to be explicitly designed as planned adaptations or in response to changing risks over time (that is, climate change impacts). The Italian case therefore further illustrates how the absence of a national framework for adaptation may constitute a hindrance or impediment for the development of local adaptation policies, as well as a limitation on local awareness or resources that could have supported the development of local actions.

To a large extent, the development of planned adaptations at the local level have drawn upon the ability to network with other levels, or 'jump scales', as has been noted more generally with regard to multi-level governance interactions (for example, Princen 2007). We show that adaptation is not only reliant on or formed in relation to the state context. Cases in Italy, Finland and Sweden in different ways show the importance and potential impact of EU funding and projects. In Italy, the measures that exist on the local level have largely been made possible through EU funding and been shaped by requirements within the EU framework, as no national framework for adaptation yet exists. While actions may thus develop locally by drawing upon various non-national frameworks, the existence of a national framework for adaptation to motivate and support local development is seen as beneficial. In Finland, planned adaptation at the local level has, lacking national funding, largely been reliant on funding in EU projects, whereas such projects for the Swedish case of Gothenburg constituted an incentive for a relatively early start in the framing of frame flood risk as an adaptation issue.

The capacities of different actors as illustrated above is dependent on how they are situated within types of states and on which capabilities they possess, for instance in terms of political and economic strength. The national system thus constitutes the context for how the different governance levels are related to one another in the four cases, and whether they reinforce each other or not. Connectivity in multi-level governance may here play a crucial role for whether policies on national level are really implemented locally, and may be supported for instance at national level by explicit priorities for the local level, as well as by indicators or grant systems (depending on the possibilities in the state system). Bottom-up indications of the role of adaptation may here also support national development of adaptation policies.

While a centralized state may – if wished – easier steer on adaptation, decentralization may make it easier for planned adaptations to develop even in the absence of strong steering from the state, as the regional or local level (depending on the level of decentralization in the particular country) may have greater leeway in the construction of local initiatives than the corresponding level of a centralized state. The study for instance illustrates that the format in which planned adaptation is developed differs between countries, where the UK's focus on steering through partnerships and performance assessment has largely shaped the UK response on adaptation. This system is currently under large transformation given the impact of the economic crisis on the UK, and the entry in 2010 of the new coalition government. Having access to resources at the national scale does, however, not necessarily translate into access to resources or at the local level. In addition, though sufficient access to resources may exist at the local level, as in Trollhättan in Sweden or Woking in the UK, planned adaptations may not necessarily emerge unless such priorities exist at the national level, or are rendered urgent at the local level (cf. Næss et al. 2006). This development of priorities may then, in turn, depend on contextual factors (for example, extreme events) as well as local political priorities and leadership.

Conclusion

This chapter contributes to the growing body of literature that analyses the emergence of adaptation across multiple levels of governance. While previous studies on this topic have paid less attention to the ways in which adaptation emerges across levels of governance, this chapter illustrates the importance of vertical linkages in adaptation policy development. The study shows that interaction does not merely happen in a top down fashion in the way government steering regularly is conducted, but that sub-national actors can also influence the policy process on higher levels of governance from the bottom up (such as Swedish regional initiatives or local UK initiatives did). This study also confirms that planned adaptation can occur without specific steering or direction from the national level and may in this be supported by levels beyond the state, in these cases notably the EU.

The findings of this chapter highlight the importance of organizational structure of different countries, and how that affects the development of adaptation policy. The chapter shows how different governance systems enable and constrain adaptation at different scales, demonstrating that a multilevel framework is a prerequisite for understanding the emergence of adaptation even in cases where this manifests as national adaptation policies. This holds certain implications for the success of adaptation initiatives; for example, committed, centralized states may be able to raise the lowest common denominator on adaptation across, for example, local authorities, and thereby create connectivity between levels on the issue. However, a centralized state with little focus on adaptation would most likely provide less room than a decentralized state for the local or regional level to develop adaptation in the absence of state policy. These important implications for policy indicate that such multi-level studies are likely to constitute an increasingly important research topic in the future.

Acknowledgements

This chapter summarizes multi-level governance aspects of adaptation on national, region and local level more extensively described in the book Keskitalo, E.C.H. (2010, ed.) *Developing Adaptation Policy and Practice in Europe: Multi-Level Governance of Climate Change.* Springer, Berlin. The project EUR-ADAPT gratefully acknowledges funding from the Swedish Research Council.

Bibliography

Biesbroek, G.R., Swart R.J., Carter, T.R., Cowan, C., Henrichs, T., Mela, H., Morecroft, M.D. and Rey, D. 2010. Europe Adapts to Climate Change: Comparing National Adaptation Strategies. *Global Environmental Change*, 20(3), 440-50.

Boland, P. 1999. Contested multi-level governance: Merseyside and the European Structural Funds. *European Planning Studies*, 7(5), 647-64.

Bulkeley, H. and Betsill, M. 2005. Rethinking sustainable cities: Multilevel governance and the 'urban' politics of climate change. *Environmental Politics*, 14(1), 42-63.

Bulkeley, H. 2005. Reconfiguring environmental governance: Towards a politics of scales and networks. *Political Geography*, 24, 875-902.

Cabinet Office. 2007. *The Pitt Review: Learning Lessons from the 2007 Floods.* London: Cabinet Office.

Commission on Climate and Vulnerability. 2006. *Översvämningshot. Risker och åtgärder för Mälaren, Hjälmaren och Vänern. Delbetänkande av Klimat- och sårbarhetsutredningen.* Stockholm: Swedish Government Official Report SOU 2006, 94.

Commission on Climate and Vulnerability. 2007. *Sweden Facing Climate Change – Threats and Opportunities* [in Swedish]. Stockholm: Swedish Government Official Report SOU 2007, 60.

DEFRA. 2009. Local Government Performance Framework. NI 188 – Planning to adapt to climate change. Retrieved June 22, 2009, from http://www.defra.gov.uk/environment/ localgovindicators/ni188.htm.

EEA [European Environment Agency]. 2010. National adaptation strategies. http://www.eea.europa.eu/themes/climate/national-adaptation-strategies (accessed 30 August, 2010).

Gagnon-Lebrun, F. and Agrawala, S. 2008. Implementing adaptation in developed countries: An analysis of progress and trends. *Climate Policy*, 7, 392-408.

Government Offices of Sweden. 2009. *En sammanhållen klimat- och energipolitik. Klimat.* Regeringens proposition 2008/09:162. Stockholm: Government Offices of Sweden.

Gupta, J. 2008. Analysing scale AQ10 and scaling in environmental governance, in *Institutions and Environmental Change: Principal Findings, Applications, and Research Frontiers*, edited by O.R. Young, L.A. King and H. Schroeder. Cambridge, MA: MIT Press.

Hooghe, L. and Marks, G. 2003. Unravelling the central state, but how? Types of multilevel governance. *American Political Science Review*, 97(2), 233-43.

IPCC. 2007. *Climate Change 2007: Impacts, Adaptation and Vulnerability.* Contribution of Working Group II to the Third Assessment Report of the Intergovernmental Panel on Climate Change (IPCC). Cambridge: Cambridge University Press.

Keating, M. and Loughlin, J. 1997. Introduction, in *The Political Economy of Regionalism*, edited by M. Keating and J. Loughlin. London: Routledge, pp. 1-15.

Keskitalo, E.C.H. 2008. *Climate Change and Globalisation in the Arctic: An Integrated Approach to Vulnerability Assessment.* London: Earthscan.

Kingdon, J.W. 1995. *Agendas, Alternatives and Public Policies.* Second edition. New York: HarperCollins.

Lijphart, A. 1999. *Patterns of Democracy.* New Haven and London: Yale University Press.

Massey, E. and Bergsma, H. 2008. *Assessing Adaptation in 29 European Countries.* IVM Institute of Environmental Studies, Vrije Universitet, Amsterdam.

Marttila, V., Granholm, H., Laanikari, J., Yrjölä, T., Aalto, A., Heikinheimo, P., Honkatukia, J., Järvinen, H.I., Liski, J., Merivirta, R. and Paunio, M. 2005. *Finland's National Strategy for Adaptation to Climate Change.* Helsinki: Ministry of Agriculture and Forestry.

Ministry of Agriculture and Forestry. 2009. Evaluation of the Implementation of Finland's National Strategy for Adaptation to Climate Change 2009. Ministry of Agriculture and Forestry, 4a/2009.

Ministry for the Environment Land and Sea (MATTM). 2007a. *Fourth National Communication under the UN Framework Convention on Climate Change.* Rome: Republic of Italy.

Ministry for the Environment Land and Sea (MATTM). 2007b. Le prime 13 azioni per l'adattamento sostenibile. Cambiamenti Climatici Conferenza Nazionale, Rome, 12-13 September.

Ministry for the Environment Land and Sea (MATTM). 2007c. Manifesto per il clima – un new deal per l_adattamento sostenibile e la sicurreza ambientale. Cambiamenti Climatici Conferenza Nazionale, Rome, 12-13 September.

Næss, L.O., Bang, G., Eriksen, S. and Vevatne, J. 2005. Institutional adaptation to climate change: Flood responses at the municipal level in Norway. *Global Environmental Change*, 15, 125-38.

Næss, L.O., Thorsen Norland, I., Lafferty, W.M. and Aall, C. 2006. Data and processes linking vulnerability assessment to adaptation decision-making on climate change in Norway. *Global Environmental Change*, 16, 221-33.

Newman, P. and Thornley, A. 2002. *Urban Planning in Europe: International Competition, National Systems and Planning Projects.* London and New York: Routledge.

Peters, B.G. and Pierre, J. 2005. Swings and roundabouts? Multilevel governance as a source of and constraint on policy capacity, in *Challenges to State Policy Capacity. Global Trends and Comparative Perspectives*, edited by M. Painter and J. Pierre. Basingstoke: Palgrave Macmillan, pp. 38-51.

Princen, S. 2007. Agenda-setting in the European Union: A theoretical exploration and agenda for research. *Journal of European Public Policy*, 14(1), 21-38.

Regione Emilia-Romagna. 2005. Piano di Tutela della Acque. Bologna: Assessorato Ambiente e Sviluppo Sostenibile, ARPA Regione Emilia-Romagna.

Rhodes, R.A.W. 2000. Governance and public administration, in *Debating Governance: Authority, Steering and Democracy*, edited by J. Pierre. Oxford: Oxford University Press, pp. 54-90.

Ribeiro, M., Losenno, C., Dworak, T., Massey, E., Swart, R., Benzie, M. and Laaser, C. 2009. Design of guidelines for the elaboration of Regional Climate Change Adaptations Strategies. Study for European Commission – DG Environment – Tender DG ENV. G.1/ETU/2008/0093r. Ecologic Institute, Vienna.

Sandford, M. 2005. *The New Governance of the English Regions*. Houndmills: Palgrave Macmillan.

Smit, B. and Wandel, J. 2006. Adaptation, adaptive capacity and vulnerability. *Global Environmental Change*, 16, 282-92.

Soini, S. 2007. *Ilmastonmuutos ja siihen varautuminen Espoossa*. Espoon ympäristökeskus Monistesarja. Espoo: 1-50.

Stern, N. 2006. *The Economics of Climate Change*. Investigation under the H.M. Treasury/Cabinet Office, London.

Swart, R., Biesbroek, R., Binnerup, S., Carter, T.R., Cowan, C., Henrichs, T., Loquen, S., Mela, H., Morecroft, M., Reese, M. and Rey, D. 2009. *Europe Adapts to Climate Change: Comparing National Adaptation Strategies*. PEER Report No. 1. Helsinki: Partnership for European Environmental Research. Vammalan Kirjapaino Oy, Sastamala.

UK Government 2008. Climate Change Act 2008. Retrieved June 22, 2009, from http://www.defra.gov.uk/environment/climatechange/uk/legislation/.

Veggeland, N. 2000. *Den nye regionalismen. Flernivåstyring og europeisk integrasjon*. Bergen: Fagbokforlaget.

Wilson, D. and Game, C. 2006. *Local Government in the United Kingdom* (4th ed.). Houndmills: Palgrave Macmillan.

Ympäristöministeriön työryhmä 2008. Ilmastonmuutokseen sopeutuminen ympäristöhallinnon toimiallalla. Ympäristöministeriö, Helsinki. 2008/20.

Chapter 5

Framing and Linking Space for the Grensmaas: Opportunities and Limitations to Boundary Spanning in Dutch River Management

Jeroen Warner

Introduction: Coping with Complexity in Water Governance

In light of the book's overall concern with connective capacity, this chapter focuses on the pointmen routing and rerouting streams of ideas and resources and the strategies they pursue seeking to achieve their objectives by way of linking, coupling and spanning across boundaries. 'Boundary spanning' (Williams 2002, Bressers and Lulofs 2010), explored in more detail in the next section, appeals here – while it does not presupposes linear transitions, it does not contradict a radical change orientation either. A competent boundary spanner manages complexity while trying to introduce, translate, and implement an innovative idea into public practice (Roberts and King 1996). Bressers and Lulofs (2010) define boundary spanning as 'adaptive governance activities of water managers linking their sector, scales, and time frames to previously independent other sectors, scales and time frames.' As we shall see, linking and (re)framing are key strategies to boundary spanning.

The literature on boundary spanning and political entrepreneurship (examples include Mintrom 2000, Williams 2002, Brouwer and Biermann 2011) has made great strides to our understanding, but paid relatively scant attention to the downsides of boundary spanning. There are also considerable risks in making boundary-spanning connections. Not only can opponents use the same tactics as proponents, the latter can also trip themselves up by taking undue risks. The case of the Grensmaas river project on the river Meuse illustrates this insight. The case study introduces the tactics of several important leaders that translated the new concept of 'nature development', developed in the 1980's, into a concrete intervention project. The analysis identifies four critical moments at which boundary spanners got into considerable trouble. At each turn, innovative ways of overcoming this were found, so that the project (so far) made it through. These critical junctures show both opportunities and limits to boundary spanning in river management.

Why Boundary Spanning?

Managing Complexity

While one-dimensional approaches can still be valid for simple tasks, multidimensional strategies are more apposite for complex tasks. For this, managers use adaptive but also connective management strategies that imply 'boundary spanning' between domains, turning borders into frontiers (Ernst and Chrobot-Mason 2010). This impels water managers to rely on material incentives and communication. Material incentives for this may be joint benefits, that is, the lure of subsidy, or a deadline in obtaining or spending money which may spur actors into action. The shadow of hierarchy remains, but mutual influence and synergy appears dominant.

Making the connections requires an enterprising mindset. Changing things when you are not boss or lack the resources to carry a plan through alone requires skill and strategy reminiscent of management literature. A growing body of literature has developed around the hypothesis that *political entrepreneurship* can change organizations from the inside by 'spreading the revolution' (Hamel 2002). Current work on political entrepreneurship (that is, Huitema and Meijerink 2010) extrapolates this to inter-organizational fields. Political entrepreneurship to change the status quo requires creating alliances and a strategy to turn others around with incentives and persuasion to establish discursive hegemony. To acquire material and/or immaterial support for a novel, boundary-crossing idea, a boundary spanner needs to couple with hegemonic discourses or new discourses that are on the ascent. It involves foregrounding or establishing structural *linkage* of issue areas and policy chessboards. It helps to establish strategic linkages with adjacent agendas, actors and arenas.

Political entrepreneurs come in two types, advocacy and brokerage, either separate or combined. Boundary spanning is the brokerage type of political entrepreneurship. Boundary spanners broker the policy streams, overcoming gaps and links with other organizations. They manage the 'structural tensions at the interface between flexible collaborative relationships and the organizational structures of statutory partners' (Stern and Green 2005: 270). This 'management of frustration' aspect will also show up in our case study. To be effective, boundary spanners need to display particular skills and abilities. Among these, Scholten (2009) highlights a claim to expertise, ability to manage complexities and interdependencies, influencing and negotiation capabilities and networking skills, and adds persistence. While entrepreneurship highlights innovation and change, boundary spanning is process-focused and collaborative.

While subscribing to the general ideas that charismatic individuals with bright ideas, connective capacity and a sense of timing can make a difference, the present chapter does not make heroic claims that boundary spanning makes revolutions, transitions and/or paradigm shifts, but maintains that in a complex adaptive environment such as the Dutch water sector (Geldof 1995), boundary spanning may have almost become a system requirement in which mono-sectoral approaches are becoming obsolete. The degree and the timing of spanning, however, are of crucial importance.

Spanning which Boundaries?

Boundaries protect a system from its environment to maintain safety. They create buffers to maintain safety (Ernst and Chrobot-Mason 2010). They result from decisions or judgments, made by a decision-maker, analyst, scientist or practitioner. As boundaries may be unclear and fluid, boundary judgments are needed. Boundary judgments concern issues such as: what is your task, your domain? These boundaries may be highly institutionalized, such as national sovereignty. 'Boundary objects' such as transboundary infrastructure, however, can incite actors to reconsider their boundaries, but also become a bone of contention. Rivers are such objects – shared by several different communities that are viewed or used differently by each of them (Jarvis et al. 2010).

Boundary spanning rarely comes naturally and requires risk-taking and strategy to persuade others in the field. This requires political, intellectual and/or structural leadership (Young 1991). Boundary spanning looks across disciplinary, institutional, geographic boundaries.

Boundary spanning in river management presents an interesting case, as rivers almost by their nature link actors that would otherwise not be involved in the same issue-area – most famously upstreamers and downstreamers in a watershed, but in a networked socio-ecological system, across much wider geographical scales in the 'problemshed': the boundaries of a particular problem defined by the issue (Allan 2001, Jarvis 2010). These connections or linkages can be promoted and prevented, the couplings can be made tighter or looser (Perrow 1984).

The present contribution pays specific attention to two types of boundary spanning: linkage and framing. Strategic linkages can be proactive or reactive. *Proactive linkage* means involving others in time, anticipating future opportunities and resistance. Linkage politics between different chessboards can enable package deals in which each other of the players accept to win some and lose some. Van der Wielen and Maskaske (2007) for example call linkage (win-win) a success or even prerequisite for making space for the river. *Reactive linkage* on the other hand is about being coupled by others after a belated understanding of others' interests or procedural needs. Reactive linkage includes linkage politics to delay or frustrate a project. We will encounter both strategies in the Grensmaas case study.

Next to linking actors and sectors, discursive linkages may be made by reframing an issue to increase the appeal of the solution. Norm entrepreneurs promote new ideas such that they resonate with the intended audience. Rather than launching new ideas, however, policy entrepreneurs tend to reformulate old ideas and combine them with new ones with a view to 'selling' the idea (Brouwer and Biermann 2011). A plan can be packaged (framed) as a frame that spans both one's own interest but incorporates the interests and agendas of a host of strategic others, phrased in terms of the general interest. Apart from manifestos and core ideas around which to rally, such formulas however also need skilled 'translators' and 'ambassadors' who spread the word in different venues (arenas) and build a hegemonic constituency. These frame merchants may be called 'entrepreneurs'.

Risks of Boundary Spanning and Political Entrepreneurship

Boundary spanning is not risk-free. Both excessive and insufficient boundary flexibility can mark a spanning initiative or role (Bressers and Lulofs 2010). Boundary spanners must not only be adept at breaking down boundaries but they must also be adept at enforcing boundaries to protect themselves from unnecessary complexity and dynamics (Huitema and Meijerink 2010). This implies, among others, a caution against making an unmanageable 'Christmas tree' of linkages.

Boundary spanners are highly mobile within and outside organizations, gathering information that can be of use within a coalition. This can raise suspicion about their loyalty, which can raise legitimation problems within the organization. They often lack formal authority to influence decision-making and specific expertise of the issue-area they are linking to. When they take too much risk, the organization may call the boundary spanner back into the fold and revoke any deals made. A risk of too much flexibility is that one's constituency or policy environment suddenly reasserts the boundaries.

Another risk is that the network arrangement is superseded by hierarchy when the project becomes elevated to a national security and sovereignty issue. When a regional project becomes a national issue, as was the case for the Grensmaas project discussed here, boundaries are redrawn. How attached actors may be to their boundaries is a function of motivation, cognition and resources (Bressers and Lulofs 2010). Involving other actors early on helps others get accustomed to the idea, aligning internal and external actors in one's own frame.

However, opening up the process to others runs the risk that others have plenty of time and information to devise a strategy of obstruction or co-optation. Political entrepreneurship and boundary spanning explore, test and sometimes crosses the boundaries of the possible. Therefore it should not be so surprising that a) the existing system fights back, and b) opponents avail themselves of similar strategies. We can expect others to be equally adept at boundary spanning and to be capable of beating the spanners at their own game.

Entrepreneurial Strategies

Bressers and Lulofs (2010) inventoried a number of strategies employed by key players in Dutch water boards. Water managers identifying themselves or identified by others as 'couplers', 'boundary spanners' or 'policy entrepreneurs' rarely start with a comprehensive plan. They invest in process: calling and visiting their 'accounts' regularly without direct occasion, to see 'what's up'. They do not carry a blueprint in their pocket, but respond adaptively, on the lookout for seizing opportunities and preventing or removing constraints. Influencing and communicating with others brings predictability of expectations, therefore lengthening the 'shadow of the future' in a complex and/or unstable environment.

While this describes the attitude of mould-breakers, they do not systematically categorize strategies. For this, it seems logical to refer to Brouwer and Biermann (2011) who found eight main tactics strategies or tactics that policy entrepreneurs employ in their efforts to pursue policy change. The main strategies are: (1) attention seeking, in order to demonstrate the significance of a problem; (2) rhetorical persuasion, to convince a wide range of participants about their preferred policy; (3) issue-linkage, to adjust problem definitions and solutions to the interests and expectations of fellow participants; (4) networking; as it helps policy entrepreneurs discover opportunities and enable them to gather reliable information in an easier and more efficient manner; (5) coalition building, because they are mostly unable to accomplish their objectives alone; (6) relational management, as the human aspect is a critical success factor; (7) game linking, because efforts to change policy are influenced by other games; and finally (8) changing gears, to speed up or slow down the process. Brouwer and Huitema (2010) extended and reorganized this list of tactics to bring about the twelve listed below, distributed across four types (see Table 5.1).

Table 5.1   Boundary-spanning tactics (Brouwer and Huitema 2010)

I. Attention-seeking Strategies	II. Linking Strategies	IIII. Relational Management Strategies	IV. Arena Strategies
Pilot projects	Coalition building	Developing trust	Timing (shifting gears)
Indicators	Selective activation and exclusion	Networking	Venue shopping (place)
Focusing events	Issue-linkage		
Correlating	Game linking		
Rhetorical persuasion			

Case Study: The Grensmaas

Introduction

Dutch water sector analysts have noted a change in water management towards the better integration of land, water and people to achieve environmental (sustainability), safety and economic goals (Bressers and Lulofs 2010). In tightly coupled policy networks such as the Dutch water sector, coercion, such as forced expropriation, is only practiced if all else fails. In the Dutch situation, local water managers depend on the cooperation or non-obstruction of a busy field of actors they are connected with horizontally, vertically and diagonally to get things done.

A characteristic of a dense playing field is that you keep meeting the same actors time and again; you cannot afford to antagonize or ignore them for too long. People regularly meet each other, in different games and-or in different policy arenas, it is seldom advisable to rub the others the wrong way.

The Grensmaas case is characterized by a strong interrelationship between local, regional, national and international (Ovaa et al. 2008). As we shall see, Limburg provincial authorities initiated the Grensmaas project, but needed to link with organizations at higher and lower levels. Boundary-spanning individuals at different levels opened windows of opportunity. The below story, based on the author's PhD research, does not claim to be comprehensive, but rather serves as an indicative example of the explanatory power of the boundary spanning concept, and its limits. In the description of the case study the boundary spanning strategies and activities mentioned in Tables 5.1 and 5.2 will be referred to.

For the purposes of this study, the case study of the Grensmaas can be analyzed as a sequence of four bright, connective ideas and their fallout – both positive and negative.

Nature Development Along Rivers

The so-called Stork plan (*Plan-Ooievaar*) for 'nature development' in rivers is normally placed at the starting point of the Space for the River 'revolution' in the Netherlands. Responding to social protest against monolithic approaches to flood defense, it is a plan that exploits the positive social, cultural and economic values of rivers to pay for river rehabilitation and enhancing riverine natural values along river banks, promoting the return of the black stork to the Netherlands. A coalition (f: coalition building) of four young, mid-ranking, ecology-minded public officers from the forestry agency within the Agricultural Department, Staatsbosbeheer (Lodewijk van Nieuwenhuijze, Dick Hamhuis, Willem Overmars and Dirk Sijmons) teamed up with an ecologist (Frans Vera) and a Water Department officer (Dick de Bruin) as well as the Dutch chapter of the World Wildlife Fund.

This provided a platform to draw attention (I) to their vision in a new arena from policymakers and practitioners (Warner 2003). The photogenic pictures of the spontaneous regeneration of a scenic area, the Oostvaardersplassen lakes, helped draw the picture that paints a thousand words in professional and popular media. The lakes evolved in only a few years' time after a development plan for the area was abandoned.

The concept of 'nature development' links two domains that were previously separate: wild, unkempt, undisturbed nature beyond the dikes and interventionism for economic development in the protected area (for example, Keulartz 1999). These domains are associated with particular actors or actor groups. As noted a coherent alliance and a coherent agenda for change usually means co-opting other's interests.

In 1987 ideas on nature management in floodplains gained considerable speed when public officers involved in the Stork Plan saw a window of opportunity to skip several hierarchical rungs when a possibility presented itself to organize a boat trip with the outgoing responsible Public Works Minister, Minister Maij-Weggen (Warner 2003). Notably Dick de Bruijn, seized his chance to skip several hierarchical levels and administrative boundaries, as outgoing Transport and Public Works was persuaded to visit the Oostvaardersplassen. The Minister was impressed with the natural values they showed her in the lakes. Once she was engaged for their concept, the policy was easily transformed inside Dutch policy world, forging blue-green coalitions between environmental engineers, NGOs and local and regional and national policymakers.

**Table 5.2   Strategies used by proponents and opponents:
The case of making space for the Grensmaas**

0 = absence of a strategy

x = strategy employed by way of opposition

I. Attention-seeking strategies	Proponents	Opponents
	I: prize winning	I: public protest
a) Pilot projects	a: Grensmaas; its pilots	
b)Indicators		
c) Exploiting focusing events	c: high-water events 1993, 95	
d) Correlating problems and solutions	d: green for gravel: employment through nature development	
e) Rhetorical persuasion	e: winning formula: flood defence, security	xe: 'BOM'

II. Linkage Strategies		
f) Coalition building	f: blue-green coalition	xf: opponents and Belgian gravel kings
g) Selective activation and exclusion	g: broad project consortium	xg: exploiting exclusion
h) Issue-linkage	h: green for gravel	
i) Game linking	i: non-linkage	

III Strategies for Managing Relations		
j) Developing trust	oj: lack of trust building until 2001	
	j: 2001 provincial countercoup after trust was lost	
k) Networking	k: well-networked engineers, environmentalists and policymakers	
IV Arena Strategies		
l) Time: (Shifting gears)	l: using setbacks to create bond w. local stakeholders	
m Place: Venue shopping	m: successful in multiple policy arenas	xm: local press, national policy and court, European Court

Stork Plan Takes Flight

The Stork plan cemented an already emerging alliance between 'green' and 'blue' networks by bringing in 'red' (brownfield) values – that is, economic activity. It promoted the strategic linkage of issues of flood safety with river restoration and regional development and departments that rarely talked (the Public Works department, the Housing and Environment department and the Agriculture and Nature and Fisheries department), thus providing new links between old issues (h: issue linkage) and policy games (i: game linkage) as it linked (spanned) the previously separated jurisdictions of the riverbed and fairway (traditionally the territory of the Public Works department) and the wider floodplain and hinterland (Spatial Planning, agriculture, nature and culture). Cultural values were linked with safety, both because works to contain the rivers have shaped the Dutch landscape and since rivers had historically been strategic in military defense against invasions.

The Stork philosophy took flight in multiple policy arenas (m: venue shopping). The group of six environmentally concerned individuals was well networked in Dutch government (k). A new policy concept after all does not 'land' by itself, but requires *ambassadors* who can translate the policy to the local context (Warner and van Buuren 2009). Hamhuis, Van Nieuwenhuize and Sijmons were involved in preparing the addendum to the Fourth Memorandum on Spatial Planning seeking to incorporate 'nature development' into it (De Jonge and Van der Wind 2009). The attention paid to the prize generated over time led to the establishment and funding of a nation-wide network of ecological zones and corridors as well as a new approach to river management.

The idea of 'natural rivers' had emerged in tandem with 'nature development': liberating rivers from their straitjackets, enabling more meandering streams and slowing down their discharge (Natuurmonumenten 1996). Ecologists and civil engineers started to put their ideas into practice in reports such as Space for Nature (*Ruimte voor de Natuur* 1994) and 'Making Space for Rhine branches' (*Ruimte voor Rijntakken* 1998) to widen rivers and develop natural values in the Rijnstrangen area. Such reports reinforced the *Space for the River* programme in the Rhine and Meuse.

The new links described above thus came with attractive labels such as: 'Making Space for..' and 'Veters los' (Untying the laces) suggesting rivers finally being released from their straitjacket.

This attractive *framing* and tailoring the message to the intended audience plays an important role in rhetorical persuasion (e). The space-making frame of the new river management approach advocated by the Stork Plan core group fits very well into the societal (middle-class) craving for freedom and wilderness in a crowded, highly planned country. The Stork Plan took off in the 1990s on the crest of an environmental wave. Environmental groups fought what they saw as the erosion of environmental, landscape and cultural values dikes, but also adopted a cooperative strategy. They recruited 'green engineers' who spoke the language of Rijkswaterstaat engineers, and over time, Rijkswaterstaat recruited more and more environmental engineers. A coalition of 'green' and 'blue' (civil) engineers became hegemonic in Dutch river management.

The rediscovery of the positive aspects of rivers however required more space, a rare commodity in the Netherlands. A policy window however opened when the 'MacSharry' reforms of the European Common Agricultural Policy instigated a move from production to socio-environmental protection, and the set-aside of agricultural lands. This created much-needed space for rivers, which could help achieve a higher level of safety combined with other desirables. The agricultural sector however would not take it lying down.

The Grensmaas: Greenery for Gravel

The concept of nature development seemed well suited to a languishing plans to unchain the Grensmaas ('Border Meuse'), a boundary river between the Netherlands and Belgium. The Grensmaas is part of the international Meuse basin, which originates in Northern France, near Nancy, and carves out a deep valley in France and Belgium before entering the Netherlands at Eijsden, over 800 kms from its source, where it is a natural border between the Netherlands and Belgium for 50 kms.

Plans to green and restore the Maas date back from the early 1980s. River restoration, however, is costly and potentially controversial, as it takes space for which land owners need to be compensated. The concept of 'agricultural nature management' however, promised an economically profitable alternative combining both agricultural and environmentalist interests. The authors of the 'Stork Plan' however felt that quarrying offered promising opportunities for 'new nature'.

The Stork idea was transferred to Limburg after the Stork group members and likeminded green engineers (Overmars, Helmer and Litjens) founded environmental consultants Bureau Stroming and Ark and developed visions for the riverine area along the Maas and Rhine (Millingerwaard). Bureau Stroming was commissioned to develop a vision for the river Maas and identified the 'untouched' the river Allier in the North of France as an ideal-type, and held it up to Limburg as a model for the Maas (Stroming 1991). The Grensmaas became a pilot project (a) for nature development as a main component of Making Space for the River. The project envisaged the restoration of the river Meuse.

The Limburg context puts the spotlight on H. Riem, Mayor of Brunssum Local Authority, delegate in the Limburg regional Parliament, as a policy entrepreneur at regional level. In 1989, Riem collaborated with the inter-ministerial Stork Plan group on a plan to bring storks back to Limburg. Riem saw great potential for issue-linkage (h). Realizing the gravellers still had a claim to 35m tons of gravel, he set about greening the way aggregates are dug up from the river bed. Due to its steep drop (45 cm per km), the Limburg Maas is the only river in the Netherlands that produces coarse material used as building materials for a resource-hungry construction industry. The Limburg population was fed up with gravel mining, which had created dozens of unsightly lakes in Central Limburg.

The idea was to grant one last concession to the powerful local gravel kings, the Panheel Group, provided the excavation would result in a wider, deeper, greener and more natural river Maas. In 1991 provincial authorities concluded a voluntary agreement with the regional gravel industry to dig up 35m million tones. The deal gave unpopular gravel kings a lease on life, but signaled the inevitable end of gravel excavation in Limburg. Connecting environmental goals and gravel digging, 'Greenery for Gravel', sounded like an excellent deal to phase out the reviled gravel excavation, in exchange for something beautiful. As a result Riem became 'Limburg's Robin Hood' (Lammerse 1995). While popular with environmentalists, however, the deal did not win over many others by rhetorical persuasion.

The Grensmaas and Maaswerken took their time to get started, but were impressively good at biding their time, awaiting or finding windows of opportunity to speed up. A window of opportunity was opened by the high-water events on the river Meuse of late 1993 and early 1995 (c). These again gave the project a lease on life as the Grensmaas could now be relabeled a flood defense project.

Focusing Event: The High-water Event of 1995

The Grensmaas project's early, green conception got several impulses, as windows of opportunity opened (c) due to the high-water events. The plan developed into something much bigger after the floods, and 'security' and 'flood defense' proved winning 'magic formulae' for rhetorical persuasion (e). Floods open opportunities for 'solutions waiting for a problem', which should however be recognized and exploited to be successful (d). The resulting security frame overruled all other concerns, not only justifying the emergency measures to sequester land for building emergency defenses. It also commanded a public support base and the social control norm to co-operate was high: no one wanted to be (seen to be) in the way of greater safety (Warner 2003). Normal *legal-administrative boundaries* lost their meaning. When the plans proved illegal or risky, 'reparation measures' were rushed through, legalizing facts on the ground.

In 1995 an emergency programme was initiated to provide flood defense infrastructure, to protect against 50-year Maas floods by 2001. Under the securitized circumstances of the emergency law (Delta Plan for the Great Rivers, DGR), This was done in an extremely informal way, as main contractors for the water management boards, Grontmij and Heidemij negotiated with citizens and companies about the exact location of the dikes. A water board spokesman (interview) felt much lay knowledge was gained from citizens who knew a great deal about past Maas flood patterns.

Post-flood, the national government took the lead to align forces and integrate the various Meuse river projects. But it chooses not to use coercive powers except in exceptional times. The 1995-97 emergency window created a bullish atmosphere. Yet the infrastructural interventions also had their detractors. The cosy fast-tracked politics of the 1995-1997 emergency flood defense plan were popular with all stakeholders involved, but lambasted by the State Comptroller, who in 1997 felt that the *kaden* program had been given a blank cheque. Unhappiness was also voiced by farmers, who had little choice but to co-operate with the land purchase needed for the Maas project, as the government had the alternative of invoking the right to expropriate under the Delta Law for the Main Rivers in the name of security provision.

The rhetorical strategy of applying a 'security' frame to a multipurpose river valley project was resisted by civil engineers, as the Maas is not below sea level and there is plenty of space to escape a flood. Regional leaders however pounced on the national level to gain inclusion in the national safety norms, and as a consequence, national responsibility. In the end, after a long fight, Limburg won, at the price of losing some sovereign power of decision and some safety. The emergency defenses, after all are an ambiguous solution as the area protected by the *kaden* is like a bathtub as there's no spillway (Wesselink, Warner and Kok 2011). The security sought therefore also brings insecurity.

The Creation of Maaswerken

The emergency law was to run out in 1997, meaning the momentum and efficacy of the flood defense program would be lost. In 1997, the Rijkswaterstaat staged a smart coup to save the Grensmaas project by linking it with the Zandmaas, the sandy stretch following the Grensmaas, which due to its slower flow promotes sand and silt, and the aforementioned shipping channel, the Julianakanaal. The pragmatic political deal now linked mining, natural values, shipping and flood safety spanning even more boundaries than before. The resulting program of work, the Maaswerken, was to be implemented by a project consortium uniquely involved private (gravellers and construction companies), public (regional and national) and civil-society (Natuurmonumenten) in a risk-bearing project – traditional boundaries were again crossed.

Framing the river deepening and widening as a flood defense project cemented an unprecedented but selective coalition of local and national authorities in multiple departments, local industry and moderate nature organizations (g). On the river Maas, an unprecedented public-private-NGO partnership was formed to implement the river Maas programme of work. This partnership however began to fray as the project took longer and longer, driving up the cost. It needed more and more gravel and was predicted to yield less and less nature in return.

This seems to be a consequence of a decision not to discuss the project's cost, which as a consequence remained the 'hot potato' of the project. In its 1997 guise of the project, funds were only discussed at the very end of negotiations, and even in the face of growing evidence to the contrary, an unrealistic expectation remained that the project was to remain self-funding. To maintain this budget neutrality, ever greater concessions were made to the gravel industry, playing into the hands of opponents. In 1998 the Junior Minister decides to stretch the allowable gravel ceiling to 53 million.

This top-up proved dangerous as trust was a major issue in the Meuse project. The pragmatic political deal underlying the river intervention (nature development through gravel excavation) was still a hard sell politically in the early 1990s.

Radio Silence

The formation of Maaswerken did not experience a happy reception outside the consortium either. Limburgers felt the project was taken out their hands, to be commanded by centralizing forces (Wesselink et al. 2011). A lengthy EIA process followed by renegotiation behind closed doors moreover meant a radio silence that eroded public support. The importance of low trust in local government, due to corruption scandals, was underestimated, and came to a head within and outside the project consortium when the deal that finally emerged gave much more scope to gravelling. Environmentalists were very disappointed at the major dilution of the environmental objectives, and locals were unhappy, leading to vocal protests nature' ranging from local street protests to administrative litigation. There was also disenchantment with the costly expansion of the Maaswerken Bureau, which was now staffed with both provincial and national officers. Brief, it appeared that not enough had been invested in trust building (j).

At different junctures, different actors become relevant. A multi-organizational project team is also likely to be loath of expanding the circle too soon, before a joint 'project culture' has been established (Craps 2003). In multi-purpose interventions like 'Making Space for the River', extremely complex compromises need to be struck between many private, NGO and administrative actors. Once all authorities and major lobbies were on board, project leaders underestimated the importance of making sufficient space for local actors. Once that feat had been pulled off, there was the expectation that the other stakeholders could be won over (selective activation).

These hopes were not to rise however, when the eventual compromise arrived at in 2001 gave the gravel industry an even bigger quota: 70 million tons. This led to a crisis in the consortium, renewed resistance from environmental and local stakeholders, and an opportunity for the Provincial government to reassert itself.

Province of Limburg Steps in

In hindsight, the province of Limburg expertly handled the crisis by shifting gears, first speeding up, then slowing down as the need arose. The Province of Limburg, fearing a crisis of legitimacy, decided that enough was enough. The license central government was prepared to give the gravel industry and the controversy this created in Limburg spurred the authorities, under strong local and NGO pressure to act, to show the Ministry the door – a provincial countercoup (Huijs 2003). The province regained the initiative by gathering the key stakeholders around the table behind closed doors, to hammer out a more agreeable deal in six months. The province of Limburg showed leadership by taking the initiative for a new plan, this time explicitly talking with concerned citizens and non-consortium environmental groups.

Indeed a new bargain was forged in the space of six months. The Province had regained the initiative and stakeholder trust. However, there was again a downside to the successful outcome – the meetings were so informal that no minutes are available, a degree of confidentiality that could have cost the province dearly. Let us go into the strategies of these dissenters.

Citizen opponents and critics of the project in a number of villages and hamlets along the Maas first staged separate protests, then organized as the BOM (*Bewoners Overleg Maaswerken*). The explosive name, which translates into English as BOMB, was well-chosen, as the protesters managed to throw metaphorical bombshells into the project. They started from an antagonistic stance towards the project from the word 'go', framing the project as pandering to greedy gravel digging interests. In this sense their opposition resembled that of the *Federatief Verband tegen Ontgrondingen* (Federation against Aggregate Excavation). Over time however the dialogue between BOM and Maaswerken became more constructive.

Opponents can be just as skilled at spanning boundaries as can proponents (Warner et al. 2010). Issue- or game-linkage were not so obviously used by opponents; they mainly stayed with the issue and the game. But antagonism can indeed be promoted by the very tactics used by proponents – selective activation also implies exclusion (g). In opposition to gravel excavation, they joined hands (*reactive spanning*) with Belgian gravel companies who felt excluded from the tendering (f). Local Limburg groups used many fora to oppose the plan, from local press to national politics and administrative courts (m). Excluded gravellers teamed up with environmentalists and disenchanted citizens to file a case with the antitrust authority, first at Dutch level, and European. This was so successful that in 2002 the project ground to a halt for a full year.

The successful if unlikely coalition of convenience between citizens and Belgian gravellers (who felt left out) led to a year of European litigation over anti-competition rules, showing opponents of interventions can use similar tactics. The Province used this time to invest in relations with the citizens, who had now united in a platform. This did a wealth of good to trust relations with the Limburg population which led to the joint development of a new deal at lightning speed (j).

When the opposition scored a victory in the form of successful European anti-trust litigation in 2002, the time was used wisely by Victor Coenen, *omgevingsmanager* (stakeholder manager), hired from a Utrecht consultancy. Coenen organized stakeholders on behalf of Limburg Province behind closed doors to get a more widely supported deal, establishing much better relations with the opposing platform BOM (*Bewoners Overleg Maaswerken*), an umbrella of various local organizations opposed to the river project. When the project succeeded in getting out of the doldrums with a deal, the dialogue continued. However no minutes were available of the behind-the-scenes bargaining, so that Limburg was taken to task afterwards. Speeding up or slowing down helped the project, but also came at a cost (see Table 5.3).

After the project's start in 2005, the most radical environmental opponent took their case up to the Council of State – hut their litigation proved unsuccessful (Warner 2011). The project works are now in full swing and recently additional funds have become available.

The different episodes are summarized on the next page in Table 5.3.

Conclusion and Discussion: Opportunities and Limits to Boundary Spanning

Framing and (de)linking

In the late 1980s, 'Nature development', along with 'spatial quality' found a ready audience among Dutch policymakers that are now widely used. Specific for Dutch river management, 'resilience' became a keyword opening the door to the political acceptance of making space for the river for flood security purposes. Such 'plastic' phrases are elastic enough to link potentially contradictory environmental, security, economic and social goals. 'Nature development' seemed a perfect fit with the multiple goals of the Grensmaas project, and found an attractive translation in the 'greenery for gravel' catchphrase legitimizing the Grensmaas project.

The project framing for the Grensmaas has been changed several times. Started as a nature development project, it needed to be *securitized* to be able to survive, changing the rationale for the project from a trade-off between nature creation and

Table 5.3   Four inspired ideas and interventions and a focusing event – and how they came at a price

	Year	Impetus for boundary spanning	Ideas and Interventions to save the Grensmaas project	Links forged between	Enterprising individual	Type of linkage and boundary	Implications
1	1987	Tension between nature conservation and economic growth	Stork Plan for 'Nature Development' wins prestigious prize	Government departments NGOs	Dick de Bruin, Frans Vera et al	Proactive	Resistance from agricultural sector, limited social support base
2	1991	Demand for phasing out gravelling; desire to renaturise the river Meuse	Regional politicians made a deal with the regional gravel kings to phase out their excavation work in a more environmentally sustainable way.	Public (nature), private (gravelling)	Mayor Mayor Hans Riem	Proactive	The deal with the gravellers was unpopular with the Limburg population. This led to consistent opposition to the Grensmaas
Event	1993 and 1995	Need for speed in handling flood peak creating considerable damage in Limburg	The flood events moved flood safety up the agenda, to which other concerns could play hopscotch.	Water boards, consultancy firms	The flood peak	Time	Informal handling, later affairs over handling of excavated aggregates.
3	1997	Need to coordinate river interventions for safety and renaturalization	The national Public Works Department steps in in 1997;	Public Works dept, province, nature NGOs, gravel companies	Not known	Proactive	The integration of the project into a much bigger project, dominated by the national level
4	2001-2002	Anger and frustration at imbalance in deal brokered, Naturmonumenten NGO walks out	Provincial authorities regain initiative, shifting gears in time. The consultant helped the provincial government save their bacon with a trust-building exercise behind closed doors.	Provincial authorities, municip-alities and local opposition	Limburg Deputy Vestjens, stakeholder manager Victor Coenen	Reactive	(non-fatal) Lack of accountability

gravel extraction to a flood protection project with environmental and economic benefits.

The resulting crises inspired initiatives to create new linkages that brought fresh air to the beleaguered project. In essence, repeated politicization pitted two main problem frames – 'green security project' versus 'quarrying project in disguise' against each other. This got worse in the course of time, since a contradictory set of project goals soon made the project run into financial difficulties even before it began, relying more and more on gravel digging to fill gaping financial holes.

Four Inspired Ideas and Linkage Strategies

The Grensmaas was a flagship river restoration project, translating a newly hegemonic idea in Dutch water management, 'nature development' to one of the major Dutch rivers. To achieve these goals, water managers will often need to negotiate and strike alliances with actors in other policy areas such as spatial planning and local and regional economic development. In the Grensmaas case, provincial and national departments uniquely cooperated with private and civil-society organizations,

The Grensmaas project needed to be saved many times over. These interventions came at a price, however: the deal with the gravellers, unpopular with the Limburg population, and the integration of the project into a much bigger project, dominated by the national level and the sidelining of farming interests.

Boundary spanners are pivotal individuals working across interorganizational frameworks of intervention/strategic alliances, networks across organizational boundaries to tackle complex problems. Individuals involved in Dutch environmental management created windows of opportunity to forge new, undreamt connections and innovations. However, the fractured story of 'green for gravel' and other episodes show the limits to boundary spanning. The deal was, in itself, an innovative compromise between public demands for phasing out gravelling and private demands to retain a profit margin. The way the deal was brokered in the early 1990's was tarred with the brush of corruption, only adding to the long history of public resentment with the preferential treatment of gravel companies. The affair exposed the thin line between spanning boundaries and completely blurring boundaries between the private and public interests.

The state of exception procured by the second high-water event gave the Maaswerken a new lease on life, fast-tracking decisions and logistics that would otherwise have been mired in lengthy procedure. However it lasted for two years only, and in many respects, the security momentum was lost early in the process, as the Maaswerken soon became like any other project. Linking up the Grensmaas, Zandmaas and Maasroute seemed an inspired move to achieve benefits, but also made it unwieldy, while its upscaling also distanced the project from its regional constituency.

This kind of cooperation takes time and requires trust relations – suspending normal boundaries – which do not conform so well with principles such as transparency and accountability to outsiders (Greenaway et al. 2007), Van der Meulen et al. (2006) conclude that the 'closed' nature of Maaswerken planning not only placed communities but also contractors in a reactive position (*reactive linkage*). Yet the authors fail to acknowledge the province's post-March 2001 efforts to do better on this count (*proactive linkage*). The second crisis of confidence indeed grew out of the isolation in which the Bureau Maaswerken worked on the project's design and EIA and the lack of access to process information (also noted in Ovaa et al. 2008). After this frustration exploded, however, the provincial authorities took the reins in bridging the gap with local stakeholders. This process led to a very fast new deal being brokered, but risked being taken to task for failing to make minutes. Limburg regained the lead in the Maaswerken, and can be credited with restoring confidence by closer consultation with stakeholders. The flipside of trust-building and deal-breaking can be an undue lack of accountability.

Disconnects and Discontents: The Risks of Non-spanning

Non-spanning across territory   Linkage can complicate things in positive and negative ways. The strategy can be used to break an impasse when a conflict leaves too few degrees of freedom for resolution when only considering obvious connections only, but can obviously also serve to create new ones. To avoid 'Christmas trees' of links, linkers and spanners have to make boundary judgments on the limits to their links.

The case shows up a conspicuous non-linkage: between Dutch and Belgian 'chessboards'. Given that the Grensmaas is a boundary, Dutch interventions easily have an impact across the border. Upstream effects are always possible as water levels are pushed up because of the intervention. For example, to avoid that the bunds around Roosteren will increase flood risk on the Maaseik (Belgian) side, it was agreed that the Meuse would be widened on the Dutch side near Roosteren. The Dutch government made itself responsible for any change in groundwater levels in Belgium.

Non- and counterspanning with farmers and townspeople   We have seen that the project's framing remained deeply contested throughout the Grensmaas/ Maaswerken's history. The hegemonic framing of the Grensmaas as a nature, gravel and flood security project voluntarily 'framed in' Limburg within the prevailing (hegemonic) Dutch system of safety and protection, saving Limburg considerable money and responsibilities in realizing its ambition (Wesselink, Warner and Kok 2011). It however also 'framed out' the agrarian sector and failed to pacify citizens worried about nuisance and as the balance between gravel mining and nature development progressively worsened with time, Limburg found it hard to shake off its image of having sold out the province to gravel companies.

From a Gramscian perspective we may note that *opponents* can follow similar strategies as policy entrepreneurs if they have a coherent policy agenda and alliance to contest hegemony (Warner 2011). When isolated local protest proved ineffective, opponents from various Limburg towns created a counter-alliance, BOM, and even concluded a temporary alliance of convenience with Belgian gravel companies (*proactive counterlinkage*). While some opponents, such as Borgharen's town council, tabled alternatives, BOM's agenda however was more coherent for its dislikes than for what it advocated. BOM's conception of 'nature' as the cultural landscape contrasted with the 'wild nature' envisaged by the Stork Plan group and their Grensmaas allies. In this important sense, the townsmen aligned with farmers, who had their own worries about the impact of the Maaswerken on groundwater levels and land tenure.

BOM kept communication lines open and became a respected interlocutor for the Maaswerken project team and authorities, cementing the rather belated connection between project and local stakeholder. In this sense they parted ways with the more radical environmentalists and anti-gravel activists, who continued to fight the project in administrative courts even after its start – in vain, as it turned out.

The case study Grensmaas shows that different boundary spanning strategies and especially discursive strategies have been employed during a long-term span by different actors, representatives of local, regional and national governments, private companies, farmer organizations, etc. Proponents and opponents of the project employ these strategies, proactively as well as reactively. Spanning has its limits; it means connection and disconnection at the same time by selective activation and participation, leading again to boundary spanning activities (counter-linkages focused at delaying the process) by non-involved actors.

Bibliography

Allan, J.A. 2001. *The Middle East Water Question: Hydro-politics and the Global Economy*. London: I.B. Tauris.

Bressers, J. and K. Lulofs (eds) 2010. *Governance and Complexity in Water Management. Creating Cooperation through Boundary Spanning Strategies*, Cheltenham UK and Northampton: Edward Elgar, also published at London and New York: IWA Publishers,

Brouwer, S. and F. Biermann. 2011. Towards adaptive management: Examining the strategies of policy entrepreneurs in Dutch water management. *Ecology and Society*, 16(4), 5.

Brouwer, S. and D. Huitema 2010. Beleidsondernemers in het waterbeheer. *H2O*, 1, 10-11.

Craps, M. 2003. *Process Facilitation and the Inclusion of Marginal Local Communities in Multiparty Domains*, in P. Hibbert, Co-creating Emergent Insight. Proceedings of the 10th International Conference on Multi-organizational Partnerships, Alliances and Networks, Co-creating Emergent Insight, 25-28 June 2003, University of Strathclyde, Glasgow, Scotland, 125-34.

Ernst, E. and Chrobot-Mason, D. 2010. *Boundary Spanning Leadership: Six Practices for Solving Problems, Driving Innovation, and Transforming Organizations*. McGraw-Hill. http://www.mhprofessional.com/product.php?isbn=0071638873.

Greenaway, J., Salter, B. and Hartht, S. 2007. How Policy Networks Can Damage Democratic Health: A Case Study in the Government of Governance, *Public Administration*, 85(3), 717-38.

Huijs, S. 2003. Het vertellen van verhalen: Een politieke manier van omgaan met onzekerheid, in *Niet bang voor onzekerheid*, edited by M. van Asselt and A. Petersen. RMNO Voorstudie, Den Haag: Raad voor Ruimtelijk, Milieu- en Natuuronderzoek (RMNO).

Huitema, D. and S. Meijerink. 2010. Realizing water transitions. the role of policy entrepreneurs in water policy change. *Ecology and Society*, 15(2), 26. [online] URL: http://www.ecologyandsociety.org/vol15/iss2/art26/

Jarvis, W.T. 2010. Integrating Groundwater Matters into Transboundary Aquifer Management. *International Conference "Transboundary Aquifers:Challenges and New Directions" (ISARM2010) 6-8 December 2010* Integrating Groundwater Boundary Matters into Transboundary Aquifer Management.

Jonge, J. de and N. v.d. Windt. 2007. *Doorbraken in het Rivierengebied: De levensloop van transformerende concepten en hun netwerken in het centrale rivierengebied 1970-2005*. Alterra, Wageningen. Online: http://edepot.wur.nl/3518 (Consulted 25 September 2011).

Keulartz, J. 1999. Engineering the environment: The politics of nature development, in *Living with Nature. Environmental Politics as Cultural Discourse*, edited by F. Fischer and M. Hajer. Oxford: Oxford University Press.

Lammerse, A. 1995. Provincie poogt bij Grensmaasproject af te komen van beschadigd imago na omkoopschandaal Limburg wil machtspositie van 'grind/cowboys' breken. *Volkskrant*, DATE.

Mintrom, M. 1997. Policy Entrepreneurs and the Diffusion of Innovation. *American Journal of Political Science*, 41(3), 738-70.

Meulen, M.J. van der, Rijnveld, M., Gerrits, L,M., Joziasse, J., Heijst, M.W.I.M. van, and S.H.L.L. Gruijters 2006. Handling Sediments in Dutch River Management: The Planning Stage of the Maaswerken River Widening Project. *Journal of Soils and Sedimentology*, 2006(3), 63-172.

Ovaa, E. et al. 2008. Grenzen aan participatie in actor-perspectief. VU-IVM and UvA/PERFORM, Leven met Water. http://www.grenzenaanparticipatie.nl/static/files/Projectflyer.pdf.

Perrow, C. 1984. *Normal Accidents Living with High Risk Technologies.* New York: Basic Books.

Roberts, N.C. and P.J. King. 1991. Policy Entrepreneurs: Their Activity Structure and Function in the Policy Process. *Journal of Public Administration Research and Theory*, 2, 147-75.

Scholten, P. 2009. Daring decisions and representative municipal democracy, An exploration within the new river management in the Netherlands. *The Innovation Journal. The Public Sector Innovation Journal*, 14(1), Article 5.

Stern, R. and J. Green. 2005. Boundary workers and the management of frustration. A case study of two Healthy City partnerships; *Health Promotion International*, 20(3), 221-35.

Warner, J. 2003. Risk regime change and political leadership: River management in the Netherlands and Bangladesh, in *Natural Disasters and Development in a Globalizing World*, edited by M. Pelling. London: Routledge, Ch. 12.

Warner, J. and W.A. van Buuren. 2009. Multi-Stakeholder Learning and fighting on the River Scheldt, *International Negotiation*, 14(4), 431-59.

Warner, J., Lulofs, K. and Bressers, H. 2010. The fine art of boundary spanning: Making space for water in the East Netherlands. *Water Alternatives*, 3(1), 137-53.

Warner, J. 2011. *Flood Planning. The Politics of River Interventions*. London: IB Tauris.

Williams, P. 2002.The competent boundary spanner. *Public Administration*, 80(1), 103-24.

Wesselink, A., J. Warner and M. Kok 2011. You gain some protection, you lose some autonomy ... paper presented at the Interpretative Policy Studies conference, Cardiff. June 2011.

Wielen, P. van der and B. Maskaske. 2007. *Succes en falen in rivierherstelprojecten: Ervaringen uit het verleden, garanties voor de toekomst?* Alterra rapport 1448, Wageningen: Alterra.

Young, O.R. 1991. Political Leadership and Regime Formation: On the Development of Institutions in International Society. *International Organization*, 45(3), 281-308.

Chapter 6

The Climate Game: Connecting Water Management and Spatial Planning through Simulation Gaming?

Qiqi Zhou, Geertje Bekebrede, Igor Mayer, Jeroen Warmerdam and Maxim Knepflé

Introduction

Policy issues in water management and spatial planning are highly fragmented because they are beset with multilevel, multi-scope, multidisciplinary, and multi-actor problems. As a result, water governance involves many governance and spatial levels, knowledge disciplines, policy actors and networks. Recent policy paradigms therefore call for more integrated approaches, as in the case of integrated water resource management. The underlying questions are what an integrated approach actually entails, and how water governance can be more connected through such an approach. These questions need to be answered in order to develop proper instruments to support integrated policy approaches. One aspect of an integrated approach is its socio-technical integration (WWC 2000, GWSP 2005).

In the domain of water management and spatial planning, there is a general transition to the use in policy making of more socio-technical integrated methods and instruments. In such a transition, stakeholder participation is often combined with scientific analysis to produce more inclusive results (Boogerd, Groenewegen et al. 1997, Castelletti and Soncini-Sessa 2006, 2007). At the same time, new technologies are being used to facilitate the communication between science and its social context, such as 3D visualization and gaming technology (Barreteau, Le Page et al. 2007, Horlitz 2007). However, more research is needed to understand how and in what ways the underlying questions are addressed in the implementation of these integrated methods. In this chapter, we examine the potential of gaming simulation as an integrated instrument to address the connection issue among water and spatial planning sectors.

In the next section, we first discuss the fragmentation and the challenge of integration among water and spatial governance sectors. Then, in the next section, we introduce and define simulation gaming as an instrument for connective capacity building. In the following two sections, we present the Climate Game: a realistic, computer-supported, multiplayer policy game that simulates a water decision process for the area of Delft, the Netherlands. Various pilot versions of serious water games have been played with professionals from water management and planning institutions in the Netherlands. We describe the general background and the gameplay, and present the first results of a validation study. In the final section, we present our conclusions.

Fragmentation and the Challenge of Integration

Fragmentation in water management and governance has characteristics at different levels, within different scopes, in different disciplines, etc. (Dixon and Easter 1986, Margerum 1995). To address these fragmented situations, integrated water resource management suggests a more interactive and interconnected approach in decision making, while taking into account, from both a natural and a societal perspective, all the affected entities related to water resource management and spatial planning (GWP 2000, Lee 1994). As related to connective governance, it emphasizes that it is "a process to promote the coordinated development and management of water, land, and related resources," and "it should be based on a participatory approach, involve users, planners and policy makers at all levels" (Geurts and Duke 2007).

In our view, the requirement of connection for governance implies that a socio-technical systems perspective in planning is necessary. In short, the technical (hydrological, ecological, etc.) aspects of water management need to be interconnected with the socio-political aspects. This implies that different forms of knowledge and different interests need to interact in order to develop a shared view among the water and spatial sectors on the complexity of the planning at hand.

There are many reasons to integrate knowledge and interests at various levels, within various scopes, and in various disciplines, and there are many modes and forms of integration. This is especially true in a socio-technical domain like water management, where hard facts, evidence, science, and models have as much credibility, usefulness, and relevance as the qualitative knowledge and insights of stakeholders. From the perspective of analysis, the inherent dilemma in socio-technical integration is that rational scientific analysis and the social interactive process are intrinsically connected; they are two sides of the same coin. Although they are sometimes considered irreconcilable because there are big differences between their scopes and methods, and there are even conflicting epistemologies, they are increasingly regarded as mutually reinforcing ways to deal with socio-technical problems. This implies that the policy analysis for integration is in need of a next generation of methods and tools that are able to analyze the technical/physical complexity and the socio-political complexity of policy problems in an interactive fashion. In recent years, considerable efforts have been made to enrich the interactive toolbox with, for example, participatory modeling, interactive model use, and gaming. In this chapter, we argue that this next generation of methods that are able to cope with the socio-technical analysis of policy problems will be derived from gaming simulation. It is assumed that by gaming, partly in a virtual environment, the socio-technical complexity of water and spatial planning, stakeholders gain a better understanding of the interconnection between the various policy subsystems and policy actors, which should enhance the connection among governance sectors in real life.

Gaming Simulation and Research Questions

A simulation game can be defined as an experimental, experiential, rule-based, immersive environment in which players can become part of the simulation and as they would in real life (Taylor 1971, Shubik 1972, Brewer 1974, Salen and Zimmerman 2004). Gameplay is an interactive learning process between players and the simulation game. Gaming is based upon the assumption that the individual learning and the social learning are induced by taking decisions and experiencing their effects through feedback mechanisms that are built into and around the simulation game (Lee 1994), and that the learning thus induced can be transferred to the real world. This transfer is largely negotiated and not immediate, thereby making a simulation game low in external risks and giving the players a sense of safety, which is a prerequisite for experimentation and creativity (Toth 1989).

It is expected that the use of game technology and concepts will revolutionize the possibilities of stakeholder interaction, collaboration and visioning. As researchers, we have used advanced forms of gaming for port planning, spatial planning, water management, sustainable urban renewal, electricity networks, rail network planning, etc. Based on the empirical experiments with simulation gaming and other interactive approaches, the characteristics of the gaming methods and approaches can be generalized as (Geurts and Joldersma 2001, Mayer, Van Bueren et al. 2005, Cecchini and Rizzi 2001):

1. Flexible and reusable: They should be usable for, or adaptable to, a range of similar situations and different learning contexts.
2. Authoritative: They should meet analytical standards (for example, of validity) and political standards (for example, safeguarding core values and timeliness) in order to increase the likelihood that the outcomes are used.
3. Dynamic: They should be able to show the "performance" of various alternatives in relation to the preferences and "behavior" of stakeholders.
4. Transparent: They should produce results that are clear and understandable to all stakeholders (that is, they should not be a "black box").
5. Fast and easy to use: The time required to apply them should be relatively short, and non-experts (for example, residents and politicians) should be able to use them.

6. Integrative: They should consider different aspects and levels of design and decision making in a holistic and systematic way.
7. Interactive: They should be able to support the negotiation process among stakeholders.
8. Communicative: They should be able to convey meaning and insight to stakeholders about problem structure, alternatives, and different perspectives.

These characteristics of the game can be addressed from different aspects. Points 1-5 in the above list are considered design elements that are required to create an immersive game environment by using all suitable gaming technologies. Points 6-8 are considered the policy relevance of game play. In the case study, we first evaluate the design quality of the game according to points 1-5. We discuss points 6-8 more elaborately to see to what extent gaming addresses the sectors' connection in water management and spatial planning.

The central question is: 'To what extent do simulation games contribute to the development of connective capacity among water and spatial sectors?' The answer to this is based on an evaluation of three aspects of the Climate Game, namely:

1. What is the validity of the Climate Game to represent the realism of decision making and planning?
2. Did the players experience the problem of fragmentation and learn to collaborate in order to arrive at integrated planning?
3. What is the usefulness of simulation gaming as an instrument to help build the connection among water and spatial sectors?

The first question concerns the ability of the game design to simulate realistic water management and spatial planning. The second question concerns the potential of simulation gaming to address the fragmentation and integration among the players. The third question generalizes the lessons learnt to use simulation gaming as an instrument to combine rational analysis and interactive process for the purpose of improving the connection among governance sectors and stakeholders.

The Climate Game

The Climate Game is a computer-based simulation game developed by RO^2, which is a joint venture by Tygron Serious Gaming and the consulting firm Ambient Advies. Original ideas for this type of simulation game originate from earlier versions of planning games developed at TU Delft, such as SimPort-MV2, which is about a major port expansion project in the Port of Rotterdam (Bekebrede

2010, Nefs and Gerretsen 2010). The main characteristics of the Climate Game are:

1. Multiplayer: usually 4 stakeholders represented by 4-6 players.
2. Computer-supported: realistic database, 2D and 3D graphics, simulation, advanced player–computer interaction.
3. Socially interactive: players interact socially in the same physical space.
4. Multi-actor, strategy games: long-term decision making, strategic behavior of the players.
5. Interactive, integrated water management: stakeholder involvement, multiple policy domains, levels, etc.
6. Urban or spatial planning: player interactions revolve around spatial planning in a shared virtual space (SimCity style).

The compu generated based on the consultation with the relevant governance sectors. A hydrological simulation model (Sobek) has been embedded in the Climate Game to represent realistic data for flood forecasting. This database is related to a set of user interfaces that provide 3D maps of the current and future situation, the actions and decisions of the players, and a multitude of performance indicators for the individual player, a subset of players, or the system as a whole. The Climate Game is characterized by high quality 3D visualization, user interaction, and continuous feedback.

The Climate Game is about integrating water and spatial planning in south-east Delft, an area that mainly consists of the campus of TU Delft (Delft University of Technology). The policy target in the game is that the stakeholders work together to develop integrated plans to deal with the changes in the environment caused by climate change, while reckoning with some budgetary constraints. The general objective is to gain better insights into the complexity of water management and spatial planning, to create policy support, and to become conscious of future developments and the influence on spatial planning in south-east Delft.

Purpose of the Game

In the current version of the Climate Game, four stakeholders are simulated: 1) the municipality of Delft, 2) the Delfland water board, 3) DUWO (a housing corporation), and 4) TU Vastgoed (a property developer). The reason for this is that the simulation game is mainly intended to simulate the socio-technical complexity, rather than the political complexity, of spatial planning. These four stakeholders are recognized as being the most active in the planning process because of their spatial interests and authorities in the real world of water management. Therefore, due to the limitation of the game design, the other stakeholders (for example, NGOs, societal actors and industries) are not included because they have comparatively less spatial interest and authority. But it needs to be realized that from the perspective of governance connection, this may constrain the potential of the game to reflect the interaction among all the stakeholders.

In the Climate Game, there is a set of objectives and interests for each stakeholder as well as for the team. As in real-life water governance, this set is a mixture of individual and collective, formal and informal, clear and ambiguous, explicit and implicit goals and interests that will become the underlying incentives of decision making during the process. The tasks and objectives for spatial development of the four stakeholders in Climate Game are:

- Municipality of Delft: The municipality is responsible for the development of Delft and for preparing this area for climate change. It must take a leading role in this process. The municipality has to cooperate with other stakeholders to increase the livability of the area, create enough water storage, improve the quality of buildings, work on the public green area and motivate the partners to realize student residences and educational buildings. The budget is 4 million euros.
- Delfland water board: The board is responsible for water storage, water levels and work on innovative water storage plans. It needs to work together with other stakeholders to create 30,000 m³ of water storage.
- TU Vastgoed: The TU Delft campus (land and buildings) is owned by the TU Delft property developer. The developer needs to ensure that the buildings and land on the campus produce as much money as possible. This can be done by selling or leasing the buildings and land to users. But it also can be done by, for example, developing multiple functions or utilizing the unused parts for water storage. The target for TU Vastgoed is to build 20,000 m³ of buildings.
- DUWO: This is the housing association for both national and international students at TU Delft. It also owns property that is used by social and cultural organizations and companies started by students. In the coming years, DUWO should build additional housing for approximately 3,100 students.

The objectives and tasks of each stakeholder are clearly defined. The purpose is to provide the players with clear information about what they should do in the game. Whoever achieves the most objectives will win the game. The role descriptions – especially that for the municipality – also address the need to work with other partners. However, the collective interests are not clearly explained. This design is realistic (in reality, the real interest is always ambiguous) and supports the aim to make the players explore the need to cooperate throughout the process.

Playing the Game

The group is divided into a number teams comprising 4-6 persons. Each team plays one round of the same simulation game. The players in a team are divided over

Figure 6.1   An impression of the game setting

four stakeholders. The decision-making process is based on the interaction with the computer simulation and the interaction among the team players. Learning is triggered by having two or more teams play the game, as their experiences and results can be compared. Picture 1 provides an impression of the game setting.

After a brief introduction to the objectives and the gameplay, the first round commences. During the various rounds, the players can make changes in the spatial environment. This spatial environment is a realistic simulation of south-east Delft using current 3D maps and data.

The players' first challenge is to make the right planning decisions. They can select from a multitude of decisions that are predefined in the game for each stakeholder. For example, the municipality can decide to improve housing conditions, develop green areas, or grant permits to other players to construct more buildings, while the water board can develop more water storage facilities or new waterworks and infrastructure. Their decisions must result in achieving their objectives and interests, such as "climate proof," "life quality," "water safety" or "profit making". The relevant information and the value of each decision considered by the player and clicked upon, are calculated and presented on the computer screen. Players use this information to compare the alternatives, and then start to realize their planning decisions.

The second challenge for the players is to realize their planning decisions in the right place. Just as in reality, each stakeholder owns some parts of the area, and thus can use them to develop their projects. In the computer simulation, the ownership of various areas is indicated by color coding and textual explanations.

Players can develop their projects on their own land if there is enough room for them. In such a case, it is often necessary to integrate the new project with the existing ones; for example, building a new water storage facility might prevent the future expansion of the car park of the building next to it. On the other hand, if a player's desired planning decision cannot be realized on his/her own land, the player needs to see whether it is possible to use another location by getting permission to use the land of other players. If not, the player needs to choose another option. During the game process, the conflict between different land use interests is the key issue for negotiation and cooperation among the players.

After some time, the players will discover that without coordination and integration, their collective objectives will most likely not be achieved by making individual decisions. They will start to realize that this affects the group performance and might also affect their long-term individual performance. Hence, communication and negotiation between the stakeholders is necessary and they need to plan integrally.

The game is paused for reflection and an intermediate debriefing. The scores of various performance indicators are shown on the players' screens and on the central screen. The indicators include the values of quality of life, climate proof, water storage capacity, and green area, the individual performance of the four stakeholders, and the team performance. For the individual performance of the stakeholders, the score is calculated on the achievement of the four indicators for each of them, together with their financial situation. If they run out of money, their score will be presented as 0 per cent. For the team performance, the score is calculated on the average of the sum of the individual scores. This allows the various players and the team performance to be compared (see tables 1-4). The players reflect on the progress made so far and on the intensity of working together. After some time, the second round starts and the same process as the first round is followed. This continues until the area is developed/redeveloped and/or the playing time is over.

At the end of the session, the participants discuss their experiences together in the debriefing, which is facilitated by the game leaders. The objective is to get a shared view of the learning experiences of all participants and to make appointments for the real-world decision-making process.

Evaluation Approach

Method

To answer the research questions, it was important to collect data about the progress of the game, the decisions and their effects, the discussions, and the insights. The following complementary data collection methods were used in the Climate Game:

1. Initial questionnaire: participants' backgrounds (age, gender, experience of gaming, etc.), their involvement with and influence on the subject, and their impressions of the real policy processes.
2. Questionnaire during the game: concerning the game play and the progress of the policy process in the game.
3. Observations during the game: the way in which the game was played, how the players organized themselves, what content-based and policy measures were taken, how the players interacted with one another, the problems they identified, and what strategies they followed.
4. Group discussions at the end of the game on: the experiences during the game, the lessons for the situation in reality, the relevant knowledge-based questions, the improvement and continued development of the game, etc.
5. Questionnaire after the game on: the players' impression of the quality of the game, the manner in which they played the game, the use of the computers, the insights and relevance to policy, etc.

The questionnaires had some open questions as well as statements with 5-point Likert scales (from totally disagree to totally agree) and the semantic differential scale (7-point). For the descriptive analysis of the quantitative data from the questionnaires (for example, means and percentages), we used the SPSS analysis program. These results were supported by the qualitative description of the behaviors and opinions of the players from the observations, group discussions, and logging data.

Players

An intensive evaluation process was implemented during a game session that involved 10 players divided into two groups (Teams 1 and 2). The players were Master's students from a spatial planning course at TU Delft. All participants completed the four questionnaires, that is, one at the start of the game, two between rounds, and one after the game. The response rate of the pre-game questionnaire was only 90 per cent, as one participant arrived too late to complete it; however, the response rate of the other questionnaires was 100 per cent. The group consisted of two female students and eight male students, with an average age of 23 (σ=.81, n=9). There were eight students from TU Delft and two participants from Deltametropool, a Dutch research organization in the field of spatial planning issues.

Although the players were not real experts, they were representative for this research because of the knowledge and information they had derived from their education. Their knowledge embraces theories on spatial planning issues, the problems in water management in this context, and the real-life general responsibility of the stakeholders represented in the game. Their knowledge and their desire to learn by playing the game immersed them in the simulation, prompting them to act as they would if confronted with the real problem.

Limitations

The effectiveness of the Climate Game, the underlying theory, and its potential effects for real life still need to be validated and form part of academic PhD research. The extent, depth, and reliability of the results and insights are still limited. The number of participants was small, particularly for extensive measurements, and the participants were not similar to professionals and experts. Their content knowledge and information, their sensitivity to the real-world problem, and their learning outcomes may therefore also be different from expert participants. However, the purpose of the research was to analyze the potential of gaming as a tool for integrating water and spatial sectors and promoting collaboration between different stakeholders. The change in the players' attitudes toward and behavior regarding cooperation and their evaluation of the game could therefore be used to analyze the potential of simulation gaming for collaborative policy making.

The accompanying evaluation and research instruments are in development in parallel with the development of the game. At the end of this chapter, we describe the way in which the Climate Game can generate more and better research data on its validity and policy insights.

Preliminary Results

Validity of the Game

In the first part of the session, we discussed the validity of the game by checking points 1-5 in the list presented: flexible, authoritative, dynamic, transparent, fast, and easy to use. To examine whether the game possesses these characteristics, we evaluated the quality of the organized process, the policy realism of the game design, and the quality of computer simulation for interaction. For each of the aspects, we analyzed the answers to related questions together with information derived from the other methods listed above. The analysis contributed to answering research question 1.

The analysis shows that the participants assessed the quality of the game as good. They agreed that the objective was clear (μ=4.3, σ =.67), the instructions were clear (μ=4.9, sd=.73), the game was built up in an interesting and motivating way (μ=4.6, σ =.69), the game was well facilitated (μ= 4.2, σ =.78), and the feedback during and after the game was good (μ=4.0, σ =.94). Besides the evaluation from the questionnaires, during the group discussion after the game, the participants also said that they liked the game because it was fun to play. All the results show that Climate Game is a fun game.

The second task was to evaluate the policy realism of the Climate Game to see whether it represented the reality, especially the real objectives and interests of stakeholders from different water and spatial sectors. To do so, we asked the participants eight questions about the validity of the simulated reality. The first three statements elicited their opinion on whether the objective of the game had been clear and whether the game was sufficiently detailed and realistic. Statements 4-6 concerned the realism of the solutions in the game and their effects. Statements 7 and 8 elicited the players' opinions of the realism of the stakeholders and their objectives. As can be observed, the participants agreed that the aim of the game had been relevant ($\mu=4.3$, $\sigma=1.67$), sufficiently detailed ($\mu=4.0$, $\sigma = .66$), and realistic ($\mu=3.9$, $\sigma=1.12$). They also agreed that the stakeholders ($\mu=3.5$, sd=1.5) and their objectives had been realistic ($\mu=3.5$, $\sigma=.97$). The students did not agree that the values of the indicators of the physical effects ($\mu=3.1$, $\sigma=1.1$) and insights into the long-term effects had become visible ($\mu=3.3$, $\sigma=.94$).

In general, we can say that the game was realistically related to the social elements in the game, and neither valid nor invalid for the physical representation of the reality. We have to be aware that the sd is still high, due to the low number of participants, which could influence the general opinion.

However, in the debriefing, the participants questioned the realism of the stakeholders in the game. Their first comment was that the objectives of the stakeholders may be too transparent; their second comment was that the limited number of stakeholders reduced the realism of their tasks. For example, when the teams had decided that coordination was necessary, they had had to select one of the four stakeholders to take on this task, while in reality other stakeholders could take this coordinating role.

It can therefore be concluded that at a higher level of abstraction, the game represents the real-world processes. However, at a more detailed level, the representation of the actors and the technical-physical indicators is limited. But as a tool to address the fragmentation issue and to answer the question about the cooperation between the stakeholders, this validity on a higher level of abstraction is considered sufficient.

The computer simulation presents spatial information and the results of policy decisions in the form of maps, figures, and descriptive messages in the computer environment. It was expected that the use of dynamic model and 3D technology would increase the transparency and understandability of the information to the players. The participants were therefore asked to give their opinion on seven statements related to the use of computers and the interfaces.

According to the participants, the 3D presentation of the future situation helped them to understand the consequences of the policy decisions taken by the different stakeholders ($\mu=4.2$ $\sigma=.92$). The other user interfaces also gave a good insight into the performance of the development of the area ($\mu=3.9$ $\sigma=.87$). The computer tool was easy to use and the computer simulation supported the understanding of the physical changes in the environment based on the decisions of the players.

Based on the validation of the game, we conclude that the Climate Game meets both the analytical and the policy standards to represent the water and spatial planning process for south-east Delft. Analytically, it provides the realistic data and information to show the immediate results of the decisions taken by the stakeholders. From the policy perspective, the game involves the relevant stakeholders in simulating the policy making process. Although the level of realism and detail is limited, the game is considered valid for the purpose of looking at the collaboration between the stakeholders.

Collaboration between the Stakeholders

Here, we discuss the playing process, whether the participants experienced the fragmentation problem and whether they learnt to collaborate and draw up integrated policy plans. We look at two aspects: the interaction among policy sectors (water and spatial) and the integrated policy plan that links different policy systems. Our analysis contributes to answering research question 2.

The gaming session consisted of three rounds. Between each round, there was a short break to discuss the process and what could be improved in the next round. The objectives, the strategies, and the individual and group scores of each round were discussed. The data from the in-game questionnaires about the player's opinion of the process and observations of the facilitators during the game were also used.

The First Round

The players first explored their individual objectives and tasks; there was no explicit requirement to collaborate or cooperate. The players started by following the game description of their tasks. They tried various policy options to see how they could achieve their objectives. They did this by selecting different predefined policy options and observing the effects on their individual scores. For example, the housing association first decided to develop student containers and student flats, and the computer simulation showed it the immediate results of its decision.

The municipality and the water board started to cooperate because their role descriptions explicitly required them to work together with their spatial partners. For example, the municipality in both teams tried to make an agreement with the developer to create more green areas. Another example of communication was observed in Team 2: the water board was able to build the required water storage facility after it received a subsidy from the municipality. However, the other stakeholders were not aware of this bilateral agreement and noted the lack of space to achieve their objectives. Except for these examples, there was no strategy for cooperation or collaboration. In most situations, the participants simply randomly talked to each other about the availability of budget and land. If there was enough space and budget money under their control, they just used it for making trade-offs.

Table 6.1   Results of the first round

	Individual score Team 1	Individual score Team 2		General score Team 1	General score Team 2
Gemeente Delft	54%	57%	Water storage	100%	100%
HHS Delfland	100%	89%	Green	10%	0%
DUWO	54%	44%	Quality of life	50%	42%
TU Vastgoed	72%	65%	Climate proof	75%	76%
Team score				**70%**	**64%**

Table 6.1 presents the game results from the first round. It shows the individual and team performance as well as the achievement of objectives. The scores show that in the first round, the water board in both teams performed the best: both boards achieved all their individual objectives. This also means that the required water storage was fully achieved. However, the results show that the other general indicators (quality of life and availability of green) are very low in the future situation. Thus, although each stakeholder achieved some of its objectives, the area as a whole does not have a high quality.

With such a low level of green and a low quality of life, nobody would want to live in this area. This "bad" result triggered a discussion, and the players started to complain about the lack of communication and cooperation. They began to realize that they needed to work together on a shared view of planning.

The Second Round

Both teams decided that, in the second round, they had to develop a better area to live in, while taking into account the other criteria. They therefore had to develop a collaborative strategy. After a brief discussion, Team 1 decided that the municipality should coordinate the new development plan. Team 2 decided to let the property developer coordinate the process, because the latter had more land use permits. However, it was soon realized that the strategies for collaboration in both teams were not going well. In Team 2, for example, the property developer soon found that its plans were too expensive to realize. It needed money, but none of its partners could provide any. So the execution of the plan was halted and none of the participants knew what to do. This situation continued until the end of the second round.

The result of the second round shows that although the amount of water storage was reduced, this did not lead to a significant improvement of the other qualities (see Table 6.2). Only Team 1 managed to improve the quality of life, and then only by 5 per cent.

Table 6.2   Results of the second round

	Individual score Team 1	Individual score Team 2		General score Team 1	General score Team 2
Gemeente Delft	58%	49%	Water storage	89%	67%
HHS Delfland	89%	67%	Green	4%	0%
DUWO	51%	37%	Quality of life	55%	42%
TU Vastgoed	76%	56%	Climate proof	75%	76%
Team score				**69%**	**52%**

We wanted to know why the participants had realized that they needed to collaborate but had failed to do so. We therefore asked their opinions about the level of their interaction during the first and second rounds. Table 6.3 presents these opinions.

Table 6.3   Analysis of the cooperation in the game process

Scales (semantic scale 1 -7, n = 10)	In-game first round Mean (std)	In-game second round Mean (std)
out of control –well managed	4.8 (1.39)	4.3 (1.6)
focus on one value – focus on multi values	4.3 (1.8)	3.5 (1.9)
individual interest – collective interests	4.0 (1.9)	4.2 (1.3)
Every one for himself – good cooperation	3.8 (1.6)	4.4 (1.2)
Conflictious – Harmonious	3.5 (1.5)	4.6 (1.8)
negotiation not successful – negotiation goes well	3.3 (1.1)	5.0 (1.4)

The results show that there was no clear formulation of a cooperative approach. For all indicators, the participants scored somewhere in between. However, a comparison of the results shows that in the second round, the players focused a little more on collective interests and cooperation. When there was negotiation, the process went better and there were fewer conflicts. Based on this result, it can be concluded that the players were willing to cooperate more in order to make decisions collaboratively.

On the other hand, the results also show that the interaction did not result in a better collaboration. The focus was somehow less on multi-values and the process was less well-managed than the first round. It was also observed that after the cooperation was stopped, the players just walked around without any concrete ideas about what to do next. None of the players could initiate an action plan to structure the process. This also explains why, in general, the scores after the second round were lower.

In the reflection session after the second round, the participants said that they were willing to cooperate, but did not know how to set up a cooperative process. The game had showed them that interaction can benefit the collective interests of both the water storage and the spatial values. For example, when the property developer decided to construct a large lake, this decreased the amount of water storage that the water board must provide. Thus, if these two stakeholders work together, both can reach their targets, while if they focus only on their own interests, they will be in conflict over the land use. For example, if the water storage project is carried out without taking into account the land's environmental value, the result might be a safe area, but also an ugly one in which nobody wants to live.

The Third Round

At the beginning of the third round, the participants discussed how they could improve their current performance. They decided to no longer focus on the green indicator, because this target could only be reached by removing all the buildings. They also agreed to support each other by exchanging budgets and areas of land to increase the scores of each individual stakeholder. The participants realized that the individual scores and the team score reinforced each other. For example, the property developer in team 1 transferred all its available land to the water board free of charge when it saw that the transfer did not reduce its score while it increased the score of the water board. Another example was observed in team 2: when the housing association was facing serious financial problems (running out of money means losing the game), all the other partners supported it with their available money. The results of the third round are shown in Table 6.4.

Table 6.4   Results of the third round

	Individual score Team 1	Individual score Team 2		General score Team 1	General score Team 2
Gemeente Delft	66%	63%	Water storage	94%	100%
HHS Delfland	96%	76%	Green	0%	0%
DUWO	77%	66%	Quality of life	100%	43%
TU Vastgoed	83%	69%	Climate proof	75%	76%
Team score				**80%**	**69%**

Table 6.4 shows that all the individual scores increased, because the score on their core value increased. This led to the increase in group performance. The general scores were also equal or higher in the third round, except for the score on the green indicator. This is because the players had learnt better to cooperate. The cooperative strategy to support each other instead of doing trade-offs helped all players better in achieving their objectives. This strategy also reduced the negotiation and conflicts among the participants, because the focus shifted from protecting their own interests to helping each other.

However, the participants realized that the cooperation strategy they implemented in the game is different from what would be implemented in reality, as the willingness to support other partners without taking into account financial and land ownership issues is not so self-evident as it is in the game. Nevertheless, the lesson that cooperating more with a good strategy can lead to a better performance was clearly learnt.

Gaming as an Instrument for Sector Connection

The final question concerned the relevance of this game to real-world water governance; that is, whether it is a potential instrument for building connections among sectors. As a policy relevant instrument, the participants said that they had gained a better understanding and more insights into the various issues of cooperation. They had obtained more insights into the interests (μ=3.9, σ =.56) and conflicts (μ=3.8, σ=.63) among stakeholders. They had seen the chance to cooperate (μ=3.5, σ =.70) and how the decisions of various stakeholders influence each other (μ=4.4, σ=.85). These insights and this understanding created a positive attitude among the participants to use the game as an interactive instrument to build connections among sectors. The results are shown in Table 6.5.

Table 6.5   The policy-relevant insights for decision making

Statement (scale 1 -5 from strongly disagree to strongly agree, n = 10	Mean (std)
Better understanding in the interests of other stakeholders	3.9 (.56)
Better understanding in the conflicts of other stakeholders	3.8 (.63)
Gained more insights to the chance of cooperation among sectors	3.5 (.70)
Gained more insights how decisions at different scales influence each other	4.5 (.85)
Climate Game could be interactive tool for stakeholder participation for all relevant sectors	4.0 (.66)
The use of this serious game is valuable for policy and decision-making	3.7 (.67)

Conclusions

Our first conclusion is that, from both a socio-political and a technological perspective, the Climate Game provides insights into fragmentation among sectors by creating an immersive simulated environment. From the socio-political perspective, the game is well formulated and it allows human players to simulate the real policy-making process and activities. Because the participants choose their objectives and decisions, they become part of the analyzing process. In this way, they realize how planning becomes a process that isolates their own activities in different sectors. From the technological perspective, the computer simulation provides immediate feedback on different policy options. The 3D environment provides a clear view of and transparent information about the effect of each policy option. By trying different policy options and seeing their consequences, it becomes clear that there is no single straightforward solution that meets all demands. Although the reality represented in the game is at the abstract level, it satisfies the requirement to generate insights into the difficulties of cooperation among sectors. The important issues that are discussed in inter-sector cooperation (for example, environmental issues) both constrain and lead to more innovative solutions, and some land use functions (for example, industry) are very hard to eliminate and they compromise overall quality to a great extent. The players experienced the challenge of addressing these issues without proper communication with other planning sectors.

Our second conclusion is that gaming addresses the need for collaboration between planning sectors, and trains participants to develop a better collaboration strategy. The game teaches them that water and spatial sectors are mutually dependent on each other to achieve their goals. It also stimulates the discussion on how to achieve the integrated policy target through a better interaction and collaboration strategy. It shows that different sectors should start communicating with each other as early as possible and to keep on communicating about the results and the new targets and tasks of each planning stage throughout the process. The game output shows participants that they need to collaborate in order to design policies that integrate different aspects. However, they also learn that even when all actors are willing to cooperate, it is difficult to form a collaboration and arrive at a good, integrated plan. The different incentives, policy targets, and ways of working become barriers to effective cooperation. After playing the game, the participants have a positive attitude toward using the game to gain insights into the chances and challenges of the cooperation among water and spatial planning sectors.

Overall, we conclude that simulation gaming is a useful instrument to facilitate the building of connective capacity among water and spatial planning sectors. It is an instrument for both policy analysis and policy learning. By playing the game together, stakeholders can gain a better understanding and experience of the need for and skills required for cooperation among sectors, which should enhance connection and integrated planning in real-life policy issues. But it must be realized that the game cannot be used to address all the aspects of connective capacity in the real world. It can deal only with a number of core actors, such as those simulated in the Climate Game, and it will ignore other important ones, such as NGOs and societal actors. Ignoring those actors may prevent us from seeing their importance and influence in the real-world context. It also needs to be realized that the impact of learning among the players is limited, because they participated in only a single game session. The experience gained from this single session shows that even in a simplified environment, it is difficult to manage individual and connected decision making at the same time.

The next step we will take to improve the Climate Game will address these limited aspects in two ways. First, the game model will be further developed to simulate more important stakeholders by using both agent-based modeling and interactive human play. Second, more game sessions will be conducted among both students and professionals. The results of the games will serve as input for a better policy for connective capacity.

Acknowledgements

This work was partly financed by the Next Generation Infrastructures (NGI) foundation. (www.nextgenerationinfrastructures.eu).

Bibliography

Barreteau, O., C. Le Page and P. Perezet al. 2007. Contribution of simulation and gaming to natural resource management issues: An introduction. *Simulation Gaming*, 38(2), 185-94.

Bekebrede, G. 2010. Experiencing Complexity: A gaming approach for understanding infrastructure systems. Faculty of TPM. TU Delft. PhD thesis.

Boogerd, A., P. Groenewegen and M. Hisschemölleret al. 1997. Knowledge Utilization in Water Management in the Netherlands Related to Desiccation. *Journal of the American Water Resources Association*, 33(4), 731-40.

Brewer, G.D. 1974. *Gaming: Prospective for Forecasting*. The Rand Paper Series. Santa Monica, California, RAND Corporation.

Castelletti, A. and R. Soncini-Sessa 2006. A procedural approach to strengthening integration and participation in water resource planning. *Environmental Modelling & Software*, 21, 1455-70.

Castelletti, A. and R. Soncini-Sessa 2007. A participatory and integrated planning procedure for decision making in water resource systems. Topics on System Analysis and Integrated Water Resources Management. Oxford, Elsevier.

Cecchini A. and Rizzi P. 2001 Is urban gaming simulation useful? *Simulation & Gaming*, 32(4), 507-21.

Dixon, J.A. and K.W. Easter 1986. Integrated watershed management: An approach to resource management. Watershed Resources Management: An integrated Framework with Studies from Asia and the Pacific. M. Hufschmidt. Honolulu: Westview Press.

Geurts, J.L.A. and F. Joldersma 2001. Methodology for Participatory Policy Analysis. *European Journal of Operational Research*, 128(2), 300-10.

Geurts, J.L.A., R.D. Duke and P.A.M. Vermeulenet al. 2007. Policy Gaming for Strategy and Change. *Long Range Planning*, 40(6), 535-58.

GWP 2000. *Integrated Water Resources Management*. Stockholm, Sweden, Global Water Partnership.

GWSP 2005. *The Global Water System Project: Science Framework and Implementation Activities*, London: Earth System Science Partnership.

Horlitz, T. 2007. The Role of Model Interfaces for Participation in Water Management *Water Resources Management*, 21(7), 1091-102.

Lee, D.B. 1994. Retrospective on Large Scale Urban Models. *Journal of American Planning Association*, 60(1), 35-40.

Margerum, R.D. 1995. Integrated Environmental Management: Moving from Theory to Practice. *Journal of Environmental Planning and Management*, 38 (3), 271-392.

Mayer, I.S., E.M. Van Bueren and P.W.G. Bots. 2005. Collaborative decisionmaking for sustainable urban renewal projects: A simulation – gaming approach. *Environment and Planning B: Planning and Design*, 32, 403-23.

Mayer, I.S. and S. Meijer, et al. 2010.*Gaming the Interrelation between Rail Infra and Station Area Development: Part 2 – Insights and results from the Serious Game 'SprintCity'*. Next Generation Infrastructures Conference, Shenzen, China.

Nefs, M. and P. Gerretsen. 2010. *Gaming the Interrelation between Rail Infra and Station Area Development: Part 1 – Modeling the Serious Game 'SprintCity'*. Next Generation Infrastructures Conference, Shenzen, China.

Salen, K. and E. Zimmerman 2004. *Rules of Play: Game Design Fundamentals*. Cambridge, MA: MIT Press.

Shubik, M. 1972. On the Scope of Gaming. *Management Science*, 18(5), 20-37.

Taylor, J.L. 1971. *Instructional Planning Systems: A Gaming-Simulation Approach to Urban Problems*. Cambridge, MA: Cambridge University Press.

Toth, F.L. 1989. Policy Exercises: Objectives and Design Elements. *Simulation Gaming*, 19(3), 235-55.

Van Houten, S.P. 2007. *A Suite for Developing and Using Business Games. Supporting Supply Chain Business Games in a Distributed Context. Systems Engineering*. PhD thesis. Delft: TU Delft.

WWC 2000. *Chapter 2: The Use of Water Today. World Water Version*. London: Earthscan Publications.

Chapter 7

Connecting Levels and Disciplines: Connective Capacity of Institutions and Actors Explored

Yvette Bettini, Jeroen Rijke, Megan Farrelly and
Rebekah Brown

Introduction

Water is an ideal resource to illustrate the theme of this book. Its role in sustaining life makes it a fundamental connector between all organisms and substances on this planet. However, the arrangements that govern its management far from account for these diverse functions, protect its sources and receiving environments, or distribute it equitably. With highly modified landscapes, dense populations and diverse consumptive needs, the urban environment adds to the complexity of water management. Within this complex setting, this chapter explores features of connective capacity, drawing together contemporary urban water governance research from Australia. The water scarcity experience of Adelaide, the capital city of South Australia, is explored to reveal how connective capacity can enable changes to water governance in response to a significant environmental driver. Through this case, two carriers of connective capacity are examined; urban water institutions and actors. Whilst the nature and interplay of these carriers is explored within an urban water supply context, the case also considers broader sectors and disciplines, including water service provision, drainage management, waterway health, spatial planning and public health. Interactions between these different disciplines reveal connective capacity within the urban water institutional settings and through processes of agency. We describe how institutions enable and bound connective capacity across different government levels and disciplines of the urban water sector, whilst actors set the magnitude and potential impact of connective capacity through interaction and leadership processes. We conclude with some key implications of connective capacity for adaptive governance.

The Australian Water Scarcity Story

Following a decade of drought across the southern Australian continent through the early 2000s, many state capital cities were driven to reassess their centralized, reticulated systems of water supply. These systems came close to failing to provide enough water after prolonged low in-flows to major reservoirs, despite a higher than average storage capacity and successful demand management campaigns. A new politically driven discourse emerged around 'drought proofing' cities for similar conditions in the future (Head 2010). Large-scale infrastructure augmentations were undertaken, including 'rain independent' desalination plants and interconnected 'water grid' pipelines to enable greater transportation flexibility between storages and consumers. These responses drew some criticism from scholars, who argued this was a 'maladaptation' (Barnett and O'Neill 2010); a solution which creates 'lock-in' to large inflexible infrastructure designed for one future scenario (Keath and Brown, 2009; Brown et al. 2011). Prolonged drought conditions challenged the reliability of current water supply approaches into the future, and the 'drought proofing' problem frame did not acknowledge the deficiencies of existing management paradigms. This view was shared by many practitioners, who noted an increasing politicization of water issues and subsequent management decisions which solved the 'supply security' problem in the short-term, at the expense of development and investment in longer-term options and planning (Head, 2010; Brown et al. 2011). Observers have argued that current water scarcity should be reframed as one example of the extreme events predicted from climate change scenarios (IPCC 2007), so that water systems can be designed to meet multiple futures. Such a problem frame suggests that increasing water supply flexibility through a portfolio of infrastructures, operating at different scales and able to deliver fit-for-purpose water, is a more appropriate solution (Brown and Farrelly, 2009b; Wong and Brown 2009). Significant water savings achieved by citizens implementing water saving and fit-for-purpose practices in their own homes, were a testament to the legitimacy of this argument. Alongside centralized system augmentations, a number of cities also instigated novel approaches to improve water efficiency at large scales, including stormwater harvesting, aquifer recharge and wastewater recycling. Pockets of lot/precinct scale recycling schemes were also implemented, including third-pipe systems and on-site harvesting and treatment of water. However, these smaller scale solutions remain secondary to the large-scale augmentation solutions, due to arguments around their financial viability, management and maintenance risks, and the level of redundancy they create in the system; conflicting with the optimization and efficiency paradigm of current water services delivery (Milly et al., 2008; Brown et al. 2011).

Water Governance in Adelaide: Exploring Connective Capacity

Adelaide has become widely recognized for its innovative uptake of stormwater harvesting for non-potable supply. Initially, a local municipality began capturing and treating stormwater to provide water for public open space irrigation and wetland regeneration through managed aquifer recharge. As the drought continued and water supplies became limited, water restrictions were imposed and prices increased. As a result, stormwater became recognized as a 'new' water source, with a greater autonomy of use than reticulated water supply. A local government-owned enterprise was established to expand stormwater harvesting volumes and develop the capacity to supply for a range of fit-for-purpose uses. These included agricultural and industrial applications and residential use (non-potable) through third-pipe systems in new housing estates. Building on this innovation in municipal-scale production systems, the South Australian Government committed to a target of supplying 60 GL of fit-for-purpose water supply by 2050 (The Office for Water Security 2010). A combined investment of AUD$150 million between the Commonwealth, State and local Governments and other partners (Wong et al. 2009) is developing stormwater harvesting technologies and knowledge in Adelaide, in recognition of the potential of this water source across the country (Kenway et al. 2011).

The dispersed nature of stormwater as a supply source entails a significant divergence from centralized reticulation systems, and the legislative, policy and regulatory arrangements that favor this type of urban water supply solution. Like all institutions, these arrangements have been formed retrospectively, modeled on past operating conditions through processes of negotiation and codification, and exist to provide order and certainty for collective endeavors (Dovers 2005). As new operating conditions and alternative supply options challenge the suitability of these institutions, many questions are raised around the governance of future water management systems (van de Meene et al. 2010). Appropriate risk management for human health concerns, infrastructure ownership, operation and maintenance, balancing cost recovery with equitability decisions and property rights to the stormwater resource itself are just some of the governance dilemmas (ACIL Tasman, 2005; Brown and Farrelly, 2009a). Many scholars have observed the 'institutional barrier' phenomenon, where these stabilizing structures maintain the past order that created them, in the face of operating conditions that challenge their suitability (Dovers, 2001; Blomquist et al., 2004; Brown and Farrelly, 2009b). However in the Adelaide case, these governance dilemmas did not preclude the acceptance and implementation of alternative water supply options. While these practice changes sit uncomfortably within the current formal institutional setting of legislation, regulation and policy, some mediating influence has resolved the contentions and conflicts with this setting to allow decentralized approaches to co-exist with traditional, centralized solutions (Bartley et al. 2008). Many scholars are suggesting that informal institutions, or the norms, values, meanings, problem frames and other social constructs, may play this mediating role (Helmke and Levitsky, 2004; Bartley et al. 2008). These tacitly known conventions enable and guide social actors to interpret, codify, enforce, challenge and change explicitly known rules documented in formal institutions (Helmke and Levitsky, 2004; Lawrence and Suddaby 2006). Thus, the combination of formal rules and regulations and informal 'rules-in-use' creates an institutional setting which is the architecture for the governance of water. The actions of actors within this setting animate these structures, translating their embedded values, beliefs, norms and codes into observed management practice. In this way, water governance results from the connections and disconnections, or connective capacity, between institutions (both formal and informal) and actors.

In Adelaide, the emergence of water supply innovation suggests the presence of some level of connective capacity, as a diverse range of actors were able to collectively navigate and challenge the formal institutions to implement and legitimize stormwater harvesting. Adelaide's water industry has been enmeshed by the immediacy of the shared water scarcity problem, bringing together actors with diverse water values, service needs, roles and responsibilities and problem frames. Also, the contemporary practice of integrated water management and the nature of stormwater itself; diffuse in location, responsible for flooding and waterway health degradation and managed through drainage infrastructure, has resulted in cross-overs with a variety of disciplines and sectors. Thus while the focal point for this chapter is on the water services sector and the government departments, agencies and levels involved, the material also draws on the linkages between the natural resource management, spatial planning, land development, public health and community sectors observed in the Adelaide case. Subsequent formal legislative reform initiated to institutionalize stormwater as a future supply source, is creating dynamics between formal and informal institutions and the agency of actors as they interpret, navigate and attempt to find stability in this new governance setting. This context offers the unique opportunity to search for and explore the connective capacity that is enabling Adelaide to adapt its urban water governance arrangements to new environmental conditions; in the dynamics of the institutional setting and the agency of its actors.

Research Approach

This chapter combines results of two unique, but highly inter-related research projects that explore adaptive governance of urban water, using Australia's contemporary water scarcity experience. Adelaide is a common case for both studies, which use multiple case study designs (Stake 1995; Yin 2009). Project A focuses on the institutional dynamics underlying urban water governance. A broad definition of institutions as social constructs (norms, shared meanings, problem frames and strategies) that prescribe, permit or prohibit actions was employed. The Institutional Analysis and Development (IAD) Framework (Ostrom 1998) was used to guide data collection and analysis. The emphasis of this project is to understand how institutional 'rules-in-use' facilitate, mediate or obstruct connective capacity, by guiding and bounding the actions and interactions of actors. Project B utilizes an agency-orientated perspective, drawing on leadership theories and the receptivity framework (Jeffrey and Seaton 2004) to explore the strategies and characteristics of the actors' navigation of these 'rules-in-use'. Thus, reminiscent of Gidden's (1984) classic arguments for the duality of both guiding structures and human capacity for agency, this chapter identifies the nature and some of the dynamics of connective capacity within the interplay of these two carriers, institutions and actors.

Data gathering was conducted for each project between August 2010 and June 2011. Both projects undertook in-depth semi-structured interviews (Project A: n = 19 and Project B: n=36 participants) and focus groups (Project A: n = 12 and Project B: n = 24 participants). Participants in both projects included practitioners from water utilities; State Government water, public health and land use planning departments; environmental regulation and natural resource management agencies; local Government; politician's consultants; private land development companies; and local researchers in Adelaide's water industry. Qualitative data analysis methods were employed to build a picture of specific attributes of Adelaide's water governance setting from institutional and actor perspectives, and to explore the dynamics of these attributes. Both projects maintained internal validity through member checking processes, extended engagement in the case and on-going contact with key informants. Using the results of these two projects, this chapter provides an empirical exploration of the connective capacity resulting from institutional-actor dynamics underlying Adelaide's water management responses to drought and evolving governance arrangements.

Institutional Carriers: Rule Dynamics and Rule Change

The institutional setting[1] of Adelaide's water sector was studied using a modified version of the IAD Framework (Ostrom, 1998; 2005). Developed in a wide range of empirical contexts and fields of study (Ostrom, 2005; Ostrom and Cox 2010), this framework is a recognized tool to map intricacies of collective action situations, such as the management of urban water, by understanding their institutional setting (Imperial 1999; Madison et al. 2010; Pahl-Wostl et al. 2010). The IAD Framework describes this setting using a generalized conceptual model (Figure 7.1) and formal and informal 'rules-in-use' which characterize and connect the components of the model (Table 7.1). By describing the nature of these rules and the ways they interact, the IAD Framework provides analytical power to understand the dynamics within the institutional setting. It is from within this interplay that connective capacity can emerge.

Interview and focus group data were coded according to the rule types in Table 7.1 and workshop participants mapped the connections, interactions and effects of the rules that were identified. This produced a picture of some of the rules-in-use and their functional dynamics in Adelaide's urban water institutional setting. The following commentary discusses the forms of connective capacity which were revealed in the rule configurations and dynamics of this institutional setting.

---

1 The formal and informal rules-in-use which describe how urban water is governed.

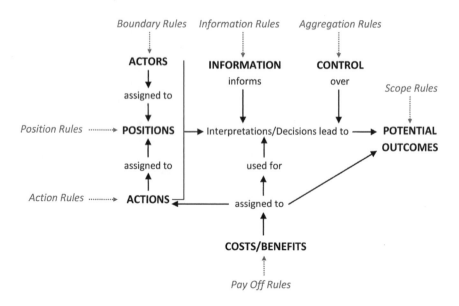

Figure 7.1   Action situation of the IAD framework. Adapted from Ostrom 2005

Table 7.1   Rules in use. Adapted from Ostrom 2005

Component	Corresponding Rule	Rule Description
Actors	Boundary	Define actors' eligibility and selection/departure process to/from positions
Positions	Position	Set the roles that can be inhabited by actors and 'hold' responsibilities and actions that can be taken to fulfill these
Actions	Choice	Determine the range of actions available (must, may, must not) and what should inform their selection
Information	Information	Set level of information available to inform choice of actions
Control	Aggregation	Determine level of control in the action situation by setting which positions can influence certain actions by other positions.
Cost/Benefits	Pay-off	Assign rewards and sanctions for particular actions
Outcomes	Scope	Set what the desirable and non-desirable outcomes are

Connective Capacity in the Rise of Sormwater Harvesting

The provision of water supply in Adelaide is the responsibility of a single water utility, SA Water. Yet municipal councils with no responsibility for water supply developed stormwater harvesting techniques. The rules-in-use underlying this story provide some explanation as to what role, if any, connective capacity played in allowing a novel approach like stormwater harvesting to develop, gain legitimacy and move toward becoming a mainstream practice.

Formal boundary rules assign one actor (SA Water) to the position of 'water supplier.' But there was enough flexibility within the institutional setting to allow other actors to step into this position. This flexibility stems from informal boundary and choice rules, which determine what role an actor can play, and the actions they should take to fulfill this role. These informal rules enabled the council to reinterpret their position of 'stormwater manager' to include 'stormwater harvester, recycler and supplier,' and allowed them to change the 'actions' they take to operate drainage infrastructure, in order to accomplish this new role. Thus, flexibility for reinterpretation of rules allowed a new actor to connect the water scarcity problem to a new solution by operating in a different way. The lack of pay-off rules to penalize the council for this reinterpretation also added flexibility. Instead, pay-off rules produced incentives for the council to become a water supplier. Community demand for green public open space created water supply responsibilities for the council, as SA Water was no longer providing reliable, cheap water for their needs, due to the drought. Community demand and the rising costs of water allied drainage engineers, environmental managers and parks and gardens staff within council around the water scarcity problem. Together they developed the capability to supply stormwater and eventually engaged planning staff to realize council's new role as 'stormwater supplier,' beyond demonstration projects, as an integral part of council's core business. This integration between urban planning and water supply provision helped to associate the stormwater harvesting innovation with normative ideas of 'best practice' urban water management.

Such a flexible institutional setting does have the potential to introduce unintended consequences. For example, with actors free to interpret their own positions, clear responsibilities and accountabilities are not established. Similarly, flexible choice rules giving actors a high degree of autonomy to select their own actions can lead to narrow assessments of the potential consequences of these choices. Actors may overlook the true costs of their actions and/or transfer costs to others. These effects did not occur to a large extent in Adelaide, due to clear scope rules counter-balancing the flexible boundary-choice rule configuration by setting clear outcomes that all actors should aim to achieve. Scope rules to delineate preferred outcomes for water management in Adelaide were broad, but clearly shared amongst the actors. The city's heavy reliance on the River Murray for water supply and a close affinity with the adjacent coastal environs had resulted in water supply management mindful of the environmental impacts associated with extracting and discharging water. Also, the sophistication of community understanding regarding water management issues had developed through long-term community participation in catchment management planning. In turn, this has given the concept of integrated water management political weight to become a normatively grounded principle for urban water management in Adelaide.

> ...to ensure the success of Water for Good and all the benefits that the community expects, water will need to be managed in a more integrated way – through what we call total water-cycle management. This recognises that water supply, stormwater and wastewater services are interrelated components of catchment systems and, therefore, must be dealt with using a holistic water management approach that is ecologically sustainable. (The Office for Water Security, 2010:129).

Thereby, a shared understanding of what water management should achieve in Adelaide through these clear scope rules tied the actors to preferred outcomes. These rules-in-use ensured that the cost/benefits beyond the individual actors were considered in their choice of actions. This precluded the need for prescriptive choice rules, providing flexibility for innovation through reinterpretation of formal rules. Thus, the rule configurations and their dynamics described above led to an urban water institutional setting with forms of connective capacity that included:

- Shared problem-frames (water scarcity) and preferred outcomes (integrated water management),
- Room for actors to reinterpret their roles and thereby find new solutions by doing things differently and finding new actors to collaborate with, and
- Incentives for actors to move outside their current roles and actions, and few disincentives for doing so.

Connective Capacity in the Change of Rules-in-use

Addressing the water scarcity crisis in Adelaide provided a common and pressing goal for all actors to work towards solving. However, their actions and subsequent novel water supply practices challenged the suitability of formal institutional rules (legislative frameworks and regulations) and prompted their review. The way Adelaide's actors worked together to reassess and alter the rules-in-use to accommodate the innovations into water management operations is of fundamental importance to understanding governance change. As institutions are socially constructed, the formation of new rules and conventions must involve a collective process of reflection, assessment, development and codification of new rules. If water governance arrangements are to adjust to future uncertainties, understanding where and how connections are made to facilitate these adjustment processes are essential. The IAD Framework recognizes this reassessment of rules governing 'operations' as occurring within a separate institutional setting known as the 'collective-choice' setting. These two settings, operational and collective-choice, represent a nested hierarchy (see Figure 7.2), where the day-to-day decisions and activities around water management are determined by the operational level setting, and activities to change the operational rules-in-use are guided by the collective-choice level setting, described by its own set of rules-in-use. In recognizing these different levels, the IAD Framework provides analytical power to explore how operational rules-in-use change.

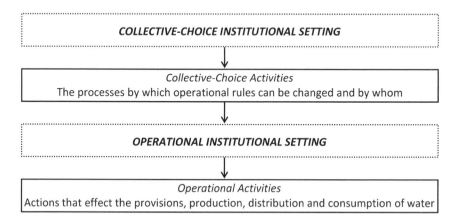

Figure 7.2   Levels of analysis of IAD framework. Adapted from Ostrom 2005

These levels within the IAD Framework provide the ability to look not only at how institutional settings and their constituent rules function to produce management practices and outcomes, but also at how these settings change overtime. Such a temporal understanding of institutions offers clues to when and why different governance arrangements become ill-suited to their operating conditions, and the role connective capacity plays in adjusting governance arrangements to these new conditions. The following commentary presents the story of collective-choice activities in Adelaide as the drought, stormwater harvesting and the politicization of water continued to question and challenge the suitability of the formal institutional setting for water management.

After a second summer of stringent water restrictions in 2008, public pressure to solve the water scarcity problem grew. There was continued media coverage and interviewees noted that the community were publically questioning the merits of current water supply solutions. The increased attention in public discourse created a political imperative to address the water scarcity situation. This political risk generated pay-off rules giving actors incentives (political and community kudos) to step outside their traditional operational level positions to start acting at a collective-choice level and examine the barriers and deficiencies in current formal operational rules (legislation, regulation etc.). Actors across water services, resource management, regulation and land-use planning began to recognize the systemic challenges to scaling up new supply solutions into mainstream practice within the formal institutional rules. These challenges included uncertainty over property rights to stormwater, difficulties justifying these types of projects within the planning system and limitations in the water quality guidelines regulating stormwater. A proliferation of committees, working groups and other collaborative forums were created at officer and executive levels to review the implications of new water management practices for current policy/guidelines/legislation and to advocate for change to these formal rules. This represented informal collective-choice rules-in-use being formed to deal with deficiencies within the formal operational institutional setting. For example, the municipal councils who had been experimenting with stormwater harvesting partnered with research institutions, regulatory agencies and private industry to monitor the water quality impacts of these schemes. The aim of this partnership was to generate the scientific basis of new guidelines that could acknowledge the different quality standards appropriate for stormwater supply along with those for the traditional reticulated sources. Many of the collaborative forums that emerged had little jurisdiction or power to address the deficiencies by altering formal operational rules. Nonetheless, individual actors collaborated in networks, and their coordinated efforts to raise the issues and advocate for change led to processes to adjust formal operational rules to be initiated. This collaborative activity was facilitated through aggregation rules, which determine how actors influence each other's efforts. A number of the interviewees spoke of the relationships they had with practitioners from a range of organizations, which had built up over their working lives. Through their interactions over time, these individuals had formed respect, trust, and knowledge of each other's skills, expertise and capacities within their own organization or other networks. This shared history created informal aggregation rules to facilitate collaboration between these individuals, enabling them to pool their capabilities in a strategic way to maintain the challenge to operational rules and progress their review and alteration. However, as the activities of different networks and groups expanded, there was increasing confusion regarding roles and responsibilities, and concern about inefficient use of effort and resources. This prompted the State Government to initiate a more systematic and formalized collective-action approach to review the formal institutions at the operational level.

The creation of an independent Commissioner for Water Security with a mandate to develop a whole-of-government 50-year plan for strategic water management, and a new State Government Department for Water with overall policy responsibility for water resources management, were the main collective-action mechanisms implemented. These initiatives aimed at consolidating collective-choice activities and providing leadership and direction to deal with water scarcity. This act represented a formalization of the collective-choice institutional setting, whereby an actor (Department for Water) had been given the position to coordinate the reforms. Furthermore, the water management plan that was subsequently developed (*Water for Good*) set out a program for activities and assigned roles and responsibilities, further formalizing the collective-choice institutional setting. Table 7.2 summarizes the rules-in-use at this level, and represents the shift from informal to formal rules in some of the rule categories.

Table 7.2   Collective-choice rules-in-use in the Adelaide case

Rule type	Summary	Example Quote
Boundary	Initially, boundary rules did not limit actors from taking part at the collective-choice level. However boundary rules were eventually established and formalized in reform processes aiming to centralize coordination.	'...started a big process of collaboration...it was such a significant issue from a political perspective that everyone wanted their piece of flesh.'
Position	Position rules at this level appeared to be absent, as collaborative activities blossomed organically between actors. Reforms are now beginning to clarify position rules.	'There was an explosion of different committees and reference groups... and it kind of all got a little bit too hard to manage there for a while. And there wasn't necessarily clear roles and responsibilities....'
Choice	With positions not clearly set, the choice of actions at the collective-choice level were limited and required actors to 'join forces' to enable action to be taken.	'My boss understood that if we wanted to get it implemented in our region, we first needed to get Adelaide sorted.'
Information	The 'crisis' response suggests a lack of information rules to collect/share monitoring data on the performance of the operational level to provide timely feedback to the collective-choice level and enable incremental adjustments.	'You can't make those good policy decisions without good science and without good information sitting behind it.'
Pay-off	With water high on the political agenda and in public consciousness, there were strong rules creating incentives for action, and costs for inaction.	'People were rightly asking questions about well, business as usual,... "Just rolling out more and more mains water from reservoirs is not necessarily the right way to go and what are you going to do about it?"'
Aggregation	Initially, the aggregation rules appeared to be informal, with long-term relationships and informal networks facilitating the collaborations needed to deal with collective-choice issues. Formal rules are to be established to facilitate cross-agency collaboration, but appear to be limited to specific issues (for example, stormwater harvesting).	'Adelaide's not that big and I think we knew most of the players around the table so I don't think things have changed that much, but it just formalized for us informal networks.'
Scope	These rules were clearly defining the goal, governance arrangements to achieve water security, and provided the focus for coordination of actor's efforts.	'The drought drove a heightened emphasis on water security as an issue; it probably drove really good collaboration and initiative-making...'

The collective-choice level of Adelaide's response to drought offers a key insight into the role of connective capacity in water governance. Governance is only transformed through alterations to the institutional rules that underpin how it is accomplished. These rules, being socially constructed, can only be altered through collective reflection on the performances of these rules and consensual development and acceptance of new, more suitable rules. The capacity of the institutional setting to join actors to these processes, and to support the processes themselves through collective-choice institutional settings, is therefore critical for suitable governance to be implemented. The analysis of Adelaide revealed the following ways connective capacity was enabled institutionally to these ends.

1. Pay-off rules incentivising reflexive actions by actors to step beyond their operational focus and question/assess how formal rules accommodate innovative and more suitable practices.
2. Initial open boundary rules to link actors across disciplines and layers of government to shared issues and allow a collective questioning of current rules across the water sector.
3. Informal aggregation rules provide capacity to collaborate and initiate action to adjust formal operational rules in the absence of jurisdiction (formal choice rules).
4. The activation of an informal collective-choice setting prompted actors with designated responsibility for this type of activity (State Government) to acknowledge the issues with formal operational rules. By building on the informal setting and formalising its collective-choice rules-in-use, a better capacity for reflexive governance has been created.

There are many more rule configurations creating institutional dynamics in Adelaide's urban water sector, but those presented here illustrate some of the key ways the institutional setting has provided structure for forms of connective capacity to emerge in Adelaide. As this commentary has suggested, the extent and impact of this capacity this will depend on how actors react, interpret, navigate and further develop rules-in-use, particularly at the collective-choice level. Therefore, we now shift our focus from the overall institutional setting to the more specific strategies and activities used by actors to navigate the institutional rules they are subject to, to understand how they carry connective capacity.

Actors as Carriers: Leaders, Networks and Actor Receptivity

The above commentary has described how institutional rules set boundaries within which actions can take place. As such, institutions as can be considered enablers and regulators of the actions of connective capacity. However, through their interaction with these rules, actors set the magnitude and potential impact of connective capacity. This will now be explored by taking a more actor-orientated exploration of the Adelaide case study.

Leadership Types and Connective Capacity

Research has shown that leadership in the Australian urban water sector relies on a combination of formal authority (that is, position and choice rules) and personalities (Taylor 2010). Consequently, leadership is determined by both the context (the institutional setting) that provide actors certain positions and opportunities to perform leadership roles, and the personalities of leaders at executive and project level in the urban water sector (Taylor et al. 2011). The Adelaide case study data revealed a number of leaders who have been responsible for recent innovation in Adelaide's urban water sector. These individuals fulfill their leadership roles through their formal positions or through their day-to-day work at a project level, and come from a variety of relevant organizations including the water utility, local Government, State Government water and environmental management departments, regional natural resource management agencies, regulatory authorities, research organizations and the private sector. Throughout the course of this research it was discovered that while a particular organization may have conventional ideas about urban water management, key individuals in that same organization may also have a clear, and sometimes different, vision for the future. This gap between the organizations vision/ objectives and the vision held by the individual leaders could be thought of in terms of different scope rules, determining different outcomes being sought. As a result, these individuals may actively build networks with different disciplines and/or organizations to find opportunities to realize these goals. In doing so, they also illustrate the legitimacy of their expanded scope rules to a wider group of actors. These individuals may even put their own reputation on the line in order to achieve breakthroughs by particular 'novel' projects that promote their different scope rules. However, this is not to suggest that there is no organizational leadership. Where government agencies have adopted a leadership role, we identified leaders at all levels of operations (practice), management (public administration) and decision-making (politics). Importantly, organizational leadership emerged from top-down, political aspirations, such as the appointment of the Commissioner for Water Security in Adelaide, and from the bottom-up. For example, the strategic cooperation between CEOs and project officers/directors in several municipal councils to persuade their elected members and state politicians about the benefits of alternative practices, can be considered an example of bottom-up organizational leadership in the Adelaide case. The majority of interviewees indicated they were aware of their leadership roles and suggested five key motivating factors for adopting such a role:

1. Recognising and exploiting opportunities for innovation
2. Frustration with current sub-optimal functioning of urban water systems

3. Opportunities for demonstrating skills in information and intellectual transfer

4. Community pressure regarding a) keeping public open space alive, and b) developing stormwater harvesting schemes because neighbouring councils are doing this, and

5. Wanting to implement a vision for the city that addressed water security

It can be seen that factors two, four and five revolve around the broadening of scope rules; current water systems only achieving limited outcomes, community expectations requiring multiple outcomes to be met, and including water security as a specific objective in future water management efforts. The interviewees also suggested that the circumstances under which they operate influence their behaviour. For example, one interviewee explained that his/her formal mandate is to adopt a leadership role, but they deliberately take a 'backseat leadership' role. Thus while their position rules assign them a leadership role, they chose to interpret this role in a way that is more likely to generate mutual respect, opportunities to listen to others and engender informal discussions. This reinterpretation of leadership was seen as important for building trust among stakeholders (that is, producing informal aggregation rules) and breeding momentum for innovation by collectively reshaping scope rules for a new shared vision and outcomes to work towards.

More prominent leadership roles were also identified. A few individuals, who are widely recognized as leaders, appear frequently in the media. This is effective for raising awareness of innovation opportunities and explaining the decisions made, and leads to greater acceptance of new approaches (hence new choice rules). This prominent leadership also attracts the attention of decision makers and politicians. In some cases this has generated tension between political aspirations and the on-ground capacity to deliver results. For example, within local government, individual leaders were identified that advocated for the uptake of stormwater harvesting systems and for stormwater to become an additional source of drinking water. The particular leaders claimed they could provide evidence that stormwater is safe for potable purposes. However, taking into account public health risk management and economics, there is little agreement amongst the industry on whether this is an acceptable policy response to water scarcity. As such, it provoked an official State Government position that direct and indirect potable use of stormwater is not on the agenda until further research has proved its economic efficacy and safety. Thus the gaps between shared scope rules and those of individual leaders may not always be reconciled, if a process to change the accepted scope rules (through collective-choice activities) does not accompany the leadership activities of these key actors.

This case analysis has demonstrated how the leadership of key actors generates connective capacity in two ways. First, by thinking 'outside the box' in terms of the outcomes being sought and using leadership strategies to bring about scope rule changes so these visions are widely embraced. Secondly, in gathering other actors together around these new visions, leaders strategically bring together people, resources and knowledge (Olsson et al., 2006; Boal and Schultz, 2007; Uhl-Bien et al. 2007) to begin to challenge or change rules of the institutional setting, thereby enabling or initiating collective-choice activity. In these ways, leaders use windows of opportunity to trigger transitions to more sustainable urban water management. However the progression of governance change to support such a transition relies on collectives of actors, developing and building consensus for institutional changes. Some insights in relation to these networks of actors will now be discussed.

Connective Capacity in Networks

The research revealed the fragmentation of urban water networks in Adelaide. A disconnect was identified between different levels of government (predominantly between local and State Government) and between water management and land use planning. This disconnect was evident in the way actors interpreted their roles (position rules) and the reach of their individual work program or organization's mandate (that is, their interpretation of choice and scope rules of the organization). As an example, State Government saw local Government as having responsibility for stormwater management, while State Government planning staff viewed water management at the periphery of their core business, which is to develop land-use plans that provide appropriate development opportunities. Informal network formation was identified as an important element in overcoming this fragmentation. Informal networks are networks of actors who interact outside the scrutiny of formal forums such as regulatory, policy and planning processes (see also Gunderson, 1999; Olsson et al. 2006). Actors in informal networks do not need to behave in a way that officially represents their organization or their authorized position. They are thus able to operate beyond formal position and choice rules, reinterpret institutional rules as an individual among like-minded colleagues, and will not be sanctioned by cost/benefit rules for doing so. Furthermore, informal networks tend to occur between different disciplines and across different organizations, thus can bring together a diverse range of actors and overcome the fragmentation of formal networks, which are typically established through organizational ties.

The research identified a number of informal networks that consisted of individuals who collectively recognized they had shared problems, similar frustrations, interests, passions and ambitions. Individuals in these networks commented that they operate on a trust basis, are building on shared interests, contain a high degree of tacit knowledge and have fluctuating levels of interactions (that is, communication may involve infrequent email communications). In relation to stormwater management, one clear informal network was identified where individuals were primarily concerned with stormwater quality management, but where experiences with stormwater harvesting and reuse were also shared. This particular network consisted largely of individuals from practice and research, had an engineering bias and involved people from organizations including municipal councils, natural resource management agencies, research bodies, consulting firms and the water utility. The individuals involved mostly have experience in the practice of planning, design, operation and maintenance of water systems, and interact on a case-by-case basis when, for example, they meet through projects, workshops, seminars or informal phone calls and/or emails. Members of this informal network are pursuing the uptake of water sensitive urban design[2] and collaborate with each other to increase their own knowledge, share experiences, and influence policy makers and politicians. Thus this network, initially relying on existing relationships built up through shared history, now exists around dissatisfaction with the current formal operational rules.

Understanding Actor Receptivity to Rule Change and Agency Processes

As described in the previous sections leadership qualities and collective efforts are important attributes for connective capacity. However, the willingness of actors to employ their 'agency' abilities to these ends should also be considered. Do network actors have a reason to connect? Is there a problem to solve or an innovative solution to apply? While formal and informal rules provide structure and guidance, it is the motivations and personal assessments of cost/benefits rules by actors (for example, 'Is this action worth risking my reputation on?) along with their interpretations of other rules, which combine to manifest in practices.. Or alternatively, to challenge or change rules through collective-choice activities. As we have described above, leadership processes are acting as a catalyst to change the rules-in-use of the institutional setting, by connecting the operational and collective-choice levels through the work of actors. Change can be initiated when actors interacting with leaders are receptive to such change. This potential receptivity of actors has been captured in a framework by Jeffrey and Seaton (2004). The receptivity framework distinguishes four non-sequential stages of receptivity to innovative technologies (for example, stormwater harvesting and reuse) or innovative processes (for example, interacting with 'new' network actors), 1) awareness about a problem or an innovation, 2) association of the problem's or innovation's values in a particular context, 3) acquisition of new competencies and skills needed to address the problem or apply the innovation and 4) creating incentives and recognition of opportunities to apply an innovative solution in practice. The research data highlighted how informal networks can increase several aspects of receptivity to integrated 'governance' approaches that contain higher levels of connective capacity amongst different disciplines and levels compared to traditional 'government' approaches (see Table 7.3).

---

2 A water management concept that aims to promote the integration of water services and protection of aquatic environments in urban design processes (Wong and Brown 2009).

Table 7.3   Aspects of connecting levels and disciplines through informal networks

Aspect	How achieved in informal networks?	Rules involved	Example Quote
Creating awareness	Putting topics on the agenda of different members of an informal network.	*Introducing new Information*	*'We are facilitators, getting different people to talk to each other to realize that we've got similar objectives and that we're trying to achieve the same sorts of things so.'*
Association with issues and values	Identifying and discussing positive and negative (side-) effects of possible solutions amongst the informal network members from different organizational or disciplinary perspectives.	*Association of costs/ benefits ('Pay-off'), identification of desirable outcomes ('Scope') and identifying which actors are involved ('Boundary') and why ('Position').*	*'I don't know how feasible it is, but that was where we came to as a sort of a brainstorming exercise.'*
Acquisition of competencies and skills	Collaborative learning about possibilities, needs and demands of different technologies, designs and processes through exchange of tacit knowledge across disciplines (mainly engineering, land use planning and natural resource management).	*Increase capacity to link information rules to new actions (choice rules) to provide guidance for actors on how to fulfill their 'positions'*	*'I'd rather have people outside the Institute come along and see what we're doing and talk to the people at our Institute, have a beer after and walk away and then be prepared to ring them up the next day and say 'saw what you're doing, can you help us out?''*
Recognition of opportunities to apply	Informing about opportunities, and negotiating needs, demands, responsibilities and the application of alternatives.	*Taking action (choice rules), identifying eligibility to perform action (boundary rules) and who should be involved (aggregation rules)*	*'I wheel and deal in anything that goes past my door provided I can make a buck out of it.'*

Overall, it could be argued that because informal networks are not constrained by bureaucratic procedures and are by their nature more responsive than formal institutional settings, they are critical to adaptive governance and should be facilitated, supported and strengthened where possible. However, as Gunderson (1999) points out, it is a challenge to create and foster informal networks, as support needs to be carefully constructed to ensure that the informal nature of these networks is not lost, as the more formalized these networks become, the less likely they are to successfully build trust. The data from Adelaide indicated that stimulating informal networks can occur through providing support for professional associations or other network organizations such as capacity building programs. For example, many of the individuals who associate themselves with the informal stormwater network suggested professional associations such as the Stormwater Industry Association or the Institute for Public Works Engineering Australia act as a platform to meet like-minded individuals, exchange perspectives and share experiences. In Adelaide, such network organizations are actively aiming to increase awareness and acquisition of competencies and skills. However, they are less successful in improving the associated values (informal rules-in-use) of innovative solutions, for example, across the urban water and planning sectors (Brown et al., 2011; Farrelly and Brown 2011). The interview data also suggested that research projects and demonstration projects are alternative mechanisms from which informal networks emerge and develop. In Adelaide such projects provided a platform on which real problems and solutions could be discussed in safe spaces without the initial scrutiny of bureaucratic forces (formal rules). However, it has been shown that demonstration projects are not always successful at diffusing such innovations. Research by Farrelly and Brown (2011) has shown that informal networks may be limited by a lack of change to the underlying rules-in-use, and require more formalized collective-choice settings to ground the changes into normative ideas of best practice through alteration to operational rules-in-use.

The results from the Adelaide case reveal the different forms of leadership actors provide in navigating and reinterpreting formal rules, and utilizing informal rules to create and enable informal networks. Further, due to informal aggregation rules such as mutual respect and trust, which bind these networks, and expanded scope rules, these actors are able to work collectively on strategies to challenge and change formal rules. In particular, harnessing collaborative projects to join different organizations and disciplines and demonstrate the multiple benefits expanded scope rules could deliver to the broad water sector. Accordingly, leadership and informal networks serve to increase the connective capacity between different disciplines (service delivery, land-use planning, research, and natural resource management) and at different levels (State and local Government, policy, regulation and operations). However, actors must also be motivated and given the authority to initiate the collective-choice activities needed for rule change, through rule configurations within the different levels of the institutional setting.

Conclusion

This case study of Adelaide has revealed some key aspects of connective capacity in institutional settings, and within actor's navigation of these societal structures. Institutional settings, or the rules-in-use guiding behavior and action, can enable and disable connective capacity through the dynamics created by the characteristics, configurations and interplay of the formal and informal rules. Therefore, these dynamics provide the potential for connective capacity. The institutional setting also generates a range of incentives and disincentives to motivate actors to enact, bend or break certain rules. The different ways actors interpret rules and strategically utilize rule configurations creates different degrees and effects of connective capacity. Actors navigate formal rules via their own interpretations and may draw on informal rules to circumnavigate constraints in the formal institutional setting. They may also draw on these informal rules to collectively change the formal rules if a consensus around the inadequacy of these incumbent rules persists. The agency of actors (both individuals and organizations) thus realizes the connective capacity inherent in institutional dynamics. Key expressions of this connective capacity are forms of leadership and the activities of networks. These bring practitioners together to recognize shared problems, the limitations of current governance arrangements, and to collectively reassess knowledge and re-vision the outcomes being sought. Once this collective problem frame is produced, networks may emerge from these interactions to further the ideas by pooling actors' skills, strengths and positions in a strategic way to effect systemic change. These connective capacities, within institutional settings and conveyed by actors, are critical for the continual adjustment of institutional rules to find 'best fit' governance arrangements in dynamic and uncertain operating conditions.

This research suggests potentially valuable insights from further work to identify informal rules, understand how actors utilize them and for what purpose, and distinguish rule configurations that build and support the receptivity of actors to adopt leadership roles and network activities. This knowledge would provide a broader understanding of the connective capacity created by these two carriers and its potential for enabling adaptive governance through more timely and systemic institutional rule changes.

Bibliography

ACIL Tasman. 2005. Institutional Arrangements in the Australian Water Sector. National Water Commission: Canberra.

Barnett, J. and O'Neill, S. 2010. Maladaptation. *Global Environmental Change*, 20(2), 211-13.

Bartley, T., Andersson, K., Jagger, P. and Laerhoven, F.V. 2008. The Contribution of Institutional Theories to Explaining Decentralization of Natural Resource Governance. *Society & Natural Resources*, 21(2), 160-74.

Blomquist, W., Heikkila, T. and Schlager, E. 2004. Building the agenda for institutional research in water resource management. *Journal of the American Water Resources Association*, 40(4), 925-936.

Boal, K. and Schultz, P. 2007. Storytelling, time, and evolution: The role of strategic leadership in complex adaptive systems. *The Leadership Quarterly*, 18, 411-28.

Brown, R., Ashley, R. and Farrelly, M. 2011. Political and Professional Agency Entrapment: An Agenda for Urban Water Research. *Water Resources Management*, 23(4), 1-14.

Brown, R.R. and Farrelly, M.A. 2009a. Challenges ahead: Social and institutional factors influencing sustainable urban stormwater management in Australia. *Water Science and Technology*, 59(4), 653-60.

Brown, R.R. and Farrelly, M.A. 2009b. Delivering sustainable urban water management: A review of the hurdles we face. *Water Science and Technology*, 59(5), 839-46.

Dovers, S. 2001. Institutional barriers and opportunities: Processes and arrangements for natural resource management in Australia. *Water Science and Technology*, 43(9), 215-26.

Dovers, S. 2005. *Environment and Sustainability Policy: Creation, Implementation, Evaluation.* Annandale: Federation Press.

Farrelly, M. and Brown, R. 2011. Rethinking urban water management: Experimentation as a way forward? *Global Environmental Change*, 21, 721-732.

Giddens, A. 1984. *The Constitution of Society: Outline of the Theory of Structuration.* Berkeley, CA: University of California Press.

Gunderson, L. 1999. Resilience, flexibility and adaptive management—Antidotes for spurious certitude? *Conservation Ecology*, 3(1), 7.

Head, B.W. 2010. Water policy—Evidence, learning and the governance of uncertainty. *Policy and Society*, 29(2), 171-80.

Helmke, G. and Levitsky, S. 2004. Informal Institutions and Comparative Politics: A Research Agenda. Perspectives on Politics, 2(04), 725-740.

Imperial, M.T. 1999. Institutional Analysis and Ecosystem-Based Management: The Institutional Analysis and Development Framework. *Environmental Management*, 24(4), 449-65.

IPCC. 2007. Climate Change 2007. *Synthesis Report.* Contribution of Working Groups I, II and III to the Fourth Assessment Report of the Intergovernmental Panel on Climate Change, edited by R.K. Pachauri and A. Reisinger. IPCC: Geneva, Switzerland, 104 pp.

Jeffrey, P. and Seaton, R. 2004. A conceptual model of 'receptivity'applied to the design and deployment of water policy mechanisms. *Journal of Integrative Environmental Sciences*, 1, 277-300.

Keath, N. and Brown, R. 2009. Extreme events: Being prepared for the pitfalls with progressing sustainable urban water management. *Water Science and Technology*, 59(7), 1271-80.

Kenway, S., Gregory, A. and McMahon, J. 2011. *Urban Water Mass Balance Analysis. Journal of Industrial Ecology*, 15(5), 693-706.

Lawrence, T.B. and Suddaby, R. 2006. Institutions and Instiutional Work, in *The SAGE Handbook of Organization Studies*, edited by S. Clegg. London: Sage Publications.

Madison, M.J., Frischmann, B.M. and Strandburg, K.J. 2010. Constructing Commons in the Cultural Environment. *Cornell Law Review*, 95(4), 657-709.

Milly, P.C.D., Betancourt, J., Falkenmark, M., Hirsch, R.M., Kundzewicz, Z.W., Lettenmaier, D.P. and Stouffer, R.J. 2008. Climate change - Stationarity is dead: Whither water management? *Science*, 319(5863), 573-4.

Olsson, P., Gunderson, L.H., Carpenter, S.R., Ryan, P., Lebel, L., Folke, C. and Holling, C.S. 2006. Shooting the rapids: Navigating transitions to adaptive governance of social-ecological systems. Ecology and Society, 11(1), 21.

Ostrom, E. 1998. The Institutional Analysis and Development Approach, in *Designing Institutions for Environmental and Resource Management*, edited by E.T. Loehman and D.M. Kilgour. Cheltenham, UK: Edward Elgar.

Ostrom, E. 2005. *Understanding Institutional Diversity.* Princeton, NJ: Princeton University Press.

Ostrom, E. and Cox, M. 2010. Moving beyond panaceas: A multi-tiered diagnostic approach for social-ecological analysis. *Environmental Conservation*, 37(4), 451-63.

Pahl-Wostl, C., Holtz, G., Kastens, B. and Knieper, C. 2010. Analyzing complex water governance regimes: The Management and Transition Framework. Environmental Science & Policy, 13(7), 571-81.

Stake, R.E. 1995. *The Art of Case Study Research.* Thousand Oaks, CA: Sage Publications.

Taylor, A. 2010. *Sustainable Urban Water Management: The Champion Phenomenon.* PhD Thesis, School of Geography and Environmental Science. Monash University. Melbourne, Australia.

Taylor, A., Cocklin, C., Brown, R. and Wilson-Evered, E. 2011. An investigation of champion-driven leadership processes. *The Leadership Quarterly*, 22, 412-33.

The Office for Water Security. 2010. *Water for Good: A Plan to Ensure our Water Future to 2050.* Government of South Australia: Adelaide, Australia.

Uhl-Bien, M., Marion, R. and McKelvey, B. 2007. Complexity leadership theory: Shifting leadership from the industrial age to the knowledge era. *The Leadership Quarterly*, 18(298-318).

van de Meene, S.J., Brown, R.R. and Farrelly, M.A. 2010. Capacity attributes of future urban water management regimes: Projections from Australian sustainability practitioners. *Water Science and Technology*, 61(9), 2241-50.

Wong, P., Rann, M. and Maywald, K. 2009. Media release—Go ahead for $150 million in stormwater projects. Australian Government/Government of South Australia: Adelaide, Australia.

Wong, T.H.F. and Brown, R.R. 2009. The water sensitive city: Principles for practice. Water Science and Technology, 60(3), 673-82.

Yin, R.K. 2009. *Case Study Research: Design and Methods.* Thousand Oaks, CA: Sage Publications*: .*

Chapter 8

Short-term and Long-term Tensions in Water Programs: The Role of Leadership and Organization

Nanny Bressers and Ytsen Deelstra

Short Term/Long Term Tensions in Water Governance

The *core aim* of this chapter is twofold. The first aim is to explore the short-term/ long-term tensions we witness in empirical water governance cases, the leadership strategies that were employed by individuals to deal with these tensions (make use of the chances or overcome the problems that arise from it) and the effects this had on handling the tensions. The second aim is to explore how current conceptualizations of complexity leadership can be helpful to understand the role of leader behavior in relation to short-term/ long-term tensions. These aims are related to the structure defined in Chapter 1 as follows: our focus lies on the agent level as a carrier (the leaders) and the short term/long term tensions as our main focal point.

The potential tension between short term and long term can be addressed through connecting agents. Agents, who will align actors around them on a shared objective, and make attempts to connect short term frames with long term frames. This is where our focal point closely relates with the focal point on frames and perceptions: it is especially these (differing) frames and perceptions that can lead to a tension between short term and long term, but a solution for addressing tensions also lies in the alignment of frames and perceptions (creating mutual receptivity, see Bressers 2011). The idea of tensions in networks is explored in governance literature (see for instance Provan and Kenis 2008), but these classic network tensions often concern matters such as flexibility versus stability, efficiency versus inclusiveness, and internal and external legitimacy (ibid.). The tensions and dynamics between scales, such as time scales, are less explored, although discussed by for instance Cash et al. (2006).

To assess these tensions and the actions and strategies of leaders to reduce these tensions, we will look at two cases on water governance. The first case, a policy program, concerns a subprogram of the Delta Program (the subprogram about the IJsselmeer area). This case departs further on in the process, and at a more regional level in comparison to Chapter 11, in which Verduijn describes and analyses the emergence of the Delta Program. This chapter will zoom in to the Delta Program as a (still ongoing) interactive policy initiative in which national government cooperates with lower tiers of government and stakeholders. Goal of the Delta Program is to make Dutch water management compatible with the requirements of future developments up until the year 2100. The second case, a knowledge program, is the program Living with Water, a recently finalized knowledge program, partially subsidized by the Dutch government. This program worked on knowledge development and dissemination and network building for innovative water management. Together, these cases give a good overview of (types of) water governance programs in The Netherlands.

Towards a Conceptualization of Short Term/Long Term Tensions and Dynamics

Policy programs and knowledge programs essentially revolve around handling (external) future developments such as sea level rise or socio-economic developments of certain areas. Their purpose is to develop plans on how to deal with predicted future developments (Van der Steen 2009). Both our cases will have a long-term outlook, but with actions that take place today and tomorrow. Furthermore, a program has to learn from past experiences to build scenarios for the future (Van der Steen 2009, Rotmans 2003). The inclusion of these lessons from the past is not always self-evident, as discussed by Pollitt (2008).

When defining short-term actions for long-term changes, one always has to deal with a large degree of inherent uncertainty that emerges from the complexity of the policy object or general situation. Hence uncertainty about which actions are required to meet the challenge is fundamental (Teisman, Van Buuren and Gerrits 2009). The amount and type of knowledge available to reduce uncertainties can help. However, Koppenjan and Klijn (2004) show that in many cases increasing knowledge does not lead to decreasing uncertainty and can even lead to increasing uncertainty. Furthermore, multi-actor cooperation in today's water governance leads to differences in perceptions about short-term and long-term challenges and goals. Firstly, actors can differ in their opinion about which moments in time belong to the short-term and which belong to the long-term (see for example Bressers, Avelino and Geerlings 2012). Secondly, actors can have different perceptions about what the short term and the long term does and should entail. In other words; their ideals and objectives differ as well as their definition of the challenge or problem. In our view this means that a definition of short term/ long term tensions cannot include a definition of what *is* short term and what *is* long term. This definition depends on the perceptions and frames of the participating actors.

Within the programs different actors co-exist, with different strategic and operational interests. Overall, we expect, based on our empirical impressions thus far, that leaders with a dominant strategic orientation will emphasize the long term more than leaders with a dominant operational orientation. Leadership styles are shaped by a mix of temporal beliefs and practices ('t Hart 2011), hence, the two are very connected. In many policy programs and knowledge programs strategic versus operational levels are, to some extent, represented by the program level and the project level. The program level is more strategic oriented and works on the bigger picture or wider message, whereas the project level is more operational and works on realizing changes in the short- to mid-term, while keeping desired long-term changes in mind. The project level is more eager to realize short-term effects, because of the private objectives of their participants (for instance profit realization for businesses).

Although we do expect to witness these divisions in both policy and knowledge programs, we do wish to state explicitly that these programs also differ on other accounts. A policy program starts from a different position than a knowledge program in the sense that it works from an already agreed upon principle (the policy plan), for which formal support is already gathered. In a knowledge program actors from all tiers of an organization (both top-level as well as lower tiers) come together to define what problems they see and what solution directions might be feasible for these problems. In general, the agreement on these problems and solutions is less than in a policy program. The problem and solution definition is therefore more formal than in a knowledge program.

As discussed above, we elaborate specifically on short term/ long term tensions in our cases. To explore these time scales we propose to explore the following working conceptualization:

1. Short-term/ long-term tensions that occur between actors are caused by the differences in perceptions and frames between participating actors. This type of tension concerns a variety of perspectives on what constitutes the short-term and what constitutes the long-term.
2. In our cases we expect to see a more long-term perspective on program level, whereas we expect to see a more short-term perspective on project level. The diverging objectives on a short-term/ long-term scale between project level and program level could lead to further tensions.
3. Leadership can diminish these tensions by connecting time scales and connecting actors and their perceptions. Connective capacity is therefore a requirement for a successful handling of time scale tensions.

Complexity Leadership for Handling Tensions

A focus on the tensions between projects and programs and the actors partaking in the project and the program level, creates a focus on the individual actors of our cases. Agents of especial importance in the programs we will study are the *program and project leaders*. Program and project leaders influence the long-term direction, the approved short-term actions, and they have the oversight required to align the short-term actions with the long-term direction. In line with *complexity leadership theory* (Uhl-Bien 2007) we assume that leaders play an important role in setting system boundaries and selecting actor networks that will be involved with the development of new policies and/or knowledge. This implies they can provide direction to direction-searching actors, can sometimes enforce or entice specific actors to undertake specific actions for the desired long-term objective and can create connections between actors and ideas.

Complexity Leadership Further Explored

In the first decade of the 21st century, scholars on leadership shifted their attention from leadership as an individual ability or quality towards leadership as a property of complex social systems. Departing from this insight, complexity leadership theory (CLT) was developed by Mary Uhl-Bien and Russ Marion (2008, 2009) (also see Uhl-Bien et al. 2007). In this contribution we will draw from the CLT approach, as the categorization of leadership roles of this approach helps to discern which individuals fulfill vital roles in managing tensions between cooperating organizations. Uhl-Bien et al. (2007: 299) state that:

> leadership should be seen not only as position and authority but also as an *emergent, interactive dynamic*— a complex interplay from which a collective impetus for action and change emerges when heterogeneous agents interact in networks in ways that produce new patterns of behavior or new modes of operating.

Hence, leaders are dependent on the system they are part of in order to be effective leaders. We are dealing with three types of leadership (ibid.). Before we elaborate on these three types, we would like to state that leaders and leadership are not entirely the same. For conceptual and analytical clarity we make a distinction between them. Reason to make this distinction is that first applications of CLT show that in some cases one person can show behavior that is related to more than one (even all three) of the discerned types of leadership (Uhl-Bien et al. 2007). In line with CLT we define leaders as persons with a certain amount of influence within a social system (not necessarily derived from a formal position). And we define leadership as behavior of these leaders in terms of the three types of Complexity Leadership). First, *administrative leadership* is about defining problems and potential solutions, project organization and setting system boundaries. In this sense, administrative leadership is closely related to traditional notions on leadership. Second, *adaptive leadership* is the kind of behavior that stimulates social systems to ensue explorative actions in order to develop new adaptive strategies. Adaptively behaving leaders work on activities such as visioning, anticipating and enthusing others for their cause. Third, *enabling leadership* provide space for persons to show adaptive leadership and adaptive networks to do their work on the one hand, and at the other hand ensure that the adaptive network does not wander of too much from existing administrative strategies and goals. At the same time enabling leadership behavior also entails preparation of administrative leaders for implementation of adaptive strategies by stretching the administrative strategies in advance towards new adaptive strategies. Their activities such as networking, connecting, and mediating create space for administrative and adaptive leadership to cooperate. Enabling leaders can employ boundary spanning activities to overcome tensions and align administrative and adaptive leaders. Boundary-spanning leaders are a specific leadership type (see for example, Bekkers, Edelenbos and Steijn 2011).

Lulofs and Bressers define boundary spanning as 'adaptive governance activities of water managers that encounter complex water challenges by linking their sector, scales and timeframes to previously independent other sectors, scales and timeframes' (2010: 11). Boundary spanning is therefore consistent with connective capacity of leaders – for it revolves around connecting actions to overcome tensions on various focal points, including time scales. Boundaries, in this sense, are not physical barriers between spatial areas or other tangible aspects, but rather socially constructed demarcations between actors (ibid.). By connecting them actors can align and become more receptive towards each other – creating space for shared objectives and tension reduction. Boundary spanners are constantly connecting scales, organizations, levels, and actors (Leifer and Delbecq 1978, Williams 2002). They do so through, sometimes ad hoc constructed, actions, always attempting to create connective capacity. Boundary spanning to us is therefore another conceptualization of connective capacity between scales (focal points). Our primary focus lies on leadership strategies on short term/ long term tensions, but we do emphasize to the leader the great overlap of our approach with boundary spanning literature.

An Explorative Framework for Assessing Policy and Knowledge Programs

In the previous section we have discussed the several leadership types of complexity leadership literature, and already mentioned several key activities and strategies of leaders, and the way they relate to each other. The table below expands this list of activities, to provide a framework of leadership activities which we will employ in our empirical studies.

Table 8.1   Strategic actions for each leader type

Leadership type	Leadership actions
Administrative	Setting system boundaries
	Define concrete objectives
	Define problems and solutions
	Managerial steering on outcomes
	Formal organization, for example, finances
Adaptive	Out of the box thinking
	Future visions
	Anticipating future problems
	Activating actors for the cause
Enabling	Connecting administrative and adaptive objectives and actions
	Seeking and visualizing mutual gains
	Stimulating trust and cooperation
	Mediating between differing leaders

We propose several related hypotheses for assessing the relation between the two.

H1: Project managers will show administrative leadership behavior more dominantly, which corresponds with a short term focus

H2: Program managers will show adaptive leadership behavior more dominantly, which corresponds with a long term focus

H3: Persons showing enabling leadership fulfill a mediating role and will take action to attempt to connect short term and long term foci.

The figure below summarizes these hypotheses in combination with the activities defined in table 8.1.

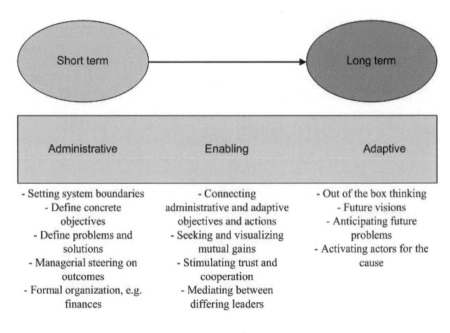

Figure 8.1   Hypothetic leadership division in policy and knowledge programs

Methodologically we will explore these hypotheses in each case through a series of interviews. In these interviews we asked respondents about the short-term/long-term they observed, their (short-term and long-term) objectives and organizational interests, the leaders in the program, and their actions and strategies. Based on this we can reflect on the short term/ long term tensions present, the employed leadership types and their actions, and through those discussions, elaborate on the interrelation of the focal point with the carrier. In each case section we will provide more information about who our respondents were and what our selection criteria were.

Case study Delta Program, The IJsselmeer Subprogram

The Delta Program is a national policy program in the Netherlands aiming at the safety against flooding and the safeguard of fresh water supplies towards the year 2100. The Delta Program emerged as a result of the advice of the second Delta Committee (chaired by professor Veerman) in September 2008.Within the program national government cooperates with lower tiers of government and stakeholders. The program is divided in 9 subprograms of which 6 have a geographical orientation and 3 have a generic policy orientation. Each subprogram has a program organization lead by a program director. Each program organization deploys a participatory process in which stakeholders jointly develop knowledge during 2010-2014 for decision-making in 2014 about the preferred long-term strategies (aiming at 2100).

This case focuses on leadership within the IJsselmeer Subprogram. This case description is based on participatory research during September 2010 – April 2011. At that time the researcher was process manager for the joint development of the long term strategies for the IJsselmeer area as part of phase 1 of the process. This participatory research is combined with interviews of ten people: five members of the program organization (including the program director), three directly participating stakeholders (water boards and provinces) and two line managers of participating organizations (provinces).

Introduction of the IJsselmeer Subprogram

The IJsselmeer is a large inland lake that came into being as a result of the closing of the Zuiderzee in 1932 (until then an open estuary) with a closure dam called the Afsluitdijk. The aim of the Afsluitdijk was (and still is) the flood protection of the land behind it. However, as a result of the closure, the IJsselmeer also became a large reservoir of freshwater that is currently used for agricultural and industrial means and for drinking water. In the current situation the river discharge of the IJssel is let out through outlet sluices in the Afsluitdijk during ebb-tide (these allow the water to run out freely).

The IJsselmeer Subprogram (operational from January 2010) is assigned to develop a long-term strategy achieving two goals. Firstly to keep save the IJsselmeer area against flooding under the conditions of increasing discharge of the IJssel river and rising sea levels. The sea level rise limits the possibility to let out water freely. The increased river discharge causes the need for an increased capacity to let out excess water from the lake. Secondly the strategy should increases the freshwater buffers for water use in large parts of the Netherlands. The assignment of the program organization is carried out in four phases that each run from April to April the next year. Phase 1 is concerned with the problem definition and possible strategies (2010-2011). Phase 2 is concerned with possible strategies (2011-2012). Phase 3 is concerned with likely strategies (2012-2013). Phase 4 in conclusion is aiming at defining preferred strategies (2013-2014).

This case describes emerging leadership and perceptions of long-term short-term tensions during phase 1.

Short-term and Long-term Tensions

All interviewees state that tensions within the boundaries of the subprogram are low during phase 1. Main causes for the absence of tensions they all mention are twofold. Firstly they mention that decision-making is not yet very concrete (no decisions about investments yet). Secondly they mention that most actors are just beginning to understand the long-term problems they are facing. In general we found two LT/ST-tensions. The first tension is characterized as an undesirable level of uncertainty – about the impact of future water management strategy (which is long term) – for short term spatial investments. The water management choices concern the adjustment of the water levels of different parts of the IJsselmeer area (that consists of several lakes due to existing compartment dams) which affect design criteria for spatial developments. The second tension is between the subprogram and other projects set outside the program. These projects regard water management infrastructure (maintenance and modifications of the Afsluitdijk), that are directly related to the ability to drain excess water. The project deadlines are planned in advance of the deadlines of the subprogram.

The Role of Leadership

Who are the leaders? All interviewees first mention the program director as *the* leader that persuades participating people to embrace the long-term challenge and goals of the Delta Program. "She appeals to the long-term goals and invites others to participate in a new and attractive way. She 'lives' the joint challenge for the future and according new ways of cooperating".

Most interviewees then mention a provincial governor and the chairman of a water board who were actively involved as co-chair of a steering committee. A few interviewees note the relative absence of the Delta Commissioner and the DG Water, the former responsible for process coordination of the whole Delta Program, the latter responsible as principal for the program organization. In third instance a number of three to five people operating at the level of direct participation (attending workshops, helping to write documents) was mentioned because of their specific contribution to build effective connections between the organizations. Hence we found in total 8 persons that are considered 'leaders' within the subprogram. It is noticeable that these persons all work for or in close cooperation with the program organization.

Administrative leadership Leaders that are entitled to make formal decisions concerning the IJsselmeer Subprogram directly seem to be not so dominant during the process of phase 1. The eight leaders central to our analysis only showed a few administrative leadership actions. The explanation we found was that administrative leadership actions such as 'setting system boundaries' and the 'definition of the policy objects' (goals) were already carried out by DG Water and the Delta Commissioner prior to phase 1. The results of these actions were captured in an assignment letter that describes the goal of the subprogram, geographical boundaries and deliverables. Furthermore DG Water carried out administrative leadership action at the start of phase 1 by 'setting the formal organization' and 'allocation of means' instituting the program organization. This was done together with (middle) managers of participating organizations (provinces and water boards). The program organization largely operated within the boundaries set by these decisions. Room for administrative leadership actions of the program director consisted primarily of the 'definition of problems and solutions' (which was carried out by developing earlier mentioned water management strategies) and 'managerial steering on outcomes' – by defining specific deliverables for phase 1 and employing actions to achieve those deliverables. Interviewees remark that they did not experience strong managerial steering from the program director and that the 'definition of problems and solutions' was primarily a joint effort of participating organizations.

Enabling leadership   The three most dominant leaders (program director, provincial governor and water board chairman) primarily showed enabling leadership. They performed almost all actions corresponding to this leadership type. All three put effort in activating participating actors that have a more short-term orientation on behalf of their home organizations for the long-term objectives of the Delta Program, hence 'connecting administrative and adaptive objectives and actions'. The program director did this by keeping close relationships with the responsible middle-managers of provinces and water boards (whose staff were participating within the subprogram). This was vital to sense whether their operational interests were met during the process. The provincial governor and water board chairman fulfilled a similar role at the level of governors, although their style differed as the first acts more front stage during meetings and the latter more backstage during bilateral contacts. These activities overlap with another type of enabling leadership actions, the 'mediating between differing leaders' which occurred primarily between water boards as they installed a platform where chairmen of all water boards within the area shared interests and information with the goal of helping the aforementioned chairmen to fulfill his role in the steering committee.

Program director, provincial governor and water board chairman also did take action to 'create trust' among participants. The first example of this behavior is holding compelling speeches at freely accessible working conferences and at a conference for all involved governors (both organized by the program organization), which all three did. The second example is attending meetings were participants were defining the aforementioned policy strategies; this was done by the program director. During those meetings she repeatedly explained how the results of the subprogram will be used for decision-making and by whom. Hence making clear where and when the home organizations of participants can formally influence the process. The result was a healthy working environment for the participants where trust could grow as formal interests could be made explicit, kept out of the discussion when inappropriate and included the discussion when appropriate.

The leadership action: 'seeking and visualizing mutual gains' was not found among the leaders. A possible explanation is that phase 1 was still of an 'exploring' nature defining the problems and not yet aimed at achieving agreement on solutions.

Adaptive Leadership   The adaptive leadership emerged at a more operational level where the program organization set the stage for a series of workshops with stakeholders to envision the future challenge, elaborate on this future challenge at a more detailed level in smaller areas (subdivisions of the total IJsselmeer area), and combining the new insights into four possible policy strategies that are considered the 'four corners of the playing field' by the stakeholders. The type of behavior of participants within these workshops differed. In fact the program organization faced a wide array of reactions, ranging from very cooperative and open to more closed and less willingness. According to the interviewees within this particular process, a few people (three to five of a group of approximately 25 persons) were notable for their connective capacities. Important qualities that were mentioned were the following. Firstly, the ability to explain complex policy content and the way the water system works, including the willingness to connect this knowledge to spatial planning issues. Secondly, interviewees mentioned the ability to leave the direct interests of home organizations 'at home' and be open about the real consequences of certain measures or effects. This type of behavior corresponds to enabling leadership actions that stimulate trust and cooperation that was needed to make future visions of the IJsselmeer area that help anticipate to future problems as a group. Hence it was this particular group that attended the workshops that jointly developed four policy strategies for the long term that showed adaptive leadership. Within the workshops they applied the following leadership actions: 'out of the box thinking' – by connecting water knowledge to spatial planning knowledge, 'made future visions' – by defining the four corners of the playing field, and 'anticipated future problems' – by translating future external developments to specific problems that have to be overcome. The four policy strategies together appealed to involved governors in a way that most actors are being activated for the larger cause of the subprogram, hence this group contributed to the leadership action 'activating actors for the cause'.

Interaction between leadership types   Persons that performed enabling and adaptive leadership actions were very closely interacting with each other in this process as the program manager and the co-chairs of the steering committee either directly participated with the strategy workshops or were informed about outcomes at a very regular basis. This close interaction helped the adaptive capacities at the operational level to grow. All interviewees mention that the involvement of formal leaders is relatively low. This points out that this group did show very little administrative leadership actions. Some stakeholders, mainly civil servants at the provincial level, perceive this lack of administrative leadership as a problem. This has two reasons. Firstly, these civil servants state that the process of the subprogram itself requires that their governors should be more directly and formally involved. Secondly, these organizations also have interests with the projects that are set outside the boundaries of the subprogram. This causes a fragmented approach for these organizations as they have to participate with different projects at the same time. Other stakeholders perceive the less formal way of working of the IJsselmeer Program as very positive and an important factor to be able to make enough headway and be innovative and be able to think out of the box. On the other hand, this way of working left members of the group that developed the long-term water management strategies in a bit of a vacuum. Should they protect their organizational interests in this process? Or should they only make clear what consequences the long-term developments have for the IJsselmeer area? The enabling leadership could not take away the feelings of discomfort some of these group members. The enabling leadership seemed not to experience a strong need to make connection with administrative leaders as the LT/ST-tension appeared low at that time.

Conclusions about the Delta Program: IJsselmeer Subprogram

In general we conclude that the three different forms of complexity leadership were found in the behavior of people involved within the IJsselmeer Subprogram that are considered influential leaders. Administrative leadership seems to be less dominant in this phase of the program. Enabling leadership, on the other hand, seems well developed and created an effective "working space" for a group at the operational level that explored the long-term challenges which showed adaptive leadership actions. The adaptive behavior did not coincide with the program manager role in this case. Enabling behavior did coincide with the mediating role considering the LT/ST-tensions. However as tensions were low as a result of the contextual situation, the mediating activities were not frequently employed. The postulated hypotheses can be partly confirmed by these conclusions. Firstly, we did find that short-term behavior coincides with administrative behavior mostly. However, in this particular context, project managers with a more short term focus worked outside the boundaries of the subprogram. As we did not study the behavior of these people we cannot reach full conclusions about this statement. Secondly, when we regard the program director of the subprogram as the program manager in this case, we partly disconfirm the second working hypothesis, as the program director showed mainly enabling leadership. At the same time however, the adaptive leadership in this case did correspond with a long term focus and enabling leadership had strong affinity with the long term focus. Thirdly we can mildly confirm the third hypothesis, as our case showed some mediating actions of enabling leaders between short term and long term foci. However in our perception the absence of a strong tension between short term and long term interests leads to smaller need to 'manage' this tension.

Case Study Living with Water

This case is primarily based on seven semi-structured interviews, done in February 2011: with six project leaders of Living with Water, and with one program manager (the director) of Living with Water. The program had approximately 100 projects. The selection of these six projects was based on previously held interviews with 46 projects in the period 2008-2009. Based on those interviews, these six projects were selected as suitable for a rather abstract discussion about time dimensions and leadership activities. Furthermore, based on the author's knowledge of the projects, these six projects were determined to be highly relevant for this discussion because their topics would make it likely they encountered short-term/long-term tensions. Aside from this primary data, the case author has studied Living with Water for four years for her PhD research (Bressers 2011), has spoken with most project leaders, has participated in countless events and meetings, and has spent many working days at the Living with Water office – to observe, interview, and participate.

Brief Introduction of Living with Water

Living with Water (LwW) was a subsidized program, which ran from 2004 till early 2010. The national government subsidized the program with money from the natural gas revenues, under the BSIK (or: ICES/KIS 3) arrangement. This arrangement intended to strengthen the Dutch knowledge infrastructure by investing money in a variety of programs, working on a diverse set of topics. The innovative water management program LwW worked on innovative knowledge development to realize a new place for water and facilitate and stimulate cooperation in the water sector. Its three prime objectives were: giving water its new place and space, connecting science and practice and creating vital alliances.

This cooperation was enhanced by the participation of a broad selection of actors in the program. The BSIK arrangement required the programs to realize demand-supply actor cooperation within the program network, in order to make sure the developed knowledge would have societal relevance and be applicable in practice. In Living with Water this requirement was carried out by setting up a tripartite participation structure. Governmental actors, knowledge actors and business actors were to participate and cooperate in the program. Furthermore, each participating actor invested money and time in its project, thereby creating commitment of the participating actors.

Short Term and Long Term Objectives and their Fit

LwW started with acquiring projects. Project ideas seeking financing would apply for subsidies in several selection rounds. Their main reason for applying to Living with Water was the possibility to jointly finance projects. Other reasons project leaders mentioned were the topics listed by LwW and the tripartite network structure. This indicates there was a proper match between projects and program at the start of the program, as mutual interests overlapped. The program also steered heavily on this fit in the project selection criteria.

The program and project objectives did differ somewhat in their short term/ long term focus, though. Based on the interviews, we see that the program level was mostly seen as either entirely long term or both short term and long term. The program manager noted: "In the end the returns are long term: we have created a direction which can be decisive for the long term". Some project leaders mentioned that Living with Water became more long term throughout the course of the program: at first they were primarily concerned with short term objectives, such as the operational aspects and the program process, starting initiatives and networks, and the tangible results. After some years the long term became more prominent, which included matters such as application of knowledge, dissemination of innovative ways of working, and content-related aspects – deemed abstract yet appealing by the project leaders.

Project objectives, on the other hand, were in general believed to be both short term and long term, or middle-long term. The focus on the long term was thus slightly less than on program level. The program manager emphasized this as well: "We as a program were like a very long train taking a very large turn (…). The projects were parts of the train, but we were concerned with the whole turn".

Short term project objectives included the development of products and pilots, operational aspects and project management, providing solutions, making plans and creating societal support. Long term project objectives included continuation after project ending, stimulating new directions in water management, providing insights, learning and connecting to long term visions of stakeholders. Sometimes these long term objectives proved very difficult and several projects came across problems in their realization of these long term objectives: "They [top-managers] didn't see how important it was. And therefore it didn't happen. Learning should take place faster, but perhaps I'm naïve, because others don't think it's strange it took so long".

In general, projects did not see many short term/ long term tensions in the program as a whole. In the projects, however, where the innovative ideas were perhaps more tangible and needed to be implemented, these tensions did arise. Sometimes these tensions had been the reason for starting the project, sometimes a project reported little tension. However, other projects did mention (significant) tensions between short term and long term. Examples of these tensions are: difficulties in looking beyond the four years the project existed and the lack of an integral awareness and approach (especially in governmental actors) and the lack of trust and support in participating or receiving actors (also mostly governmental actors). Two project leaders stressed that the water world in general knew tensions between short term and long term, and that these tensions existed relatively little in Living with Water: "In daily practice these tensions are more eminent and more complex". Overall, the degree of short term/ long term tension thus differed between each project, with the comment that on the program level these tensions remained relatively absent, especially when compared to the wider sector.

The Role of Leadership

Who are the leaders? The leaders in the projects were from a variety of backgrounds. In all interviewed projects more than one leader operated and often these leaders came from both practice and science worlds. Important backgrounds for leaders in the interviewed projects were organizations operating on the edge of government, business and knowledge-development, universities and formal principals. The leaders in the program Living with Water were the people from the Living with Water office. Mentioned by all six project leaders was the program director. Mentioned second most often were the most recent scientific director and the most prominent program secretary.

What do they do? Project leaders fulfilled a variety of roles. In order of importance, stemming from the interview data: connecting and networking, integrating and developing knowledge, organization and process management, providing direction and vision, promoting and supporting, creating support bases, stimulating creativity and innovativeness and inserting structure. These roles were therefore a mixture of complexity leadership activities. This mixture could easily exist within one person: "My own role was mixed: it was connective ... but also aimed at targets: we needed an outcome, say, the 'hard project leader' role. Another aspect of my role was to think outside the box, be creative and innovative". This project leader thus demonstrated all three leadership types. In each project the emphasis in terms of leadership types would differ, but overall we witnessed a relatively strong emphasis on adaptive and, especially, enabling leadership, and less emphasis on administrative leadership. A potential risk of this can be that a group of connected actors does proceed to long term thinking, but without connecting adequately to today's problems, interests and issues.

On program level we also witnessed a mixture of roles. The director of the program, who was seen as *the* program leader by the project respondents, was active in networking and connecting projects and project participants, enthusing others, and stimulating innovativeness and project functioning. The program director fulfilled the role of program sponsor: to a great extend he became the face of the program, and Living with Water relied heavily on his skills, expertise and enthusiasm. His role combined adaptive leadership (the provision of direction, the motivating) and enabling leadership (the networking actions). Another program leader was the scientific director who was active in scientifically connecting ideas and people and providing scientific interpretation of project outcomes and inter-project topics, thereby demonstrating a clear example of adaptive leadership. The project secretary of the program was active in stimulating project functioning, providing contacts to project participants, and improving project organization. His role was therefore mostly administrative and enabling. The top three leaders of the program level together therefore combined the leadership styles, but, just like the project level, administrative leadership was relatively underrepresented, although not absent.

These roles were organized through multiple tangible activities. Most mentioned actions were 'mentioning names, organizations and examples' (for building connections), 'thinking along and co-writing', 'project management activities such as planning and agreements', 'communication and consultation', 'direction and structure', and 'promotion and support through enthusiasm and offering a stage for project'. The program manager placed greater emphasis on visioning, convincing, storytelling, and process management. In doing this he could 'assemble diverging interests' of project participants for increased project success: "You have to assemble interests, by networking, by exploring each other's interests. You assemble by knowing interests, accepting them and recognizing them. … Assembling interests often works out, because there is money. With 40% co-financing you can assemble, with only 10% you can't". In doing so, program leaders could steer the projects somewhat in the intended direction, although steering appears to have been limited and not unwelcomed by project leaders: "Those were directly welcome – Living with Water was well aware of the issues in the project and they didn't come with sudden and unwelcome surprises, it always fitted the context of the project".

Conclusions about Living with Water

The program Living with Water knew relatively little short term/ long term tensions, although they were not absent. What we witnessed in our case is that especially the project level ran the risk of these tensions, whereas the more strategic program level remained relatively little touched by tension. The hypotheses we formulated earlier in this chapter indicate that a program with little tension would generally know a good mixture of leadership types, with administrative and adaptive leadership connected by enabling leadership. The variety in leadership types would increase connectivity between short term and long term objectives, and make sure that both the short term and the long term have their place in the program.

In the program and its projects we witnessed indeed a mixture of leadership types, as discussed sometimes even embodied in one person. This appears to confirm our hypotheses. We did note in our empirical discussion of the Living with Water case that the degree of administrative leadership was relatively low. This would mean attention for the short term was less than attention for the long term. Although Living with Water did have attention for short term objectives (for example, the operational project start-up, proper finances, solid organization, etc.) it did primarily pay attention to the long term, especially on the program level. This is confirmed by previous research on the Living with Water case, in which it was concluded that participation of business actors in LwW remained limited, due to, amongst others, the rather abstract nature of the program (see Bressers 2011). 'Abstract' was often used by business actors to indicate 'too long term'.

Patterns we witnessed overall in the case include a large degree of enabling leadership activities such as consensus building and connecting interests. The program appears to have consisted of many enabling leaders, or at least leaders who fulfilled this role from time to time. Enabling leadership could for instance be seen in actions such as organizing exchange meetings, bridging projects, and challenging projects to think bigger than their own project. In projects we saw many combinations of leadership types. However, as one project leader commented: "Our project was very good in informal leadership but in crucial moments we were short of formal leadership". Formal leadership here refers to, for instance, the connection with governmental agencies, the anchorage. The relatively little degree of administrative leadership (sometimes also called formal leadership) meant that the short term was less naturally part of the discussion in projects and program than the long term.

This means the first hypothesis is partially confirmed. A lack of administrative leadership does indeed create a lesser focus on short term action. We did indeed witness relatively more administrative leadership on the project level, but it must be noted that adaptive and enabling leadership were more present on the project level than administrative leadership. The second hypothesis is also partially confirmed by this case. Just like in the Delta Program case, the program managers demonstrated a lot of enabling leadership, although, different from the Delta Program case, they also showed much adaptive leadership. They had indeed a long term focus. Enabling leadership was seen much in both projects and programs, and indeed helped to connect time orientations, as far as tensions existed at all. The third hypothesis is therefore mildly confirmed.

Reflection and Lessons for Connective Capacity in Water Governance

We found a connection between leadership type and time orientation, as proposed in our hypotheses. Administrative leadership coincided with short-term orientations and adaptive leadership coincided with long-term orientations. Both our cases knew relatively little tension between short term and long term. In the IJsselmeer case this was caused by administrative leaders who did choose boundaries that decreased tensions for the moment. Within the Living with Water case tensions were low in most projects and on the program level. In both cases this meant that enabling leadership required little effort in terms of managing conflicts arising from differences in time orientations. In as far as tensions did arise, however, we witnessed that the role of enabling leadership, spanning boundaries, indeed served as a tool in connecting time orientations, albeit with varying degrees of success. For instance, in the IJsselmeer case the platform for civil servants to envision the future, created by enabling leaders, functioned well. At the level of governors, enabling leaders did not succeed yet in generating active involvement of other governors in the area. In the Living with Water case, enabling leadership was organized through various activities, such as meetings designed to bridge projects, but also individual project steering by program management. Short term oriented projects were asked to think broader and about the implications for the wider water sector. Intriguingly, long-term oriented projects were less asked to think more short term. The steering on connecting time scales was therefore predominantly oriented at increasing attention for the long term.

The relation between leadership type and presence of tensions remains somewhat of a 'chicken and the egg' puzzle, as both cases knew high degrees of enabling leadership, which may have been a cause of the low tensions. Alternatively, the limited presence of tensions could have been a cause of enabling leadership, as this becomes a rewarding task when parties are open to connecting time scales. Our data does not allow us to determine a direct causal relationship about this, as we cannot rule out other influences.

We did not completely confirm the second part of our hypotheses – the part in which we connected project versus program management roles to leadership types. Within the IJsselmeer case the distinction between program management and project management was hard to make due to organizational boundaries. Within the LwW case the distinction was more relevant. In this case we found that enabling leadership played a significant role on both levels and adaptive and administrative leadership could be seen on both levels. The overall relative low levels of administrative leadership in both cases create risks for connecting long term visions to today's actions and ideas as enabling leaders did not succeed in creating conditions for administrative leaders to become more active in the process. As we propose that enabling leaders focus on connecting short term and long term, the short term (represented by administrative leadership) should be present in order to be connected.

Leadership can, all in all, be an instrument in addressing time scale tensions. However, the current research cannot be conclusive about exact causality in this effect. We do see that enabling leadership is of vital importance in connecting time scales. The connection between administrative leadership with its short-term focus and adaptive leadership with its long-term focus can then be made, given that these two leadership types are also present. Realizing connectivity between short term and long can be brought about by facilitating discussion in bridging meetings and envisioning platforms, individual steering on projects and attempts to involve wider circles of decision-makers, such as the governors in the IJsselmeer case. Through including a variety of leadership styles and activities (see Table 8.1) a program can steer towards greater connectivity.

Bibliography

Bekkers, V., Edelenbos, J., Steijn, B. 2011. Linking Innovation to the Public Sector: Contexts, Concepts and Challenges, in *Innovation in the Public Sector. Linking Capacity and Leadership*, edited by Bekkers, V., Edelenbos, J., Steijn, B. Houndmills: Palgrave Macmillan.

Bressers, N.E.W. 2011. *Co-Creating Innovation. A Systemic Learning Evaluation of Knowledge and Innovation Programmes*. PhD thesis. Rotterdam: Erasmus University Rotterdam.

Bressers, N.E.W., Avelino, F. and Geerlings, H. 2012. Short- versus Long-term and other Dichotomies: Applying Transition Management in the A15-project, in *Transition towards Sustainable Mobility: The Role of Instruments, Individuals and Institutions*, edited by H. Geerlings, Y. Shiftan and D. Stead. Surrey: Ashgate.

Bressers, H. and Lulofs, K. (eds) 2010. *Governance and Complexity in Water Management. Creating Cooperation through Boundary Spanning Strategies*, Cheltenham UK and Northampton: Edward Elgar, also published at London and New York: IWA Publishers.

Cash, D.W., Adger, W.N., Berkes, F., Garden, P., Lebel, L., Olsson, P., Pritchard, L. and Young, O. 2006, Scale and Cross-Scale Dynamics: Governance and Information in a Multilevel World, *Ecology and Society*, 11(2), 8-21.

Goldstein, J., Hazy, J.K. and Lichtenstein, B. 2010. *Complexity and the Nexus of Leadership: Leveraging Nonlinear Science to Create Ecologies of Innovation*. Englewood Cliffs: Palgrave Macmillan.

Hart, P.'t. 2011. Reading the Signs of the Times: Regime Dynamics and Leadership Possibilities, *The Journal of Political Philosophy*, 19(4), 419-39.

Hazy, J.K., Goldstein, J.A. and Lichtenstein, B.B. (eds). 2007 *Complex Systems Leadership Theory*. Mansfield, MA: ISCE Publishers. Table of Contents.

Hazy, J.K. 2006. Measuring leadership effectiveness in complex socio-technical systems. *Emergence: Complexity and Organization (E:CO)*, 8(3), 58-77.

Hazy, J.K. 2008. Toward a theory of leadership in complex systems: Computational modeling explorations. *Nonlinear Dynamics, Psychology, and Life Sciences*, 12(3), 281-310.

Koppenjan, J. and Klijn, E.H. 2004. *Managing Uncertainties in Networks – A Network Approach in Problem Solving and Decision-making*, Routledge, London.

Leifer, R. and Delbecq, A. 1978. Organizational/environmental interchange: A model of boundary spanning activity. *The academy of management review*, 3(1), 40-50.

Pollitt, C. 2008 *Time, Policy, Management: Governing with the Past*. Oxford: Oxford University Press.

Provan, K.G. and Kenis, P. 2008, Modes of Network Governance: Structure, Management, and Effectiveness, *Journal of Public Administration Research and Theory (JPART)* 18 (2), 229-52.

Rotmans, J. 2003. *Transitiemanagement: Sleutel naar een duurzame samenleving*, Assen: van Gorcum Uitgeverij.

Steen, M. van der. 2009. *Een sterk verhaal: Een discoursanalyse van vergrijzing*, dissertation, University of Tilburg.

Teisman, G.R., Buuren, M.W. van and Gerrits, L. (eds). 2009. *Managing Complex Governance Systems. Dynamics, Self-organisation and Coevolution in Public Investments*. New York and London: Routledge.

Uhl-Bien, M. and Marion, R. 2009. Complexity leadership in bureaucratic forms of organizing: A meso model. *The Leadership Quarterly*, 20, 631-50.

Uhl-Bien, M., Marion, R. and McKelvey, B. 2007. Complexity Leadership Theory: Shifting leadership from the industrial age to the knowledge era. *The Leadership Quarterly*, 18(3), 298-318.

Williams, P. 2002. The competent boundary spanner. *Public Administration*, 80(1), 102-24

Chapter 9
Connecting Long and Short-term via Envisioning in Transition Arenas

Josee van Eijndhoven, Niki Frantzeskaki and Derk Loorbach

Introduction

The main issue of this book is connectivity in water governance. The central question is: *which connective capacities in water governance are to be developed in order to face water problems in an integrative way?* Connectivity is important for bridging various interests, and connecting long term aspirations with short term actions. In water management, such a connection is important because of the long term infrastructural investments that are needed, whereby short term choices determine long term directions as discussed in Chapter 1.

In addition to this, the interest on how water and spatial development are related is growing (Van Buuren et al. 2010). The involvement of not only economically driven actors becomes important where water and spatial development, certainly in urban environments, get more and more intertwined. As stated in Chapter 1, many government layers and levels are involved in water issues; the number of domains involved is increasingly growing, from the public as well as the private spheres. Consequently, diversity of perceptions to be taken into account is of growing importance.

As various contributions in this book show, water professionals developing flood defense infrastructures started to consider interdependencies and dynamics of both nature and ecosystems. Despite the efforts of scholars practicing different water paradigms, the issues that prevail for water governance (for example, institutional fragmentation, lack of coordination) remain unresolved due to: (a) the rigidity of existing paradigms within communities of practices and the relative closedness of water-expert communities to other policy domains, and (b) due to the increasing complexity of problems that relate to water in view of climate change. These two factors also result in a disconnection of water as an issue from other governance agendas.

The water sector still very much stands on its own as a separate epistemological sector, although water governance generally has become more integrated. It is relatively seldom that water is visible on more general political agendas. In the third World Water Assessment report (WWAP 2009) this was the most important conclusion: to better integrate water with other policy issues, it is necessary to get out of the water box. This is an important statement that is easier made than realized, as the developments discussed in this chapter will show.

To improve governance responses to complex water problems, the current research effort focuses on connective capacity. Connective capacity relates to the efforts to create actor or organizational networks between scales and levels and to connect long-term visions and short-term actions, so as to buffer impacts and issues in the view of increasing complexity of water problems. Understanding how to improve the connective capacity of governance structures is essential for dealing with mis-integration and institutional misfit. Part of the problem of institutional misfit results from the fact that water experts consider water-related issues as the core of the agenda, neglecting or being limited in their understanding of how those issues relate to other policy domains (for example, spatial planning, housing).

We propose that water experts can increase connective capacity when not considering water as the central issue but rather as one of the connecting issues in regional or urban sustainability. We aim to understand how water issues can be integrated in an urban policy agenda through processes of envisioning. The overarching research question is: Does envisioning connect long-term and short-term thinking and actions within water governance processes? Using two empirical cases we show how envisioning processes can increase the connective capacity of urban related issues, interests and policy agendas, and to connect long-term vision and action.

The governance instrument used is the transition arena approach (Loorbach 2010, Frantzeskaki et al. 2012) which combines a selective process philosophy with developing visions based on the notion of transitions as processes of fundamental systemic change that can be initiated by change agents (policy and social entrepreneurs). We argue that a specific form of selective participatory envisioning can enhance connective capacity via connecting:

- actors from different policy domains when co-creating a vision
- abstract long-term desires to strategic short-term and medium-term actions
- time scales while specifying feasible actions
- innovative and transformative capacity of change agents to policy reality and practice.

Visioning can be done in various ways. Traditionally acquainted with long-term planning, water-related visions are often developed by officially appointing expert committees that get a formal assignment from a government. Examples are the Tielrooij committee in 2000 (Van der Brugge 2009) or the Veerman committee (see Chapter 11). The compilation of such a committee is made in such a way that the various perspectives that are considered relevant are in the committee. These types of vision inform water policy but neither break out of the waterbox nor explore how other domains might take up or facilitate water-related issues. These types of water policy-oriented visions primarily strengthen the existing system and seek to improve water systems in light of possible water and climate scenarios.

We argue that an increasing number of areas are 'spilling-over' into the water domain, thereby posing external pressure on the waterbox to open up. Developments in areas such as housing, energy, spatial planning and agriculture are developing sustainability innovations that influence the water sector. This requires responses that not only reason from within the waterbox towards the outside world but also from the outside in. This implies open, explorative, uncertainty- and multi-perspective-based envisioning processes. An approach less directly connected to current ways of operating can be important when faced with grand challenges such as developing adaptive water systems, in which threats and opportunities are unclear, as well as who the relevant actors are. The transition management approach is one possible perspective to take up such a challenge.

Methodology

In this chapter we start from the perspective that water related issues to be handled effectively can best be addressed from a broad perspective of which water forms only a part. We do this by using the city of Rotterdam as an example in which water is of great importance and is, on the other hand, seldom seen as *the* central issue on the agenda. We present two case studies with two different transition arenas.

Case 1: Conceptualization and development of the Water vision for the city of Rotterdam to be realized in 2030. The vision was first formulated in 2005, and started to be implemented from 2007 onward. In several of the visioning activities that took place in Rotterdam, water was an important underlying issue and arena-like activities were conducted to develop a long term vision from which short term activities were deducted. This was the case in the vision Rotterdam Watercity 2035 (and the ensuing Waterplan 2) and in Cityports (Stadshavens in Dutch).

We employed three different research methods to conduct the first case study. First, document analysis and literature review provided a basis of the case study. Materials include: Van Eijndhoven et al. (2009), Van der Brugge (2009), Van der Brugge and De Graaf (2010) and additional information, for example, taken up at the Water week of the Province South-Holland, June 2010 at the World Exposition in Shanghai. Second, interview material (transcripts) by researchers of DRIFT during the monitoring the different projects were re-assessed and revisited for writing the current chapter.

Case 2: The second case is the development and management of the area Cityports, an area that was the most important harbor area of Rotterdam in the 19th century, but lost much of this function during the second half of the 20th century. In this case DRIFT was asked to support the transition process. The information used in the case study is mostly derived from the people directly involved (hence the method employed is action research) and from document analysis. The researchers from DRIFT who were involved in the project of Cityports changed over time. We made use of information generated in a number of projects, personal information from those involved and document analysis.

The chapter unfolds in four sections. The next section includes the background of transition management and of envisioning. The following section presents the water related envisioning in Rotterdam. The chapter then goes on to present our conclusions in relation to connective capacity.

Transition Management, Transition Arena and Envisioning

Transitions Approach in a Nutshell

Transitions are conceptualized as societal processes of fundamental change in the structure, culture and practices of a societal system (Frantzeskaki and De Haan 2009). Many historical transitions (e.g those forming part of the industrialization era and the post-war emergence of mobility), were partly driven by the promise of solving societal problems such as poverty, inequality, education and so on.

The transitions that formed our modern society have brought with them, as a side-effect, the current environmental problems. Solving these issues will require major changes to existing structures (for example, institutions and markets), cultures (for example, consumerism) and practices (for example, resources exploitation). The needed transitions can neither be fully planned nor fully steered, since they are societal processes of fundamental change taking place in societal systems that are inherently complex. The transitions approach offers conceptual frames for better understanding the dynamics of transitions and how they develop (Smith et al. 2010).

Transition Management and Transition Arena

Transition management comes down to creating space for frontrunners (niche-players and regime-players) in transition arenas (Frantzeskaki et al. 2012). In transition arenas, a vision, an agenda and a social commitment to sustainability values for a specified issue are formed. A transition arena is based on the promises of increased group-learning and group-effectiveness of small-groups and it agrees with the best practices indicated by the literature on small-group negotiations (De Dreu and West 2001, Van Knippenberg et al. 2004) and social learning writings (Grin et al. 2004). A transition arena aims at creating a network of change agents that identifies and reframes a persistent problem, develops a sustainability vision and a shared agenda for moving in this direction (Voss and Bornemann 2011). The common discourse developed in the transition arena relates to the shared belief in the possibility of transition in the near future and the need to develop strategies to guide this transition towards sustainability.

This implies a selective participatory approach to bring together policy and social change agents, that is, actors that have an explicit ambition and interest in sustainability-oriented innovation. The actors that are involved in the transition arena participate on a personal basis and not as delegates or representatives of their institution. The actors participating in the transition arena need to have the following competencies: (i) understanding the complexity of the persistent problems at hand, (ii) ability to reflect upon existing practices, cultures and structures, and (iii) an understanding of how these practices relate to persistent problems. Actors need to represent the different ways of thinking, different values and stakes present in the society. They need to be already active in developing or stimulating innovations. The transition arena group needs to be limited in size so as to allow quality of debate and productive group-dynamics.

Experiences with transition arenas show that frontrunners' groups can have an impact when receiving time to develop a novel narrative and vision, when the timing is right, and when the interaction between the arena and the regime is strategically managed (De Graaf and Van der Brugge 2010, Heiskanen et al. 2009, Hendriks 2008, Kohler et al. 2009, Loorbach and Rotmans 2010). 'Impact' in this context, can be interpreted in different ways, meaning impact through influencing regular policy, influencing and inspiring concrete projects, influencing participants that diffuse ideas within their own daily professional context, and articulating a shared promising perspective to which many, to date uninvolved, participants can relate. These different forms of impact are only achieved (or rather discovered) as the process evolves.

A Transition Arena Process

Problem structuring   The actors in the transition arena are stimulated to reflect upon their everyday routines. This active engagement in the problem (re) structuring phase results in a deeper understanding of problem's complexity. The outcomes of the first phase are: (a) the basic transition narrative that is a mapping of the pathologies of the current system, (b) the sustainability guiding principles that are the conditions under which the same societal function can be provided in a sustainable way in the future; and (c) the formulation of domains of change that are areas that require changes so as to achieve a more sustainable system state.

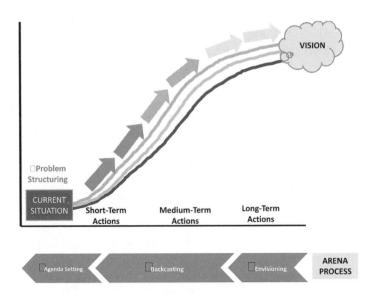

Figure 9.1   The transition arena process and its outputs

Envisioning   The process of envisioning itself and the group dynamics in it create a selection environment. This means that the group dynamics may result in some actors exiting the transition arena, while other actors may be invited to join depending on their alignment to the vision and to the produced group-dynamics. The objectives of envisioning include:

    a. to bring forward the potential of the city or region as represented by change agents
    b. to understand and fore-face the desirable directions or images that are associated to sustainability (of the city or region),
    c. to communicate local desires and connect local actors with policy practitioners (Sheppard et al. 2011: 410)
    d. encourage new ways of thinking and pave the ground for change by exposing complexity of interests and possibilities (Ozkaynak and Rodriguez-Labajos 2010, 996).

The transition vision depicts the common desires of the transition arena group and is an outcome that has a guiding role for the following activities. When actors formulate the vision, they reflect on the way short-term actions can impact and shape the pathway to achieve the long-term vision.

Backcasting   In the backcasting phase, the arena group builds upon the shared problem definition and visions (points of departure and destination, guiding principles, visionary images) to develop actions and targets. For every vision image, different sets of actions for short-term, medium-term and long-term are listed. The combined actions form transition pathways. Transition pathways depict social objectives (for example, cohesion) or themes (for example, liveable cities). In the transition arena, holistic thinking is activated by reflecting that a transition to a sustainability vision requires synergy and synthesis of all the different pathways generated with backcasting.

Developing transition agendas   At this phase, actors who can contribute to the realization of the visions are invited. For those new entrants, the selection criteria differ from the previously presented criteria and concern: (a) their involvement or power in the different transition pathways and (b) their role in specific institutions and organizations that can catalyze the realization of (any of) the transition pathways.

The outcomes of a transition arena group have no formal power. The transition agenda can only be realized through the voluntarily stewardship and diffusion within and along the networks of the actors involved as well as via the adoption of the agenda (or of elements of the agenda) by policy practitioners. The transition arena aims to stimulate the formation of new coalitions and partnerships that coagulate around a new way of thinking and operating.

Transition experiments   Transition experiments may be initiated by the transition arena group as outcome follow-up activity. Transition experiments can focus on new institutional arrangements so as to enable new sustainability-oriented pathways or innovations. Transition experiments can be employed by policy developers to test new innovations. Transition experiments can function as innovation and testing spaces providing evidence for the effectiveness of new ideas that can facilitate their (future) diffusion or adoption.

Experience with Transition Arenas

A relatively large number of transition arenas have been organized during the last ten years in the Netherlands. Some of them include: Parkstad Limburg (Van Buuren and Loorbach 2009), Northern Frisian Woodlands (part of TransForum program) (Beers et al. 2010), Healthcare (Van den Bosch 2010), the Roofing sector (Loorbach and Rotmans 2010), the Dutch energy arena (Hendriks 2008) and Sustainable Living and Housing (Loorbach 2007).

In practice, arenas do not completely follow all of the principles described in all cases. Trajectories may last longer than foreseen and/or have a more diverse 'ownership' than wished for (both of these elements occurred in the Zuidvleugel arena (Van Eijndhoven et al. 2009). Even then, the generated visions and the transition pathways may influence ensuing developments. In this chapter, we describe two trajectories based on the transition arena methodology in which envisioning took place with developments around water in Rotterdam.

Rotterdam

Rotterdam as an Urban Innovation Harbor

The city of Rotterdam provides an example of what visioning trajectories can bring about, given that it is confronted with grand challenges, water related, but not water dominated. These challenges have to be addressed in a dynamic environment in which globalization as well as being part of an urbanizing delta has important implications for the way in which the city strives for resilience (Wardekker et al. 2010).

Rotterdam hosts 650.000 inhabitants in the south western part of the Netherlands. The city hosts the largest port in Europe and was the largest port of the world. Rotterdam is a city located below sea level, and water is not only important because of the harbor, but also because climate change will challenge its deltaic character.

Socio-economic Dynamics

The world is globalizing very quickly. This means large shifts in the transportation sector. In order to keep up with these shifts, the Rotterdam harbor is restructuring. The development of the Tweede Maasvlakte sees to it that the capacity of the harbor keeps in line with the growing number of shipments. Not only is the number of shipments an important factor, but also the size of the ships. Due to the growing size of Atlantic ships, many harbors can no longer be reached. Rotterdam wishes to retain its role as a big container port.

The Tweede Maasvlakte is the next step of the city development in the Western direction, due to the need for more space for the harbor, more space per ship, and more room that was once needed in the city itself. Consequently, the original harbor function of the Cityports has vanished and it is a challenge for the city to re-develop this partly-used area. The visioning trajectory that will be discussed later in this chapter is a result of reflections on the possible futures of Cityports.

Ecological Dynamics

The economic challenge for the Rotterdam harbor has many relationships with another important challenge: the possible consequences of climate change. In 2006, the KNMI (The Dutch Meteorological Institute) developed a number of scenarios for possible future climate developments in the Netherlands, based on the Fourth IPCC assessment report (KNMI 2006, IPCC 2007). These scenarios led to the conclusion that the area around Rotterdam could get more water from four sides: behind (the rivers), upfront (sea), above (rain) and underneath (salt water intrusion). This combination of potential threats urges the city to address the water issues coming up.

Institutional Dynamics

When confronted with this situation, the city was already developing its current approach towards water management in the city, inspired by ways in which other cities had redeveloped their harbor areas to become attractive parts of their cities. Another incentive to start rethinking the water governance of the city was a shift in the responsibilities of the institutions involved in the water management of the city (Van der Brugge 2009).

The city of Rotterdam supported this envisioning process from the start due to the challenge to become a more attractive city in which the waterfront would no longer be a dividing line between parts of the city, but a factor connecting people and attracting highly educated citizens. The case studies unravel how envisioning succeeds in connecting spatial planning with water issues and how envisioning connects short-term and long-term time horizons via recommended policy actions that form a transition agenda.

Rotterdam Watercity 2035 (Rotterdam Waterstad 2035, in Dutch)

In this section we discuss the envisioning process that took place around the International Architecture Biennale Rotterdam in 2005. We firstly discuss the political and circumstantial background against which it took place. Secondly, we describe the envisioning and its relationship to the above described transition arena. Third, we analyze what this process did and did not accomplish. The process did not use the ideas behind transition arenas, however, the ideas behind the set-up had so much in parallel with the transition arena set up that that we use it as an example for assessing the outcomes of a transition arena set-up.

The main actors in urban water management in Rotterdam are three district waterboards[1] and the Rotterdam municipality. The waterboards are responsible for water quantity and quality management. The municipality is responsible for urban planning and thereby responsible for the amount of surface water, the sewer system and groundwater. This division of responsibilities came about after 1989. Till that time, the waterboards were mainly focused on rural areas (Van der Brugge 2009). Recently the emphasis has shifted to urban surface water. In Rotterdam, the first attempt to transfer responsibilities from municipality to the waterboards took place in 1996. This attempt failed due to a conflict over the price of the assets. It succeeded at the second try in 2001.

---

1   The three waterboards are Hollandse Delta in the south, Schieland and Krimpenerwaard in the northeast and Delfland in a small part of the northwest.

In the meantime the municipality had developed a first water management plan (WP1) in 1999 for two reasons: (1) the upcoming transfer of responsibilities for urban surface water management and (2) the sewer system, rebuild after 1945, had to be renewed. WP1 formulated future ambitions for the water system for the first time. WP1 targeted the *improvement* of the existing infrastructure, hydraulic functioning and water quality.

Around the same time the possible future effects of climate change started to be discussed in the Netherlands, partly in response to a period of fluvial flooding in 1998 in western Holland. This led to the appointment of the committee Tielrooij (Tielrooij-committee 2000) which argued that water retention was the main problem. The ensuing National Water Treaty of 2003 following Tielrooij, specifies the objectives and responsibilities of the individual authorities. For Rotterdam, this amounted to 600,000 m^3 of additional water retention capacity before 2015 and 900,000 m^3 in 2050. These objectives are often referred to as the *water assignment*. This water volume could not be accommodated by the current infrastructure. The Rotterdam municipality realized that simple adaptation of the water infrastructure would not suffice. Thus the municipality was eager to be involved in the International Architecture Biennale of 2005.

The Envisioning Process

In 2005, the International Architecture Biennale Rotterdam (IABR) had the theme 'The Flood' due to the growing attention for climate change and water retention in urban areas (Van der Brugge 2009). As part of the Biennale, NEPROM (Vereniging van Nederlandse Projectontwikkelingsmaatschappijen, Dutch Alliance for Development Projects) organized a contest of water related projects.

Four projects were developed in this frame[2], of which one was taken up by the Municipality of Rotterdam in cooperation with two waterboards (Delfland and Hollandse Delta). Three departments of the Rotterdam municipality were involved: the Urban Planning and Design Department, the Public Works Department, and the Economic Development Department. The project developed during a period of two months intense cooperation, during which 16 participants and two facilitators worked together for two days a week. The process was referred to as 'master-case'.

The group was formed by a strict selection procedure and official interviews. Fifteen project members were selected from various backgrounds: six designers, five water management experts, one member from the economic management department of the city and three external members from the waterboards. The different backgrounds of the members were expected to stimulate the cross-pollination of ideas.

The resulting Rotterdam Watercity 2035 design (IABR 2005) argues that surface water in the city can contribute to the urban challenge by creating a high

---

2   The four projects were: Meerstad Groningen, Wieringerrandmeer, an Integral development Perspective for the coast of South-Holland, and Rotterdam Waterstad 2035.

diversity of social environments and by attracting higher educated residents, thereby contributing to the gentrification of degraded neighborhoods. Additionally, water could improve the connection of the city with the surrounding areas and could contribute to an attractive city centre. The actual urban design encompasses three images: River city in the city centre, Water network city in the south and Canal city in the north (IABR 2005, Van der Brugge 2009). Each of the three images is elaborated, showing practical examples, for example, water-squares that can retain water in heavy rainfall. The level of detail of the images was such that the route from the present to the future appeared very accessible.

Follow up

Watercity 2035 received much political and public attention from the regional government, waterboards and the ministry responsible for water management. Within the municipal council it led to the Kuyper-motion which proposed development of a feasible program based on the design and time strategy of the plan (Van der Brugge and de Graaf 2010).

The ensuing Water Plan 2 took Watercity as its starting point and inspiration. Formally it was a follow up to Water Plan 1 and connected to the City Vision 2030 (hence the time span for the plan was 2030). In practice, the main lines of the Watercity report were taken over, including a number of practical examples like options related to River City: water mobility and floating housing. It was emphasized that innovative options were necessary for the water challenge to be met. Examples included underground water storage, green roofs and water squares. In transition terms, this phase can be seen as a (second) backcasting phase.

What the Visioning did Change and What not

Rotterdam Watercity 2035 was developed in a context of architecture. The contest in 2005 was water related (themed 'The Flood'). The initiative in Rotterdam was not initially coming from a waterboard but from the municipality of Rotterdam. The context of a contest led to the formation of a temporary group consisting of a variety of people, not all connected to water issues. The composition of the group contemplates the (suggested) composition of a transition arena. People in the group have (for the larger part) no institutional ties to policy.

An important difference between the situation before and after the visioning process is the framing of the issues. Three kinds of reframing resulted from the visioning process (Van der Brugge 2009: 199),

1. The problem perception
2. The perspective of the water manager vs. the spatial planner
3. Solutions and measures.

The original problem perception took climate change as a threat. In Watercity 2035, climate change was presented as an opportunity to adapt and to improve the city's fabric. This was an important factor for the proposal to become attractive. The visioning process was an important learning process for those involved. They learned to view the challenge for the city from each other's perspective and to value each other's measures to the challenge.

The measures proposed focused on linking the space for water retention to urban renewal projects. This resulted in two main strategies. First, since the harbor activities were in the process of being removed from the inner city docks (Cityports) to new locations outside the city, there are opportunities for water related entrepreneurial activities in the old docks. Second, urban plans for rebuilding deteriorated neighborhoods could create opportunities for water retention spaces.

The visioning process therefore led to reframing with regard to problem perception, the perspective and the measures. Water is now seen as a means to add quality to the social environment and to contribute to solving urban problems. This is a radical shift in thinking in which water management is no longer seen as an independent policy field, but as an integral part of the city and as such has an important function in improving the city. The envisioning led to the uptaking of innovative and non-conventional projects by the assessment of the feasibility of the examples included in the Water City Report. Therefore, over time, the short term options were adapted whereas the long term vision stayed as the overall perspective and inspiration.

Even if a plan is taken up, the question is how it will be implemented. This can be illustrated using developments around the three innovative options mentioned above, that each can be seen as a transition experiment.

Underground water storage in Museum Park   In the museum area of the city, an underground car park was planned. It was decided that this car park should have a dual function: car park and underground water storage. The expectation was that different actors should cooperate in a new way. One of the interviewees related this to (in 2008), water managers do calculate in square meters. In this case they should learn to use cubic meters. The car park finally opened four years later than planned (in 2010) and at a cost more than double the original estimate. During construction, its nickname was: the blunder hole.

Green roofs   Since July 2008, the municipality of Rotterdam has had a subsidy scheme for green roofs. This scheme falls under the responsibility of the Rotterdam climate adaptation program entitled 'Rotterdam Climate Proof'. The municipality of Rotterdam promotes green roofs as a means for climate adaptation and as one way of dealing with the water challenge. Waterboards are less enthusiastic, because the retained amount of water cannot be precisely measured.

Water-squares: change the name!   The first attempt to develop a water-square was taken up in Feijenoord in 2009, a relatively low-income area of Rotterdam. The plan was generated by the municipality in cooperation with the waterboard and it was to be realized in Bloemhof. However, people living there considered such a square dangerous for their children[3]. Even if the square is filled with water only a few days per year, people tend to fear for their children because of the risks of drowning. Additionally, residents did not understand why the square should be redeveloped, since it was not so long ago that it had been restored[4]. Finally the attempt to develop the first water-square in Bloemhof was halted.

A new attempt started in 2010 in another area in Rotterdam, namely in Spangen on the Bellamy square. In this square there were already problems with water: during heavy rains the square became a mud pool. It was decided that this square could be used for retaining water. In the case of the Bellamy square, discussions were started with the people living around the square to decide what were in their view, the important issues to be taken into account in redeveloping the square. Not all wishes could be completely taken into account; however (at the moment of writing this chapter) it seems that the redevelopment will go on.

For the waterboards, the Bellamy square is viewed as the first water-square to be implemented, and as such, in the visualization of the water-square on the internet, attention is given not to water, but to safety and better quality.[5] The Bellamy square however, did not function as a 'water square' considering the retention capacity. A new square is in development now (the Benthemplein), that will function as a water square. A large difference with the first try at Bloemhof is that the ideas are being developed very interactively with the people in the environment.

Alternatives from the Watercity 2035 vision that were considered most practical were taken up as experiments. Additionally, even if a vision exists and is taken as a starting point, the implementation of new solutions necessitates new ways of thinking and cooperating. The interactive execution that was seen as a necessary condition by one of the members of the original master-case team[6] did not always develop as needed. However, the long term perspective that was developed clearly gave focus and direction to the ensuing developments and the needed ways of interaction are becoming clearer over time

Cityports

Developments related to Cityports were already part of the vision Watercity 2035, but the challenge here is not primarily related to the 'water assignment'. Here,

---

3   www.nieuwbank.nl/inp/2009/11/25/R221.htm?fmt=INPRINT
4   Various sources during the South-Holland water week in Shanghai.
5   http://www.youtube.com/watch?v=luWaxrboquA&feature=player_profilepage#t=716s
Approached March 30, 2011.
6   www.geldofcs.nl/pdf/Artikelen/Harde_realiteit.pdf. Approached April 3, 2011.

the primary challenge is area redevelopment. The case represents a more typical challenge on policy agendas in contrast to primarily water related challenges.

The Cityports is an area in Rotterdam of about 1600 hectares located on both banks of the river Meuse and within the city limits. It is still largely used for harbor activities, but will transform the next 25 years as harbor activities move outward to the sea. The municipality and the Port of Rotterdam Authority started a joint program in 2006 to facilitate this transition aiming at transforming the area into an urban area. It is the largest urban development area within the urbanized western part of the Netherlands and defined as a project of national importance. The first years, the municipality and port authorities were in a confrontation about who was in charge, what strategy to use and where to start. They did create a vision for the area, mainly identifying the need to allow for harbor activities as long as possible, to accommodate some 15.000 houses and to improve accessibility of the area. The majority of the stakeholders in the area and the involved city officials felt that this vision was too mediocre for such a unique historic area. The project management was completely renewed and transition researchers were asked to help develop the project into a transition program.

The Envisioning Trajectories

First round   This new approach started by a broad envisioning process in which innovative stakeholders were involved at the strategic level to develop a more ambitious long-term perspective and multiple groups were formed at the tactical level, discussing specific parts of the area or specific sub-themes. A vision of sustainable cityports was created, referring to an innovative mix of living, working and recreation. This vision, 'Creating on the edge', emphasized the need for experiment and innovation while considering the unique features of the location in terms of the entanglement with the water, the availability of space and the urgency to ensure its sustainability[7]. Some of the guiding principles defined were: energy self-sufficiency, closed material loops, living on and with water, new communities and clean mobility.

The vision explicitly positioned the area development as a transition process. It tied the economic development to sustainable innovation for the area and therefore makes a strong case to see the area development itself as booster for the regional economy and development. The area was presented as experimental zone and a lobby started to create as much space in terms of finance and regulation as possible. The envisioning and strategy development involved over a hundred representatives from different municipality departments (economic, housing, mobility), the Port of Rotterdam Authority, local business and industry, research and NGO's. During these processes, the discussion on the vision, the need for structural change and the required governance approach created enthusiasm and gained political support.

---

7   http://www.het-portaal.net/sites/default/files/gebiedsvisie_stadshavens.pdf

The overall vision is now in the process of being translated to different areas on a lower level (Cityports is divided into 5 sub-areas), which all have their own specific characteristics and time-horizon upon which harbor activities will gradually disappear. The area of Merwe-Vierhavens has been designated as pilot zone, where a lot of space will become available in five years. A number of experiments have started around 2009 and have been developing. Some examples include:

- A floating city. In fall 2009, the building started on a first module of what could evolve into a floating city. The basic rationale is that increasing water levels in the river and of groundwater will necessitate innovative living concepts that are able to adapt to these conditions. In the Cityports, thousands of people could possibly live on water. The so called floating pavilion opened its doors in 2010. The Floating Pavilion serves as a location for events, hosts an exposition about the area development and is a new city-attraction frequently visited by delegations from all over the world.
- Mobility over water. Key to the area development is accessibility and clean mobility. Since the area is located on the river bank and much is expected of new housing concepts on water, a plan was developed for a new infrastructure of public transport over water. The first waterbus line started late 2008 and is connecting the different areas with each other and with the inner city.
- Sustainable communities. In one of the areas, a small village in the midst of the harbor industry needs a large reconstruction the coming decade. The 1500 houses are planned to be largely replaced by more sustainable ones. A project has started to involve frontrunner consumers that search for an adventurous environment (close to harbor activities), are willing to accept some of the disadvantages that would normally block housing development (e.g noise, traffic), and want to co-design their own houses. A consortium of construction companies' experts in sustainable housing will conduct the design and construction. Harbor and city are exploring ways to create symbiosis between harbor and living (sharing resources and facilities, exchanging waste-heat and more).

These are some of the initiatives that came out of the transition arena processes of the last three years. They are examples of how long-term visions and ambitions can be linked to short-term innovative experiments. The envisioning created mental, physical and financial space for projects that would otherwise never have been developed so quickly or at this level of ambition. In the following years, it seems that the strategy of experimental development is gradually delivering results and opening up space for greater and larger scale innovation. The Floating Pavilion has paved the way towards planning of a Floating Neighborhood. More specifically, Merwe-Vierhavens is expected to transform from a desolate port area to a flourishing city district in the coming decades. DRIFT was asked to start a limited arena process, restricted to problem structuring and envisioning. The aim was to create an inspiring vision and transition pathways, giving extra attention to area's sustainable development (DRIFT & DSA 2011).

A group of 20 frontrunners was selected. This group consisted of experts in very diverse fields, who shared a passion for sustainability and for the future of Rotterdam. Three creative sessions provided an open setting for the emergence of innovative ideas. Many ideas emerged, some were embraced, some needed elaboration and some were rejected. A number of very interesting building blocks for a future vision of the Merwe-Vierhavens were produced.

A transition team formed by employees of DRIFT and Doepel Strijkers Architects (DSA) prepared and facilitated the meetings. The arena sessions were fuelled by street interviews, a historic analysis, an analysis of existing plans and the identification of the core values of the area. After each session, the transition team elaborated the arguments and the views and used them as starting points for the next session.

The process resulted in an inspiring vision document describing two intertwined development paths for the area: the "Free Zone" that facilitates pioneers and attracts investments and the "City Oasis" that accommodates communities that develop parts of the area as a place to live, work and co-production. The ultimate goal is that the vision affects the thinking of diverse actors involved in the development of the Merwe-Vierhavens area so as to become more future-oriented and more sustainable-minded.

By choosing for the highest economic benefits on the short-term, usually city development leads to sub-optimal development from the perspective of sustainability. The city tries to counterbalance this by stressing the importance of quality and sustainability.

Conclusions

Water is an important issue for Rotterdam. Rotterdam city faces challenges as a deltaic city in an urbanizing world with an important harbor with globalization aspirations. It is a city facing long-term challenges that have to be dealt with at the short-term.

In this chapter we analyzed two cases: Watercity 2035 and Cityports. In these cases envisioning took place in an arena-like setting. Watercity 2035 was an initiative for the Biennal 2005. In the Cityports case the researchers were supporting the arena setting that was set up by the Cityports project team. We use the cases to explore how transition arena works in practice, to discuss the way it may link short-term and long-term challenges and what role water plays.

Does envisioning connect long term and short term thinking and actions? From our analysis and assessment of the case studies, we argue that envisioning taking place in a transition arena succeeds in connecting long-term perspective and short-term action. We saw that the vision was taken as a guiding direction and some of the suggested practical options were considered as starting points for experimental action. Although the experiments were not always fruitful, they were guiding the implementation.

Does envisioning broaden the vision and connect water with urban agendas? Envisioning aided urban planners to understand water issues, include them in the agenda and view water as a brokering issue and opportunity issue rather than a constraint. We observe that disciplinary barriers are too strong to break with one successful policy project. Broadening the scope and connecting urban planning with water management are activities that need to be done in every project and in every action in policy reality.

What are the lessons learnt from the Rotterdam case concerning connective capacity in urban deltas? Envisioning as a tool for connecting short-term and long-term thinking and actions brought forward innovative solutions in terms of function (for example, water-square) and in terms of feasibility (for example, floating pavilion). At the same time, envisioning resulted in perspectives change: from water as a threat to water as opportunity creator. For the case of Cityports, water was seen as an opportunity from the start of the envisioning, leading in this way to fruitful discussions and visions. In line with this, we observe that a negotiated positive starting point for the envisioning is a success factor for envisioning to be fruitful and to improve connective capacity.

The experience with envisioning in transition arenas shows that the involvement of people with diverse perceptions is important so as to have an integral vision that yields a variety of pathways and short-term actions. This is depicted in the vision Watercity 2035, which is not simply about water quality but seeks for accommodating water and in this way achieve a liveable city. The clarity of the pathways was a success factor in adopting the vision and moving towards action. An integral vision is produced that was not empty in content but included multiple actions and pathways that addressed the short- and medium-term capabilities in realizing the long-term vision.

An Early Paradox for Connective Capacity

A reflection concerns how the innovative projects and programs that are realized in Rotterdam connect to the urban context. Connecting the different actors and interests of spatial planning domain with water, created the opportunity for innovative projects and programs towards urban renewal and urban innovation. These innovative projects can be seen as urban innovation niches that are disconnected from their urban context since they function on their own loci with project-specific objectives. It is a paradox of connectivity: by connecting interests and actors of spatial planning and water domains, the urban innovation projects (and the associated change agents) are the frontrunners that sometimes remain disconnected from the Rotterdam urban practice.

The envisioning placed water challenges in perspective by showing how water can be a connecting link that offers new opportunities and insights for innovation in urban areas. Instead of de facto prioritizing water, envisioning created space for reflection and 'egalitarian' prioritization between water, economic, spatial and mobility issues.

Policy Implications and Suggestions to Policy Makers for Increasing Connective Capacity via Envisioning

We argue that besides breaking out of the waterbox, there is need to develop strategies that deal with other actors 'breaking into' the waterbox. We present two cases in which water experts and issues were part of a spatial envisioning and strategy development process, through which water came to be defined more practically and as part of the broader context. The cases show the importance of opening up, exploratory processes, engaging frontrunners and how these might lead to innovative outcomes that are included in the formal policy process. The cases thus show that there is another way to inform policy and produce real-world innovation, besides the dominant expert- and institutions-based planning and envisioning in the water sector. Arguably, a more open approach offers opportunities for new connections between water and other issues: rather than seeking to convince other domains that water is a really important issue, it might be more fruitful to actively seek for openings in other sectors and networks to present water as an opportunity.

Bibliography

Beers, P.J. et al. 2010. Future sustainability and images, *Futures*, 42, 723-32.

De Dreu, C.K.W. and West, M.A. 2001. Minority dissent and team innovation: The importance of participation in decision making, *Journal of Applied Psychology*, 86, 6, 1191-201.

Frantzeskaki, N. and de Haan, H. 2009. Transitions: Two steps from theory to policy, *Futures*, 41, 593-606.

Frantzeskaki, N., Loorbach, D. and Meadowcroft, J. 2012. Governing transitions to sustainability: Transition management as a governance approach towards pursuing sustainability, *International Journal of Sustainable Development*, 15 (1-2), 19-36.

De Graaf, R. and Van der Brugge, R. 2010. Transforming water infrastructure by linking water management and urban renewal in Rotterdam, *Technological Forecasting and Social Change*, 77, 1282-91.

DRIFT and DSA, 2011. *Merwe-Vierhavens, Van Woestijn naar Goudmijn*.

Grin, J. et al. 2004. Practices for reflexive design: Lessons from a Dutch programme on sustainable agriculture, *International Journal of Foresight and Innovation Policy*, 1(1-2), 126-48.

Hendriks, C.M. 2008. On inclusion and network governance: The democratic disconnect of Dutch energy transitions, *Public Administration*, 86(4), 1009-31.

Heiskanen, et al. 2009. Designed to travel? Transition management encounters environmental and innovation policy histories in Finland, *Policy Sciences*, 42, 409-27.

IABR 2005. *Rotterdam Waterstad 2035*.

IPCC 2007. Climate change 2007: Synthesis Report. Contribution of working groups I, II, and III to the Fourth Assessment Report of the Intergovernmental Panel on Climate Change [Core Writing Team, edited by R.K. Pachauri and A. Reisinger. IPCC, Geneva, Switzerland, 104 pp.

KNMI 2006. KNMI Climate Change Scenarios 2006 for the Netherlands, KNMI Scientific Report WR 2006-01, 22 May 2006, www.knmi.nl.

Kohler, J. et al. 2009. A transitions model for sustainable mobility, *Ecological Economics*, 68, 2985-95.

Loorbach, D. 2007. *Transition Management: New Mode of Governance for Sustainable Development*. Utrecht: International Books.

Loorbach, D. 2010. Transition Management for Sustainable Development: A Prescriptive, Complexity-Based Governance Framework, *Governance: An International Journal of Policy, Administration, and Institutions*, 23(1), 161-83.

Loorbach, D. and Rotmans, J. 2010. The practice of transition management: Examples and lessons from four distinct cases, *Futures*, 42, 237-46.

Ozkaynak, B. and Rodriguez-Labajos, B. 2010. Multi-scale interaction in local scenario-building: A methodological framework, *Futures*, 42(9), 995-1006.

Sheppard, S.R.J. et al. 2011, Future visioning of local climate change: A framework for community engagement and planning with scenarios and visualization, *Futures*, 43, pp. 400-13.

Smith, A., Voss, J.P. and Grin, J. 2010. Innovation studies and sustainability transitions: The allure of the multi-level perspective and its Challenges, *Research Policy*, 39, 435-48.

Van Buuren, A. and Loorbach, D. 2009. Policy innovation in isolation?, *Public Management Review*, 11(3)3, 375-92.

Van Buuren, A., J. Edelenbos, E.H. Klijn 2010. *Gebiedsontwikkeling in woelig water*. Den Haag: Boom/Lemma.

Van der Brugge, R. and de Graaf, R. 2010. Linking Water policy innovation and urban renewal: The case of Rotterdam, The Netherlands, *Water Policy*, 12, 381-400.

Van der Brugge, R. 2009. *Transition Dynamics in Social-ecological Systems, the Case of Dutch Water Management*, Erasmus Universiteit Rotterdam.

Van den Bosch, S.J.M., Brezet, J.C. and Vergragt, Ph. J. 2005. How to kick off system innovation: A Rotterdam case study of the transition to a fuel cell transport system', *Journal of Cleaner Production*, 13, 1027-35.

Van den Bosch, S.J.M. 2010 Transition experiments, Exploring societal changes towards sustainability. PhD thesis. Erasmus University Rotterdam.

Van Eijndhoven, Josee et al. 2009. Connected People and Entwined Activities, DRIFT,Transumo.

Van Knippenberg, D., De Dreu, C.K.W and Homan, A.C. 2004. Work Group Diversity and Group Performance: An Integrative Model and Research Agenda', *Journal of Applied Psychology*, 89(6), 1008-22.

Voss, J.P. and Bornemann, B. 2011. The politics of reflexive governance: Challenges for designing adaptive management and transition management, *Ecology and Society*, 16(2), 9 (www.ecologyandsociety.org/vol16/iss2/art9).

Wardekker, J.A. et al. 2010. Operationalising a resilience approach to adapting an urban delta to uncertain climate changes, *Technological Forecasting and Social Change*, 77, 987-98.

WWAP 2009. Water in a changing world, 3rd UN World Water Development Report.

Chapter 10

Connecting Time Spans in Regional Water Governance: Managing Projects as Stepping-stones to a Climate Proof Delta Region

Corniel van Leeuwen and Arwin van Buuren

Introduction

Climate adaptation is essentially a long-term challenge. The impact of climate change only becomes visible within fifty or hundred years. Decisions for adaptation strategies thus have to be based upon estimations of the expected situation in for example 2050. Budgets for adaptation strategies are therefore scanty and political attention is often rather low and unsteady (Giddens 2010).

At the same time regional planning processes (in which climate adaptation is only one of the relevant aspects) deal with much shorter time horizons. The criteria used by decision-makers to take decisions are usually based upon short-term issues like available finances, grassroots support, procedural deadlines et cetera. Furthermore, these planning processes are executed by project organizations which have to do with fixed terms in terms of time and budget (Crawford et al. 2003). And finally, planning processes comprise many actors with many divergent values and stakes. Realizing consensus between these actors is necessary to get projects implemented but also means that short-term ambitions frequently push aside long-term considerations.

The tension between climate adaptation on the long term and the urgency of public investments on the short term in infrastructure, recreation, housing and so on, is widely felt. Therefore, the search towards useful institutional arrangements to make regional planning processes more future-oriented takes off. Some are pleading for new frameworks which can be used to reconsider spatial planning decisions. Others develop economic instruments to take into account long-term costs and benefits of urgent public investments (Staff Delta Commissary 2011).

In this chapter we will look at the Steering Group Southwest Delta as an institutional arrangement aimed to help short-term planning processes to become more future-proof. This Steering Group can be seen as a regional governance arrangement in which local, regional and national governmental actors collaborate. The Steering Group has developed a program management approach to realize its objectives: the Implementation Program Southwest Delta. Within the Netherlands, regional program management is more and more applied as an umbrella arrangement for regional planning processes with the aim to organize cohesion, mutual enforcement and adjustment to more generic regional ambitions (as for example climate adaptation on the long term).

Figure 10.1   The area of the program Southwest Delta

The program organization Southwestern Delta is involved in many inter-municipal and regional planning processes. Recently this program organization developed the so-called Implementation Strategy which is aimed to set in motion a transition process with regard to the Lake Volkerak Zoom and the Lake Grevelingen, to solve the merely ecological problems in these lakes like the lack of oxygen in the Lake Grevelingen and the presence of the toxic blue green algae in the lake Volkerak Zoom. The Steering Group tries to realize this by initiating and connecting small scale interventions and projects which together can constitute a gradual development towards a more climate-robust water system in the long term.

In this chapter we first discuss both project and program management as devices to organize decision-making around complex spatial issues. We reflect upon how they cope with the issue of time and their relative value with regard to taking the long term into account. Then we zoom into the way in which the long and the short term can be aligned by developing a vital program-project connection. In the second part we present and analyze our case study of the Implementation Strategy developed and accomplished by the Steering Group Southwest Delta and we reflect upon its value in developing connecting capacity between the short and the long term.

We use our empirical study to find out which strategies are used to aligning time horizons and deduct from our analysis some building blocks for connecting capacity with regard to the relation between the short and the long term as it can be mobilized by establishing and maintaining institutional arrangements for collaboration and steering.

Project and Program Management

The Emergence of Complexity in our Contemporary Society

Our contemporary society is dominated by networks of actors who all defend their own stake. In these networks, long-lasting conflicts can be detected (Radford 1977). Actors are confronted with a lack of capacity to solve perceived problems on their own. Cooperation between actors becomes necessary to find feasible solutions for problems actors are facing. This is especially true in the policy field of water governance (Van Buuren et al. 2012). Water issues are confronted by a high degree of complexity because of the different agendas, perceptions and interests of actors involved in the policy making process. The compounded and interconnected character of water problems urges actors to a joint approach and the mutual resource interdependency between actors urges them to take the aims and ambitions of others also into account, creating even more compounded problem definitions and ambitions.

Due to this growing complexity in the field of water, the traditional so-called top-down strategies to solve societal problems dissatisfies in terms of their effectiveness. Water problems cannot be solved in line organizations of central government agencies anymore. Other organizational arrangements have to be found to face these challenges. This development has been defined as the transition from 'government to governance' (Pierre 2000, Sørensen en Torfing 2005). It is not the single intervention of one actor, but the joint effect of the interventions of a set of actors that generates guidance and developments and that contributes to the ability of societies to deal with water issues.

The Emergence of Project Management to Deal with the Observed Complexity

One of the management strategies to deal with this new governance context, which was developed in the middle of the former century, is called project management. The main goal to develop this management approach was the presence of fragmentation within line organizations (Meredith and Mantel 2009). Kor and Wijnen (2005: 66) describe a project as a unique complex of proceedings focusing on an in advance defined result which has to be realized with limited resources. Managing approaches to realize the project goal focuses mainly on defining the budget, on defining the time schedule and the desired quality (Crawford et al. 2003). These activities and targets are the main criteria to indicate whether a project manager is successful.

In the public domain, that means that project management is used when the competent public authorities have defined a specific problem. Project organizations then are used to design strategies to solve this problem. They are composed of civil servants from various agencies and get a certain degree of autonomy to prepare decisions and execute them after formal approval. From an institutional perspective they can be seen as temporal arrangements that facilitate joint problem-solving. Especially when it comes to inter-organizational projects with a major societal impact, project teams are accompanied by (temporal and light) institutional arrangements that facilitate intergovernmental dialogue and collaboration. In these projects there is (semi-) structural cooperation between officials of various public agencies and there is an arrangement (Steering Group, Board) in which the responsible authorities are represented.

The Shortcomings of Project Management in Dealing with Long-term Challenges

However, project management has not proven to be the panacea for fragmentation and conflicts. Delays and cost overruns have shown that project management is facing its limits (Flyvberg 2003). It has become clear that the aims of projects are often contradictory to other ambitions represented by other line organizations and other project teams and to goals of (other) government policies. So, while project management was introduced as a solution to fragmentation, it also forms a cause of new fragmentation on the level of projects which do set and defend their own organizational boundaries. So the fragmentation between line organizations is now (to some extent) replaced by fragmentation between project organizations. Societies now seem to evolve into a next decade in which the project management approach no longer is a satisfactory answer to fragmentation. According to Licht (2005) the changed context causes that project management is not always effective anymore.

In this chapter we will especially focus upon the shortcomings of project approaches when it comes to long-term challenges and we evaluate how overarching institutional collaborative arrangements can mitigate these shortcomings. Project management approaches are for several reasons not well equipped to deal with ambitions which are related to long-term developments and urgencies like climate adaptation. There are at least three reasons for this:

1. Project management approaches are forced to focus upon the short term due to their restrictive project targets (procedures, budget, formal deadlines);
2. Project management approaches are forced to focus upon the short term due to external demands and network complexity (to realize agreement upon a combination of short-term ambitions is already difficult enough, and it is almost impossible to also take into account other – less urgent or articulated issues);
3. Project management approaches are inherently aimed at realizing short-term ambitions which can be clearly defined and which do have enough urgency (projects are only formulated when there is a clear problem definition and thus a strong focus upon the goal to be realized).

One of the main focus points of project management is its clearly bounded time span. This element can be seen as one of the main strengths of project management: this management strategy is especially used to generate enough pressure to realize a certain task within a specific (tight) time frame. But it can also be seen as one of its weaknesses, because it also generates pressure to neglect complicating issues which makes realizing the deadline more difficult. As a consequence, project management approaches are in general not very suitable to deal with long-term challenges like climate adaptation, because these challenges lack clear-cut problem definitions and solutions.

The Emergence of Regional Governance with Program Management Orientation

Regional collaborative governance arrangements can be identified as an answer to the fragmentation caused by the large amounts of loosely coordinated and partly conflicting project management actions in western societies (Murray-Webster and Thiry 2000, Maylor et al. 2006, Van Buuren et al. 2010).

Within the Dutch context regional governance coalitions often rely upon program management as a concrete steering approach to realize their joint agenda. A program is aiming to overcome the fragmentation of loosely coupled projects in an interdependent context by integrating the knowledge and aims of different projects into a multi-project program activity. De Graaf (2008) describes a program as a series of projects with the goal to realize a mayor change over a long time span. The goal of the program is not the same as the sum of the goals of the projects. Programs are about creating a development that cannot be the responsibility of the project leaders that are part of the program.

Program management is also more and more applied in Dutch regional water governance. Here, programs are not aiming to facilitate existing or initiating new projects. They are aiming for project adaptations and combinations in such a way that the ecology of projects together generates a climate proof region in the long run.

Although the literature does not explicitly deal with the question whether program management is a useful approach to realize long-term ambitions, we will argue that there are good reasons to suppose this. These reasons are:

1. Programs (within governance contexts) are ideally not focused upon realizing specific projects, but upon safeguarding certain values (on various scales of time, place and government) within these projects;
2. Programs are less inclined to deliver concrete results in the short term and do have more room to maneuver when it comes to trying to realize more intangible results;
3. Programs find themselves in the lee, compared to most projects. They do have a more administrative and explorative character what makes them less interesting for stakeholders and give them more room to formulate strategies inclined to anticipate on less urgent long-term ambitions.

In contrast to project management, blessed with a tight scope and aim, the playing field for program management is wider (Buijs and Edelenbos 2012). Programs for regional development are characterized by broad and general targets, dynamic and changing sets of stakeholders and a long term orientation in a short term erratic societal and political context. The regional governance coalition which supports a program is – contrary to project arrangements – a more structural arrangement with a more inclusive agenda, which functions as a forum for informing, deliberation and mutual adjusting.

The ability to combine a variety of content strived for by a variety of actors is a core capacity of program management, as it is applied by regional governance coalitions (Van Buuren et al. 2010). Program management can be described as targeted managing on content cohesion (De Graaf 2008). According to Ferns (1991) a program is 'a group of related projects that are managed in a coordinated way to gain benefits that would not be possible were the projects to be managed independently'. In program management, the focus of the management is on the relations between projects and relations between projects and the program, gaining mutual benefits beyond boundaries of responsibility and adding missing elements in order to improve robustness of spatial developments. Effective program management is able to realize synergetic solutions and is – more than project management – able to integrate the challenges of the changing environment over a longer time span in its focus (De Graaf 2008).

According to Buijs and Edelenbos (2012), building connective capacity is a key element of program management. In the first place there is the program-line nexus. Projects and programs have their embedding in line organizations of the involved stakeholders. Effective program management is defined by a strong program-line nexus. In this situation there is a fertile integration of line activities with program activities which contributes to the legitimacy of program managers. Moreover, effective program management is characterized by a strong project-program nexus. This connection is about individual projects and the program and between projects which are part of the program. The effectiveness of a program can be based upon the extent to which it is successful in aligning projects and realize cohesion and synergy. It is this latter nexus which is the focus of this chapter. Program management in relation to water governance, as applied by regional governance coalitions, is often an attempt to strengthen the program-project nexus. We are especially interested in the way this nexus can contribute to the alignment of short term project ambitions and long term program ideals.

Transcending Time Horizons by Strengthening the Program-project Nexus

In general the time orientation of projects is relatively short. This is caused by the clearly defined task, budget and quality of the project. In contrast, regional programs in general have a much wider time span. They are aimed at stimulating a couple of regional objectives for the long run (like economic development, climate robustness or livability) which have to be realized by setting the right but small steps via a variety of single projects (Van Buuren et al. 2010). Therefore program management can be used to influence the short-term focus of projects in such a way that they fit in the long term ambition of the program.

There are various appearances of project-program connections aimed at integrating short and long term ambitions. In this chapter we focus upon the interpretation in which projects are seen as 'stepping stones' to a 'dot on the horizon' which programs try to reach. In other words, a long term orientated program is only effective when the short term projects fit and in the more ideal situation contribute to the long term ambition of the program (Mosakowski and Earley 2000, Sharpe and Van der Heijden 2007, Hulme and Dessai 2008). This angle provides the need to connect short term projects to long term programs. Program management can use various strategies to strengthen this program-project nexus. In using these strategies the program aims to sketch a path towards the future. Projects have to fit in this path in terms of content and process and need to contribute to this path.

In order to establish a binding direction which connect and adjust individual projects, we suppose program managers can apply various strategies.

1. directly or indirectly adjust the project ambitions in such a way that they fit in the long-term ambition;
2. influence the timing and sequence of projects in such a way that they can take each other into account in terms of process, scope, procedure and strategy;
3. create interfaces between projects and program to support mutual alignment and information exchange.

In our empirical analysis we will discover in more detail which management strategies are used to align time horizons between projects and program.

Analyzing Project-program Connections

In this chapter we will explore a specific regional governance arrangement: the 'Steering Group South Western Delta' that aims to connect a series of projects in such a way that a long-term adaptation strategy can be realized. Within this arrangement, projects are seen as stepping stones which can result in the desired long-term programmatic ambition. But therefore it is necessary to adjust their scope, timing and way of implementation in such a way that they enforce each other and fit within the overarching program ambition with regard to the long-term development of the whole area. The arrangement used to realize this is called the 'Implementation Strategy'. In this chapter, we introduce this strategy and explore it in-depth.

This chapter is the result of an in-depth case study in which we started with a desk study in which all relevant policy documents with regard to the Implementation Strategy have been analyzed. Next to this, ten interviews have been conducted as part of a participatory research. The first author was actively involved in implementing the 'Implementation Strategy'. This meant that he worked hand and hand with practitioners and followed their work closely. We were able to observe the strategies used by the program management in relation to the concerned projects by attending meetings of the program organization as well of meetings of the individual projects. This made it possible to observe the program steering activities with regard to the various projects.

In our case study four questions are put central:

- What are the main characteristics of the program and project management context in which the Implementation Strategy is implemented,
- What are the main objectives of this Implementation Strategy and what are its main characteristics,
- How does the Steering Group Southwestern Delta try to manage the

program-project nexus in general and more specific when it comes to connecting long term and short term ambitions with help of the Implementation Strategy,
*   Which elements of connective capacity can be distinguished, based upon our analysis of the Implementation Strategy used by the Steering Group Southwestern Delta?

The Context of the Program Southwest Delta

As a reaction on the major flooding disasters in 1906 and 1953 in the Southwest part of the Netherlands, the national government executed some major interventions in the water defense system (De Schipper 2008, Slager 2010). As a result of these interventions, which are known as the 'Delta works', the Southwest Delta with its characterizing estuarine dynamics transformed in a series of lakes losing its dynamics and connection with the North Sea and the rivers. As a result of this, several ecological problems arose (like: the anoxic lake Grevelingen and toxic blue-green algae in the lake Volkerak Zoom). As a consequence, at the end of the 20th century, recreation and tourism started to decline, marshes and mud flats were disappearing and shellfish culture became more difficult because of a shortage of nutrients originally coming from the rivers. Furthermore, because of the prevalence of the blue-green algae in the lake Volkerak Zoom, the freshwater is (especially in the summer) not suitable anymore for sprinkling farmlands on the adjacent islands.

Alongside these merely ecologic orientated problems in the Southwest part of the Netherlands there are also economic problems. As a part of the Delta works, several locks were created. These locks (Volkerak and Krammer locks) were built for the shipping industry to connect the several lakes. However, these locks were built in 1967 (Volkerak locks) and 1983 (Krammer locks) of the former century. In the last decades the shipping industry has grown enormously. Inlands ships have grown and transportation between the ports of Rotterdam and Antwerp has multiplied. As a result of this, the Volkerak Locks suffers from a capacity problem. Boatmen sometimes have to wait for more than an hour to pass the Volkerak Locks. This is causing economic damage to the transport domain.

Beside these ecologic and economic problems there is a safety issue in the lake Grevelingen and lake Volkerak. Because of the changing climate, storms and high sea levels become more prevalent (Deltacommittee Veerman 2008). At the same time, because of the more extreme weather conditions, high river discharges become more prevalent. A coincidence of these two circumstances causes a 'bath tub' effect. Because of the low altitude with respect to the sea level, the Southwest part of the Netherlands is vulnerable to this.

In recent years the national government started several separated projects for the various basins to further explore the problems. At the same time, governments on other scales (regional, local) have initiated projects in the lake Grevelingen and Lake Volkerak to enhance the economic, recreational and ecological value of these lakes. These projects are projected in the figure below. In the next part of this paragraph we will illuminate two projects to provide further insight in these problems.

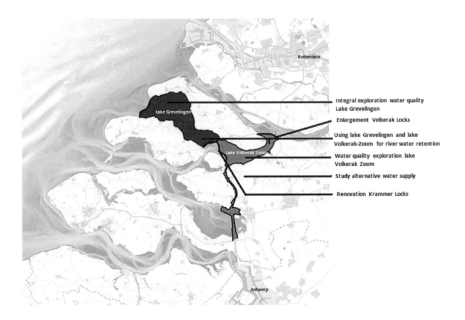

Figure 10.2   Projects in the lake Grevelingen and lake Volkerak Zoom

In the first place, in 2002, Rijkswaterstaat (the national water management agency) started a problem exploration for the freshwater lake Volkerak Zoom. After a studying period of several years, salinization in combination with a reintroduced estuarine dynamic proved to be the solution to solve the problem of the blue green algae. However, this solution seemed to cause new problems because the fresh water in the lake is used by farmers for sprinkling farmlands. Another problem was that the renewed salt lake Volkerak-Zoom would cause a salt leak in the Volkerak locks leading to side effects in another fresh water basin – Haringvliet, Hollandsch Diep – also used for sprinkling farmlands and industries. So, the solution could only be executed when an alternative fresh water supply would be realized.

Another project was started in the lake Grevelingen. In contrast to the lake Volkerak Zoom, the Grevelingen is a salt water basin because of a little culvert in the Brouwersdam (created in 1978), connecting it with the North Sea. However, this culvert proved not to be enough for providing the lake Grevelingen with enough oxygen. This led to deterioration of the water quality of the lake. Because of this, in 2006, Rijkswaterstaat started an exploration of the consequences of reintroducing estuarine dynamic in the lake Grevelingen. Because of the positive outcomes, the Secretary of State asked in 2010 for a further exploration of reintroducing estuarine dynamics on the lake Grevelingen in combination with a tidal plant, a renewed waterway to the North Sea and a connection with the lake Volkerak Zoom which can be used to increase the water retention capacity of the Southwest Delta in case of high river discharge.

Because of these explorations, the regional administrators started to realize that the problems in the different basins had to be seen in its interdependence. Nevertheless, this insight was not totally new. Already in 2004, regional governments and the national government started to work together in a Delta Council with the ambition to bring back the estuarine dynamic in the South West Delta (Delta Council 2004). However, the Delta Council functioned merely as a debating and agenda-setting platform. In 2008 the Delta Council transformed in the Steering Group Southwest Delta and embraced the ambition to create an ecologically resilient, economically vital and safe delta. From this moment on, the Steering Group became more and more a steering unit and transformed in the program Southwest Delta. The cooperation between the actors involved intensified. The program Southwest Delta, in its current form, can be described as an intergovernmental policy program. Within the program the national government, regional governments and water boards are working together to realize a climate proof, ecologic resilient and economic vital Southwest Delta in the Netherlands (Steering Group Southwest Delta 2010).

The above described projects nevertheless were still standing on their own with their clearly defined boundaries and project demarcations in time and focus. From 2008 on, the program organization more and more started to interfere in the individual projects by widening their problem perspective and showing the interdependence with other projects with the aim to create more content and process cohesion in the different project initiatives. Furthermore, in 2009, the program got a new mission. As a consequence of the more and more felt urgency of climate change, the national government gave the program organization the mission to analyze the problems (and strategies to solve them) which were to expect in 2050/2100. For the Steering Group, this was the moment to start thinking about the very long term issues in the Southwest Delta.

Table 10.1   Institutional arrangements in the Southwest Delta

Year	Name arrangement	Characteristics
2004	Delta Council	Debating and agenda setting platform
2008	Steering Group Southwest Delta	Steering unit, interfering in individual projects, defining interdependences between individual projects
2009	Steering Group Southwest Delta	Long term climate adaptation thinking

One of the main results of this long term problem analysis is that the weather is going to be extremer in the Netherlands, with more droughts and wet periods. Especially the wetter periods can in the long run become a major problem for the Southwest Delta. But also the urgency of more river water retention became more prevalent to prevent flooding. In contrary, the more prevalent droughts can also have enormous implications, especially for the lake Volkerak Zoom. More common droughts cause a process of salinization of the lake and this is a threat to the fresh water supply for sprinkling and drink water installations. In short, the problem analysis for the long run, carried out by the program organization, provided new insights for the short term decision making processes of the individual projects. For the program Southwest Delta this problem analysis led to ambitions in terms of content:

- Creating a climate robust fresh water supply for the Southwest Delta as a whole;
- Creating enough water retention capacity in the Southwest Delta to prevent the 'bathtub effect'.

One of the main contributions of the program is the created insight that the Southwest Delta needs to be seen as a whole to deal with the complexity of the problems in the Southwest Delta. This means that individual water related problems cannot be solved apart. Doing this will cause problems in other basins (for example because of salt leaks and the disability of using fresh water for sprinkling farmlands). Next to this insight, the economic crisis in the Netherlands in combination with a new national government in 2010 (with less focus on ecological issues) makes clear that financing the individual projects was not possible anymore. The individual projects were no longer able to attract money from the central government (which has the main responsibility for the lakes). So, the projects were vulnerable to fall apart with the consequence of letting the prevalent water problems unresolved. These developments contributed to the awareness of the program organization in that it is wise to influence the short term orientated projects in order to contribute to the solution of the long term ambitions. For these reasons, the Steering Group Southwest Delta developed a new strategy to overcome these difficulties: the so called *Implementation Strategy* which will be the subject of the next paragraph.

The Implementation Strategy

The Implementation Strategy is an attempt of the Steering Group Southwest Delta to set in motion several developments which together have to result in a climate robust Southwest Delta. The ambitions in terms of content focus on realizing enough water retention to prevent for flooding, to enlarge the capacity of the Volkerak locks, to improve the water quality in the lake Grevelingen and lake Volkerak Zoom (by reintroducing estuarine dynamics) and to create a robust fresh water supply. The goal thereby is to find the most efficient/effective solutions and a contrived timing of the various steps. The Steering Group tries to realize these ambitions by making use of several building blocks:

• Focusing on fundamental, guiding and element decisions;
• Bringing no-regret measures to the implementation phase;
• Arranging decisions in the most efficient sequence.

In the first place the Steering Group focuses with the Implementation Strategy on making three fundamental choices: introducing tide on the Lake Grevelingen, salinization the lake Volkerak-Zoom and finally using the lake Grevelingen for river water retention or not. By doing this, the Steering Group aims to force fundamental decisions around these three issues and prioritize them as the most important decisions in the Delta. These three fundamental decisions are constitutive for the whole delta system. Herewith, the program organization of the Steering Group tries to narrow the scope of the many decision making processes running in the Delta.

Furthermore, these three fundamental decisions are aimed as attractors for smaller decision making processes dealing with sub choices. To realize this ambition the Steering Group focuses in the Implementation Strategy on the decision which makes it possible to realize estuarine dynamic in the future. So, because of the financial and political circumstances, the Steering Group does not primarily focus on a decision to implement measures right now. It focuses on decisions which give direction to future decision making processes (guiding decisions). In case of the ambition to reintroduce estuarine dynamics, it focuses on the decision which says estuarine dynamics are possible in the future for the lake Volkerak Zoom and lake Grevelingen. These guiding decisions function as a trigger for smaller decision making processes in the near future on their way to the attractor (the fundamental decision of reintroducing estuarine dynamics). However, before making the guiding decision, it is necessary to make decisions about further explorations, execute preparing measures and pilots (for example a tidal test centre in an old spuicelock). In sum, the Implementation Strategy makes use of three types of decisions:

1. Fundamental decisions;
2. Guiding decisions;
3. Element decisions.

The fundamental choices function as an attractor for many smaller decisions about investments, pilots, explorations and preparing measures. These smaller decisions (stepping stones) pave the way for guiding decisions which in turn function as triggers for further decision making processes and make the future more feasible. With the Implementation Strategy the Steering Group tries to anchor this path by making use of a National Planning Document. This framework helps to fix the long term ambition of program and the path towards the future proof Southwest Delta.

In the second place the Steering Group steers on bringing no-regret measures to the implementation phase. These are measures which are attractive in all circumstances. By doing this it wants to set in motion a transition to a more robust Southwest Delta. In relation to the fundamental decision of reintroducing estuarine dynamics, this means that these relative small measures, like the pilot 'tidal test centre' and an innovative bubble curtain near the Krammer locks to prevent a salt leak are brought to the implementation phase. The Steering Group does this for example by preparing a regional offer of the regional governments in the Steering Group in combination of investments of the private sector. This regional offer (a substantial amount of money and administrative support) is intended to seduce the national government for co-finance. This is necessary because the national government has the main responsibility for the Delta waters while the regional governments benefit from these measures (in terms of more opportunities for regional development). Because of the precarious financial situation of the national government it is necessary to demonstrate the joint willingness of the regional governments to invest in the proposed measures. The regional offer is a concretization of this. The Steering Group uses the no-regret measures (in its Implementation Strategy) to set in motion a transition to a more sustainable Southwest delta. Implementing fresh water measures for example, prevents negative consequences of climate change for the freshwater supply around the two lakes in the long run. Thus, these measures anticipate on the realization of the long term ambition.

In the third place the Steering Group tries to arrange decisions in the most efficient sequence. Hereby it prioritizes measures in terms of efficiency and effectiveness. Within the Implementation Strategy this is done by determining the 'extreme' decision making moments. These are the moments on which *windows of opportunities* in decision making processes are closing. From these moments on, possibilities to keep open the future disappear or the costs of delaying a measure becomes more expensive than taking a decision. An example of this is the decision to invest in more drainage capacity in the Volkerak locks which is necessary to use the Lake Grevelingen for river water retention. Not making this decision will lead to 101 million euros costs in surplus when the locks need to be adjusted in a later phase (Stratelligence 2011a). Realizing this extra drainage capacity in combination with enlarging the capacity of these locks is the most efficient strategy. To realize this most efficient sequence of decisions, it is necessary to continuously monitor the regional governance system for opportunities to make or delay a decision.

By making use of these building blocks, the Steering Group strives for an integral approach whereby the sum of projects, explorations, measures and pilots needs to provide a development that fits in the long term perspective of a sustainable Southwest Delta. Within the Implementation Strategy, projects are seen as stepping stones which can result in the desired long-term ambition. To realize this, the program tries to adjust their scope, timing and way of implementation in such a way that they enforce each other and fit within the overarching program ambition. In sum, the Steering Group strives for a stepwise efficient decision making process which is bending the impossibility of financing large infrastructural measures now in a possibility to finance those in the future.

How Institutional Arrangements can Contribute to Connecting Time Lines

As we have seen in the previous section, the institutional arrangement 'Steering Group Southwest Delta' and its supporting program management office tries to connect the long and the short term. In this section we derive a number of program management insights from the activities performed by the Steering Group.

Playing with Project Boundaries

First of all, connecting long-term ambitions and short time developments in the context of the Southwest Delta is about transcending and adjusting project boundaries. Short time urgencies which dominate projects sometimes conflict with long term ambitions. Realizing long term ambitions is thus about adjusting these project boundaries. Project scopes sometimes need to be adjusted so that their goals fit in the long term ambition of the overarching program. The Steering Group uses this principle in its Implementation Strategy. The individual projects all form ingredients in the overall strategy. The individual goals of the projects are adjusted by positioning them in the overall perspective of the Steering Group on the two basins Volkerak Zoom and Grevelingen. The projects still hold their own project management but their boundaries and project goals are adjusted by the Steering Group. The Steering Group was able to do this because of the changed financial and political situation in the Netherlands. Individual project organizations were not able anymore to get money from the central government. So, for realizing their project goals, they became more dependent on the program organization of the Steering Group which took the opportunity to bring the various projects together within one convincing narrative and strategy/time-path for implementation.

Playing with Time

Secondly, connecting long term ambitions and short term developments essentially have to do with playing with time. It has to do with arranging a specific sequence of decisions. This sequence is based upon two considerations:

- Which decisions are effective, irrespective of any future development?
- Which decisions set in motion a specific path-dependent development?

The first consideration tries to find out which decisions are "no-regret". These decisions can be taken in any case and fit within various future scenarios. They try to set in motion several other decisions which together form a transition to a more sustainable future. In the context of the Southwest Delta in the Netherlands, this is done by focusing on for example the innovative bubble curtain to prevent salt leaks. This decision paves the way for future decision making processes. The second consideration looks for critical connections between decisions. Because we have to do with a physical system which is highly connected, interventions in such a system can have significant impacts on related (sub-)systems and can be difficult to rescind. From a climate adaptation perspective in which much is uncertain, it is highly important that decisions which exclude certain (possible desirable) development paths are prevented and decisions which can provoke certain desirable developments are advanced. In the Implementation Strategy we see that, due to changed political and financial circumstances, decisions which were thought to be made in the near future are now positioned on the long-term. With smaller projects the route towards the preferred future state is demarcated.

Playing with Complex Systems Characteristics

Third, connecting long term and short term has to do with playing with complex system characteristics. Within the Implementation Strategy, the Steering Group makes use of specific (small-scale) decisions which do have the ability to set in motion a more large-scale development. To plan these decisions, it is highly important to understand the behavior of the complex system in question. Not understanding the complex character of the system can lead to decision with a high *regretness* in the future. Reintroducing estuarine dynamic and salt water in the lake Volkerak Zoom leads for example to a salt leak in the Volkerak Locks with negative consequences for the adjacent lake. Noble decisions which are not taking into account the complex character of the physical system can lead to a chain reaction of negative consequence.

Playing with Energy and Attention

Fourth, connecting long-term ambitions and short-term developments is about keeping the energy of actors involved. The urgency of long-term ambitions can easily evaporate. It is thus necessary to think about possibilities to take small steps (which gives actors the impression that the 'great transition' is still ongoing) in the right direction. These small steps can trigger the enthusiasm necessary for the larger development. In the Implementation Strategy the pilot 'tidal test centre' is used for this. It uses the attention which is given to this measure to put it in the long term ambition for the Southwest Delta. The tidal test centre is seen as an integral solution which improves the estuarine dynamic on the Grevelingen, provides the lake Grevelingen with more oxygen and provides the region with employment and a chance for international exportation. The pilot fits in the ambition of the national government to stimulate innovation in water and sustainable energy. The Steering Group makes use of this window of opportunity by using the pilot to illustrate the necessity of this measure for a future proof Southwest Delta. So, the Steering Group mobilizes support and legitimacy for projects that fit into the long-term ambition and contribute to it. This also characterizes the flexibility of the institutional arrangement: it is able to allow for new issues on its agenda and is willing to devote energy to them when they seem to be promising. So, flexibility is also a necessary characteristic of institutional arrangements to connect time lines and to realize connective capacity.

Playing with Scarce Resources

Finally, when it comes to realizing long-term ambitions, the availability of the necessary resources (in terms of money, organizational capacity, etc.) is a problem. It can be helpful to accelerate decisions on issues which do have the necessary resources to get implemented and to postpone decisions for which these resources are lacking. The Implementation Strategy makes use of this principle. An example is the innovative bubble curtain. The national government arranged money for this measure and so the implementation received priority. In the Implementation Strategy this measure is positioned as a pilot that paves the way for the guiding decisions. The other way around, postponing decisions is also a principle which is used in the Implementation Strategy. We see this with regard to the salinization of the lake Volkerak Zoom. Already in 2002, the national government started explorations to solve the water quality problem. After all these years of study the project only awaited a go/no-go decision. The availability of resources defines the timing of projects and the sequence of decisions.

Conclusion

From our explorative analysis of the Implementation Strategy, developed by the Steering Group, we can deduct a couple of building blocks for connective capacity when it comes to connecting time spans.

Firstly, connective capacity has a strong knowledge component. Connective capacity is based upon knowledge about how complex physical systems behave and how they are interconnected with other subsystems. This knowledge is necessary to think about the optimum sequence of decisions and about how to trigger specific evolutions. Without this knowledge, connecting time scales is impossible. Taking a wrong decision in terms of the physical system characteristics can cause a chain reaction of negative consequences. As a result, the long term ambition can get out of sight because of the high recovery costs. Institutional arrangements thus have to invest in a robust knowledge base as departing point to think about meaningful connections between short and long term ambitions.

Secondly, connective capacity is also based upon the capacity of regional arrangements (such as the Steering Group Southwest Delta) to develop a convincing narrative in which various developments and investments are meaningfully connected to each other as part of a transition path towards a sustainable future. In other words, a program management strategy possess connective capacity when it is able to create a coherent and attractive path towards the future in which project and program ambitions are connected and mutually enforce each other. In our analysis, we showed the way the Steering Group is doing this by focusing on three fundamental decisions which together will lead to a climate proof Southwest Delta. The narrative used focuses on the opportunities (in terms of economic opportunities, flood risk reduction and ecological quality) which can be cashed when the Delta moves towards a more dynamic, open and tidal system in which the current freshwater dominance is replaced by thinking about the opportunities of saltwater lakes.

Thirdly, connective capacity has to do with program management competencies to contain the opportunities for competent timing and sequencing. These managerial competencies also have to do with understanding the logic of complex governance systems, especially when it comes to proposing additional decisions which can become attractors that trigger other decisions that builds up to a transition. To do this, it is important to understand the drivers for local and regional politicians and to set them in motion by formulating the right proposals. Connective capacity in this sense assumes political and administrative sensitivity of the program manager. Absence of this sensitivity can cause triggers that cross the path towards a sustainable future and lead to a negative chain reaction.

Fourthly, connective capacity also consists of organizational arrangements as such, which are able to bring together relevant actors and organizations responsible for the various components of a long-term governance transition. These arrangements have to be able to exercise the power to enforce decision-making on the right moment (and thus to postpone some decisions and to accelerate others). These arrangements are thus both vertically and horizontally inclusive: they unite relevant authorities from the various governance scales (national, regional, local) as well as from the various functional domains (water safety, ecology, recreation, etc). Within the Steering Group we can witness this inclusiveness although it is a difficult job to get the national government committed to the regional agenda.

Fifthly, connective capacity also has to do with authority and legitimacy of and within arrangements such as the Steering Group. Program management blessed with connective capacity needs to have this authority and legitimacy of the representatives from the various participating agencies to sketch a path towards the future. Other actors in the complex governance system with more authority will interfere in projects ambitions and processes. As a consequence of this, outcomes of decision making processes will be different than expected and desired. Due to this, the proposed attractor can get out of sight and will not be a trigger for future decision making processes.

Finally, connective capacity has to do with using the right procedural devices to consolidate current agreements on long-term ambitions. In our case the instrument of the National Planning Document is used by the Steering Group to record the ambitions on the long-term transition towards restoring estuarine dynamics in the

Southwest Delta. Such a planning procedure can help to secure the commitment of the involved actors in institutional arrangements. Institutional arrangements, procedures and structures are essential to secure that the common developed framework will hold stand in the future. This is necessary to prevent the developed path from conflicting influences like volatile politics.

Bibliography

Buijs, J-M. and Edelenbos, J. 2012. Connective capacity of program management: Responding to fragmented project management. *Public Administration Quarterly*, 31(1), 1-20.

Buuren, M.W., Buijs, J-M. and Teisman, G.R. 2010. Program management and the creative art op coopetition: Dealing with potential tensions and synergies between spatial development projects. *International Journal of Project Management*, 28, 672-82.

Buuren, van M.W., Klijn, E-H, Edelenbos, J. 2012. Democratic legitimacy and new forms of water management. *International Journal of Water Resources Development*, 28(4), 629-45.

Delta committee Veerman. 2008. *Samen werken met water. Een land dat leeft, bouwt aan zijn toekomst.* 's-Gravenhage.

Crawford, L., Costello, K., Pollack, J. and .Bentley, L. 2003. Managing soft change projects in the public sector. *International Journal of Project Management*, 21(6), 443-8.

Deltacouncil 2004. *Deltamemorandum.* Middelburg.

Ferns, D.C. 1991. Developments in program management, *International Journal of Project Management*, 9(3), 122-43.

Flyvberg, B., Bruzelius, N., Rothengatter, W. 2003. *Megaprojects and Risk: An Anatomy of Ambition.* Cambridge: Cambridge University Press.

Giddens, A. 2010. The Politics of Climate Change. Cambridge: Polity Press.

De Graaf, D. 2008. *Integraal Programmamanagement. Grip op de sturing van proces, inhoud en verandering.* Den Haag: Sdu Uitgevers.

Hulme, M. and Dessai, S. 2008. Predicting, deciding, learning: Can one evaluate the 'success' of national climate scenarios? *Environmental Research Letters*, 3(4), 139-54.

Kor, R. and Wijnen, G. 2005. Project-, programma- of procesmanagement: Een kwestie van kiezen voor de passende aanpak. *Holland Management Review*, 103, 61-71.

Licht, H. 2005. *Programmamanagement: Regievoering zonder macht.* Assen: Koninklijke Van Gorcum.

Maylor, H., Brady, T., Cooke-Davies, T. and Hodgson, D. 2006. From projectification to programmification. *International Journal of Project Management*, 24(8), 663-74.

Meredith, H. and Mantel, S. 2009. *Project Management: A Managerial Approach*, 7th ed., New York: Wiley.

Mosakowski, E. and Earley, P.C. 2000. A selective review of time assumptions in strategy research, *The Academy of Management Review*, 25(4), 796-812.

Murray-Webster, R., Thiry, M. 2000. Managing programmes of projects, in *Gower Handbook of Project Management*, edited by R. Turner and S. Simister. Aldershot: Ashgate, 47-63.

Pierre, J. 2000. *Debating Governance, Authority, Steering, and Democracy*. Oxford: Oxford University Press.

Radford, K.J. 1977. *Complex Decision Problems. An Integrated Strategy for Resolution*. Virginia. Reston Publishers.

Schipper, P. de 2008. *De slag om de Oosterschelde. Een reconstructie van de strijd om de open Oosterschelde*, Amsterdam/Antwerpen: Atlas.

Sharpe, B. and van der Heijden, K. 2007. *Scenarios for Success: Turning Insights into Action*. Chichester: Wiley.

Slager, K. 2009. *Watersnood,* Ouwerkerk.

Sørensen, E. and Torfing, J. 2005. The democratic anchorage of governance networks, *Scandinavian Political Studies*, 28(3), 195-218.

Stratelligence 2011. *Structurering keuzes en waardering alternatieven voor borging veiligheid benedenrivierengebied.* Den-Haag.

Stratelligence 2011a. *Aanzet uitvoeringsstrategie op basis van een analyse van mogelijkheden.* Rotterdam.

Steering Group Southwest Delta. 2010. *Uitvoeringsprogramma Zuidwestelijke Delta 2010-2015+.* Middelburg.

Chapter 11

Framing Strategies and Connective Capacity in Water Governance Policy: The Case of the Second Delta Committee

Simon Verduijn

Introduction[1]

In this chapter I explore the meaning and relevance of connective capacity for framing and agenda setting aimed at integrating climate adaptation in water governance policy. In general connective capacity is conceived as essential for realizing adaptive capacity in water governance, since dealing with climate and water is dealing with complex and uncertain developments (Pahl-Wostl 2007, Pahl-Wostl et al. 2007). Mankind is largely dependent on the way nature displays itself. Excessive rainfall or long periods of droughts can have immense influence on the way our canals, rivers and lakes are managed. Because of that, Edelenbos, Bressers and Scholten (see Chapter 1) argue that connective capacity in water governance is needed to cope with these uncertain and complex processes. Even though I will argue that connective capacity is of importance, I will also argue that to successfully gain high agenda priority status and support for an issue, a strong coherent one-dimensional policy frame is needed and not primarily the creation of connections with other discourses, frames or actors. In the rest of this chapter I reflect on these points by looking at a committee that, without a concrete cause like flooding, succeeded in setting the agenda for climate adaption in water governance policies in the Netherlands. It did that by employing, in a connective way, framing strategies and advancing a strong dominant coherent policy frame in which climate adaption and water safety have the highest priority.

In 2007, the Dutch cabinet installed the Second Delta Committee, named after its famous predecessor, the Delta Committee, which was established after the dramatic storm surge of 1953 that killed 1,835 people. The Second Delta Committee, chaired by the former Minister for Agriculture, Cees Veerman, was asked to formulate recommendations for strategies for long-term flood protection and freshwater management and issued its advice 'Working together with water; A living land builds for its future' in 2008 (Veerman 2008). The Committee's main recommendations were that the Dutch government should prepare and implement

1 This chapter is partly based on the analysis as presented in Water Alternatives (Verduijn et al. 2012). I am thankful to the Nieuw Land museum+archive+study centre in Lelystad, the Netherlands, which provided financial support for the study.

a second Delta Program aimed at maintaining and improving water safety and freshwater availability, establish a Delta fund to provide the necessary resources for implementing the second Delta Program and appoint a Delta Commissioner to supervise the program's implementation. The Committee has contributed much to the awareness of the potential impact of climate change on Dutch water management and the Dutch Cabinet accepted all the main recommendations. The report was also warmly accepted in the media and by politics. Unlike the closure of the Zuiderzee after the 1916 sea flood, the first Delta Program, which was drafted after the dramatic storm surge of 1953 (Meijerink 2005), and the new 'Room for the Rivers' policy issued after the 1993 and 1995 (near) river floods in the Rhine and Meuse rivers (Meijerink 2005, Roth, Warner, and Winnubst 2006), the Second Delta Committee did not draft its advice in the aftermath of a disaster. There had been no flooding when the committee was installed or when it presented its report. The committee itself is aware of the rather unusual circumstances in which it had to issue recommendations: "Our Committee's mandate is therefore unusual: we have been asked to come up with recommendations, not because a disaster has occurred, but rather to avoid one" (Veerman 2008: 7). For this case, this raises the question how the agent managed to be successful in framing perceptions and influencing the public agenda and changing governmental policies in the absence of a shock event, which would have clearly demonstrated a need for change in governmental policies. I set out the hypothesis that the committee's success is attributable to its behavior as a policy entrepreneur, its strong coherent policy frame and its use of specific connective framing strategies.

The core of our methodology is a discourse analysis of the report of the committee and media communications, such as the press release and a short video that supports the report. In addition, we looked at other newspaper articles on the committee and selected newspaper articles containing the Dutch word "*deltacommissie*" from LexisNet (a digital database for Dutch newspapers). These were articles published after the presentation of the report in September 2008. We checked these articles to see whether the report was being accepted or not. It would take at least a ten years' time period to make a full assessment on the degree of policy change or change (Birkland 2004, Sabatier 2007), so we were only able to make a preliminary assessment of the impact of the committee. It will be shown that the committee used various framing strategies[2] to develop and communicate a coherent and powerful problem frame and that the committee's recommendations were nurtured by the fear of future flooding and in a broader perspective the danger of climate change as a whole.

---

2   Next to framing strategies, other types of strategies are also possible to study. Strategies like networking, coalition building, venue exploitation, et cetera.

Policy Entrepreneurs and Framing

Policy Entrepreneurs

A policy entrepreneur is an actor who advocates and seeks to change policy by exploiting opportunities and employing strategies (Kingdon 1984, 2002). Policy entrepreneurs have several characteristics in common. First, a policy entrepreneur is an advocate for policy proposals or ideas (Kingdon 1984, 2002, Mintrom and Norman 2009, Roberts and King 1991). Second, a policy entrepreneur is involved throughout the policy change process and tries to have influence on every part of that process, or the policy entrepreneur has a well-chosen focus (mostly in the agenda setting stage of the policy process) (Kingdon 1984, 2002, Mintrom and Norman 2009, Roberts and King 1991). Third, a policy entrepreneur has certain skills and knowledge on when to intervene and risk failure which involves seizing moments to promote change (Kingdon 1984, 2002). Fourth, a policy entrepreneur exhibits a significant amount of perseverance during his or her career (Huitema and Meijerink 2007, 2010, Kingdon 1984, 2002, Meijerink and Huitema 2010). Fifth, a policy entrepreneur can best be identified by his actions and not by the position he holds (Kingdon 1984, 2002, Mintrom and Vergari 1996). We will regard the undertaking of actions as the employing of strategies. Although policy entrepreneurs have received a lot of attention in political and social sciences over the past decades, there is a limited understanding of the strategies that change agents employ in their efforts to pursue policy change (Brouwer et al. 2009; Roberts and King 1991). Mintrom and others (Mintrom 2000, Mintrom and Norman 2009, Mintrom and Vergari 1996) state that there is need for further study on the conceptual and empirical relationship between policy entrepreneurs and policy change. I regard strategies as the link between policy entrepreneurs and policy change and therefore choose to focus on these.

In this chapter I view policy entrepreneurs as actors who advocate and seek to change policy by exploiting opportunities and employing strategies. Although in literature the policy entrepreneur is mostly regarded as an individual, I will choose otherwise. In this approach we will regard the Second Delta Committee as one actor, consisting of a group of individuals. Now we are able to study the actions of the Delta Committee as such, but not the actions of every individual Committee member. Although future study may focus on the function of the Delta Committee as a venue for promoting (individual) policy ideas. Nevertheless, the Second Delta Committee as one actor meets the description of a policy entrepreneur at various points. The committee is an actor that advocates new policy proposals, is involved in the agenda setting stage of the policy process and tries to raise public, policy and political attention. Also, it at least seemed to choose the right moment to present the report and employs strategies to raise attention and set the agenda for policy change. The close reader will notice that we skipped the fourth characteristic of a policy entrepreneur. This is because the committee was founded out 'of nothing' by the state in 2007 and relieved from its task after presenting the report one year later. As mentioned, we would need another approach if we want to know whether individual committee members exploited the committee as a venue to push forward their own career or interest and ideas.

Framing Strategies

We define 'framing strategies' as strategies aimed at managing perceptions and creating awareness and possible support for a particular presented frame. Presenting a frame in a certain way can create awareness, recognition, acknowledgement and support. Therefore, change agents try to connect or link issues or topics that are part of the problem or solution and fit them within their frame. Hence, frames are organizational principles that transform fragmentary information into a structured and meaningful whole that "(..) governs the subjective meaning we assign to social events" (Goffman cited in Fischer 2003: 144). Schön and Rein point to the way in which public policies rest on frames that supply them with underlying structures of beliefs, perception and appreciation (Schön and Rein 1995). In their view, therefore, a frame is understood as a normative-prescriptive story that sets out a problematic policy problem and a course of action to be taken to address the problematic situation. It provides conceptual coherence, a direction for action, a basis for persuasion and a framework for collecting and analyzing data – that is, order, action, rhetoric and analysis. Frames also determine what actors consider the facts to be and how these lead to normative prescriptions for action. According to Entman, frames "*define problems* – determine what a causal agent is doing with what costs and benefits, usually measured in terms of common cultural values; *diagnose causes* – identify the forces creating the problem; *make moral judgments* – evaluate causal agents and their effects; and *suggest remedies* – offer and justify treatments for the problems and predict their likely effects" (Entman 1993). Thus, frames help to define problems, state a diagnosis, pass judgment and reach a conclusion in a specific social context (Fischer 2003: 144).

The Use of Narratives and Storylines

Stone (2002) distinguishes two types of policy narratives or stories. The first focuses on the story of 'decline or crisis'. The second addresses human helplessness and the need for 'social control'. In the first type, things are getting worse while in the second, that which has previously seemed to be a matter of fate or accident is now portrayed as an issue for change through political or policy action (Stone 2002, Stone in Fischer 2003). Creating alternative and new stories or storylines, which in fact are still linguistic constructions, help to convince an audience of the necessity of political action or policy measurements. Or, as Fischer (2003: 169) says, stories "help to identify both the responsible culprits and the virtuous saviors capable of leading us to high ground", and a storyline is "a generative sort of narrative that allow actors to draw upon various discursive categories to give meaning to specific or social phenomena" (Hajer 1995: 56 in Fischer 2003: 86).

The primary function of narratives and storylines is that these suggest a unity on which people can rely. One can voice narratives and storylines through the use of rhetoric, symbols and artifacts and crisis exploitation. These strategies, which we discuss in the next sections, help to spread the policy frame in an appealing way and to raise support.

The Use of Rhetoric

Rhetoric is the art of persuading, influencing or pleasing people through the use of spoken or written speech. As such, rhetoric consists of structuring and presenting the arguments made. The arena in which rhetoric is used most obviously is political debate. There, it can be important in forging or disrupting (political) coalitions. Rhetoric used by politicians can resemble political manipulation, which has negative connotations. But, in itself, the art of rhetoric is a way of telling your story or making your point, regardless of any moral judgment. You could say that it depends on the verity of the content, the reliability of the storyteller and on his intended objective, whether or not the rhetorical strategies are used to inform and persuade, or deceive and manipulate. Howarth (2009) describes rhetoric as follows: "[P]oliticians use a variety of strategic devices to bring about favorable outcomes. (.) [I]nventing new actions and political practices that circumvent existing ones; framing and reframing the evaluation of outcomes by others so that actors can improve their prospects of achieving goals; altering the perceptions and character of individual preferences by various rhetorical operations and interventions; and so on". Examples of rhetoric include metaphors (an implied comparison, understanding and experiencing one kind of thing in terms of another, which can also be made visual), trade-offs (any situation in which one thing must be decreased for another to be increased) or paradoxes (statements that appear contradictory or absurd, yet in fact may be true). As mentioned in the previous section, rhetoric can support narratives or storylines in spoken or written speech.

The Use of Symbols and Artifacts

Symbols and artifacts may be helpful in communicating and gaining support for a specific problem frame. A symbol can be defined as anything that stands for something else. A symbol's meaning is not intrinsic: meaning is invested in a symbol by those who use it – its meaning is created collectively. An important feature of symbols is their potential ambiguity because they can refer to more than one thing at the same time. Or as Yanow (1996: 9) says: "The power of symbols lies in their potential to accommodate multiple meanings. Different individuals, different groups, may interpret the same symbol differently". Symbols unite those who share the meaning and create distance from those who do not. Artifacts are physical objects that represent a frame or (problem) perception by a specific group. They are recognized by both supporters and opponents.

Exploiting Crises and Focusing Events

Crises or focusing events are one of the most successful opportunities for advancing policy ideas. Crises are "events or developments widely perceived by members of relevant communities to constitute urgent threats to core community values and structures" (Boin et al. 2009: 83-4). A focusing event is "an event that is sudden, relatively rare, can be reasonably defined as harmful or revealing the possibility of potentially greater future harms, inflicts harms or suggests potential harms that are or could be concentrated on a definable geographical area or community of interest and that is known to policy makers and the public virtually simultaneously" (Birkland 1997, cited in Birkland 2004: 181). A crisis or focusing event can create or trigger a 'window of opportunity' by dramatically highlighting policy failures (to which government or other institution might respond) and provide opportunities for policy learning or for issues to gain attention and move up the agenda (Boin et al. 2009, Kingdon 1984, 2002). This opening of windows creates an opportunity for change agents to link problems and solutions and to advance new policy plans. Change agents that seek change try to exploit the opening of a window and stimulate institutional attention for an issue when no other actors are exploiting the event to raise attention. Foreseeing the opening of windows of opportunities can play a crucial role in changing policy because focusing events can only create opportunities when the timing is right.

As stated in the introduction, the Second Delta Committee was not commissioned in response to a crisis or focusing event, but in anticipation of that. And this is different in regard to most literature on crises exploitation. We will therefore additionally need to see how the committee tried to create awareness in the absence of a recent crisis, focusing event or window of opportunity. We expect that the frame itself and the framing strategies, like telling narratives and storylines, the use of rhetoric, the use of symbols and artifacts and the exploiting of crises and focusing events, helped by to manage public, policy and political perceptions.

Case Study of the Second Delta Committee

Below we will discuss and analyze the different types of framing that are employed by the committee.

Adherence to the Climate Adaptation Narrative

According to the committee: "The Netherlands delta is safe, but preserving this safety over the long term involves action now" (Deltacommissie 2008b). We call this story, to which the committee adheres and contributes, the "climate adaptation narrative". There is a stream of research and literature emerging on the need for adaptation to climate change, from the global to the local (Driessen, Leroy and

Van Vierssen 2010, Gupta et al. 2010, Termeer, Meijerink and Nooteboom 2009). The logic is that the climate is undeniably changing and that we should adapt to these changes. "Climate change is now forcing itself upon us: a new reality that cannot be ignored" (Veerman 2008: 5). Even if the international community were to meet the goals set down in the Kyoto Protocol and its successors, and even if greenhouse gas emissions worldwide were to be cut drastically tomorrow, global warming would continue for centuries (Veerman 2008: 45). "The predicted sea level rise and greater fluctuations in river discharge compel us to look far into the future, to widen our scope and to anticipate developments further ahead" (Veerman 2008: 5). In the committee's view, the best opportunity for both people and nature to stay abreast of changing conditions involves working with natural processes, and building with nature, where possible: "The best long-term strategy to keep the Netherlands safe and a pleasant place to live is to develop along with the changing climate. Moving with and utilizing the natural processes where possible leads to solutions that allow humans and nature to adapt gradually. This further affords better opportunities for combined, multifunctional solutions for functions such as constructing infrastructure, reserving land for housing and business parks, using land for agriculture, recreation and nature" (Veerman 2008: 5, Veerman 2008: 45, 88).

By using the climate adaption narrative as its starting point, the committee succeeded in raising awareness for their problem definition and solutions. This story unites the Netherlands and the global community, because climate change is evident both globally and locally. The strength is that the story is presented as if it cannot be denied and that we, therefore, need to take action.

Using the Story of our Delta Identity

The proposed measures for adapting to climate change are backed by a relatively implicit story of the historical legitimacy of our delta identity. Throughout the report, the Delta itself, with its dikes, dams, mounds, sluices and pumping stations are the symbols and artifacts of which the Dutch are told to be proud, because they defend us against water and show that we have been able to 'live, work, invest and recreate' in a once vulnerable delta, for centuries. Our entire delta system, which is said to be the safest in the world, is presented as a success story, a symbol of which we can be proud, and which sets us apart from other countries: "One cannot conceive of the Netherlands without water. Through the centuries, and still today, the inhabitants of our delta have made great efforts to struggle from the grasp of the rivers and the sea, and it is this that sets our country apart" (Veerman 2008: 5). At the same time, this symbol of our Delta is used to remind us that we also depend on it. In some sense, the committee is trying to communicate a double message. On the one hand there is no reason for panic but on the other we should feel the urgency of taking action. The dike, as a symbol of our defense, is used to tell us these two messages: the dike is safe (as are we), but not safe enough. This corresponds with Stone's descriptions of the 'story of social control' and the 'story of decline and crisis'.

The 'story of social control' is that we have always been able, in our interaction with water, to ensure the country is a safe place to live: "In our interaction with the water, we, the country's residents, can ourselves shape the Netherlands of the future – just as our forefathers have always done throughout the centuries" (Veerman 2008: 97). Based on our long tradition and experience with living in a Delta, we manage. Since we "master the long-term challenge of keeping the Netherlands a safe, attractive country" (Veerman 2008: 97), we are able to "keep the Netherlands a prosperous, safe country with sufficient clean water for humans and livestock: we have the time, the knowledge and the means" (Veerman 2008:37). So, even though the undeniable force of climate change is upon, it may also offer us new prospects, chances and opportunities. If we cleverly combine multiple functions, such as water safety, energy production and nature development, we will be able to strengthen our defense system, create new energy, and create new forms of nature. The committee wants us to have this mentality of control and future prosperity: "It is for an attitude like this that the Committee is pleading; let everybody dare to form a clear picture of what we can expect and think ahead to the way we can cope with these challenges. Even better: how can future opportunities be created?" (Veerman 2008: 37). Like our forefathers, with their challenging creations (such as the world-famous Eastern Scheldt storm surge barrier), we will be able to secure the Netherlands, create new space for living and, in addition, put the Dutch on the map again. The committee hopes to open the door for engineering enterprises and energy production companies to showcase their innovative products and solutions and at the same time boost the Netherlands' image and economy.

The committee also tells a 'story of decline and crisis' alongside its story of control. The historical disasters in 1916 and 1953 help us to remember that taking good care of our water defense system remains our responsibility: "The disastrous floods of 1953 are still etched into our collective memory" (Veerman 2008: 7). The Netherlands is home to a rich natural environment and has a wealth of history and culture that we must not run the risk of losing (Veerman 2008: 46). In the committee's 18-minute video that supports the report (Deltacommissie 2008a), this story of decline is promoted and backed up with an explicit use of symbols and artifacts. The film recalls and frames the flooding in 1953 to warn us of the threats of climate (change). The film includes original black and white footage of the flooding with ominous background sounds. Next, the voiceover moves directly to the measures taken by the Dutch government to prevent that flooding from happening again. At the same time, the images smoothly change from black and white into color images. Then, the video switches to the present day and informs us about today's global warming and climate change. The (near) river floods in 1993 and 1995 in some parts of the Netherlands are recalled to link climate change and the current threat of flooding. While showing the high level of water next to the dikes at that time, the voiceover says: "Fortunately it didn't come to a catastrophe, but the message was clear [silent for 2 seconds]". Then, the film quickly moves to the commissioning of the Second Delta Committee in 2007. The remainder of the film is devoted to explaining the committee's 'frame'. This is also backed up with images of the storm in 2005 in New Orleans. The voice over tells us: "If we don't anticipate the future, if we do nothing, floods *just like this one* [emphasizing voice], could also hit the Netherlands, causing enormous damage and suffering and years of disruption of our society". Then, a map is shown of the Netherlands with potential flooding impact if we were to do nothing. It explains and shows all the critical problems this will cause. The next step is to tell us that water also offers significant opportunities, before moving on to the recommendations the committee deems necessary. The video ends by repeating the committee's main objective: "How can we create the conditions that will make this country an attractive place to live, work, invest and recreate, for many generations to come? As far as this committee is concerned, we can start realizing those conditions, today".

We see that the use of symbols and artifacts, in this specific order, support the story and image of our delta system that is under threat. The disasters, examples, footage, the 'facts' of climate change, ominous sounds and the warning pictures serve to make us aware of the urgency and necessity of taking action. The committee aims for us to accept this frame by using a certain climate change and threat rhetoric, vocabulary, argumentation and language, to convince people that we should turn the tide of this 'story of decline and crisis'. On the other hand, in the last few seconds of the video, we see that the committee wants to close with a positive message of 'control'. There we see, as the quotation above shows, that the committee wants to assure us that we have the means available to make this country an attractive place to live work, invest, and recreate for many generations to come.

This story of our delta identity has been what binds us together in the Netherlands throughout the centuries. Apart from the crisis anticipation, we *are* able to exert control. History has shown that we need to adapt and have always been able to do so. The strength of the committee's framing is that it was able, both in the report and in the video, to support this compelling story. The delta becomes part of our own identity. We all live in this delta and we all share the same identity: "The sea and the rivers have shaped our identity and the country itself: its nature and landscape, its prosperity and economy, and the way it is governed (water boards; the polder model)" (Veerman 2008: 5). If we want to uphold our identity we cannot lose our delta system to climate change. The delta symbolizes our identity. It is as if the committee is saying that no self-appreciating nation or human being would want to lose grip of its identity and that we therefore need to join forces to keep the spirit of our delta identity alive: at least over the coming decennia, but preferably throughout the coming centuries. The committee's own recommendations are presented as 'the logical next step' in our history of living with water. We should embrace the urgent challenges we face in the future collectively.

Creating a Sense of Urgency and Collectiveness

The title of the Press Release was indicative of one of the main conclusions that the committee wants to communicate: "Wide ranging intervention for water security urgent: Decisiveness and investment needed" (Deltacommissie 2008b). At the moment, the Netherlands is, according to the committee, unprepared for climate change because, "the flood risk will increase and the freshwater supply will come under pressure if no extra measures are taken" (Veerman 2008: 29). The committee seems to know very well that, in order to press forward, immense measures with huge costs in times of financial crises and a sense of urgency are needed. Therefore the committee keeps reminding us that the Netherlands faces an urgent, but not acute, threat: "For us, the Second Delta Committee, the threat is not acute, but our mandate is nevertheless urgent. There is absolutely no reason for panic, but we must be concerned for the future" (Veerman 2008:5). This is included in the report several times (Veerman 2008: 10, 23).

In the report, we see that the committee chose the worst case scenario caused by climate change (including full societal damage and dislocation) by taking the highest-end calculation concerning temperature and sea level rise in the future as the basis for its policy recommendations. However, by taking all climate change as a driving force for the problems the Netherlands as a whole faces in the future, the committee has broadened its assignments and, accordingly, their recommendations. The committee was appointed by the Cabinet as a Committee of the State, called the Sustainable Coastal Development Committee. Its mandate was to formulate a vision of the long-term protection of the Dutch coast, not the Netherlands as a whole. In the report we see that the committee does take a broad view of the coast and proposes an integral approach for the Netherlands as a whole:

> "The Committee takes a broad view of the coast: it includes the sea and the coastal zone as well as the low-lying hinterland, the interaction with the rivers and the IJsselmeer lake, and the cross-border aspects of the rivers and the coastal zone. This broad interpretation is necessary because, to a great extent, the system forms a single hydrological, ecological and economic entity" (Veerman 2008: 17).

By broadening the scope, and viewing the challenges the Netherlands faces as a whole, the committee succeeds in making the report and the task at hand a matter of national interest and of utmost priority[3].

---

3   One of the interesting choices made by the committee was to use the word "Delta", which seems in the Netherlands to be becoming synonymous with matters of "national interest and urgency". We saw the word "Delta" being used in other policy domains as well (Doorduyn and Herderscheê 2008).

Creating a Crisis Narrative

In the introduction, we stated that, prior to the commissioning of the Second Delta Committee, there had been no disaster, which made it additionally tough to create the sense of urgency and collectivity required for such drastic measures to adapt to climate change. The committee is well aware of this and says the following:

> The Committee realizes that its message is a difficult one: after a disaster, there tends to be a widespread feeling of urgency, that something must be done to prevent a repetition of events. … The general public takes it for granted that government guarantees its protection against flooding, but the public does not see the matter as urgent, or of high political priority. The people of the Netherlands are not apprehensive of a natural catastrophe; the risks of climate change are only gradually becoming manifest and there is a general feeling that effects will only be felt in the distant future (Veerman 2008: 77).

Therefore, the committee exploits several crises and focusing events to create its own crisis narrative. First, it recalls a number of historical examples. Second, recent examples elsewhere are named. Third, it points out possible future disasters due to current climate change trends.

Historical examples   To create a sense of urgency and urge people to take action, the committee tries to recall past focusing events. The floods in 1916 (Zuiderzee) and 1953 (southwest Delta) are recalled to show the impact of such flooding. The floods are also recalled to highlight the positive influence the measures had in response to those events. The 1916 and 1953 floods led to radical policy measures to shorten the coastline: construction of the Afsluitdijk (the IJsselmeer's sealing dam) and the Delta Works. Nowadays, the Wadden Sea and the Western Scheldt are the only two natural systems that remain open to the influence of currents, tides and waves. Implementing these measures, which were multifunctional and integral, provided major benefits for the freshwater supply (via the IJsselmeer), agriculture (vast tracts of new land) and flood protection (up to and including Amsterdam). The committee continues that the measures also resulted in the islands in Zeeland being connected to the mainland and each other and to the development of recreation, water sports and nature reserves (Veerman 2008: 47).

Recent examples   Apart from recalling historic focusing events, we see in the report that the committee also makes a connection to recent disasters around the globe. Although it is almost 5,000 miles away from the Netherlands, New Orleans is mentioned as a focusing example of climate change worldwide and how that lower delta region was unprepared for climate change (Veerman 2008: 22). In 2005, hurricane Katrina caused a tropical storm to which at least 1.464 people lost their lives in the actual hurricane and in the subsequent floods (Anonymous 2010b). The Delta Committee focuses on the severe economic damage this hurricane caused. Prior to the hurricane Katrina disaster, potential damage in New Orleans was estimated at US\$ 16.8 billion. Following the disaster, direct damage to dwellings, government buildings and public infrastructure alone was estimated at US\$ 27 billion (Veerman 2008: 22).

Future disasters   After recalling historical and recent disasters in its report, the committee moves on to the possible harm caused by flooding and climate change in the future. They state, for instance, that an estimated 65 per cent of national wealth is located in flood-prone areas, so that the wealth potentially under threat is in the order of EUR 1,800 billion. This gives an impression of the capital that needs to be insured against flood risk (Veerman 2008: 22). We are warned that future flooding in the Netherlands could result in more severe damage than past and recent disasters.

In this regard, it is important to emphasize that the committee exploits potential disasters as a means of introducing a combination of measurements that need to be implemented in the Netherlands. The fundamental premise also adheres to the risk management approach that the first Delta Committee raised, whereby flood risks are managed by a combination of measures that reduce the *probability* (such as high and strong flood defenses) and those that limit the *consequences* (such as regulating spatial planning, or zoning, compartmentalization, early warning, crisis management and contingency planning). The committee states that the combination of measures is adjusted to the nature of the potential disaster and the characteristics of the relevant dike-enclosed area (Veerman 2008: 41, 42).

We see that, by exploiting historical and recent crises and anticipating future disasters, the committee succeeds in creating a sense of urgency and collectiveness.

The absence of a framing contest   What is remarkable about the dissemination of the committee's report in politics and the media is that it was accepted warmly (Anonymous 2008). In newspapers we found discussions about the scenario of the sea level rise that the committee uses in telling the story of climate change. Some skeptics claim that the committee exaggerated the numbers and purposefully neglected the uncertainties that surround predictions about climate change (Hazeleger 2008, Huisman 2008). However, these discussions were instigated and led by academics and not so much by politicians or civilians (Warner 2008, Warner and Vink 2008). An aspect that elicited greater opposition was the financing of the Delta Program by the Delta Fund, but not so much whether a Delta Program was really necessary (Anonymous 2008b). In addition, there was some critique about the need to improve the safety level for all dike-enclosed areas by a factor of at least 10 (Anonymous 2008a). Furthermore, some warned that the committee's focus was too much on preventive measurements instead of on consequence-reduction measures or crisis management (Warner and Vink 2008). However, apart from these 'minor' points, we saw that, in terms of the 'frame' the committee presented, the problem definition, diagnosed causes, moral judgments and suggested remedies were (in general) accepted relatively easily and quickly (Anonymous 2008a).

The Prime Minister at the time said: "The government takes on the challenge"[4], after which he announced the establishment of a Delta Act and Delta Fund: "If we take on the challenge wisely, the Netherlands will emerge from this fight stronger against water (…). [The report] forces us to face facts about what must be done in the Netherlands to maintain water safety". The Secretary of State for Transport and Public Works agreed with the message the committee presented: ''We are from after the flood. Therefore, we must take action now and not wait for the next disaster. Let 2008 go down in history as the year in which the future of this low country was placed high on the agenda". The opposition in the lower chamber also accepted the policy frame of the committee. In contrast, we saw no opposing coalition of actors trying to raise attention for an alternative frame. The only recommendation by the committee that elicited practical discussion concerned raising the water level of the IJsselmeer due to the immense impact this would have on the region and surrounding municipalities (Schreuder 2008). It is possible, therefore, that once the implications of the policy advice become clear to the public with the implementation of the Delta Program that the public will join forces and oppose.

Conclusion

The agent in our case was very successful in framing the climate change issue in such a way that it was possible for the committee to connect climate change to all different kinds of more or less related issues such as the collective history and relationship with water in the Netherlands. However, the frame itself was very strong and one-dimensionally based on the assumption that climate changes and that we need to adapt to these changes in the way we manage our water system. This message stood out strong and was taken over by the media, the public and politics. Opposing frames were not put forward or considered. How can this be explained and does this then mean that connective capacity was not practiced? No: connective capacity was practiced but not for the reason to be connective and relate to other actors in an equal and horizontal manner but to create support and make the committee's frame and climate adaption narrative dominant in water governance policies.

We conclude that the Delta Committee, by employing the discussed framing strategies in the absence of an actual crises or focusing event, succeeded in doing two things. First, the committee managed to create awareness, set the agenda for climate change adaptation and the issue of safety in Dutch water management and to certain degree have its recommendations translated into policy programs by employing connective framing strategies. Second, the committee managed to a large extent to get the media, the public and politics to accept their frame and framing of the problems, causes, moral judgments and suggested remedies because it was presented as a strongly one-dimensionally focused frame. Therefore, as I

---

4   All these quotes are my own translations from Anonymous (2008a).

conclude below, a strong policy frame can benefit from connective capacity as long as the strategies are used in a connective way to support the main frame.

In our discussed case we found that climate change became a topic of discussion due to connective framing strategies and elicited a great deal of media attention even though no actual flooding occurred. We saw that all the framing strategies were closely related and used in an integrated and intertwined matter. Narratives, symbols, rhetoric and crises were used in cooperation to adhere to the climate adaption narrative, to build on the story of our delta identity, to create a sense of urgency and collectiveness and to create a crisis narrative due to the absence of a concrete crisis event. The committee obviously sought for an integral, adaptive and flexible approach given their responsiveness to economic welfare, tourism, nature, ecology, landscape and culture. The facts, examples, figures and images were all presented in such a way to strengthen the committee's main assumption and frame that climate change is a pressing issue to which we need to adapt. This resulted in a coherent frame in which water safety and climate change had the highest priority as a matter of national interest that should be protected, at arm's length, against daily politics. This appealed policy makers and politicians, making it easy to have the committee's recommendations being translated into policy plans quite fast. There was significant consensus between all parties that there is urgency for joining forces, taking action and 'working together with water'. This shows that the committee offered enough focal points in its report for policy makers to relate to. This has also been, as I see it, the connective capacity and strength of the committee's framing because it offered the opportunity for other actors to relate to, even though the conclusion, 'climate adaption in water management is needed', would be the same for all actors and in all situations and could not be meddled with.

Apart from this, far more than the report of the Second Delta Committee does, the Delta policy Program connects actors and instruments. This might be explained by the differences in goals; the Second Delta Committee's Report was aimed at raising attention and getting agenda status for a single issue, while the Delta Program needed to be implementable for various actors involved in the implementation process. For our notion of connective capacity in regard to water governance, I therefore conclude that 'connective capacity' is essentially an organizing principle, while in this chapter we focused on the process of agenda setting prior to that. So, to set ground for a policy program that breathes connective capacity, it is needed to set the agenda first by advancing a strong coherent policy frame that needs to become dominant. Later, when ready for translation to policy and implementation, a governance perspective for connective capacity, connecting all actors and instruments involved, can be strived for.

Bibliography

Anonymous. 2008a. Positieve reacties op Deltaplan II Retrieved 2010-11-09, from http://nos.nl/artikel/76399-positieve-reacties-op-deltaplan-ii.html.

Anonymous. 2008b. Nieuwe Deltawerken; Commentaar, *NRC Handelsblad*, 4 September.

Anonymous. 2008c. Niets doen maakt 't straks nog veel duurder. *Het Parool:* 7.

Anonymous. 2010a. Factsheet Room for the River; a safer and more attractive rivers region Retrieved 2010-11-08, from http://www.ruimtevoorderivier.nl/media/19174/factsheet_uk.pdf.

Anonymous. 2010b. Reports of Missing and Deceased; August 2, 2006 Retrieved 2010-10-30, from http://www.dhh.louisiana.gov/offices/page.asp?ID=192&Detail=5248.

Baumgartner, F. and Jones, B. 1993. *Agendas and Instability in American Politics*: Chicago, IL: University of Chicago Press.

Birkland, T. 2004. "The World Changed Today": Agenda-Setting and Policy Change in the Wake of the September 11 Terrorist Attacks. *Review of Policy Research*, 21(2), 179-200.

Boin, A., t Hart, P. and McConnell, A. 2009. Crisis exploitation: Political and policy impacts of framing contests. *Journal of European Public Policy*, 16(1), 81-106.

Brouwer, S., Huitema, D. and Bierman, F. 2009. *Towards Adaptive Management: The Strategies of Policy Entrepreneurs to Direct Policy Change*. Paper presented at the Amsterdam Conference on the Human Dimensions of Global Environmental Change, Amsterdam. http://www.earthsystemgovernance.org/ac2009/papers/AC2009-0365.pdf.

Deltacommissie. 2008a. Film that supports the recommendations of the Delta Commision, from http://www.deltacommissie.com/en/film.

Deltacommissie. 2008b. Press Release: Delta Committee: Working with water. Retrieved from http://www.deltacommissie.com/doc/pressrelease_080903.pdf.

Doorduyn, Y. and Herderscheê, G. 2008. Tweede Kamer stort zich op 'de jeugd'; Rapportage over jeugdproblematiek als 'bom onder de samenleving' heeft Den Haag wakker geschud, *de Volkskrant*, 15 September, 3.

Driessen, P., Leroy, P. and Van Vierssen, W. 2010. *From Climate Change to Social Change. Perspectives on Science-Policy Interactions*. Zeist: International Books.

Entman, R. 1993. Framing: Toward clarification of a fractured paradigm. *Journal of Communication*, 43(4), 51-8.

Fischer, F. 2003. *Reframing Public Policy: Discursive Politics and Deliberative Practices*: Oxford University Press, USA.

Gupta, J., Termeer, C., Klostermann, J., Meijerink, S., van den Brink, M., Jong, P. and Bergsma, E. 2010. The Adaptive Capacity Wheel: A method to assess the inherent characteristics of institutions to enable the adaptive capacity of society. *Environmental Science & Policy*, 13(6), 459-71. doi: DOI: 10.1016/j.envsci.2010.05.006.

Hajer, M. 1995. *The Politics of Environmental Discourse: Ecological Modernization and the Policy Process*: Oxford University Press, USA.

Hazeleger, W. 2008. Zoveel haast is niet nodig bij kustverdediging; Een zeespiegelstijging van 1,30 meter in komende eeuw komt alleen voor in het zwartste scenario, *NRC Handelsblad*, 11 December.

Howarth, D. 2009. Power, discourse, and policy: Articulating a hegemony approach to critical policy studies. *Critical Policy Studies*, 3(3), 309-35.

Huisman, J. 2008. De zeespiegel stijgt, maar niet zó hard; Berekening Veerman is dubieus, *NRC Handelsblad*, 8 September.

Huitema, D. and Meijerink, S. 2010. Realizing water transitions: The role of policy entrepreneurs in water policy change. *Ecology and Society*, 15(2), 26.

Huitema, D. and Meijerink, S. (eds). 2009. *Water Policy Entrepreneurs: A Research Companion to Water Transitions around the Globe*. Cheltenham: Edward Elgar.

Kingdon, J. 1984. *Agendas, Alternatives, and Public Policies*: Little, Brown and Company.

Kingdon, J. 2002. *Agendas, Alternatives, and Public Policies (Longman Classics Edition)*. New York: Longman.

Meijerink, S. 2005. Understanding policy stability and change: The interplay of advocacy coalitions and epistemic communities, windows of opportunity, and Dutch coastal flooding policy 1945-20031. *Journal of European Public Policy*, 12(6), 1060-77.

Meijerink, S. 2008. Explaining continuity and change in international policies: Issue linkage, venue change, and learning on policies for the river Scheldt estuary 1967-2005. *Environment and Planning A*, 40(4), 848-66.

Meijerink, S. and Huitema, D. 2010. Water transitions, policy entrepreneurs and change strategies: Lessons learned *Water Policy Entrepreneurs: A Research Companion to Water Transitions Around the Globe*. Cheltenham: Edward Elgar Publishing.

Mintrom, M. 2000. *Policy Entrepreneurs and School Choice*: Washington, DC: Georgetown University Press.

Mintrom, M. and Norman, P. 2009. Policy Entrepreneurship and Policy Change. *Policy Studies Journal*, 37(4), 649-67.

Mintrom, M. and Vergari, S. 1996. Advocacy coalitions, policy entrepreneurs, and policy change. *Policy Studies Journal*, 24(3), 420-34.

Pahl-Wostl, C. 2007. Transitions towards adaptive management of water facing climate and global change. *Water Resources Management*, 21(1), 49-62.

Pahl-Wostl, C., Craps, M., Dewulf, A., Mostert, E., Tabara, D. and Taillieu, T. 2007. Social learning and water resources management. *Ecology and Society*, 12(2), 5.

Roberts, N. and King, P. 1991. Policy entrepreneurs: Their activity structure and function in the policy process. *Journal of Public Administration Research and Theory: J-PART*, 1(2), 147-75.

Roth, D., Warner, J. and Winnubst, M. 2006. *Een noodverband tegen hoog water; Waterkennis, beleid en politiek rond noodoverloopgebieden*: Wageningen Universiteit en Researchcentrum.

Sabatier, P. 2007. *Theories of the Policy Process*. Colorado: Westview Press.

Schreuder, A. 2008. Plan met IJsselmeer wekt discussie; Deltacommissie krijgt alom bijval, maar niet in pittoreske Zuiderzees-tadjes, *NRC Handelsblad*, 4 September: 3.

Schön, D. and Rein, M. 1995. *Frame Reflection: Toward the Resolution of Intractable Policy Controversies*. New York: Basic Books.

Stone, D. 2002. *Policy Paradox: The Art of Political Decision Making*. New York: WW Norton.

Termeer, C., Meijerink, S. and Nooteboom, S. 2009. Klimaatneutrale of klimaatbestendige bestuurskunde? *Bestuurskunde*, 4, 2-16.

Veerman, C. 2008. *Working Together with Water; A Living Land Builds for its Future*.Verduijn, S.H., Meijerink, S.V. and Leroy, P. 2012. How the Second Delta Committee Set the Agenda for Climate Change Adaptation: A Dutch Case Study on Framing Strategies for Policy Change. *Water Alternatives*, 5(2), 469-84.

Warner, J. (2008-06-02). Kalm aan met die wateroorlog, *de Volkskrant*, 7.

Warner, J. and Vink, M. (2008-09-19). Leven met water is leven met risico: Verband temperatuur met stijging zeespiegel is nog erg onduidelijk, *Het Parool*, 30.

Waterschappen twijfelen aan nut peilverhoging IJsselmeer. (03-09-2008). *NRC Handelsblad*.

Yanow, D. 1996. *How does a Policy Mean?: Interpreting Policy and Organizational Actions*: Washington, DC: Georgetown University Press.

Chapter 12

Bridging Knowledge Frames and Networks in Climate and Water Governance

Art Dewulf, Marcela Brugnach, Catrien Termeer and Helen Ingram

Introduction

Addressing the challenge of water governance in view of climate change requires the best of available knowledge, sensible ways to deal with the inherent uncertainties, and, as we will argue in this chapter, bridging diverging knowledge frames and networks. The fate of diverse knowledge frames and networks in the climate domain is directly relevant for water governance – why investing in for example, hydropower or water storage capacity if climate change isn't much of a problem, as climate skeptic activists and political parties claim. In a field as knowledge-intensive as water and climate policy – without sophisticated models, climate change wouldn't even be recognized as an issue – a thorough understanding is needed of how knowledge is produced in networks, how knowledge links to conflicting perspectives or frames and how diverse ways of knowing can be bridged.

The type of connective capacity we address in this chapter focuses on connecting knowledge frames and, as we will argue, therefore also knowledge networks. By combining knowledge and frames into the concept of knowledge frames, we stress the point that frames embody particular kinds of knowledge and that knowledge implies a specific frame of reference about what is important and what not. The variety of different knowledge frames that different stakeholders bring with them cannot be reduced in a straightforward way (Brugnach et al. 2008). Adding more and more information is likely to increase ambiguity instead of reducing it. What is needed then is more and more varied cues and mechanisms that enable debate, clarification, and enactment more than simply provide large amounts of data in order to create meaning through discussion and joint interpretation (Dewulf et al. 2005b). The goal is to achieve frame connection (Dewulf et al. 2011) rather than frame integration, because complete integration would do away with the valuable differences and creative tension between frames. The connective capacity that focuses on knowledge frames can be carried by institutions and arrangements such as boundary organizations, but importantly also by instruments such as boundary objects and by the agency of individuals or groups through boundary experiences. In this chapter, we first outline a dynamic view on knowledge frames and networks, by connecting conceptual developments on knowledge creation, interactive framing, ways of knowing and configuration theory. Second, we identify key dimensions of frame diversity in the climate change debate, on the basis of a secondary analysis of a range of peer-reviewed empirical studies. Then, in our discussion, we elaborate on the connective capacity needed for bridging knowledge frames and networks and the potential of boundary organizations, objects and experiences.

Towards an Interactional Theory of Knowledge Frames and Networks

When knowledge is conceived of as an abstract body of statements, stripped of uncertainties and perspectives and inscribed into the brain of the rational actor, we cannot understand how knowledge is actually created, how scientific turf wars and policy controversies emerge and how multiple knowledge frames and networks could be connected. In this section, we connect different strands of literature, namely interactional framing theory (Dewulf et al. 2009), relational concepts of knowledge and uncertainty (Brugnach et al. 2008, Cook and Brown 1999), configuration theory (Termeer and Koppenjan 1997) and ways of knowing theory (Feldman et al. 2006, Van Buuren 2009), to construct a much more dynamic view on knowledge frames and networks. These theories are situated at the cross-roads between organization science and policy science and share a focus on interactive sensemaking (Weick 1995): how people produce knowledge in their interactions with issues, artifacts and each other.

The process by which decisions, policy issues or events acquire different meanings from different perspectives has been studied as *framing* (Benford and Snow 2000, Chong and Druckman 2007, Dewulf et al. 2009, Entman 1993, Schön and Rein 1994). By highlighting certain aspects of the situation at the expense of others, by drawing different boundaries around the issue and by putting different elements at the core of the issue, people from different backgrounds construct frames about the situation that may differ considerably from how others frame the issues. We use the term *knowledge frames* to indicate that knowledge implies a specific frame of reference about what is important and what not, and to indicate the links between how people understand their life world, what they know about it and how they relate to it (Brugnach et al. 2008).

Why would frames be important for climate and water governance, one might query? Shouldn't we focus rather on actions? To address this issue, it is important to point out that framing not only relates to action but is in itself a form of action in a specific context, for example, in a multilateral negotiation, in a press release, in a court plea or in a hallway conversation between a civil servant and the minister. Framing is an action with consequences for policy. Whoever is able to set the terms of the debate steers the debate in a certain direction and the framing of the questions fed into commissions or working groups bounds the range of resulting policy recommendations (Pielke 2007).

The shift in framing from 'global warming' to 'climate change' is a case in point. Global warming started as a scientific concept and did not immediately catch on or inspire action. Later, the term climate change was promoted by environmentalists as a more encompassing term and has become much more productive than its creators could have imagined. Climate change has become a breakthrough frame, a discursive bridge connecting all kinds of ideas and events that were not previously understood as connected" (Brick and Cawley 2008). Previously isolated phenomena like hurricanes, heat waves or floods acquired a new and coherent meaning in the light of climate change, linking "seemingly random events into a single interpretive schema" (Brick and Cawley 2008). This went together with an increasing expansion and diversification of the climate change research network, including more aspects and disciplines than were initially involved, and with wide ramifications for water governance.

We argue that theory development and further research on framing, knowledge and networks are needed to better inform policy debates (see also Boykoff et al. 2010, Scrase and Ockwell 2010). In order to move forward we need to better understand the nature of knowledge frames and how these are tied to networks.

The idea that knowledge is embedded in networks and practices is central to our argument. Wenger speaks of *knowing-in-practice* and argues that 'as a regime of competence every practice is in some sense a form of knowledge, and knowing is participating in that practice' (Wenger 1998: 411). Knowledge as enacted in practice implies a strongly relational underpinning of knowledge, tied to specific communities. This kind of relational knowledge comes from connecting, leads to further connecting and is reciprocal, not only because the parties involved know each other but also because it grows from interaction (Dewulf et al. 2005a). Related to this are two different conceptions of knowledge: 'knowledge-as-substance' and 'knowledge-as-participation' (Bouwen and Taillieu 2004). The knowledge-as-substance metaphor considers knowledge as substance or content that can be transferred from one mind to another mind. The knowledge-as-participation metaphor conceives knowledge as being formed and enacted in the interaction among different actors. Knowledge is situated in the coordinated actions among actors that engage in some form of collaboration.

Although framing is often associated with cognitive processing or individual mental models, the *interactional approach to framing* can contribute significantly to our understanding of how knowledge is created in interaction (Dewulf et al. 2009). An important difference between the two approaches to framing is that the cognitive approach considers frames to be representations stored in memory (and framing is the process of applying cognitive frames to situations), while the interactional approach considers framing to be the dynamic enactment and shaping of meaning in ongoing interactions (and frames are transient communication structures). In the cognitive approach, meaning is located 'between the ears' of each individual and ultimately depends on their private understandings and interpretations of information communicated and processed. In contrast, in interactional framing theory, meaning is located 'between the noses' of people and ultimately depends on their reactions to each other's communication.

Linking framing to knowledge emphasizes the point that knowledge implies perspectives (Dewulf et al. 2007). The presence of multiple knowledge frames can result in ambiguity (Brugnach et al. 2008), referring to the situation where there are different, and possibly conflicting, views about how to understand the system, resulting in conflicting knowledge (Van Buuren and Edelenbos 2004). It is important to note that these different knowledge frames may all be plausible and legitimate. Ways of understanding a system can differ on where to put the boundaries of the system or what and whom to put into the focus of attention. Multiple knowledge frames are linked to multiple networks of actors engaging in different practices, in which knowledge is created, enacted and transformed.

A similar way to conceptualize the relations between meaning, knowledge and action can be found in *ways of knowing* theory (Feldman et al. 2006, Lejano and Ingram 2008). This assemblage of heterogeneous elements and relationships constitute a response or understanding of a specific situation, problem or policy. Ways of knowing are dynamic networks of social "sensemaking" and are created through communication, discourse and relationships. Ways of knowing an issue, policy or problem are most often multiple even for a single individual. A way of knowing embeds a rationality that serves as a vehicle for making sense of reality. While rational self-interest has been the dominant paradigm adopted in policy analyses, this is only one way of knowing about a problem, and this way of knowing may or may not be relevant in particular issue situations. People have a large repertoire of cognitive and emotional tools beyond self-interested rationality such as authority, intuition, moral reasoning, direct experience, logic, belief or faith, mysticism, etc. that contribute to their capacity for comprehending a problem situation in multiple ways, rather than just as one stable, established way. Any one of these perceptual lenses may become more or less relevant through continuous discourse, engagement and learning. The ways of knowing approach implies that multiple rationalities are possible.

Knowing is a social process, and it is formed and molded by interacting with others in a specific, grounded situation. To understand disagreements, misalignments and tension in policy processes, insight is needed in the diverging ways of knowing from which these arise (Van Buuren 2009). The ways of knowing approach contrasts sharply with the cognitive approach to framing, because "WoKs constantly are in flux from the sheer interaction of objects (artifacts, reports, forums, etc.) in a policy space" (Lejano and Ingram 2008). The interactional approach of framing (Dewulf et al. 2009) is very compatible and complementary with the notion of ways of knowing.

As do interactional framing and ways of knowing theories, *configuration theory* (Termeer and Kessener 2007, Van Dongen et al. 1996) captures dynamics, but in addition provides also a way of conceptualizing how knowledge is bounded by networks. People are continuously in contact with other people. In interaction with each other, they negotiate the meaning they give to their surroundings: what is happening, what do we know about it, what do we think of it, what don't we know yet, what does that mean for our actions, which outcomes do we expect, and so forth. By constructing stories with others, actors make sense of themselves and others and of their actions. Besides shared meanings, in interactions, they also develop shared rules about who they include, to whom they assign power, how to deal with third parties and about what is allowed in their relationship. In processes of sensemaking, both realities and interaction rules are constructed.

A social-cognitive configuration is characterized by a group of people with an intensive interaction pattern, agreed-on interaction rules, and shared meanings (Termeer and Kessener 2007). Configurations arise because people not only develop shared meanings in interactions but also tend to get and remain in contact with people with similar meanings. It's a circular causal process in which a group of people (a social structure) produces content (a cognitive structure) and, vice versa, content produces a group. The social structure is both the precursor and the result of the cognitive structure. Configurations do not have to correspond to existing divisions such as organizations, departments or neighborhoods. Configurations are always a snapshot of a historical and ongoing process: they come into being, crystallize, fall apart or fuse together. Dynamics arise through the confrontation with other realities, people or interaction rules. At the same time, the process has the tendency to stagnate. Whenever people talk primarily with people who have similar realities and only assign meanings in those interactions, the configuration closes. The internal homogeneity increases and the external borders become more pronounced (Termeer and Kessener 2007).

Although configuration theory uses the concept of 'cognitive structure' to refer to the social construction of issues among a group of people, the label 'cognitive' captures the content aspect of the interaction, as opposed to the 'social' or relational aspect, and does not claim that content is hard-wired in people's mental structures. The emphasis on how interaction processes shape perspectives on a situation is very much in line with the interactional approach to framing. Groups of people that develop intensive interactions start framing issues in similar ways. The configuration theory idea that the interactional context is crucial for how people frame issues and that the same people might frame issues in different ways when they interact in other configurations, is much closer to the interactional approach to framing than to the cognitive approach, which is characterized by its emphasis on mental structures.

In sum, ways of knowing and configuration theory help to conceptualize change and stability in interactive framing. In these conceptualizations it is the pattern of interactions among people and objects in networks that provide continuity to how issues get framed – rather than invoking the individual mind as accounting for stability. If knowledge is as much action (a practice) as representation (a body of statements), then the ways it becomes embedded in frames, ways of knowing and configurations becomes important for both research and policy practice. A crucial challenge for present day water governance consist of dealing with climate change, a domain that has become somewhat controversial. Multiple ways of framing climate change did and do co-exist in parallel and partially overlapping networks or configurations, and have increasingly resulted in controversy.

Knowledge Frames and Networks in the Climate Debate

Making sense of climate is not a new activity. Throughout history people have developed knowledge about climate and attached specific meanings to the phenomenon (Hulme 2008a). During the late Middle Ages and early modern era in Europe, climate was associated with fear through the connection of extreme weather events with divine retribution or demonology, thereby framing climate as judgment. Adverse weather could both be an expression of God's will or the work of the devil or witchcraft – it seems likely that witches were on occasions burnt as scapegoats for climatic anomalies (Hulme 2008a). Disputes about whether the hand of God, the devil or witchcraft caused these anomalies were resolved by the religious elite. The weakening of this dominant way of framing climatic disaster was already in evidence by the late eighteenth century, when naturalistic explanations of climate competed with religious explanations. The current framing of climate is undoubtedly very different from this historical example, but the accompanying discourse of fear is similar (Hulme 2008a). The language used refers to "catastrophe chaos and havoc, and the tone is often urgent. It employs a quasi-religious register of doom, death, judgments, heaven and hell. It also uses language of acceleration, increase, intractability, irreversibility and momentum" (Retallack et al. 2007: 55, cited in Hulme 2008a). Interestingly the early identification of global warming through the work of Svante Arrhenius in the 1900s and Guy Callandar in the 1930s was not cast in these terms, but rather predominantly portrayed as benign or beneficial (Hulme 2008a). A salient aspect of the current ways of framing climate change is the human impact and the ensuing attempts at controlling climate change, changing the image from 'mankind surrendered to the elements or the gods' to 'mankind engineering the future climate' – quite literally so, if we consider the proponents of geo-engineering solutions to climate change.

The current framing of climate change is not unitary, however. In the next paragraphs we discuss three dimensions on which framings of climate change differ, their link with the involved knowledge networks, and their implications for water governance.

Framing Climate Change as an Emissions Issue Versus an Impacts Issue: Climate Neutrality or Climate Proofing?

A recurring discussion in climate science and policy is the one about mitigation versus adaptation (Biesbroek et al. 2009, Hulme 2008b, Pielke Jr 2004, Pielke et al. 2007, Termeer and Meijerink 2008). These strategies correspond to different ways of framing, what is problematic about climate change and involve different knowledge networks. From the point of view of mitigation, the problem is framed as human-induced climate change through greenhouse gas emissions. From the point of adaptation, the problem is framed as climate change impacts on vulnerable environments or social groups. These problem framings and action strategies can be seen as complementary. Some even claim that "for decades, the options available to deal with climate change have been clear: we can act to mitigate the future effects of climate change by addressing the factors that cause changes in climate, and we can adapt to changes in climate by addressing the factors that make society and the environment vulnerable to the effects of climate" (Pielke Jr. 2004). However, mitigation and adaptation have entertained a tense relation through their links with different sectors, policy arrangements, international bodies and scientific research communities.

The implications of framing climate change as an emissions problem versus an impacts problem are potentially far reaching. With climate change as an emissions problem, the solution is to reduce (or capture and sequester) greenhouse gas emissions. This turns the climate change problem largely into an energy problem, and points towards solutions such as reduced or more efficient energy use and more sustainable energy production. The concept of *climate neutrality* is linked to this, used to qualify activities that do not provoke a net increase in greenhouse gas emissions. At the global level, mitigation policy arrangements have been agreed upon in the Kyoto-protocol, including emission caps and emissions trade. The global dimension of climate change is thus put on the foreground. Even if very local interventions are framed as part of the solution (for example, using energy-saving light bulbs or not using a car for short distances), the locality of these interventions is basically irrelevant, because it doesn't matter where in the world emissions are produced or reduced. There is one global parameter for the problem, which provides clarity and seems to put all global citizens at the same level. Although effects in terms of reduced emissions can be achieved and measured in the short term, the crucial effects on climate change are only achievable and measurable on a long term time scale.

With climate change as an adaptation problem, the solution is to deal with climate impacts, especially in vulnerable environments and societies. Impacts such as changes in precipitation patterns, extreme weather events and sea level rise turn the climate change problem to a large extent into a water governance problem. This emphasis is somewhat less pronounced than in the case of mitigation as an energy problem, because of the multiple and regionally differentiated climate impacts on for example, water, agriculture or biodiversity. The concept of *climate proofing* becomes the crucial one here – are environments, societies and human activities able to cope with climate impacts? Global policy arrangements to address adaptation are far less developed than for mitigation. Climate change impacts are mostly framed as local or regional problems and so are adaptation strategies. According to Pielke et al. (2007), "The focus on mitigation has created policy instruments that are biased against adaptation". Tensions between mitigation and adaptation in the climate governance domain, often fuelled by fears that investing in adaptation will undermine commitment to mitigation, are likely to affect the water governance domain. Changes in water governance that are justified by a climate adaptation rationale, for example, can potentially be criticized by mitigation proponents, as well as by climate skeptics – the issue that we will turn to now.

Framing Climate Change as Certain Versus Uncertain:
'Alarmism' or 'Skepticism'?

Uncertainty has played a pivotal role in framing climate change. Uncertainty, referring to what is not known about a system, has been used to justify certain policy courses or to defer others. For example, when the Bush administration and the Russian government noted the economic disadvantages of participating in the Kyoto Protocol, they continued to point to scientific uncertainty as a basis for their decisions, setting the stage for their opponents to argue certainty as the basis for changing course (Pielke Jr. 2004). When the latter strategy involves framing away the uncertainties, there is a risk that public support for climate policy could crumble when inevitable uncertainties do catch public attention. The question can be asked: "Even if we are correct about human-induced climate change, what if we are wrong about the timescales, the severity or the extent of climate change?" (Keeling 2009). In this way, uncertainty –or its counterpart certainty– becomes the foundation for claiming the legitimacy of policy action and inaction.

Uncertainty plays different roles in framing of climate change: the framing of climate science as valid or controversial, the framing of climate science as certain/uncertain at the science-policy interface and the framing of climate change as leading to more uncertainties about weather conditions. We consider each of these roles in the paragraphs below, and then take up the framing of uncertainty itself.

Antilla (2005) identified four frames in newspaper coverage of climate science: valid science, ambiguous cause or effects (questioning the gravity of climate change), uncertain science and controversial science. Under the valid science frame, scientific findings are emphasized, covering a broad range of issues such as climate change impact, extreme weather events and effect of climate change on certain species. Contrarily, ambiguous cause or effect deemphasized science by restating findings to convey a different message. Uncertain science frames are used to point out biases or incompatibilities in the way in which science addressed certain issues (for example, different definitions of climate change used by the UNFCCC and IPCC). Finally, controversial science frames reflect skepticism about climate change science, stating it as speculative and proposing natural variability as a main cause. Each of these frames prioritizes the production of different types of knowledge and triggers a different political response (Pielke Jr. 2004).

Different ways of framing uncertainty can play an important role at the science-policy interface, involving scientists, politicians and the media (Boykoff 2008). According to Weingart et al. (2000), "in the German discourse on climate change, scientists politicized the issue, politicians reduced the scientific complexities and uncertainties to CO_2 emissions reduction targets and the media ignored the uncertainties and transformed them into a sequence of events leading to catastrophe and requiring immediate action". As Latour (1998) observed, uncertainties are at the core of collegial discussions among scientists in their daily work (the "research"), but when moving towards more formal and public settings (for example, international conferences or publications), and especially towards policy and media settings, uncertainties are progressively removed from the stories, leaving only what are supposed to be certainties (the "science").

From an analysis of framing in the recent "climategate" debate between 'alarmists' and 'skeptics' (Nerlich 2010), it appears that climate skeptics are not only challenging climate knowledge by claiming it to be uncertain. Through religious framing, anthropogenic global warming theory is likened to religious dogma, scientific consensus to orthodoxy and scientists to preachers or evangelists. In this rather paradoxical way, climate knowledge is challenged by climate skeptics as being all too certain and this certainty is alleged to be manufactured in a quasi-religious way.

Framing Climate Change as a Technical Issue Versus an Inequity Issue: Technical Efficiency or Social Justice?

Equity concerns compound the ambiguity that arises from the previously discussed framing dimensions. The privileging of highly technical framing of climate change discounts relational facets of knowledge about the fairness or equity of various mitigation or adaptation strategies. Technical framing slights the issue of international equity as it treats emissions from developed and developing countries the same regardless of the century or more during which developed countries have had the luxury of enjoying energy intensive enterprises without challenge (Demeritt 2001). A fair and socially situated consideration of the pace and trajectory of economic development means framing the issue to give more weight to the perspectives of developing countries that often lack the scientific expertise to argue their case in technically dominated international arenas. Some critics contend that "the threat of future climate change holds little meaning for developing nations and the poor people in them struggling daily in face of crippling structural adjustment policies with more basic and immediate needs of sanitation, health, and hunger" (Demeritt 2001: 313). Framings of climate change as a technical rather than an inequity issue have implications for the adaptation discussion as well. According to O'Brien et al. (2007), "The dominance of the scientific framing of climate change has meant that the scope of adaptation policies has been interpreted quite narrowly ... Increased attention to the human-security framing of climate change may raise the relevance of climate change to broader communities".

A particularly thorny issue in the relations between Northern and Southern countries in the UNFCCC negotiations is the framing of climate change as a matter of current and future emissions versus a matter of historical responsibility (Friman and Linner 2008). The issue was raised by Brazil in the pre-Kyoto negotiations, but after referral of this issue to the Subsidiary Body for Scientific and Technological Advice, the discussion became confined to technical calculations – the historical responsibility issue became stranded on problems of how to correctly represent the physics in climate models. Contrasting with this technical framing of historical responsibility is a framing in terms of equity. The latter has become marginalized, with consequences in terms of lower participation of Southern countries in UNFCCC meetings. With equity and historical responsibility not being part of the official negotiation frame, the political-economic issues are not thoroughly addressed and at the same time the concept serves as an easy excuse for rapidly developing Southern countries not to cut emissions.

Context becomes much more important in framing that focuses on equity, while technical framing tends toward reductionist and linear cause-effect reasoning (O'Brien et al. 2007). The Cities for Climate Change Campaign, an international network engaging hundreds of cities, has been successful in framing climate as a local problem and situates cities a part of the problem as well as part of the solution (Lindseth 2004). CCPC focuses on contextual problems like air quality, health effects and transportation because city residents feel in their bodies actual effects of changing climate (Lindseth 2004: 329). Recognizing of the importance of context suggests that one size fits all policy solutions deriving from templates, models, lists of best practices, and uniform standards are ill advised (Lejano and Ingram 2007). Climate policies must be framed to "fit" local communities' agendas and capacities. A program based on joint community management of common property forests or fisheries may not work where there are serious divisions within the community or where a local boss commands most of the resources (Lejano and Ingram 2007). Injecting issues of fairness into the climate debate calls for more detailed knowledge of power structures, economic inequality and other inequities that affect human-climate interactions.

In summary, our analysis has identified three key dimensions of frame diversity in the climate change debate: (1) framing climate change as an emissions issue versus an impacts issue, (2) framing climate change as certain versus uncertain science and (3) framing climate change as a technical issue versus an inequity issue. These dimensions of how climate change gets framed do not capture the full spectrum of meanings of climate change. They are, however, based on a secondary analysis of a broad range of studies and they do pinpoint key dimensions with potentially far reaching implications for policy directions and arrangements.

Discussion: Bridging Knowledge Frames and Networks

Bridging is a connective activity that occurs at boundaries. Bridging a diversity of knowledge frames and networks need decision spaces that enable people to work towards new ways of knowing and that promote mutual understanding and the development of reciprocal relationships (Brugnach and Ingram 2012). We discuss the potential of boundary experiences (joint activities that transcend boundaries between individuals), boundary objects (physical objects that enable people to understand other perspectives) and boundary organizations (collectives that are drawn together from different ways of knowing) for bridging different ways of knowing (Feldman et al. 2006). In discussing these carriers of connective capacity, we will use examples from other domains and from there illustrate and discuss how these mechanisms could play a role in bridging the particularly challenging "alarmism" versus "skepticism" divide in the climate debate.

Boundary Organizations

Originally conceived with the purpose of protecting but also transcending the divide between science and practice, boundary organizations perform four critical functions (Tribbia and Moser 2008): (1) convening: bringing stakeholders together for face-to-face contact to foster trust-building and mutual understanding, (2) translation: assuring that information and resources are comprehensible for co-operating individuals and organizations, (3) facilitating collaboration: bringing together groups for transparent dialogue and co-production of relevant, credible and applied knowledge and (4) mediating: assuring that various interests of stakeholders, information producers and users are taking into account.

More generally, boundary organizations (Berkes 2009, Feldman et al. 2006, O'Mahony and Bechky 2008) or bridging organizations (Berkes 2009) can facilitate the connection between different types of knowledge, provide an arena for co-production, trust building, sensemaking and learning, vertical and horizontal collaboration and conflict resolution. Beyond connecting scientists and policy makers, bridging organizations can serve as a catalyst and facilitator between different levels of governance, and across resource and knowledge systems – particularly relevant for water and climate change governance.

An example where a municipal organization functioned as a boundary organization is Kristianstads 'Biosphere Office' (Olsson et al. 2007). The Kristianstads Vattenrike Biosphere Reserve (Sweden) is of high importance for biodiversity, agriculture and water resources and is of interest to stakeholders on different scale levels – from local farmers to international nature organizations. A shift in management regime had its beginnings in the early 1980s. Multiple individuals from different organizations observed problems in the area, including declining bird populations, decreased water quality and decreased use of flooded meadows for grazing. Personal links developed among these individuals, resulting in an emerging informal network. Some of the actors realized that these problems were interrelated while the governance structures and processes for dealing with the problems were not. Through the leadership of the newly established Ecomuseum the initial local network reframed the wetland area issue from a problem ("water sick") into a valuable resources with multiple uses ("water rich") and expanded itself to include regional, national and international actors (for example, WWF and a national research council). This cross-scale policy network gained enough momentum to convince the executive board of the Municipality of Kristianstad to adopt a more adaptive new management approach, making use of the window of opportunity consisting of the search for a new identity by Kristianstad. The Biosphere Office as a municipal organization formed a key node in the adaptive co-management network, but without having authority or power to enforce rules.

Rather its role consists of linking and coordinating multiple scales and levels as a boundary organization.

A boundary organization functions as a new venue introduced in a governance system. Boundary organizations range from quasi informal task forces that exist during a period of time and then dissipate, to much more formal government sponsored organizations intended to bring together multiple perspectives.

They can have two distinctive purposes: for boundary work (for example, allowing science being separated while at the same time engaging with public policy actors). Or to blur boundaries and create new ways of knowing. The alternative labels of bridging organization (Berkes 2009) and boundary organization (Feldman et al. 2006, O'Mahony and Bechky 2008) reveal an interesting duality of function: they both separate (gatekeeping at the boundaries) and connect (bridging across the boundaries). Their value lies in allowing different knowledge frames and networks to retain their unique properties and at the same time connecting those. This differentiates bridging from integrating, because the latter refers to combining the original elements into something new or more complete.

Two long-standing boundary organizations at the science-policy interface for Dutch climate governance are the IPCC (Intergovernmental Panel on Climate Change) at the international level and the PBL (Netherlands Environmental Assessment agency) at the national level. PBL is the primary policy advisor to the national government regarding climate policy and is also a prominent participant in the IPCC, having served as the Technical Support Unit for Working Group III (Edwards et al. 2011). In the controversy that sprung from the release of e-mail correspondence between climate scientists at the University of East Anglia (now known as "climategate") and from the identification of alleged errors in the IPCC report, including one regarding the percentage of Dutch territory lying below sea level, these organizations played very different roles in connecting between climate 'believers' and 'non-believers'. While the IPCC, finding itself under fierce attacks, did not engage with climate skeptics, the PBL took active steps to invite climate skeptics to present their views and to set up a website inviting people to submit issues or errors in the IPCC report, which were subsequently investigated.

However, an organizational form such as a boundary or bridging organization will not be sufficient in and of itself to bridge diverse knowledge frames and networks. An otherwise very successful institution like the IPCC, which was awarded the Nobel Peace Prize, hardly fulfilled any bridging function in the debate with climate skeptics. The PBL did so by acting as a forum or meeting place between the contending parties, thereby creating the boundary experiences that we will come back to in a later section. In and of itself "a boundary organization per se is no guarantee of "success" no matter how it might be measured. It is the processes, dynamics, relationships, and leadership style that matter" (Schneider 2009). As can be expected given our interactional approach to knowledge frames and networks, the nature and context of interactions plays an important role in successful bridging of knowledge frames and networks. Therefore, in the next section, we zoom in on boundary objects and boundary experiences.

Boundary Objects

Boundary objects provide an artifact such as a model, scenario, template, prototype or the like, upon which people from different knowledge networks can project different knowledge frames. In this way, boundary objects can become focal points for interactions that support mutual understanding among different ways of knowing.

The use of models as boundary objects in the upper Guadiana experience is an example. Participatory modeling, or group model building, is a modeling technique that can be used as a boundary experience to facilitate dialogue and communication in a group. In this case, the modeling process becomes the venue through which participants make explicit what are their views on the problem, identifying points in common or in disagreement. When the conditions for collaboration are present, this process can lead to the development of a shared view on the problem and solution. In the Upper Guadiana River Basin, a participatory modeling exercise using Bayesian Belief Networks was carried on. The aim of this exercise was to increase the understanding of the basin by improving the communication and knowledge exchange among different stakeholders. These developments lasted for almost two years and, what started being a controversial and conflictive situation in which stakeholders disagree about what the problem of basin was (Brugnach et al. 2011, Henriksen et al. 2011, Martínez-Santos et al. 2010), resulted in an increase capacity for accepting differences and collaborating for finding a solution.

In the climate discussion in the US, where 'climate denial' is used more than 'climate scepticism' and where climate scientists have been targeted in law suits, a dataset of temperature data and measurement stations seem to have functioned as an interesting boundary object. Initiated by Anthony Watts, meteorologist and author of one of key climate sceptic websites, a project was set up to survey surface temperature stations across the US with the aim of identifying biased (that is, higher) temperature measurements due to increased urbanization around the surface stations. At www. surfacestations.com they claim to have surveyed over 80 per cent of the US stations through the help of numerous volunteers' assessments and pictures. Although they were often dismissed as 'climate deniers', their empirical work has been taken up by scientists to verify and correct the US temperature record and their results were recently published in a scientific journal (Fall et al. 2011).

Boundary Experiences

Boundary experiences are "shared or joint activities that create a sense of community and an ability to transcend boundaries among participants" (Feldman and Khademian 2007). Examples include field trips, bus tours, joint problem solving activities or community visits. Boundary experiences bring us to the level of interactions where knowledge is developed across boundaries.

In an example about a joint bus trip as a boundary experience (Feldman and Khademian 2007), simply seeing the same things at the same time of year and time of day provides a common reference point to which different perspectives can be connected. It also provides a basis to refer to in future conversations. Also, on the relational level, the trip created connections between people and dispelled stereotypes that enable people to keep their distance from one another. It was like a 'traveling reception', providing many opportunities for people to meet others who understand the issue differently from them (Feldman and Khademian 2007).

The concept of relational practices (Bouwen 2001) similarly captures the interactional quality required for bridging diverse knowledge frames and networks. A relational practice is an interactive activity between at least two actors: it has consequences for the mutual relationships and some perceivable outcome. Concrete and simple examples of a relational practice are: a jazz improvisation, a spontaneous celebration or a good conversation. Any meeting or group activity that is aimed at bridging can be considered from its potential as a high quality relational practice. The meeting of a project group or a management team, an occasional meeting in the parking lot or in the elevator, the joint setup of a field experiment – all these interactive moments have a potential for creating high relational qualities. To characterize the quality of a relational practice, one can look at the extent of reciprocity between the actors' contributions, the openness and concreteness of communication, the mutually energizing and engaging character and the shared ownership of the activity.

In the Dutch climate debate, the following event can be cited as an example of a boundary experience, connecting a skeptic journalist and a parliamentarian in a public event (quoted from Edwards et al. 2011).On 15 November 2010, a small ceremony took place in the press centre of the Dutch parliament in The Hague. The climate spokesperson of the social democratic parliamentary party in the House of Representatives (the Tweede Kamer) received the first copy of the book De staat van het Klimaat (The State of the Climate), which was written by a climate skeptical science journalist (Crok 2010). The author is also one of the initiators of the website Climategate.nl, which was established one year before, following the hack into climate scientists' e-mails at the University of East Anglia's Climatic Research Unit. The parliamentarian, Diederik Samsom, complimented the author, Marcel Crok, for his 'intelligent and scrupulously careful analysis of theories on climate change'. He expressed his particular appreciation for the book's view on the relationship between science and politics, stating that he shared the author's concern regarding 'what political interests have done with science'.These kind of boundary experiences allow for personal but task-relevant connections between people that can form the basis for a more a constructive debate or collaboration across boundaries.

Conclusion

Addressing the complex and varied challenges for water and climate policy requires contributions from a wide range of sometimes disconnected knowledge frames and networks. When frame differences remain unrecognized or unaddressed in these processes, dialogues of the deaf, intractable controversies and stagnations are likely to occur (Dewulf et al. 2005b, Gray, 2004, Schön and Rein 1994, Termeer 2009, Van Eeten 1999). These conflicts are often as much about knowledge as they are about frames. Report wars ensue when rivaling coalitions commission one report after the other from different researchers (Koppenjan and Klijn 2004), when a minimal agreement on the important questions and parameters is lacking. Interestingly, the crucial barrier in science-policy relations is not always at the border between policy makers and researchers in a particular policy domain but between policy makers and researchers from different policy domains (van Buuren and Edelenbos 2004), or in other words: between different knowledge frames and networks.

Establishing collaborative links between different networks, crossing the boundaries of different ways of framing climate change and bridging existing configurations will be necessary. In that sense, designing policies that purposefully draw from and appeal to different framings and perspectives is preferable to coherent policies that are more singular in focus and intent. Some authors argue that 'socially robust knowledge' (Nowotny 2003) or 'clumsy solutions' (Verweij et al. 2006) are needed to tackle ambiguous issues like climate change. Water and climate policies ought not to strive for elegance, singular definitions of problems and consistency of goals, values and policy tools. It might be better to have clumsy policies in which none of the existent framings are excluded. Such policies are likely to attract more support and be more easily implemented. Although these concepts have been around for some time, they critically hinge on bridging knowledge frames and networks. This is still a huge challenge, both within the scientific realm in the form of inter- or transdisciplinary knowledge creation as in the political realm where policy makers and societal actors create and contest knowledge as well.

In our view, bridging both knowledge frames and knowledge networks is crucial. Linking knowledge frames alone can result in a nice conceptual or theoretical integration and linking networks alone can result in increased cohesion between people, but bridging different ways of knowing requires an intertwining of contents (knowledge frames) and relations (knowledge networks). There are a number of promising research paths that start to address this challenge of connective capacity. Through boundary experiences between different knowledge frames and knowledge networks, new meanings about the situation can emerge and strategies can be devised that acknowledge and capitalize on the various forms of knowledge – including equity frames which are essential to forging implementable solutions to problems. Boundary objects can provide a joint reference point through which interaction remains or becomes possible between knowledge frames and networks that would otherwise remain disconnected. The organizational form of a boundary organization, finally, can function as a meeting place on more or less neutral ground for connecting diverse knowledge frames and networks. We argue that connections in the form of organizations, objects and experiences will be simultaneously needed to really bring different frame regarding climate and water together. In the end this may all be a matter of what the theorist of knowing-in-practice Etienne Wenger (1998) has called the interplay between two ways of negotiating meaning: reification and participation. Reification is the process of producing objects (physical or conceptual artifacts) through which communities give their practice an embodiment in the world, like in organizations or objects. Participation refers to the active involvement of people in a particular practice. At each moment of engaging with the world, these two processes come together to negotiate the meaning of our experience. It is at this profound level that boundary organizations and object are in need of boundary experiences to bring them to life and that boundary experiences need boundary organizations and objects to structure them and carry them forward to the next occasion.

These issues deserve a place on the climate and water governance research agenda and we are convinced that an interactional theory of knowledge frames, along the lines we discussed above, will prove useful to address them.

Bibliography

Antilla, L. 2005. Climate of scepticism: US newspaper coverage of the science of climate change. *Global Environmental Change*, 15, 338-52.

Benford, R.D. and Snow, D.A. 2000. Framing processes and social movements: An overview and assessment. *Annual Review of Sociology*, 26, 611-39.

Berkes, F. 2009 Evolution of co-management: Role of knowledge generation, bridging organizations and social learning. *Journal of Environmental Management*, 90, 1692-702.

Biesbroek, G.R., Swart, R.J. and van der Knaap, W.G.M. 2009 *The Mitigation-adaptation Dichotomy and the Role of Spatial Planning*. Habitat International In Press, Corrected Proof.

Bouwen, R. 2001. Developing relational practices for knowledge intensive organizational contexts. *Career Development International*, 6, 361-9.

Bouwen, R. and Taillieu, T. 2004. Multi-party collaboration as social learning for interdependence: Developing relational knowing for sustainable natural resource management. *Journal of Community and Applied Social Psychology*, 14(3), 137-53.

Boykoff, M.T. 2008. The cultural politics of climate change discourse in UK tabloids. *Political Geography*, 27, 549-69.

Boykoff, M.T., Frame, D. and Randalls, S. 2010. Discursive stability meets climate instability: A critical exploration of the concept of 'climate stabilization' in contemporary climate policy. *Global Environmental Change*, 20, 53-64.

Brick, P. and Cawley, R.M. 2008. Producing political climate change: The hidden life of US environmentalism. *Environmental Politics*, 17, 200-18.

Brugnach, M., Dewulf, A., Henriksen, H.J. and van der Keur, P. 2011. More is not always better: Coping with ambiguity in natural resources management. *Journal of Environmental Management*, 92, 78-84.

Brugnach, M., Dewulf, A.R.P.J., Pahl-Wostl, C. and Taillieu, T. 2008. Toward a relational concept of uncertainty: About knowing too little, knowing too differently, and accepting not to know. *Ecology and Society*, 13, art. no. 30.

Brugnach, M. and Ingram, H. 2012. Ambiguity: The challenge of knowing and deciding together. *Environmental Science and Policy*, 15, 60-71.

Chong, D. and Druckman, J.N. 2007. Framing Theory. *Annual Review of Political Science*, 10, 103-26.

Cook, S.D.N. and Brown, J.S. 1999. Bridging Epistemologies: The Generative Dance between Organizational Knowledge and Organizational Knowing. *Organisation Science*, 10, 381-400.

Demeritt, D. 2001. The construction of global warming and the politics of science. *Annals of the Association of American Geographers*, 91, 307-37.

Dewulf, A., Craps, M., Bouwen, R., Abril, F. and Zhingri, M. 2005a. How indigenous farmers and university engineers create actionable knowledge for sustainable irrigation. *Action Research*, 3, 175-92.

Dewulf, A., Craps, M., Bouwen, R., Taillieu, T. and Pahl-Wostl, C. 2005b. Integrated management of natural resources: Dealing with ambiguous issues, multiple actors and diverging frames. *Water Science and Technology*, 52, 115-24.

Dewulf, A., Gray, B., Putnam, L., Lewicki, R., Aarts, N., Bouwen, R. and van Woerkum, C. 2009. Disentangling approaches to framing in conflict and negotiation research: A meta-paradigmatic perspective. *Human Relations*, 62, 155-93.

Dewulf, A., Mancero, M., Cárdenas, G. and Sucozhañay, D. 2011. Fragmentation and connection of frames in collaborative water governance: A case study of river catchment management in Southern Ecuador. *International Review of Administrative Sciences*, 77, 50-75.

Dewulf, A.R.P.J., Francois, G. Pahl-Wostl, C. and Taillieu, T. 2007. A framing approach to cross-disciplinary research collaboration: Experiences from a large-scale research project on adaptive water management. *Ecology and Society*, 12, 14.

Entman, R.M. 1993. Framing: Toward Clarification of a Fractured Paradigm. *Journal of Communication*, 43, 51-8.

Fall, S., Watts, A., Nielsen-Gammon, J., Jones, E., Niyogi, D., Christy, J.R., Pielke Sr, R.A., Parodi, A., Foufoula-Georgiou, E., Emanuel, K. 2011. Analysis of the impacts of station exposure on the US Historical Climatology Network temperatures and temperature trends. J. Geophys. Res 116, D14120.

Feldman, M.S. and Khademian, A.M. 2007. The Role of the Public Manager in Inclusion: Creating Communities of Participation. *Governance*, 20, 305-24.

Feldman, M.S., Khademian, A.M., Ingram, H. and Schneider, A.S. 2006. Ways of knowing and inclusive management practices. *Public Administration Review*, 66, 89-99.

Friman, M. and Linner, B.O. 2008. Technology obscuring equity: Historical responsibility in UNFCCC negotiations. *Climate Policy*, 8, 339-354.

Gray, B. 2004. Strong opposition: Frame-based resistance to collaboration. *Journal of Community and Applied Social Psychology*, 14, 166-76.

Henriksen, H.J., Zorrilla-Miras, P., de la Hera, A., Brugnach, M. 2011. Use of Bayesian belief networks for dealing with ambiguity in integrated groundwater management. Integrated *Environmental Assessment and Management*, 7.

Hulme, M. 2008a. The conquering of climate: Discourses of fear and their dissolution. *Geographical Journal*, 174, 5-16.

Hulme, M. 2008b. Governing and adapting to climate. A response to Ian Bailey's Commentary on 'Geographical work at the boundaries of climate change'. *Transactions of the Institute of British Geographers*, 33, 424-7.

Keeling, S.J. 2009. What if? Media, celebrity and climate change. *Weather*, 64, 49-50.

Koppenjan, J. and Klijn, E.H. 2004. *Managing Uncertainties in Networks: A Network Aapproach to Problem Solving and Decision Making*. London: Routledge.

Latour, B. 1998. Essays on science and society: From the world of science to the world of research? *Science*, 280, 208.

Lejano, R. and Ingram, H. 2007. Place-Based Conservation: Lessons from the Turtle Islands. Environment. S*cience and Policy for Sustainable Development*, 49, 18-27.

Lejano, R.P. and Ingram, H. 2008. *Collaborative Networks and New Ways of Knowing*. Environmental Science and Policy In Press, Corrected Proof.

Lindseth, G. 2004. The Cities for Climate Protection Campaign (CCPC) and the framing of local climate policy. *Local Environment*, 9, 325-36.

Martínez-Santos, P., Henriksen, H.J., Zorrilla, P. and Martínez-Alfaro, P.E. 2010. Comparative reflections on the use of modelling tools in conflictive water management settings: The Mancha Occidental aquifer, Spain. *Environmental Modelling and Software*, 25, 1439-49.

Nerlich, B. 2010. 'Climategate': Paradoxical metaphors and political paralysis. *Environmental Values*, 19, 419-42.

Nowotny, H. 2003. Democratising expertise and socially robust knowledge. *Science and Public Policy*, 30, 151-6.

O'Brien, K., Eriksen, S., Nygaard, L.P. and Schjolden, A. 2007. Why different interpretations of vulnerability matter in climate change discourses. *Climate Policy*, 7, 73-88.

O'Mahony, S. and Bechky, B.A. 2008. Boundary organizations: Enabling collaboration among unexpected allies. *Administrative Science Quarterly*, 53, 422-59.

Olsson, P., Folke, C., Galaz, V., Hahn, T., Schultz, L. 2007. Enhancing the Fit through Adaptive Co-management: Creating and Maintaining Bridging Functions for Matching Scales in the Kristianstads Vattenrike Biosphere Reserve, Sweden. *Ecology and Society*, 12(1), 28.

Pielke Jr, R.A. 2004. What is climate change? *Issues in Science and Technology*, 20, 31-4.

Pielke, R. 2007. The honest broker: Making sense of science in policy and politics. Cambridge: Cambridge University Press.

Pielke, R., Prins, G., Rayner, S. and Sarewitz, D. 2007. Lifting the taboo on adaptation. *Nature*, 445, 597-8.

Schneider, A.L. 2009. Why do some boundary Organizations result in new ideas and practices and others only meet resistance? Examples from juvenile justice. *American Review of Public Administration*, 39, 60-79.

Schön, D.A. and Rein, M. 1994. Frame reflection: Toward a resolution of intractable policy controversies. New York: Basic Books,.

Scrase, J.I. and Ockwell, D.G. 2010. The role of discourse and linguistic framing effects in sustaining high carbon energy policy-An accessible introduction. Energy Policy, doi:10.1016/j.enpol.2009.1012.1010.

Termeer, C.J.A.M. 2009. Barriers to New Modes of Horizontal Governance. *Public Management Review*, 11, 299-316.

Termeer, C.J.A.M. and Kessener, B. 2007. Revitalizing Stagnated Policy Processes: Using the Configuration Approach for Research and Interventions. *Journal of Applied Behavioral Science*, 43, 256-72.

Termeer, C.J.A.M. and Meijerink, S. 2008. Klimaat bestendig of klimaat neutraal bestuur? Een essay over het adaptief vermogen van instituties voor de Raad voor Verkeer en Waterstaat. Raad voor Verkeer en Waterstaat, Den Haag.

Tribbia, J. and Moser, S.C. 2008. More than information: What coastal managers need to plan for climate change. *Environmental Science and Policy*, 11, 315-28.

van Buuren, A. 2009. Knowledge for governance, governance of knowledge: Inclusive knowledge management in collaborative governance processes. *International Public Management Journal*, 12, 208-35.

van Buuren, A. and Edelenbos, J. 2004. Why is joint knowledge production such a problem? *Science and Public Policy*, 31, 289-99.

Van Dongen, H.J., De Laat, W.A.M. and Maas, A.J.J.A. 1996. Een kwestie van verschil (A matter of difference), Conflicthantering en onderhandeling in een configuratieve integratietheorie. Eburon, Delft.

van Eeten, M. 1999. Dialogues of the deaf on science in policy controversies. *Science and Public Policy*, 26, 185-92.

Verweij, M., Douglas, M., Ellis, R., Engel, C., Hendriks, F., Lohmann, S., Ney, S., Rayner, S. and Thompson, M. 2006. Clumsy solutions for a complex world: The case of climate change. *Public Administration*, 84, 817-43.

Weick, K. 1995. Sensemaking in Organizations. Thousand Oaks, CA: Sage.

Weingart, P., Engels, A. and Pansegrau, P. 2000. Risks of communication: Discourses on climate change in science, politics, and the mass media. *Public Understanding of Science*, 9, 261.

Wenger, E. 1998. Communities of practice: Learning, meaning and identity. Cambridge: Cambridge University Press.

Chapter 13

Values Connecting Societies and Water Systems

Jacko van Ast, Jan Jaap Bouma and Mansee Bal

Introduction

Water systems such as rivers and lakes have many important values for ecosystems and human societies. Both economic, social-ecological, cultural and political values are met by the water systems, connecting different activities in human society and ecosystems. Water systems with low water quality serve different values than healthy water systems and have huge impact on the society. For example, for drinking water, biodiversity or recreational open space, a healthy water system is crucial.

The values of the water systems are interlinked. The interlinking and overlapping values of the water systems at the spatial and temporal scales have determined a connective capacity in the water governance, be it the coordination between the values or the competition between the values and its linked governance approach. The challenge is: values of water systems change with the change in the societal development and consequently influence the water governance approach. A reverse process is also evident. Unfortunately, today, water systems in many cities have slowly reduced in their total value for society. The revival of the water systems, such as river and lakes, thus seems to be urgent in order to enhance the values generated by these systems for the society.

The concept of connective capacity can be applied to the values generated by water systems, where these values bring activities, and on a higher level the ecological and social systems, together. This can be illustrated with the historical development of changing values of water systems. Main questions are what we can learn from the connecting capacity of values and if these values play a role in (inter)connecting societies and water systems. The chapter provides analyses of the changing values in water management in The Netherlands and in India, illustrated with examples of urban lake systems. It discusses how values of the water systems (inter)connect societies and water systems and in turn influence the water governance and vice versa. The findings are based on literature review and broad stakeholder analysis conducted from repeated field visits to the lakes sites in Tilburg and Ahmedabad from 2005-2010. The field visits included semi-structured and open ended interviews with the stakeholders, backed up by document analysis.

Dynamics in Values and Water Governance

Values of Ecosystems

The multiple objective approaches in current water management are derived from the different values of the water systems. The term 'value' is broad and multidisciplinary and has different interpretations in different disciplines. In the total economic value (TEV) framework, Pearce and Moran (1994) divide values in instrumental value (or use value) and intrinsic or passive (or non-use) value. The instrumental value is subdivided into direct use value, indirect use value and option value and the intrinsic value is subdivided into existence value and bequest value. In case of rivers and lakes, ground water recharge, swimming and washing are the direct use values. Experiencing the water, the landscape, the fauna and the flora are examples of the indirect use value, while planning of recreation or real estate development belongs to the option value of natural water systems. The non-use values are slightly more problematic in definition and estimation. Conserving it for its very being/identity as an asset is referred as the existence value and conserving the lake for future generations is the bequest value.

The use and non-use values combined can be considered in alignment to the definition of sustainability by the World Commission on Environment and Development, development that meets the needs of the present without compromising the ability of future generations to meet their own needs (WCED 1987). The use values and non-use values can be categorized depending in which domain the use and non-use values are referred to and related to, such as ecological values, economic values, social values, cultural values and political values. The ecosystem values encompass all the goods and services generated from the ecosystem of water. The 'value' in this chapter refers to the array of functions performed by the water systems from its source of generation to the consumption and the waste water generation. It encompasses all kinds of values discussed in the TEV. The choice of values by the society at a certain time period is usually reflected in the governance of the specific water systems such as lakes.

Water Management

Water management and water governance is defined in different ways (Teclaff 1996, Biswas 2004, Biswas 2008, Hooper 2005). The Dublin Conference on Water and the Environment uses "Integrated Water Resource Management", based on a participatory approach, safeguarding availability and vulnerability of water and taking into account affordability and equity criteria (ICWE 1992). The concept was elaborated in the United Nations Conference on Environment and Development in Rio de Janeiro (UNCED 1992).

The modern multiple objective approach is known as "adaptive management" where water managers continually adjust their actions in response to monitoring data and insights that informs about changes in the characteristics of a water system, its catchment area, economic conditions and social preferences with respect to the values a water system is expected to fulfill. Water managers no longer dominate the decision-making process related to managing the flow of the river, its quantities and its quality. They are now more open for support from stakeholders within the process of participation (Van Ast 2000). In this respect, currently the concept of water governance is used. Taking the stakeholders into account means that the costs and benefits of the different values of water systems are to be balanced. This in turn leads to a request for insight into the processes of valuation and its institutionalization. Examples are Cost Benefit Analysis, Multi Criteria Analysis, Co-valuation (Van Schie and Bouma 2008, Schuijt 2003, Bouma et al. 2008, Van der Veeren and Van Cleef 2008). In contrast to the traditional water management approach, it advocates the need for coordination, integration and synchronization of values, interests, responsibilities and tasks within water management and governance (Biswas 2008).

The Involvement of Values in Governance

The way values play a role is for a large part dependent on the way government organizes the use of the goods and services of the water system by different stakeholders. To some extent it is coordinated by market mechanisms based on financial (monetary) value (maximization of profits) as the value paradigm. The role of the market mechanism however is subject to an ongoing debate. Stakeholders compete for accessibility to the water systems. In this respect, different values and the chains of stakeholders (like drinking water producers, distributors and consumers) that make use of them, may be organized in different ways under different market conditions. The overall coordination of the relevant value chains within one state and between states connected to a water system is regarded as problematic. Different countries have often different traditions and sets of values associated with water systems. They also vary in the way how property right systems are embedded in legal and institutional environments. Different value chains may be characterized by their own governance model or framework. In regional and urban planning many values are involved. In this context historical, cultural, recreational and other economic values may overrule or consolidate the ecological values of a water system. However, the coordination of a water system is not overarching all other coordination systems that in the end of the day explain the quality of a water system, especially in an urbanized region. It becomes even more complex because over time, different coordination systems responsible for the quality of a water system or parts of it, change.

An innovative approach of 'virtual water' or 'water footprint analysis' may allow water to be channeled towards those value chains and those units within these chains that provide the highest value (Hoekstra 2008). However, it is still a new concept and unclear how this valuation process should be organized and woven into practical governance models or frameworks and which values are to be included in the value concept that is relevant in the governance of a water system.

General notions on the role of institutions in the coordination mechanisms in infrastructures of Williamson (1979, 1998) or North (1990) consider the impacts of relevant mechanisms of processes of institutionalization (DiMagio and Powell 1983). It is still fuzzy if and how current and future adaptive strategies for governing water systems embed the values that are reflected in the theoretical framework and acknowledge the performance measures (outcomes) policy makers aim for (Valkering and Offermans 2008). The impacts of Climate Change on water systems and their values introduced a permanent degree of uncertainties on the final effects on societies. In the current urban water governance approaches, the challenge in formulating adaptive water strategies is how to deal with potential conflicting value-concepts of the stakeholders and the costs and benefits.

The governance of water systems depends on local and contextual variables. Some of these variables are the involved traditional and economic values that are at stake. Other variables are related to the institutional arrangements that embed the specific values into the management of water systems. Sometimes this may result into the dominance of some economic sectors that have the ownership and consequently use the specific water system according to their preferences. Local tendencies towards or away from integrated and sustainable water management approaches are key characteristics of water governance. These contextual variables are discussed in the following studies of Dutch and Indian water management and illustrated by the Tilburg and Ahmedabad settings as they are identified by the stakeholders.

Water Governance in the Netherlands

Values and Paradigms

The history of Dutch water management shows a long development of change in values and governance (Van Ast 1999, Van der Brugge and Rotmans 2010). The early intervention with water in the Netherlands was primarily associated with the fear of flooding and later with fear of diseases. Many efforts were made to fight the water and its health risks. At first, mounds were formed; small hills of a few meters, where the water could not reach the houses. Later, the construction of dikes became the major strategy to keep the water away from the land. After some centuries of experience with dikes and drainage ditches, the combination with windmill technology created a very successful strategy against flooding. It appeared that it was even possible to create land from the sea, by making a ring of dikes and consequently pump the water out (Dubbelman 1999). The efforts result from the dominating values of the times when productive land was increasingly important. The population increased and agriculture needed more space to feed all inhabitants. The other fight came with awareness of the risks of polluted water and the value of clean drinking water for human health. It resulted in physically dividing the contaminated water from the people. In no time, the water systems obtained religious value in the society.

Looking at the economic value of water, fishing had the earliest focus. The existence of water bodies ensured the availability of food for people. With modernization, due to over harvesting and pollution, the fish stocks collapsed which changed the food habits of the people. From Medieval times, water as a mode for transportation gained importance in river systems. It resulted in a large water infrastructure connecting cities and villages through existing natural lakes and rivers. Due to its geographical position, the Netherlands always enjoyed the connective capacity of rivers for transport.

The field of interest of the water manager has followed the value perception in society and consequently broadened considerably with time. During the 20th century, the specific water sector policy made many new values explicit, like the recreational, ecological and aesthetical values. The environmental value became significant due to the high pollution loads in the water. Conflicts with upcoming values like nature and ecology and the awareness that the use of water as waste collector is unavoidable became apparent. It also brought the realization that the physical division of water does not avoid all the health risks. With new technology, cleaning of water systems became possible and many values depending on clean water turned realistic. This is the time of the paradigm shift in water governance from "fighting the (dirty) water" towards "living with (clean) water".

When in the mid-eighties the awareness increased that sector optimization created major drawbacks, the concept of integrated water management took off at the Ministry of Water Management and Infrastructure (1985, Saeijs 1995). It is based on a water systems approach, transcending environmental compartments. The integration not only refers to surface water and groundwater or to water quality and water quantity: it includes the various uses and the connected policy. In this phase, significant changes in thinking emerged in the society and the water managers. First, the change was from the protection of humans against the water to the protection of the water against humanity. Perhaps the most important insight is that ecology was considered the basis of managing water, that is, the ecosystem approach in water management (Allen et al. 1992).

In the nineties of the last century, a further broadening of thinking occurred with the implementation of the concept of sustainable development WCED (1987) and the Water Framework Directive (EU 2000). Dutch water governance intensified the approach towards nature protection and environmental regulation. It leads to the concepts like dynamic or adaptive water management (Geldof 1994), total water management (Van Rooy et al. 1997), participatory and interactive water management (Van Ast 1999). A large system of institutions evolved in governing the water systems with different actors on different levels and scale belonging to various policy fields. In general, the State (ministry) is responsible for the main lakes, rivers and canals, while a specific layer of democratic water boards manages the regional water infrastructure. Ministries, provinces, regional water boards and municipalities own the water systems. Only in rare cases, smaller physical water bodies that do not have a function in the main water infrastructure are sold to the private sector, but the State always sets conditions for their maintenance. Privatization in the drinking water has not taken place. Traditionally, the role of market mechanisms in the water sector are low (EUROmarket 2003) except the exploitation for recreational purposes. Waterworks and the maintenance of water systems have arrangements. Some rely on local taxation schemes (water board taxation) that are designed as a logical consequence of a relatively restricted role of market mechanism with its dominance of market priced values. Others, especially those works that are of safety importance are financed out of collective national funds.

Despite the trend to connect the different values and related expectations, the optimization of the realized value is not yet a proven case. In summary, it can be observed that the surface water changed from a primarily negative value due to flood and health risks to a positive value in terms of ecology and aesthetics.

Case: Changing Values of Small Lakes in Tilburg

In the following, an illustration of the changing values is given by small lakes, situated in the city of Tilburg. They have fulfilled many different values for ages and spatial planning reveals that safeguarding of the primary value of recreation is the key. The integration of the value of water systems into spatial planning initiatives started from the economic perspective. Possible impacts of water streams are controlled to maintain the water quality and quantity for the recreation. High water quality standards go along with the swimming water standards. It is observed that the conditions for the recreational swimming function even underpin the need for complying with the legal ecological standards. In recent times, the recreational value is challenged by urbanization and became less important as a result of increased supply of competing recreational arrangements. This is visible particularly when:

- water quality and quantity standards are to be met;
- the number of visitors and the entrance fee they pay can outweigh the costs of maintenance and opportunity costs of not using the area for further urbanization.

At this stage all the stakeholders with their own values are considered in the benefit-cost assessments. It is questionable to what extent such decision-making processes are open to those stakeholders with unknown values and stakes. It is the on-going challenge to keep the decision making process open to let new stakeholders into it as they may be innovators in the field of managing urban lakes.

Water systems may connect different knowledge suppliers with old and new users of this knowledge that may be embedded in completely other fields than of managing water systems. For example, to safeguard the recreational value of the lake, the private company who holds the concession introduced an innovative finger scan technique that is also applied in many economic sectors with a need for such kinds of security and entrance control systems.

This case shows that the decision on water quantity and water quality characteristics of a lake is spatial and temporal specific. Most recent developments demonstrate a stronger dominance of the market mechanism. A lake in Tilburg now offers a natural swimming surrounding with recreational facilities. The local governments believe that the natural swimming facility and the future existence of the lake will depend on the economic feasibility of the recreational facilities offered at this lake.

Stages of Water Governance in the Netherlands

Historically, abundance of water in the Netherlands made safety an essential value, since the low-lands were very vulnerable to flooding from the rivers and from the sea (Van Ast 1999). Later, values like safety oriented water quantity management lead to land reclaiming projects, besides the improvement of inland navigation.

In the twentieth century, an acceleration of the use of functions of water systems was realized. In this stage, sectoral water management like agriculture, industry, drinking water etc., all called for specific attention from the water managers. Even the quality of water formally got its sectoral place in 1970, when a specific law was published, followed by an explosion of water quality policy documents. The State is the service provider and community, agriculture and industries are the users. Water systems had to follow the social systems, that is, governmental planning. In the eighties of the twentieth century, the sectoral approach reached its limits. It became necessary to make decisions about the water system as a whole. This urged for integrated water management, aiming at the ability of the total water system to supply the optimum of the many demanding sectors.

In the beginning of the 21st century, a paradigmatic shift, or transition (Van der Brugge and Rotmans 2010) is taking place. Terms like resilience, participation, adaptation, and transition management refer to the practice of sustainable water management, generally characterized as "adaptive water management". In this approach the water managers adapt to the values the water system provides. If values change, their management will change. Nowadays, the concern (in itself a value) that has been given to the climate change issues plays an important role. Again the development is directed to more complexity, where land planning increasingly follows the natural systems, not in the last place in order to avoid additional costs. But more and more, social systems (and planning) follow the water systems.

The Dutch history of water governance consists of three main stages in which in every new historical phase, new values emerged. The dominance of specific values of water systems can be identified on how and to what extent these values are safeguarded in legislation and other policy instruments. Table 13.1 provides insights in the relative values identified. They are embedded into the policy design of the successive generations of EU water directives, which directly shape the

Dutch water governance approach (Euromarket 2003). It can be argued that all values are fully embedded into current governmental policy approaches. However, the overview does not reflect the market prices and the role of market mechanism.

Table 13.1   Changes in value perception in the Netherlands

Relative value (importance related to other values)	Importance: * little, ** significant, ***high		
	Historical (+- before 1900)	Modern (+- 1900- 2000)	Recent (+- after 2000)
Religious/spiritual			
Drinking water	**	**	**
Fish production		**	**
Transportation by ship	**	**	**
Sand and clay		*	*
Transportation by pipes		*	*
Recreation		*	***
Cooling water		*	**
Electricity production		**	**
Ecology		*	**
Attractive for housing (aesthetics)		**	***

Water Governance in India

Values and Paradigms

From the early civilization, environmental values linked to the water systems were veiled behind the socio-economic and cultural values that are linked to the direct use value. Since antiquity in India, water enjoyed a respectable and unique status amongst all the natural resources. Like air, wind and sunlight, water was considered to be an unlimited resource in ancient India. The existence value and the bequest value did not appear at the centre of the water management; however, in the traditional community water management was embedded as a fundamental factor.

The first reference to the hydrological cycle in the world came from the Chandogya (Agarwal et al. 2001). Chandogya is part of one of the principle philosophical texts of Hindu religion called the Upanishads. The main agenda of water management was to meet the demand of water for domestic and irrigation purposes and for the protection against floods and droughts (Bansil 1991). Since agriculture became part of civilization, land management interlinked with water management was in the forefront of water system governance (Bal 1999). With water as a deciding factor for growth and prosperity, indigenous practices of water conservation, water harvesting and transportation of water from remote areas emerged. These practices were given shades of ritualistic overtones and were woven into the religious and social-cultural habits resulting into a widespread practice at community level.

An important aspect of socio-cultural values is that rivers and lakes are considered to be sacred till date. Every religious and ceremonial occasion have some association with the rivers and lakes (Agarwal and Narain 2001). Rivers/ lakes are referred by the names of a female goddess, such as the five main holy rivers of the country are called by *Ganga, Jamuna, Godavari, Narmada* and *Kaveri*. It is believed that a dip in any of these five holy rivers washes ones sins away. The sacredness is testified by the fact that even today thousands of pilgrims perform the holy pilgrimage of Circumbulation (called Parikrama) to these rivers every year. Other rivers and lakes enjoy a similar holy status in India. Traditional fairs like Kumbh Mela at the banks of river Ganges and Pushkar Mela at Pushkar Lake are still very popular across the country and even got attention internationally.

In earlier days, the social processes followed the water system. The values of the water systems were directly linked to the people of the community and the management of rivers/ lakes was inherently integrated in the community life. Although the property rights of rivers and lakes remained with the government, formal and informal rules were usually crafted by the community for water usage, maintenance, sanctions etc. (Ostrom 1990). The hydrological cycle, the water balance principles and the community water management systems were known to the community through wisdom and experience passed from one generation to the other (Bansil 1991).

The economic values such as fishing, transportation and irrigation were always embedded with other values. Pilgrimage to sacred rivers and lakes for socio-cultural events involved many economic activities such as religious fairs, trade fairs, animal fairs and even bride/groom fairs. Popular traditional events are still organized in the honor of rivers and lakes and held at their banks. The economic value of water increased by the mid twentieth century with tourism linked to recreation, ecotourism and water sports. In addition, the use of water in hydropower, industry and municipal consumption gained prominence. Technological developments such as dams linked to rivers and lakes for energy generation and irrigation are considered to be the key economic drivers of the society. Water management with scientific and sophisticated tools aimed at optimal utilization and management of the water systems and to make the development more complimentary to the environment and economy became usual.

Water became a significant concern by the end of twentieth century in terms of lack of availability and accessibility because it started affecting economic growth and even the balance of human life. The state of rivers and lakes, the community and the water governance changed. Rivers and lakes became a politically contested resource at city level, state level, national level and even international level. Reclamations of land from the rivers and lakes for urban development activity became common at city level. Urban development and planning began to dominate over the existence of the water systems (Bal 1999). Governing surface and ground water separately became a challenge, adding more complexity with water quantity and quality management (World Bank 1998). The growing demand and competition between municipal consumption and industry due to the rapid urbanization, the uncontrolled access to surface water and groundwater and the lack of proper institutional arrangements led to pollution and degradation of surface water and ground water sources. The water exploitation indiscriminately affected the health of rivers and lakes and droughts and floods became common in many cities. The river and lake beds turned into large cesspools and became the recipients of industrial and domestic wastes, generated from the cities. In addition, land encroachments and squatting by the residents, industries and sometimes even by the state organizations affected the rivers and lakes systems.

The growing disagreement on sectoral water management led to the integrated water resource management (IWRM). IWRM as a process to promote coordinated development and management of water, in order to maximize economic and social welfare in an equitable manner, without compromising the sustainability of vital eco-systems (Bansil 1991). Although there was an overtone of socio-economic values in IWRM in the form of peoples' participation, employment generation; the mindset that water is a government's business prevailed in the society. This was the time when the slogan of 'access to water was considered to be a fundamental right of every citizen'. The state being the authority was obliged to take care of 'water as a good', with the citizens as end users. Narain (2000) advocated institutional reforms in India's water governance through: securing greater coordination and integration within the water management organizations, restructuring water bureaucracies as inter-disciplinary, financially autonomous organizations and defining water rights and dual accountability between user groups and the bureaucracy.

In the last decade, sustainability of lakes and rivers became high in the water governance agenda because of the growing threat to the existence of rivers and lakes. Water gained more focus on environmental grounds when the concepts of climate change and global warming came in the forefront of global environmental agendas. The National Water Policy of 2002 puts emphasis on integrated water resource development and management for optimal and sustainable utilization of available surface and ground water resources, the creation of sound information systems, the use of traditional methods of water conservation and non-conventional methods for water utilization and demand management and also to have a synergy between the government and non-governmental organization for water conservation and utilization (MoWR 2002). The year 2003, declared as the 'International Year of Freshwater' by the United Nations, made water the subject of most environmental and developmental discourses. National and international water initiatives became very active in India, such as the formation of the National Lake Conservation Plan (NLCP) in 2003, the promotion of River Basin

Organizations (RBO) in the line of integrated river basin management (IRBM similar approach as IWRM) and many wetlands were declared as Ramsar sites for conservation. The legal institutions and community based organizations are also more active over environmental concerns of water (Reddy and Char 2006).

The concept of sustainable water management (SWM) is now common in the policy and research domain in India. The catch is who uses it and what values are attached to it. The use-value in terms of social-economic values are driving however, the bequest value and intrinsic value in terms of ecological values are slowly gaining momentum. Sustainability of rivers and lakes are linked to the sustainability of cities. It is also the time of bringing people back into the issue of water governance. Water Users Association (WUA) formations for managing canals, lakes and ponds, portion of rivers and irrigation systems are considered an efficient way to get better outputs in water management (Narain 2000). The WUA became effective and functioning in many rural areas but still face problems to take-off in urban areas. The urban lifestyle and occupation keeps urban people away from direct interaction to the water systems, rivers/lakes are perceived as places of recreation and water as a 'service' for which people pay tax or user charges (Bal 2006).

The several values involved in the water governance in India are reflected in the several sectors and institutions involved in governing the river and lake systems. Reddy and Char (2006) present a comprehensive list of institutions linked to water governance and show concerns over the fragmentation of responsibilities and coordination amongst the organizations and policy implementations.

One of the prominent ways in which water governance is reflected in the society is in spatial development. Plans and projects for river/lake regenerations and redevelopments, rehabilitation of slums encroaching the river/lake beds, waste water treatment plans and rain water harvesting are exceedingly seen as important in addition to the modern water quantity and quality management (Bal 2006). Since developing new sources of water is costly, the logic of re-using the waste water generated from municipal consumption and industry also rose as new domain in the water governance. Waste water is now realized to be an alternative source of water. Such initiatives are underway within the Jawaharlal Nehru National Urban Renewal Mission, JnNURM (AMC and AUDA 2005). Under this scheme, river/ lakes are addressed through the infrastructure (waste water and/or storm water) development. The privatization and public-private partnership (PPP) initially took off with lot of promises since international organizations such as World Bank, International Monetary Fund and Asian Development Bank promoted private sector-led growth in water works and services. PPP was promoted as vehicle to achieve the required growth in most infrastructures, including the water sector. Soon serious criticisms and disapproval rose from the civil society groups and experts regarding the priorities and strategies of the private sectors. PPP's further crumpled with the global recession when government finances were used to bail out many PPP projects. However, PPP probably will not disappear anymore but their nature may change over time (Dwivedi 2010).

Case: Revival of Lakes in Ahmedabad City

An illustration is given with some urban lakes in India. Just like many other villages in the earlier days, habitation in the region of Ahmedabad was strategically located at the edge of lakes and ponds. The lakes and ponds of Ahmedabad served several needs of rural life such as impounding the surplus of rain water, recharging the ground water reservoirs and feeding the wells, providing irrigation, supplying drinking water for human beings and cattle, providing places for bathing, washing, cultivation of water demanding produces, and a number of other functions. The governance of the lakes and ponds was therefore directly in the hands of village people. In the mid twentieth century, when the villages started getting engulfed in Ahmedabad's urban development, the functions of the lakes and ponds slowly changed. They became recipient of human and waste squatting. This was the phase of neglecting lakes and ponds in the city. The governing responsibility was under the national government, to which control and management was a farfetched work. At the same time, the local government was reluctant to go through the bureaucratic process to take over its development. Moreover, the community was by far the least interested in development, since the urban occupation and life style had no direct association with the lakes. However, in the last decade, many lakes in Ahmedabad are revitalized for mainly city's infrastructure functions such as storm water collections points for the storm water drainage system of the city, for recreational development and for the creation of real estate property in the form of land reclamation from the lake area (AMC and AUDA 2005). The quality and quantity of the water in the lakes was less priority to the agenda of the development of the area. The property prices of the surrounding areas of the lakes that are developed rose very high. The governance is in the hands of local government, which is trying to reach partnerships with both private sectors and community based organizations.

Stages of Water Governance in India

Learning from what was described above, it appears that in historical India, the human health value related to water and food demands is reflected in domestic use, irrigation, safety from flood and drought protection. They were given shades of rituals and are linked to socio-cultural values. Ecological values were the underpinnings of the socio-cultural values. Spatial development followed the existing rivers, lakes and other water bodies. State owned water was usually managed by the community. Social systems followed the water system.

In the 20th Century, apart from the traditional economic values, benefits for larger developments at the core such as large and small dams for water reservoirs, energy generation, municipal and industrial consumption. Spatial development manipulated the existence of rivers, lakes and other water bodies that were State owned. The State is seen as service provider while community and industries are the users. Water systems follow the social systems.

Recently, periodical risks and consequences of degradation of water resources brought ecological and sustainability values high on the water governance agenda. Economic-socio-cultural values are considered necessary for ecological sustainability. Political value is considered prime in the aversion of the degraded state of water resources. State owned waters are managed increasingly in partnerships, with participation of community and NGOs. Integrated water management and sustainable water management are the main conceptualizations of the attempt to find balance between the social systems and water systems.

A kaleidoscopic overview of the value of water and water governance focusing on the river and lakes in India, which is presented above, is represented in Table 13.2:

Table 13.2   Changes in value perception in India

Relative value (importance related to other values)	Importance: * little, ** significant, ***high		
	Historical (+- before 1950)	**Modern (+- 1950-2000)**	**Recent (+- after 2000)**
Religious/spiritual	***	**	**
Drinking water	***	**	*
Fish production	***	**	*
Transportation by ship	***	**	*
Transportation by pipes	*	**	***
Sand and clay	*	**	***
Recreation	**	**	***
Cooling water			
Electricity production	*	**	***
Ecology	***	*	**
Attractiveness for housing (aesthetics)	**	**	***

Large similarities between the development in domination values in India and the Netherlands can be observed. After basically life threatening values, during modernization the economic values came into the picture, only recently followed by non-use values.

Discussion and Recommendations

Over centuries there has been a strong relation between the value of water systems, like rivers and lakes, and the way these water systems are governed. Several values are associated with rivers and lakes, such as socio-cultural values, economic values, ecological values and environmental values. Values connect individuals, empower stakeholders and frame the water governance in a more comprehensive manner than before. Multiple sectors dealing with water governance is an outcome of the demand for different values by the society and consequently the water managers. From the examples it is reflected how the expected and realized values of lake systems result from the functions of the water system and the people of the society who bring in and have knowledge to manage water systems accordingly. Connecting values and the knowledge brought into the management scope have enlarged the possibilities for multi-functionality of the system and have helped in maximizing the total value of the water system.

Societies have exploited water systems in such a way that these have reached their ecological limits. The governance emphasis tends to co-evolution between ecological and economic values. In a transition towards sustainability, a trend is observed to ground human use on the limits of the natural water system, leading to practices like adaptation, participation and strengthening of resilience. Table 13.3 presents the change of values and the water governance approach over time.

Table 13.3   Developments in the concept of water management

Phase	Concept	Value
historical times	• flood control (wet areas) drinking water supply (dry areas) • water quantity management	• human health • land use/food production
modernization	• sectoral water management • integrated water management	• human use • water system health
recent times	• sustainable water management adaptive water management	• sustainability (long term) interaction, adaptation, resilience

In general, the differences between the governance systems in The Netherlands and in the Indian society are large. Some differences in the governance of water systems appear to be temporal, corresponding with some national or local conditions that will disappear in the long run as a result of overarching trends reflecting on-going modernization processes. In this respect, similarities in water management between Netherlands and India are likely to increase. Considering the transition, further research could identify the values that connect or compete with each other over time and space. A scheme that could give some guidance is presented in Table 13.4.

Table 13.4   Changes in water management

FROM traditional water management	TO Modern water management
Water as an 'enemy'	Water as a 'friend'
• 'fighting against water'	• 'living with water'
• Sectoral water management	• Integrated water system management
• Effective and efficient	• Sustainable: long term responsibility
• Supply Management	• Demand Management
• Water systems follow social processes	• Social processes follow water systems
• Water follows spatial development	• Spatial development follows water
• Technocratic:	• Ecosystem based:
• build and maintain	• support resilience and self-regulation
National	**International and regional**
• Government lead water management	• Participative water management
• 'Command and control' water policy	• Interactive water management

These changes are the outcome of which values are attributed to water systems. 'Beauty' and 'Nature', for example, are for a large part aesthetical values that increased their weight in post-modern times of relative luxury. In this way, the transition corresponds with the change from exploiting the nature for human use to approaching nature as an independent value that can upgrade civilization in various ways. The awareness that society depends on large ecosystems of which they are part of made a contribution to the increase of the ecological value. It also resulted in governance approaches that take the characteristics of the ecosystem into account. In addition, it has brought the equal access to consumption of water and the access to mechanisms of influencing the decisions about water systems to the forefront. These values are considered to be responsible for the revival of the water systems in recent times. Although their nature is completely opposite, both in times of 'living with water' and in times of 'fighting the water' the connective capacity of the water systems is large. In both situations water systems connect people and societies via the many positive and negative values that they possess.

Values are a driving factor for changes in water management, but which value(s) will connect in the future in times of increasing urban population density everywhere? The answer depends mainly on the values that will lead human behavior. There is a risk for urban societies where the opportunities to interact with water systems are limited. It could be one of the main factors that determine the paradox of on the one hand the high value that generally is attributed to water and on the other hand the current state of many rivers and lakes. At the same time the deteriorated state can also accelerate the transition towards sustainability, and again this value proves to be a connector in societal development today as it was during traditional water management practices.

Bibliography

Agarwal, A. and Narain, S. 2001. *Dying Wisdom*. Centre for Science and Environment, Delhi: CSE.

Agarwal, A., Narain, S. and Khurana, I. 2001. *Making Water Everybody's Business: Practice and Policy of Water Harvesting*. Centre for Science and Environment, Delhi: CSE.

Allen, T.F.H., Bandurski B.L. and King A.W. 1992. *The Ecosystem Approach: Theory and Ecosystem Integrity*, Washington D.C. (USA): International Joint Commission United States and Canada, Boulder, CO: Westview Press.

AMC and AUDA. 2005. *Jawaharlal Nehru National Urban Renewal Mission: City Development Plan Ahmedabad* 2006-2012. Ahmedabad: Ahmedabad Municipal Corporation and Ahmedabad Urban Development Authority.

Anderies, J.M., Janssen, M.A. and Ostrom, E. 2004. A Framework to Analyze the Robustness of Social-ecological Systems from an Institutional Perspective, *Ecology and Society*, 9(1), 18.

Bal, M. 1999. *Open Spaces in the Urban Context – Lakes as an Opportunity*. Thesis: Post Graduate Diploma in Urban Design, School of Architecture, CEPT University, Ahmedabad, India.

Bal, M. 2006. *An Assessment of the Case for Increase in Public Amenity and Space*. Thesis: MPhil in Planning, Growth and Regeneration, Department of Land Economics, Cambridge University, UK.

Bansil, P.C. 1991. *Water Management in India*. New Delhi: Concept Publishing Company.

Biswas, Asit K. 2004. Integrated Water Resources Management: A Reassessment, *Water International*, 9(2), 2004, pp. 248-56.

Biswas, Asit K. 2008. Integrated Water Resources Management: Is It Working?, *Water Resources Development*, 24(1), March 2008, pp. 5-22.

Bouma, J.J., Francois, D., et al. 2009. Assessing socio-economic impacts of wave overtopping: An institutional perspective, *Coastal Engineering*. Elsevier, 56(2), 1-6.

Braungart, M., MacDonough, W. and Bollinger, A. 2007. Cradle-to-cradle design: Creating healthy emissions – a strategy for eco-effective product and system design, *Journal of Cleaner Production*, 15, 1337-48.

DiMagio, P.J. and Powell, W.W. 1983. The Iron cage revisited: Institutional iso-morphism and collective rationality in organizational fields, *American Sociological Review*, 48, 147-60.

Dubbelman, H. 1999. *Maatschappelijke golven in de waterbouwkunde*, dissertation Delft University of Technology, Delft: Delft University Press.

Dwivedi, G. 2010. *Public-Private Partnerships in Water Sector: Partnerships or Privatisation*? Manthan Adhyayan Kendra, Badwani, India.

Euromarket 2003. Water Liberalisation Scenarios. *Analysis of the European Union's Explicit and Implicit Policies and Approaches in the Larger Water Sector*, Euromarket Group, EU: Brussel. Website: http://www.unesco-ihe.org/ Project-Activities/Project-Portfolio/EUROMARKET-Water-Liberalisation-Scenarios.

European Union 2000. *Water Framework Directive*, Directive 2000/60/EC, Brussel: EU.

Geldof, G.D. 1994. Adaptief waterbeheer, in *Het Waterschap, juni 1994*. Deventer: Tauw.

Hoekstra, A.Y. 2008. Human appropriation of natural capital: A comparison of ecological footprint and water footprint analysis, *Journal of Ecological Economics*, doi: 10.1016/j.ecolecon.2008.06.021. Elsevier.

Hooper, B.P. 2005. *Integrated River Basin Governance*, Learning from International experience, London/Seattle: IWM Publishing.

ICWE 1992. International Conference on Water and the Environment, *Development Issues for the 21st century*, The Dublin Statement Report of the Conference, ICWE Conference January 26-31, 1992, Dublin Ireland, Dublin: ICWE.

Ministry of Water Management and Infrastructure 1985. *Omgaan met Water, naar een integraal waterbeleid* (Dealing with Water, towards an integrated water policy). Den Haag: SDU.

MoWR 2002. Ministry of Water Resources. *National Water Policy*. New Delhi: Government of India.

Narain, V. 2000. India's water crisis: The challenges of Governance, *Water Policy*, 2, pp. 433-44.

Narain, V. 1998. Towards a new Ground Water Institution for India. *Water Policy*, 1(3), pp. 357-65.

North, D.C. 1990. *Institutions, Institutional Change and Economic Growth*. Cambridge: Cambridge University Press.

Ostrom, E. 1990. *Governing the Commons: The Evolution of Institutions for Collective Action*. New York: Cambridge University Press.

Pearce, D.W. and Moran, D. 1994. *The Economic Value of Biodiversity*. In association with the Biodiversity Programme of IUCN- The World Conservation Union. Earthscan, London.

Reddy, M.S. and Char, N.V.V. 2006. *Management of Lakes in India*. Lakes and Reservoirs: Research and Management 2006, 11, 227-37.

Saeijs, H.L.F. 1995. *Levend water en een Wereldstad, ecologie als economische factor in het waterbeheer,* oratie Erasmus Universiteit Rotterdam, Rotterdam: Erasmus Studiecentrum voor Milieukunde.

Schuijt, K. 2003. *Valuation of Water: The Process of Economic Valuation of Ecosystems in Water Management*, PhD dissertation, Erasmus University Rotterdam.

Teclaf, Ludwik A. 1996. Evolution of the River Basin Concept in International Water Law, *Natural Resources Journal*, 36(2), Spring 1996.

UN 1987. United Nations, Register of international rivers and lake basins, (Department of Economic and Social Affairs), *Water and Supply Management*, 2(1), pp. 1-58.

UNCED (United Nations Conference on Environment and Development), *Agenda 21*, Declaration of Rio de Janeiro, New York: UN.

Valkering P. and A. Offermans 2008. *Inspelen op verandering: Naar een robuuste en flexible strategie voor waterbeheer*. Eindrapportage van de pilotstudie Perspectieven in Integraal Waterbeheer, Maastricht: International Centre for Integrated assessment and Sustainable development.

Van Ast, J.A. 1998. Trends Towards Interactive Water Management; Developments in International River Basin Management, *Physics and Chemistry of the Earth (B)*, 24(6), Elsevier Science. Oxford, blz 597-602; 1999.

Van Ast, J.A. 2000. Interactief watermanagement in grensoverschrijdende riviersystemen (Interactive water management in transboundary river systems), Delft: Eburon.

Van der Brugge, R. and Rotmans, J. 2010. Towards Transition Management of European Water Resources, *Journal Water Resource Management*, 2010.

Van der Veeren, R. and R van Cleef 2008. *Ervaringen met MKBA in het natuur- en milieubeleid*, Tijdschrift H20/17, pp.17-19.

Van Rooy, P.T.J.C., van Sluis J.W., Tolkamp H.H. and de Jong J. 1997. Op weg naar totaal waterbeheer (7) AUTUNNO, *H2O, 11 (30)* 1997, 348-55.

Van Schie, N. and Bouma, J.J. 2008. *The Concept of Covaluation: Institutionalisation the Involvement of Local (Public) Values in Regional Planning on Water.* Competition and Regulation in Network Industries, 9(4), 361-92, Intersentia.

WCED 1987. World Commission on Environment and Development, *Our Common Future*. Oxford: Oxford University Press.

Williamson, O.E. 1998. Transaction costs economics: How it works, where it is headed, *The Economist*, 146(1), pp. 23-58.

Williamson, O.E. 1979. Transaction costs economics: The governance of contractual relations, *Journal of Law and Economics*, 22 October, pp. 3-61.

World Bank 1998. *India. Water Resources Management Sector Review: Report on Inter-sectoral Water Allocation, Planning and Management*, New York: UN.

Chapter 14

Creating Legitimacy in Water Governance Networks through Complexity Sensitive Management

Jurian Edelenbos, Ingmar van Meerkerk and Erik Hans Klijn

Introduction

Water projects are of complex nature, because these projects cross different governmental, jurisdictional, geographical and functional boundaries (Pahl-Wostl 2007, Edelenbos 2010). Moreover, these projects are often developed and implemented in governance networks of interdependent actors, which employ dynamic interaction and negotiation processes with each other in order to find effective and legitimate solutions (Edelenbos et al. 2010b). The multi-faceted aspects of water projects stress the interconnected nature of these projects. Water touches upon the issues and interests of spatial planning, environment, nature and livability. The connection of different interests in package deals is important to realize legitimized outcome from water governance processes as already stressed in the first chapter of this book.

Network management is of major importance for the functioning and the performance of governance networks, including their democratic legitimacy (see for example Koppenjan and Klijn 2004, Edelenbos and Klijn 2006, Klijn et al. 2010, Meier and O'Toole 2001, 2007). Network management is especially focused on organizing connections between different actors in different spheres, political, governmental and societal (Edelenbos et al. 2011). However, empirical insights in water governance network about the relationship between a connective style of network management and legitimacy is lacking.

In this chapter we will investigate this relationship by elaborating *connective management* style through the concept of *complexity sensitive management* and its effect on *different kinds of legitimacy*. Data is gathered through survey research (N=166), which was conducted in 2010 among respondents involved in water projects in the Netherlands. These water projects are developed in complex governance networks, because they touch on the interests of a variety of public and non-public actors and their realization is dependent on these same actors (for example, Koppenjan and Klijn 2004, Sabatier et al. 2005, Lubell and Lippert 2011, Edelenbos and Teisman 2011). Throughout the chapter we will illustrate the survey results with qualitative case material. These cases were also part of the survey. This case material is collected by interviews and document analysis and is part of a study on water governance in The Netherlands (see Van Buuren et al. 2010).

This chapter is structured in the following way. In the next section, we elaborate the concept governance networks and its relationship with legitimacy. Subsequently, we discuss the relationship between complexity sensitive management – and legitimacy and formulate three research hypotheses in the next section. The following section is dedicated to our research methods and techniques. We finish this chapter by drawing conclusions and further discussing the findings.

Water Governance Networks and Legitimacy

Governance Networks and the Issue of Legitimacy

Within contemporary public administration theory, it is recognized that many decision-making processes take place within interdependent sets of actors (for example, Marsh and Rhodes 1992, Rhodes 1997, Kickert et al. 1997, Pierre and Peters 2000, Sorensen and Torfing 2007). This also applies for the sector of water (resource) management (Pahl-Wostl 2007). We therefore depart from a view on networks, which approaches networks as loosely coupled interrelationships between governmental, societal and private actors around policy problems.

Although the literature on governance networks is not well-developed on the topic of legitimacy, it does suggest that governance networks represent a threat to representative democracy, but is not necessarily a threat to democracy as such (Sørensen and Torfing 2007b: 233). Governance processes in governance networks offer "...new ways of connecting public policy-making to citizens and stakeholders, overcoming the constraints and limitations of representative democracy and party politics" (Klijn and Sklecher 2007: 588). There is however very little empirical work on the democratic nature of governance networks although theoretical work on this is growing (see Sorensen and Torfing 2007).

Governance Networks and Different Sources and Forms of Legitimacy

Regarding defining the concept 'legitimacy', it is important to make a distinction between two levels: (1) the legitimacy of governance networks as a *system*, and (2) the legitimacy of *governance practices* unfolding in governance networks. Systemic legitimacy is about the acceptance of a governance regime or political institutions (for example, Held 2006) and is often the focus of political science oriented research. Governance practice legitimacy is focused on the legitimacy of concrete policy and decision-making processes. In this chapter we focus on the latter definition. Building on Scharpf (1999), we distinguish three different types of legitimacy: (1) output, (2) throughput, and (3) procedural legitimacy. Instead of input legitimacy we focus on procedural legitimacy. Input legitimacy is about mechanisms or procedures to link preferences of citizens to political decision-making and accountability structures

(Scharpf 1999, Van Kersbergen and Van Waarden 2004). However, because governance networks are a-constitutional (Mathur and Skelcher 2007: 229), it is less easily to locate loci of power. We therefore focus on following formal procedures as an instrument to gain accountability. In the proceeding paragraphs, we further elaborate these three types of legitimacy.

In literature, output legitimacy is built up out of two dimensions. The first dimension is about the problem solving capacity of policy outputs generated by governance processes. Political choices and public policies are legitimate if they will generally represent effective solutions to common problems of the governed (Scharpf 1999). The second dimension of output legitimacy is about the acceptance of policy outputs by citizens and stakeholders (for example, Edelenbos et al. 2010). Some scholars argue that legitimacy comes from pragmatic consideration when stakeholders (citizens, NGOs, etc.) believe that decision-making outcomes are relevant and in their own interests (Held 2006, Kooiman 1993, 2000).

Throughput legitimacy is about the democratic quality of the process (Dryzek 2000). Openness, accessibility and transparency are often-mentioned aspects of this kind of legitimacy (Macpherson 1979, Berry et al. 1993, Scharpf 1999, Hirst 2000, Young 2000, Held 2006). By involving more actors (and certainly citizens), decision-making acquires a less closed character, leading to more transparency, deliberative quality and mutual understanding (Dryzek 2000).

Procedural legitimacy means that democratic legitimacy is gained by following formal governmental procedures and rule of law (see Luhmann 1969, Esmark 2007). Legitimacy is achieved if decisions are made according to procedures that include some forms of accountability such as the rule of law (Van Kersbergen and Van Waarden 2004: 156). It "…implies that some actors have the right to hold other actors to a set of standards, to judge whether they have fulfilled their responsibilities in light of these standards and to impose sanctions if they determine that these responsibilities have not been met" (Grant and Keohane 2005: 29).

How the different forms of legitimacy are unfolding in practice is highly dependent on the specific context. O'Toole (1997: 458) argues that network management "..provides both complications and opportunities to facilitate parts of the democratic ideal". In the next section we elaborate this thought, focusing on the role of network management.

Network Management and its Influence on Legitimacy

Network management is in essence an inter-organizational activity (Hanf and Scharpf 1978, Gage and Mandell 1990, Kickert et al. 1997). Network management is about connecting people and is focused on enabling interactions and relationship building in order to develop and explore content and attempt to come to an agreement on sharing resources and joint action (Rogers and Whetten 1982, Scharpf 1978). Research on network management shows that network management activities that are focused on developing relations between actors from different organizations through, for example, selective (de)activation and boundary spanning activities have an (significant) impact on achieving good (process and content) outcomes (Klijn et al. 2010). The management of complex water issues is about making meaningful connections between a wide variety of actors from different layers, domains and sectors (Edelenbos 2010). Thus, connecting is an important network management strategy in water (resource) management.

Management in governance networks often clashes with institutions of representative democracy (Edelenbos 2005). Representative democracy provides the democratic foundations of hierarchical-instrumental policy making (Wagenaar 2007: 41). This way of policy-making often conflicts with the horizontal processes in governance networks (for example, Kickert et al. 1997, Klijn and Skelcher 2007, Wagenaar 2007, Teisman et al. 2009). Managers operating in governance networks have to deal with this tension; they have to deal with institutions which are based on traditional foundations of representative democracy on the one hand and the fragmented and complex reality of governance networks with all kind of actors (citizens, NGOs, companies, etc.) on the other hand (Klijn and Skelcher 2007). This tense full context requires an adaptive or a complexity sensitive network management style (Edelenbos and Klijn 2009, Teisman et al. 2009).

A complexity oriented, or *complexity sensitive management style* as we call it in this chapter, is considered to be more suited to solving complex issues within governance networks (c.f. Teisman et al. 2009). This management style is based on approaching complex phenomena in a holistic manner (Uhl-Bien et al. 2007, Edelenbos et al. 2009, Jackson 2000, Rosenhead 1998, Senge 1990). It is therefore more oriented at the interactions and the interdependencies between parts of issues and networks. It means that managers do not draw strict lines between different parts of complex issues and policy processes, but are rather oriented towards making meaningful connections and embeddedness (Edelenbos 2010). A complexity sensitive management style is oriented at creating the context in which effective and legitimate governance processes could unfold.

In line with the literature on complexity management, one can argue that a complexity sensitive management style will enhance certain forms of legitimacy and will undermine other forms of legitimacy. Firstly, the focus on stakeholder diversity and stakeholder interaction contributes to "..the flow of experiential knowledge through the system so that they enable actors in the system to produce, appreciate and select productive intervention strategies and arrive at the coordination of problem solving and decision making" (Wagenaar 2007: 18). Hence, including different stakeholders and organizations could result in solutions which cover the diversity of functions and interests, touched by the complex issue at stake, – leading to relevant and supported outcomes (Teisman et al. 2009, Edelenbos 2010). Giving room for other interests could stimulate governance processes in which stakeholders are thinking, along with policy initiators and solving the policy issue at stake, rather than organizing resistance against policy initiators. Furthermore, it enhances the chance of the emergence of unforeseen combinations of viewpoints, and therefore innovative solutions (Uhl-Bien et al. 2007). In all we expect higher output legitimacy through a complexity sensitive management style in governance networks:

H1: A complexity sensitive management style within governance networks dealing with complex water projects will lead to higher output legitimacy.

Moreover, complexity sensitive network management is focused on the involvement of a broad range of stakeholders. Instead of reducing the administrative complexity by focusing on a few parties who are in charge, the manager involves different stakeholders with different interests (Hazy 2008, Edelenbos et al. 2009). The management style is focused on inclusion of stakeholders and transparency of the process. This means that a complexity sensitive management style should provide more opportunities for interaction, deliberation and debate (Dryzek 2000, Edelenbos et al. 2010b). Therefore, we expect a positive relationship between complexity sensitive management style and throughput legitimacy.

H2: A complexity sensitive management style within governance networks dealing with complex water projects will lead to higher throughput legitimacy.

A complexity sensitive management style takes the dynamics around a project into account and provides opportunities for stakeholder interactions and influence on the course of action (Edelenbos et al. 2009). We expect that the manager is mainly focused on the environment of the project; adapting initial preferences to emerging demands of stakeholders in the environment of the project. This outward orientation comes at the expense of the inward orientation, i.e. the way shareholders (the core actors in the governance network) approach problems and solutions and normal procedures that are being followed, which are focused on efficiency and control (Schreiber and Carley 2008: 294). Hence, we expect that the needed flexibility for a complexity sensitive management style contrast with the institutionalized way of working within traditional public bureaucracies. This leads to our third hypothesis.

H3: A complexity sensitive management style within governance networks dealing with complex water projects will lead to lower procedural legitimacy.

Research Method, Sample and Measurement

Research Method: Survey Approach

To examine complex water issues in governance networks we conducted a survey among participants in water projects with a spatial land use character in The Netherlands. In The Netherlands, spatial planning projects and water projects are often related because of the strong presence of water and water related issues. These 'water related land use' projects have often a complex nature, because a variety of spatial functions (for example, housing, infrastructure, agriculture, nature development and water retention) are included and different domains (policy sectors), governance levels and private/societal actors are involved (for example, Van Buuren et al. 2010).

We collected data from a web-based survey held in 2010 (April-May). We were able to acquire 874 e-mail addresses of people from our target group, by utilizing the mailing list of 'Living with Water'. This is a national research program directed at developing and sharing knowledge about management of complex water projects which are being developed in interaction with spatial/environmental functions in the Netherlands. Different types of organizations collaborate in this program, including municipalities, water boards, environmental interest groups, building contractors and project management organizations. Furthermore, individual participants, such as residents living in project areas are also part of the mailing list. The mailing list is, among other things, used for providing information on certain water projects and policies. Considering the variety of actors on this mailing list, we argue that our respondents represent different organizational backgrounds actors have in networks around complex water projects. The respondents also represent different levels of participation: they include managers, closely involved participants, and bystanders (see below).

Population, Sample and Unit of Analysis

Table 14.1 describes the population and sample used for the survey and the number of respondents who have returned the questionnaire. A total of 272 questionnaires (31.1 per cent) were returned. After conducting a missing value analysis, 200 respondents were included in the analysis. The removed questionnaires (72 cases) were not completed.

We asked the respondents at the start of the questionnaire to name the project of which they have been mostly involved and to answer the questions regarding this project. The 200 respondents were involved in 166 different water projects. These water projects are geographically dispersed over the Netherlands. Because there are several respondents who are involved in the same water project and thus the same

Table 14.1   Population and sample

Number of people on Living with Water List (after removing researchers, communication and marketing bureaus, etc.)	874
Returned questionnaires	272
Sample after removing questionnaires with too many missing data	200
Analyzed questionnaires (1 respondent per project)	166

governance network, we randomly selected one respondent for each project. In this way we made sure that the data from the different respondents are independent.

Characteristics of our Respondents

Because the different respondents have different backgrounds, considering the different types of organizations on the mailing list, we made a general distinction in the role of the respondent in the project. The majority of our respondents (75 per cent) are the most active actors in the project. This group consists of managers (36 per cent of total sample) and respondents who are actively participating in the project (39 per cent of total sample). The other quarter of our respondents (25 per cent) consists of people who are less actively involved in the project (respondents who think along in certain parts of the project or bystanders). Because these different positions could influence the perceptions of the way in which the manager operates and how the legitimacy of the projects is judged, we included the position of the respondent as a control variable in our regression analyses (see below). Furthermore, we asked for the experience of our respondents in complex projects. On average, the respondents of our survey have been involved in complex projects for twelve years. This shows that the respondents are quite experienced in dealing with governance networks. However, the standard deviation is high (8.81), which means that large differences exist. Therefore, we also included experience as a control variable (see below).

Characteristics of the Water Projects and the Governance Networks

To measure the complexity of the projects and of the networks we asked several questions concerning the project and network characteristics (see Agranoff and McGuire 2001, Kickert et al. 1997, Klijn et al. 2010a, Koppenjan and Klijn 2004, Sørensen and Torfing 2007). In Table 14.2, an overview of the outcomes is provided. 92.2 per cent of the respondents respond that 'their' water project is related to other projects. On average about 3 planning activities or spatial functions are combined in the project. However, the standard deviation of 1.5 is quite high, indicating that in some projects considerably more planning activities are combined than in others. In 50.9 per cent of the cases 3 or more spatial functions (such as nature development, housing, water retention, recreation etc.) were involved and in 25.5 per cent of the cases 4 or more spatial functions were involved. 90.4 per cent of the respondents participate in a water project with more than 5 actors involved; in 53 per cent of the cases more than 10 actors are involved and in 27.7 per cent of the cases even 20 actors or more are participating. 76.7 per cent of the respondents state that they are strongly dependent on other actors within the network. These results indicate that the projects in which the respondents participated are developed in governance networks.

Table 14.2   Characteristics of the projects (N=166)

Number of different activities	Mean = 2.73 (sd: 1.5)	Includes water storage, houses, business terrain, environmental development, commercial development, infrastructure (rail and public highways)
Project includes: Water storage Construction of houses Nature development	95.8% 47.2% 82.2%	
Experienced dependency	M = 3.90 (sd: 0.90)	5 point Likert scale
Level of conflict	M = 2.89 (sd: 1.09)	5 point Likert scale
Unexpected events	M = 3.33 (sd: 0.94)	5 point Likert scale

Measurement

Core Variables

In this chapter we look at four core variables:

1. output legitimacy,
2. throughput legitimacy,
3. procedural legitimacy and
4. complexity sensitive management style.

All the answers on the different items concerning these core variables were given on a five-point Likert scale ranging from totally disagree to totally agree or ranging from certainly not to certainly yes. Because we make use of a survey we actually only could make use of the perceived outcomes of the different involved participant of the projects.

Measuring our independent variable: complexity sensitive management (CSM) The managers in our survey are public managers working in or for governmental organizations. In our conceptualization, complexity sensitive management means that the manager is sensitive for the interdependencies and interactions between different parts of complex issues (Choi et al. 2001, Teisman 2005, Edelenbos and Teisman 2008). We measured this variable by four different items, (see appendix I for the concrete survey questions) (Koppenjan and Klijn 2004, Edelenbos and Klijn 2006, Teisman 2005):

1. A complexity sensitive manager is aimed at connecting different spatial functions in the development of the project;

2. The manager tries to adapt the project to the demands and wishes of the stakeholders;
3. The manager tries to keep the project in line with the expectations of the involved stakeholders. It therefore creates enough time for representatives to discuss the developments with their grass-roots;
4. A complexity sensitive manager tries to connect the different interests which are present in governance networks.

The Cronbach's alpha of the four items was 0.71.

Measuring our Dependent Variables: Legitimacy

Output legitimacy As described above, we distinguish two dimensions of output legitimacy: the problem solving capacity of the policy outputs and the acceptance of these outputs by stakeholders. Building on prior survey research (Edelenbos et al. 2010, Klijn et al. 2010a) we have used the following four items to measure output legitimacy. These items formed a reliable scale, with a Cronbach's alpha of .72. The concrete questions can be found in appendix I. The two items concerning the problem-solving capacity:

1. The extent to which the solutions really address the problem, the responsiveness (see Innes and Boohler 2003. Scharpf 1999);
2. The robustness of the results, that is, the future robustness (time frame) of the results (see Koppenjan and Klijn 2004);

The two items concerning the acceptance of the policy outputs and decisions (Edelenbos et al. 2010):

1. The support for the results of the governance process;
2. The support for the substantiation of the decisions.

Throughput legitimacy As we described above throughput legitimacy is about the quality of the process. We used six items (see appendix I) to measure three different aspects of the democratic quality of the process (Bekkers and Edwards 2007. Dryzek 2000. Edelenbos and Klijn. 2006. Edelenbos et al. 2010. Klijn 2009. Scharpf 1999):

1. Voice. This refers to the depth (the intensity and the influence of stakeholders) and width (how many stakeholders) of participation;
2. Due deliberation. This aspect focuses on the quality of the deliberation process: the extent to which there were real opportunities for debate and the quality of the argumentation process;

3. Transparency. This aspect focuses on the availability and accessibility of information. In this way participants are better able to make well-informed judgments and arguments.

The six items of throughput legitimacy resulted in a scale with a Cronbach's alpha of .80.

Procedural legitimacy   Procedural legitimacy is about gaining legitimacy from institutionalized governmental procedures and rule following behavior (Koppenjan and Klijn 2004, Edelenbos 2005). In our questionnaire we distinguished therefore two items measuring to what extent the governance process has been structured by following formal procedures (see appendix I):

1. Determination of the governance process by a priori determined procedures and rules; and
2. Emphasis on compliance to formal rules and procedures.

These items formed a scale with a Cronbach's alpha of .75.

Control Variables

Of course, legitimacy could be influenced by a lot of other variables. To test the influence of specific respondent and project characteristics on the outcomes, the following control variables are involved in the analysis.

Project phase   The phase of the project can also influence the perception of management style and/or level and form of legitimacy. For instance, almost by definition, there will be fewer outcomes in the first phases of a spatial project and therefore influence output legitimacy. We distinguished seven different phases in the activities around the water/spatial projects (see the appendix for the items). In most of the cases (65.5 per cent) the project plan is developed and realized by elected representatives. In 29.6 per cent of the cases construction activities are already taken place. To include this variable in the analysis we added the different finished activities per respondent.

Characteristics of the environment of the network   The characteristics of the environment of the network could probably influence management style and legitimacy. We asked respondents to indicate the environment of the governance network. They could indicate on a five point Likert scale the a. stability of the environment, b. the relationship with other projects and c. the level of differences of opinion about the project. 69.8 per cent of the respondents indicates that the governance network of which they are part operates in a changing (political, social, and/or economical) environment. 92.2 per cent of the respondents responds that the

Table 14.3 Descriptive statistics and correlations between variables

	CSM	OuLe	ThLe	PrLe	PF	RoP	SN	In	DO	MA	Pa	Ot	YE
CSM	1												
OuLe	,378**	1											
ThLe	,393**	,475**	1										
PrLe	-,131	-,212**	-,218**	1									
PF	,064	,226**	,098	,232**	1								
RoP	,152	,007	,079	-,106	,003	1							
SN	,194*	,033	,211**	-,063	-,058	,117	1						
In	,129	,135	,172*	-,097	-,045	,134	,046	1					
DO	-,167*	-,403**	-,143	-,006	-,129	,083	,001	,186*	1				
Ma	,175*	,156	,067	-,113	,185*	,138	,120	,026	-,100	1			
Pa	-,055	-,040	,070	,027	-,196*	-,002	-,099	,044	,150	-,596**	1		
Ot	-,133	-,130	-,152	,096	,014	-,151*	-,023	-,076	-,057	-,438**	-,461**	1	
YE	-,050	,094	,027	,086	,073	-,059	-,029	,110	,013	-,068	,103	-,039	1

Notes: CSM: Complexity Sensitive Management, OuLe: Output Legitimacy, ThLe: Throughput Legitimacy, PrLe: Procedural Legitimacy, Tr: Trust, PF: Project Phase, RoP: Relationship with other Projects, SN: Size Network, In: Interdependency between network parties, DO: Differences of opinion between parties, Ma: Position respondent: manager, Pa: Position respondent: participant, Ot: Position respondent: Other, YE: Years of experience respondent with complex projects. Depending on the number of missing values, N is between 153 and 166, ** p <0.01; * p<0.05

water project is related with other projects. 33.8 per cent of the respondents indicate that there are many differences in opinions concerning the direction of the project.

Characteristics of the governance network   Regarding the differences in the characteristics of governance networks, we selected three control variables: the size, the degree in which there are differences in opinions and the interdependencies between actors. The characteristics of the governance network could probably influence management style and the level and form of legitimacy in the projects. The descriptive results of these variables have already been discussed above (see also Table 14.2).

Characteristics respondent   Because both managers and other participants in the project are surveyed, it is important to check if managers perceive their style and the outcomes of the project differently compared to other participants in the project. For the analysis, we made a distinction between three kinds of involvement: (a) respondents who followed the project from a distance or who were thinking along with the project (25 per cent), (b) respondents who actively participated in the project (39 per cent), (c) managers of the project (36 per cent). Furthermore, we asked respondents to indicate their experience with complex projects. This could possibly influence the perception of the management style and/or legitimacy. For example, participants who have more experience possibly know the difficulties of managing such projects and have a kind of reference for judging the managers' style. The mean experience of our respondents was 12.09 years, with a standard deviation of 8.81.

Findings

Table 14.3 shows the correlations among all the variables included in the analysis. The table shows that complexity sensitive management is strongly correlated with output and throughput legitimacy: a positive correlation of 0.38 and 0.39 respectively. These correlations are in line with our hypotheses. However, there is no correlation between management and procedural legitimacy, which is not in line with hypothesis 3. Furthermore, the correlation table shows that output and throughput legitimacy are highly correlated (0.48). This is not surprising: when respondents are satisfied with the process, then they are also often satisfied with the output or vice versa. The relationship between output and throughput legitimacy on the one hand and procedural legitimacy is negatively correlated (-0.21 and -0.22 respectively). Although there is no correlation between management and procedural legitimacy, these outcomes are in line with our theoretical argumentation that the creation of output or throughput legitimacy could hamper procedural legitimacy or vice versa. Apparently, these different forms of legitimacy could contradict each other.

Furthermore, the level of conflict in the networks (differences of opinion) is negatively correlated with output legitimacy (-0.40). This is not surprising. In networks with a high level of conflict stakeholders are likely to be more sceptical regarding the acceptance and valuation of policy outputs. Interestingly, the level of the respondent's involvement did not really matter regarding the perception of the different core variables. Only managers are a bit more positive regarding their sensitivity towards complexity in the governance networks we examined.

In the remainder of this section we subsequently focus on the three research hypotheses by using OLS regression analyses. First we pay attention to our first hypothesis: a complexity sensitive management style within governance networks dealing with complex water projects will lead to higher output legitimacy. We used OLS regression analysis with output legitimacy as dependent variable. Table 14.4 shows the results of this analysis.

Output Legitimacy

Table 14.4 shows that there is a significant, positive relationship between complexity sensitive management style and output legitimacy. We also see that there is negative significant relationship between level of conflict (differences of opinion, a characteristic of the specific governance network) and output legitimacy. In sum, our first hypothesis can be confirmed: complexity sensitive management leads to higher output legitimacy.

Table 14.4   Results of ordinary least squares regression analysis with output legitimacy as dependent variable (N = 153)

Model	B	Beta	Sig
(Constant)	3.087		,000**
Complex sensitive management	.224	,285	,000**
Characteristics project			
- Project phase	.046	,147	,043*
- Relationship with other projects	-.026	-,037	,609
Characteristics network			
- Size	-.007	-.018	,805
- Interdependencies	.089	.150	,041*
- Differences of opinion	-,179	-.366	,000**
Characteristics respondent			
Position			
(manager = reference category)			
- participant	-.008	-.007	,931
- other	-.134	-.110	,176
Years of experience with complex projects	.004	.070	,327
	R2 =,329		
	R2adj =,286		

Case study from the survey: The case Noordwaard

The Noordwaard is a polder of nearby 2,500 hectares alongside the river New Merwede in The Netherlands. It has a mainly agricultural and residential function and consists of 75 farm and non-farm households. The Noordpolder area is located between the river New Merwede and the natural reserve area Biesbosch. By making the Noordpolder available for retention during high river discharges a water level fall could be realized of about 60 centimeters in the Merwede and 30 centimeters near Gorinchem, a city threatened during river flooding.

Two managers from the national department of Infrastructure and Environment were appointed to organize and implement the project. They implemented a highly open and stakeholder oriented process. The managers implemented a complexity sensitive management style, in which all kind of stakeholders (NGOs, citizens, farmers, etc.) got the opportunity to get involved in the process and to provide information, thoughts, interests and wishes. Through interactive design sessions, workshops and discussion meetings a kind of alternatives were explored. In these sessions of civil servants, external experts and stakeholders the "Noordwaard option" was born. In several interactive sessions the 'run-through' alternative emerged, which makes the inner part of the area available for temporary water retention when the river Merwede needs more space. The outer parts (left and right) are protected against flooding and available for land use (residential and agricultural functions). At the same time, the stakeholders managed to enforce a couple of conditions for developing the Noordwaard option:

inhabitants have the opportunity to stay;
inhabitants are given clarity within two years. The Noordwaard project should become a front-runner project (see above);
people who have to move out will get reasonable compensation;
inhabitants and landowners (mostly farmers) are actively involved in planning.

Especially the first point was a victory for farmers and residents. In case of people moving out, the national government had to provide new locations in the same area.

In all, the Noordwaard option was considered an effective solution in coping with flooding. This option was the result of an extensive interactive, stakeholder oriented process. The output was broadly accepted by the stakeholders. This case illustrates how a complexity sensitive style of management resulted in high output legitimacy.

To give this finding on output legitimacy more qualitative flavor, we shortly discuss one of the projects, case Noordwaard, in the box below.

Throughput Legitimacy

Now we turn to our second research hypothesis: a complexity sensitive management style within governance networks dealing with complex water projects will lead to higher throughput legitimacy. We used an Ordinary Least Squares (OLS) regression analysis with throughput legitimacy as dependent variable. Table 14.5 shows the results of this analysis.

Table 14.5 shows that there is a significant positive relationship between complexity sensitive management style and throughput legitimacy. Hence, our second hypothesis can be confirmed. Furthermore, we see a positive significant relationship between size of network (as a governance network characteristic) and throughput legitimacy. We can conclude that process legitimacy gets higher when the network size, i.e. the actor relationships, increases. Interaction among more actors in the network seems beneficial for realizing throughput legitimacy.

Table 14.5   Results of ordinary least squares regression analysis with throughput legitimacy as dependent variable (N = 154)

Model			
	B	**Beta**	**Sig**
(Constant)	2.262		.000**
Complex sensitive management	.262	.319	.000**
Characteristics project			
- Project phase	.028	.085	.272
- Relationship with other projects	-.002	-.003	.966
Characteristics network			
- Size	.063	.157	.043*
- Interdependencies	.082	.133	.092
- Differences of opinion	-.063	-.122	.123
Characteristics respondent			
Position			
(manager = reference category)			
- participant	.120	.105	.235
- other	-.070	-.055	.524
Years of experience with complex projects	.001	.012	.875
	$R^2 = .223$		
	$R^2adj = .173$		

Case illustration: Bypass Kampen IJsseldelta

The project IJsseldelta-South is focused on the area between the city Kampen, the river IJssel en the Dronterlake in The Netherlands. The goal of this project is the improvement of water safety, the living and working conditions and the infrastructure. Moreover, the project wants to improve the agricultural sector in the area. To keep the area safe from the water from the sea or river - the IJssel - the project IJsseldelta-South anticipates on the realization of a bypass river from the IJssel to the Dronterlake. This bypass makes it possible to retain and recover the quality of the national landscape in the IJssel area.

In the first round of the process started in 2000 the orientation was mainly on the inclusion of governmental actors (like water board, municipality, central agency Rijkswaterstaat and the province of Overijssel). In a relative closed arena five alternatives for the bypass were developed. This resulted in fierce resistance from a local association, which was against this location because it would geographically divide two communities in the area. This resistance became apparent in an informative meeting with stakeholders. In response, the delegate of the province of Overijssel gave the association the opportunity to develop their own alternative, and promised support from his administration in developing this alternative. As result a 6th scenario was born. This scenario consisted of a blue bypass on a different location, nearby the city of Kampen in a green area. The province of Overijssel took the role of process manager. The province implemented organizational arrangements, like the steering board (for deputies from the governments), the project organization (civil servants from the governments) and the sounding board (for stakeholders). Stakeholders were informed periodically about the project and they were given opportunity to give input. This process approach led to a change in the way stakeholder perceived and valued the process. The change from an exclusive, inward oriented process approach towards an inclusive, outward oriented process approach was highly appreciated by the stakeholders.

In all, a complexity oriented management style emerged in which transparency and voice were important conditions. This led to high valuation of process legitimacy of the project.

Table 14.6   **Results of ordinary least squares regression analysis with procedural legitimacy as dependent variable (N = 160)**

Model			
	B	Beta	Sig
(Constant)	3.124		,000**
Complex sensitive management	-.130	-,096	,255
Characteristics project			
- Project phase	.141	,264	,002**
- Relationship with other projects	-.070	-,058	,478
Characteristics network			
- Size	.000	,000	,991
- Interdependencies	-.097	-,095	,251
Differences of opinion	.020	,023	,782
Characteristics respondent			
Position			
(manager = reference category)			
- participant	.233	,125	,185
- other	,260	,125	,177
Years of experience with complex projects	,006	,061	,451
	$R^2 =,110$		
	$R^2_{adj} =,054$		

Procedural Legitimacy

There is no significant correlation between complexity sensitive management and procedural legitimacy. Hence, our third hypothesis cannot be confirmed. There is a correlation between project phase and procedural legitimacy. This indicates that in the end of complex water governance processes following and sticking to procedures becomes more important.

Conclusion and Discussion

In this chapter we focused on connective capacity by investigating the complexity sensitive management style regarding the development of legitimacy in complex water governance networks. Complexity sensitive management is especially focused on the compounded and integrated whole of a network and tries to interconnect different parts (actors, arenas, etc.) in this network. Water governance networks are characterized by horizontal relationships between actors, which raises questions concerning the legitimacy of these networks and the relationship with existing institutions of politics and policy making based on the foundations of representative democracy and vertical accountability structures (Koppenjan and

Klijn 2004, Wagenaar 2007). The literature on governance networks is ambiguous regarding this relationship and is empirically not well developed. Building on the literature on legitimacy, we distinguished three forms of legitimacy in this chapter, which we considered to be of importance for studying water governance networks: output legitimacy, throughput legitimacy and procedural legitimacy.

Furthermore, given the complex, erratic and unpredictable nature of governance networks, we argued that a complexity sensitive management style is more effective for realizing output and throughput legitimacy. Such a management style is aimed at creating the context in which effective and legitimate governance processes could evolve (Uhl-Bien et al. 2007, Teisman et al. 2009).

Before drawing conclusions from our research, we stress that care must be taken in making generalizations from this research. Firstly, this study has focused on specific kinds of governance networks: all the networks studied were in the field of water resource management. These results cannot automatically be assumed to also hold for other types of public projects or policy domains, such as (social) service delivery networks (Meier and O'Toole 2001, 2003). Each field, domain or network has its own characteristics and contextual features, which might influence the results found in this study. Secondly, the study was conducted in The Netherlands and the projects are all Dutch. The results may differ in other countries with different decision-making cultures. Despite these limitations we believe that we provided useful new insights regarding the management and legitimacy in the context of complex governance networks.

Our first conclusion is that complexity sensitive management has a positive impact on the output legitimacy of the water projects. A complexity sensitive management style is focused on actor interdependencies in the water governance networks and has an eye for emerging dynamics occurring in such networks. The manager is focused on exploration and connection of different aspects and viewpoints regarding the complex issue (Uhl-Bien et al 2007, Edelenbos et al. 2009). The inclusion of the diversity of interests and values in solutions leads to relevant and supported outcomes.

Our second conclusion is that complexity sensitive management has a positive impact on throughput legitimacy. The relationship in our survey-research is very strong. A complexity sensitive management style is focused on inclusion of stakeholders, on transparency of the process and on creating opportunities for interaction, deliberation and debate. This leads to higher (perceived) throughput legitimacy in governance networks. The complexity sensitive manager plays an important role in connecting practices in governance networks with deliberative forms of democracy and could in this way enhance the legitimacy of governance networks.

The relationship between procedural legitimacy and complexity sensitive management could not be confirmed. We did find, however, that procedural legitimacy is negatively correlated with output and throughput legitimacy. This indicates that different forms of legitimacy could contradict each other. Further research is needed in order to discover under which circumstances this occurs. For example, the level of conflict or trust within governance networks could be such conditioning factors. A low level of trust as starting condition, for example, could imply that actors are more inclined to procedural legitimacy and less to throughput legitimacy because they want security from written agreements and less from process based rule-making (c.f. Das and Teng 2001).

Overall we can conclude that connective capacity via complexity sensitive managerial strategies is important for bringing societal and governmental spheres in water governance networks together and enhancing the legitimacy of the working and functioning of governance networks in the field of water (resource) management. A complexity sensitive style is therefore an important factor for connective capacity building in complex water governance networks.

Bibliography

Bekkers, V. and A. Edwards 2007. *Legitimacy and Democracy: A Conceptual Framework for Assessing Governance Practices*, in *Governance and the Democratic Deficit. Assessing the Democratic Legitimacy of Governance Practices*, edited by V. Bekkers, G. Dijkstra, A. Edwards and M. Fengers Aldershot: Ashgate.

Berry, J.M., K.E. Portney and K. Thomson 1993. *The Rebirth of Urban Democracy*. The Brookings Institution, Washington DC.

Buuren A. van, J. Edelenbos and E.H. Klijn 2010. *Gebiedsontwikkeling in woelig water. Over water governance bewegend tussen adaptief waterbeheer en ruimtelijke ontwikkeling*. Boom/Lemma, Den Haag.

Das, T.K. and Teng, B. 2001. 'Trust, control, and risk in strategic alliances: An integrated framework', *Organization Studies*, 22(2): 251-83.

Dryzek, J.S. 2000. *Deliberative Democracy and Beyond; Liberals, Critics, Contestations*. Oxford: Oxford University Press.

Edelenbos, J. and G. Teisman 2011. Symposium on Water Governance. Prologue: Water Governance as a Government's Actions between the Reality of Fragmentation and the Need for Integration. *International Review Of Administrative Sciences*, 77(1), 5-30.

Edelenbos, J. 2010. *Water as Connective Current, inaugural speech*. Den Haag: Boom/Lemma.

Edelenbos, J., B. Steijn and E.H. Klijn 2010. Does Democratic Anchorage Matter? An Inquiry into the Relation between Democratic Anchorage and Outcome of Dutch Environmental Projects. *The American Review of Public Administration* 2010, 40, 46-63.

Edelenbos, J.E.H. Klijn and M. Kort 2009. Managing Complex Process Systems: Surviving at the Edge of Chaos, in *Managing Complex Governance Systems*, edited by G.R. Teisman, A. van Buuren and L. Gerrits. London: Routledge, 172-92.

Edelenbos, J. and Klijn, E.H. 2006. Managing stakeholder involvement in decision making: A comparative analysis of six interactive processes in the Netherlands. *Journal of Public Administration Research and Theory*, 16(3), 417-46.

Esmark, A. 2007. Democratic Accountability and Network Governance: Problems and Potentials, in *Theories of Democratic Network Governance*, edited by E. Sørensen and J. Torfing. London: Palgrave.

Gage, R.W. and M.P. Mandell (eds) 1990. *Strategies for Managing Intergovernmental Policies and Networks*. New York: Praeger.

Grant, R.W. and R.O. Keohane 2005. Accountability and Abuses of Power in World Politics. *American Political Science Review*, 99(1), pp. 1-15.

Hanf, K. and F.W. Scharpf (eds) 1978. *Interorganizational Policy Making; Limits to Coordination and Central Control*. London: Sage Publications.

Hazy, J.K. 2008. Patterns of Leadership. A case study of influence signaling in an entrepreneurial firm, in *Complexity Leadership, Part 1: Conceptual Foundations*, edited by M. Uhl-Bien and R. Marion. Charlotte: Information Age Publishing, pp. 379-415.

Held, D. 2006. *Models of Democracy*. Polity Press.

Hirst, P. 1997. *From Statism to Pluralism: Democracy, Civil Society and Global Politics*. London: UCL Press.

Jackson, M.C. 2000. Systems Approaches to Management. Kluwer/Plenum: New York.

Kersbergen, K. van and F. van Waarden 2004. "Governance" as a Bridge Between Disciplines. *European Journal of Political Research*, 43(2), 143-71.

Kickert, W.J.M., Klijn, E-H. and Koppenjan, J.F.M. (eds). 1997. *Managing Complex Networks: Strategies for the Public Sector*. London: Sage.

Klijn, E.H. 2010. *Creating (output) Legitimacy by Interactive Decision-making*. Paper for the section 'Interactive Governance, Policy Innovation and Democracy', panel Is interactive governance democratic?', 9-11 September 2009, Potsdam, Potsdam University

Klijn, E.H., B. Steijn and J. Edelenbos 2010. The Impact of Network Management on Outcomes in Governance Networks. *Public Administration*, 88(4): 1063-82.

Klijn, E.H. and C. Skelcher 2007. Democracy and Governance Networks: Compatible or Not? *Public Administration*, 85(3): 587-608.

Kooiman, J. (ed.) 1993. *Modern Governance: New Government–Society Interactions*. London: Sage.

Kooiman, J. 2000. Societal Governance: Levels, Models and Orders of Social-Political Interaction, in *Debating Governance: Authority, Steering and Democracy*, edited by J. Pierre. London: Sage.

Koppenjan, J. and Klijn, E.H. 2004. *Managing Uncertainties in Networks*. London: Routledge.

Lubell, M. and L. Lippert 2011. Integrated regional water management: A study of collaboration or water politics-as-usual in California, USA. *International Review Of Administrative Sciences*, 77(1), 76-100.

March, J.G. and J.P. Olsen 1995. *Democratic Governance*. New York: Free Press.

Marsh, D. and Rhodes, R.A.W. (eds), 1992. *Policy Networks in British Government*. Oxford: Clarendon Press.

MacPherson, C.B. 1979. *The Life and Times of Liberal Democracy*. Oxford: Oxford University Press.

Meier, K.J. and L.J. O'Toole 2001. Managerial strategies and behavior in networks: A model with evidence from U.S. public education', *Journal of Public Administration and Theory* (11)3, 271-93.

Meier, K.J. and L.J. O'Toole 2007. Modelling Public Management: Empirical Analysis of the Management-Performance Nexus. *Public Administration Review*, 9(4), 503-27.

Pahl-Wostl, C. 2007. Transitions towards Adaptive Management of Water Facing Climate and Global Change. *Water Resources Management*, 21(1), 49.

Pateman, C. 1970. *Participation and Democratic Theory*. Cambridge: Cambridge University Press

Pierre, J. (ed.) 2000. *Debating Governance; Authority Steering and Democracy*. Oxford: Oxford University Press.

Pierre, J. and B. Guy Peters. 2000. *Governance, Politics and the State*. Basingstoke: Macmillan.

Rhodes, R.A.W. 1997. *Understanding Government*. Buckingham and Philadelphia: Open University Press.

Rogers, D.L. and D.A. Whetten 1982. *Interorganizational Coordination: Theory, Research and Implementation*. Ames, Iowa: Iowa State University Press.

Rosenhead, J. 1998. *Complexity Theory and Management Practice. Science as Culture*, http://humannature.com/science-as-culture/rosenhead.html.

Scharpf, F.W. 1999. *Governing in Europe: Effective and Democratic?* Oxford: Oxford University Press.

Schreiber, C. and K.M. Carley 2008. Network Leadership. Leading for Learning and Adaptability, in *Complexity Leadership, Part 1: Conceptual Foundations*, edited by M. Uhl-Bien, and R. Marion. Charlotte: Information Age Publishing, 291-331.

Senge, P.M. 1990. *The Fifth Discipline: The Art and Practice of Organizational Learning*. New York: Doubleday.

Skelcher, C. 2007. Does Democracy Matter? A Transatlantic Research Design on Democratic Performance and Special Purpose Governments, *Journal of Public Administration Research and Theory*, 17(1), 61-76.

Sørenson, E. and J. Torfing (eds) 2007. Theories of democratic network governance, Cheltenham: Edward Elgar.

Teisman, G.R., M.W. van Buuren and L.G. Gerrits 2009. *Managing Complex Governance Systems*. London: Routledge.

Uhl-Bien, M., R. Marion and B. McKelvey 2007. Complexity Leadership Theory: Shifting Leadership from the Industrial to the Knowledge Era. *The Leadership Quarterly*, 18, 298-318.

Wagenaar, H. 2007. Governance, Complexity, and Democratic Participation: How Citizens and Public Officials Harness the Complexities of Neighborhood Decline. *American Review of Public Administration*, 37(1), 17-50.

Young, I.M. 2000. *Inclusion and Democracy*. Oxford: Oxford University Press.

Young, I.M. 2001. 'Activist Challenges to Deliberative Democracy'. *Political Theory*, 29(5), 670-90.

Appendix: The Items of the Core Variables

1. Measurement of the Independent Variable: Complexity Sensitive Management

Table 14.7   Measurements of complexity sensitive management

Dimension	Item
1. Complexity of the project: connecting multiple spatial functions	1. The manager is aimed at connecting different spatial functions in the development of the project
2. Complexity of the actor environment (a): adapting the project to the environment	2. The manager is aimed at adapting the project to the demands and wishes of the stakeholders
3. Complexity of the actor environment (b): keeping the project in line with stakeholders' expectations	3. The manager creates enough moments for the representatives of the different involved parties for feedback to their grassroots
4. Complexity of the actor environment (c): connecting different interests	4. The manager is aimed at connecting different parties with different interests as much as possible

2. Measurement of the Dependent Variables: Legitimacy

Table 14.8   Measurements of output legitimacy

Dimension	Items
1.a Problem solving capacity: effectiveness solutions	Do you think that the solutions that have been developed really deal with the problems at hand?
1.b. Problem solving capacity: robustness of the results	Do you think that the developed solutions are durable solutions for the future?
2.a Acceptance of policy outputs: support for the results	Do you think that – in general – the results of the governance process are supported by the involved parties?
2.b. Acceptance of policy outputs: support for the decisions	Do you think that the substantiation of the decisions are – in general – supported by the involved parties?

Table 14.9 Measurements of throughput legitimacy

Dimension	Items
1.a Voice: Width participation	There are a lot different stakeholders involved in the project
1.b.Voice: Access project for participation	The process is good accessible for all stakeholders
2.a. Transparency: Organization of information	The information services concerning this project are well organized.
2.b. Transparency of decision making process	The decision-making process concerning this project is characterized by a high transparency (insight in concrete decisions)
3.a. Due deliberation: Opportunities for debate	During the process there are a lot of possibilities for debates and discussions
3.b. Due deliberation: Quality of argumentation	The argumentation concerning this project is careful

Table 14.10 Measurements of procedural legitimacy

Dimension	Items
1. Determination of the process by procedures and rules	The interaction process is largely determined by formal and a priori legal procedures and rules
1.The emphasizes on procedural rules	In the project there is an emphasizes on the compliance with formal rules and procedures

Chapter 15

The Influence of Connective Capacity on the Legitimacy of Flood Management

Miriam Cuppen and Joanna Pardoe

Introduction

This chapter continues the exploration of the relationship between connective capacity and legitimacy, started in the previous chapter. As these two concepts are both central to successful flood management policy making, we believe their relationship is of interest to policy sciences. We argue that as actors consciously or unconsciously employ connective strategies they not only influence the connective capacity of the project and policy sectors, but also their legitimacy. This chapter focuses on how connective strategies employed to connect various actors in two flood management projects in Oxford influenced the legitimacy of these projects and the legitimacy of the flood management policy sector in Oxford at large.

This chapter adopts the following structure: first the concepts connective capacity and legitimacy will be discussed, followed by a description of the methods used. Then, we will describe flood management in Oxford which forms this chapter's case study. Third, we will discuss the support and legitimacy levels of the "Oxford-Flood-Risk-Management-Strategy" project and of the flood management policy sector in Oxford at large. Fourth, we analyze which connective strategies were employed and how these influenced legitimacy.

Connective Capacity

Like other water policy sectors, flood management is a complex policy sector involving the interests of a wide range of different actors and policy sectors. In flood risk management there is an increasing recognition that flooding cannot be tackled through structural measures that focus solely on preventing flooding. Such approaches are seen as inadequate as they cannot achieve 100 per cent protection against all floods. The shift to non-structural/spatial measures emphasizes the need to approach flooding in a connected way, accounting for interlinkages with other domains. For example, an urban flood water management scheme enables urban functions to be carried out whilst being protected from the disruption of flooding. However, such a management scheme would require space to be constructed, which could compete with other land use pressures (Mitchell 1990: 1, Penning-

Rowsell et al. 2010, Pardoe et al. 2011). The challenge in flood risk management lies in connecting these different domains to develop measures that recognize and accommodate the other policy issues interconnected with flood management. In the UK, flood management responsibilities are fragmented, but flood management is highly connected to issues such as nature conservation and urban planning. In addition, the public affected by flooding form a key stakeholder group. Integrated Water Resource Management (IWRM) clearly advocates the need for "coordinated development and management of water, land and related resources" (GWP 200: 22). In addition, Mitchell (1990: 1) asserts the need for simultaneous consideration of the "various dimensions of water". In a fragmented situation, this calls for the development and enhancement of connections between the different actors, interests and policy sectors. Since a policy sector is constructed and operated by human actors, it can be expected that the "connective capacity" of the policy sector is dependent to a great extent on the actions of the most relevant actors who act as carriers of connective capacity (see Chapter 1).

Lichtenthaler and Lichtenthaler (2009: 1320) state that connective capacity refers to "the ability to establish links to other elements, and these connections facilitate knowledge access". In the context of IWRM, connective capacity may then be viewed as the ability of the various stakeholders/actors (including government actors, consultancies and residents in the affected area) to work together in collaboration, sharing knowledge, ideas and opinions to effectively manage and address a complex water problem. Theoretically, an optimum exists in the number of connections in a policy sector (Buijs 2010). Too many connections can cause stagnation of the policy development, while too few connections can hamper the necessary flow of knowledge. Achieving the correct number of connections is one of the main challenges in IWRM (Mitchell 2005). Stakeholders play a central role in making the necessary connections and are able to employ "connective strategies" such as collecting information from various sources or establishing working relationships with other stakeholders through joint activities, to enhance the connective capacity of the sector. These connective strategies may not always be employed consciously, but may still have an important impact on increasing the connective capacity.

The case study explored in this article highlights the extent to which connective strategies have been employed in Oxford and how this has influenced the connective capacity and the legitimacy of the policy sector. By exploring the connective strategies and capacities in this case study, this article will highlight the successes and failures of stakeholder integration on connective capacity and legitimacy in flood risk management.

Legitimacy

Connective capacity alone is not a sufficient factor to successfully implement and operate water management policies. Since policies seldom serve the interests of all they impact and sanctioning is an expensive method of social control (Grimes

2006), it is important for policy makers to understand how water management can develop and maintain legitimacy. Through legitimacy, actors can accept policies for reasons other than self-interest or fear of sanctions (Fallon 2005, Beetham 1991). Legitimacy is a group-construct developed in the group of influencing and impacted actors (Connelly 2011), and is rooted in the attitudes of individual members of the community towards water management (Scharpf 1997, 1998). Legitimacy can be defined as "the prestige of policy making that it is morally justifiable and therefore authoritative. (Weber 1980).

We take a slightly different approach to assessing the legitimacy of water management than chapter 14 by Edelenbos et al. that assessed the legitimacy of water management projects through measuring how actors perceived a number of predetermined aspects. However, in governance it is not self-evident which aspects of policy making lead to legitimacy (Connelly et al. 2006, Van Kersbergen and Van Waarden 2004). An actor group can attribute legitimacy to water management for many different reasons, and therefore, we assess legitimacy through studying actor's overall-attitudes towards water management and through their assessments of the overall-attitudes of the other actors. In this manner, we heed the advice of public opinion research not to rely merely on simple aggregation (Taber 2003) in assessing a group-level construct such as legitimacy. To this purpose all respondents (both of structured and in-depth interviews) were asked 1) how they themselves felt about flood management in Oxford, and 2) how they thought other people around them felt about flood management in Oxford (perceived legitimacy).

An attitude is a "psychological tendency that is expressed by evaluating a particular entity with some degree of favor or disfavor" (Eagly and Chaiken 1993: 1). Actors can have different attitudes towards policy making. For instance, actors can feel differently about a project's content than about its process, leading actors to be ambivalent about the project. As Figure 15.1 shows, four possible project attitudes can be distinguished: support and rejection, and two more ambivalent attitudes: contesting only the process, and contesting only the content.

Both participating and non-participating actors can develop attitudes towards a project and a policy sector. Social psychology suggests that personal experiences are strong triggers for forming attitudes (Fazio and Zanna 1981, Eagly and Chaiken 1993). Participating actors in flood management projects develop attitudes towards projects and policy sector mainly through their personal experiences. Attitudes can diffuse through society through the media and interpersonal discussions (Johnston and Bartels 2010, Yin 1999, Wu and Huberman 2004, Watts and Dodds 2007). In this way, the attitudes towards policy sector or projects could diffuse from participating to non-participating actors. Therefore, we will look at the attitudes of participating and non-participating actors.

Flood management projects are not developed in isolation, but are part of broader developments made in the flood management policy sector. It can thus be expected that the legitimacy of the flood management policy sector and of flood management projects are interrelated. Since projects are among the most

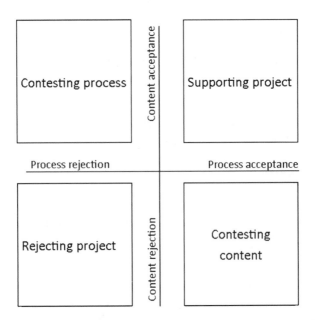

Figure 15.1   Four possible project and policy sector attitudes (adapted from Cuppen, Broekhans and Enserink, 2011)

visible components of a policy sector, it can be expected that actors' perceptions of projects influence their attitudes towards the broader policy sector. Because of this possible interaction between projects and the policy sector, this chapter considers both levels of policy making.

Since in governance the reasons for attributing legitimacy are not self-evident, it is a pressing question how legitimacy can be developed and maintained in the flood management sector. Various authors (Engelen, Keulartz and Leistra 2008, Wallner 2008, Woltjer 2002, Enserink and Monnikhof 2003, Monnikhof and Edelenbos 2001) have suggested that participation, in particular having a voice, being taken seriously, and believing that the concerns of all actors are taken into account, could be grounds for attributing legitimacy to a project or policy sector. Given this, it could be suggested that connective capacity with its ability to provide a platform for the development of the components of legitimacy may contribute positively to increasing legitimacy and policy acceptance.

Methods

For the purposes of this case study, 12 in-depth interviews were conducted between April 2009 and February 2010 with participating stakeholders in an ongoing urban flood management project in Oxford, called 'the Oxford flood risk management strategy'. The respondents for the in-depth interviews included those involved in the Environment Agency consultation process for the development of the Oxford Flood Risk Management Strategy, a representative from the consultancy firm tasked with the Oxford flood risk management strategy and key civil servants from the Environment Agency. These in-depth interviews were open interviews in which respondents were invited to describe their involvement in the OFRMS and flood management in Oxford in general. At the end of most of the in-depth interviews, respondents described their project and policy-sector attitudes along with their perceptions of the project and policy sector attitudes of their acquaintances. The open interviews allowed for thick analysis of the data in which theory was inferred from data (Partington 2000). Grounded theory advocates an analysis scheme consisting of various rounds of coding (Charmaz 2006). The in-depth interviews were analyzed using grounded theory coding principles: initial codes were sentence long summaries of heuristic parts of the interview. These initial codes were subsequently divided in three categories: "content-aspects", "process-aspects" and "stakeholder-aspects" and each initial code was recoded into a code of a single word reflecting the central aspect of it.

In addition, 18 structured interviews were held with residents of Oxford in the summer of 2009. For the structured interview, the respondents were selected from the telephone book (approximately every 5th listed person). The selected respondents were ordered by "region", based on their proximity to the flood plain, as indicated in Figure 15.1: area 1, which is the floodplain; area 2, which is the area close to the floodplain; area 3, which is the area to the back of Oxford away from the floodplain; and area 4, which is the area downstream of Oxford. The response rate was 7.2 per cent. Of the respondents 22 per cent lived in the floodplain, 33 per cent were from region 2, 16.7 per cent were from region 3 and 27.8 per cent lived downstream in region 4. Thus a reasonably equal distribution of respondents across the regions was reached. The structured interviews contained questions on awareness and involvement in the OFRMS, attitudes towards project and policy sector and evaluations of some aspects of the content and process of the OFRMS and the common practices in the policy sector at large. The structured interviews were analyzed through descriptive statistical methods.

Furthermore, project documents of the Oxford flood Risk Management Strategy project were consulted, mainly for validation purposes of the events and issues described in the in-depth interviews.

In the last decade, flooding has become a common occurrence in England. Since 1998 there have been several large scale (national) flood events, in 2000, 2003 and 2007, affecting several regions of the UK at once. Oxford, a city of 149.300 citizens (Oxford city council 2010a) approximately 90 kilometers north east of London, was one of the areas affected by these floods with some properties being hit for the third time in ten years in 2007 (British Geological Survey 2010). The built-up area has expanded over time with suburbs developing in the floodplains. Consequently, it is estimated that around 3600 houses currently lie in the Thames and Cherwell floodplains in Oxford and of these 2700 properties are at risk of flooding from the 1/75 year flood event (Environment Agency 2009).

In response to the 2003 floods, the Environment Agency (EA) began to develop the Oxford Flood Risk Management Strategy (OFRMS), to provide a scheme that could reduce the frequency and impact of flooding in the city. In response to the floods of 2007, society and national government further increased their pressure on the Environment Agency to develop this flood prevention scheme. The developed OFRMS provided recommendations for flood management measures to be taken over the next 100 years. It proposed a conveyance channel on the western floodplain running from Botley Road south to Sandford lock, an upstream storage near Chimney (East of Oxford) to account for climate change and finally a series of smaller short term measures. (Environment Agency 2009). Other options listed in the consultation document were variations of this option (larger or smaller watercourses, maintenance only, small or large storage areas, etc.)

In order to secure access to essential knowledge and create goodwill among key stakeholders, the Environment Agency informally consulted with some of the main stakeholders during the development of the Strategic Environmental Assessment (SEA). Consultees included the councils of the city, the districts and the county and some large land owners such as the nature conservation organization BBOWT and the Oxford Preservation Trust (OPT). In addition, the Environment Agency followed the best practice guidelines for SEA's by organizing a 12 week consultation period, including public exhibitions, sending consultation documents to subscribers of the flood warnings register and publishing the consultation documents in the local newspaper, on the internet, in local libraries and council offices. The Oxford Flood Alliance and local councilors were also asked to distribute copies within their communities (Environment Agency 2011). To assist an effective consultation, the consultation document comprised a description of the problem and various options. In addition the full SEA was available on internet. In addition, consultants attended public meetings to explain technical aspects of the OFRMS. The public was asked which alternative they preferred of the nine alternatives listed in the consultation document. These alternatives ranged from do nothing, to the composite of measures described above.

In addition to the OFRMS, the Environment Agency began another flood management project in the intervening time before the OFRMS would be approved and constructed. This other project, "short term measures 1", consisted of a number of measures which were low cost, no regret measures that could decrease the flood risk. The Oxford flood Alliance (OFA), a citizen flood action group, put forward ideas for STM-1, which were subsequently taken up by the Environment Agency and executed. STM-1 concentrated on removing blockages near Redbridge and replacing the culverts there. The measures were implemented from 2009-2010.

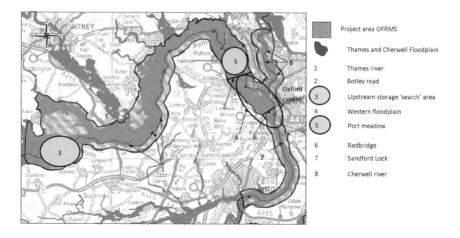

Figure 15.2 **'Search area' Oxford flood risk management strategy, including key spatial features (adapted from: Environment Agency 2009: 3)**

Issues Specific to Food Management in Oxford

A number of issues complicate the development of flood management measures in Oxford. Some of these issues are natural constraints to flood management, such as the bottleneck south of Oxford and others relate to socio-economic activities such as the presence of the railway connection to London and a main by-pass road in the flood plain. There are also some interests which could be negatively impacted by flood management measures, such as archeology, the city view and nature conservation (especially in Port Meadow). Lastly, there is continued pressure for further urban development in the floodplain, which could raise the flood risk. Table 15.1 shows an overview of these interests.

In order to design a viable scheme, which can be implemented in reasonable time, all of the constraining issues need to be taken into account in the design of the OFRMS. This calls for an integrated approach (IWRM/AWM) whereby the various issues would be represented by stakeholders who could highlight the implications of the OFRMS plans for that particular interest.

The integrated and holistic approach was present from the outset and evidenced by the employment of an interdisciplinary team of consultants. Consultants were contracted to conduct work on the project under the management of the Environment Agency who oversaw the project. In addition to the interdisciplinary consultancy, external experts on different issues were also consulted on a regular basis. For instance, the county archeological service was approached for information about possible archeological sites in the search area, and a well-respected biologist was asked to study possible effects of flood management measures on Port Meadow.

Table 15.1   Issues at play in flood management in Oxford

	Details	Constraint imposed
Soikom-position	Flat land consisting of gravel results in groundwater flooding	Bunding not possible due to seepage and nature of groundwater flooding.
Topography	Natural bottleneck created by topography	Bottleneck limits the speed of water flowing from the floodplain, large flows can back up causing flooding.
Man-made obstructions	Railway bridge	Cannot be easily moved, provides further obstructions, limiting the speed of water flows.
Preservation issues	Famous views of 'City of Dreaming Spires'	The Oxford Preservation Trust is exploring mechanisms to protect this view. This could implicate technical solutions such as diversion channels, which may impact on the beloved view.
	Port Meadow Site of Special Scientific Interest (SSSI) status and listed monument.	Such status creates serious restrictions on changes to the environment. Any proposed works will have to ensure that they do not adversely affect the protected features.
	Archaeological interest in "Red bridge" (remains of D'Oilly's stone causeway believed to be present in the bridge)	Site would need to be protected.
Transport infrastructure	Railways connection to London	Crosses the flood plain and cannot be easily moved, restricts flood flows further but also requires protection from flooding as an important transport link.
	City By-pass functioning at full capacity	Crosses the flood plain and cannot be easily moved, restricts flood flows further but also requires protection from flooding as an important transport link. Possibly a constraint for implantation speed, since resources need to be transported to and from the project area via this route.
Residential Development	Pressure for increase housing stock	Development has already taken place on the flood plain and new development (whilst discouraged) may still take place, displacing water and increasing flood risk for existing buildings.

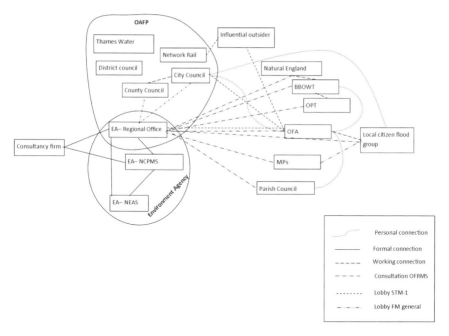

Figure 15.3   Flood management stakeholder network in Oxford (depicting relationships referred to in in-depth interviews)

The Stakeholder Network in Oxford

The stakeholder network in the Oxford Flood Management policy sector is complex. Figure 15.3 shows an overview of the stakeholder network and its connections. Noteworthy is the central position the Environment Agency takes in the network. This position reflects the central role the Environment Agency plays in the consultation. The Environment Agency approach of one-to-one consultation with stakeholders, as opposed to group consultation, limits development of connections between other stakeholders.

The Environment Agency is a fragmented organization in which various departments have roles to play in flood management in Oxford. In addition to complexity within the EA, there is also a multitude of other organizations with flood management responsibilities, for example, Thames Water, the District Council, the County Council, the City Council and Network Rail. In 2003, "the Oxford Area Flood Partnership" was set up as a platform organization where representatives from these organizations can meet to discuss flood related matters and coordinate action (Oxford city council 2010b). Annual public meetings are held by the Oxford Area Flood Partnership to inform the public of developments in flood management and to offer further opportunity for flood related issues to be raised.

Meanwhile, the community flood action group Oxford flood alliance is able to apply further pressure by lobbying for flood measures and taking community action to increase flood resilience in neighborhoods. Various flood action groups had been set in neighborhoods in Oxford as a response to flooding. In 2007, these groups joined forces to form the Oxford Flood Alliance. The Oxford Flood Alliance focuses on developing working relationships with civil servants of the various relevant governmental bodies, especially the Environment Agency. It also develops ideas for small, short term flood defense measures which were successful at being taken up as part of the short term measures 1- program (Interview with Oxford Flood Alliance members 2009).

Support and Legitimacy for Flood Management in Oxford

The goal of this chapter is to assess how the connective capacity of the Oxford flood management policy sector has influenced its legitimacy. Above we discussed that legitimacy can be studied by understanding the dominant attitude in a community, through looking at the attitudes of members of the community and their perceptions of the overall attitudes of their community. The following section discusses the local community attitudes towards the OFRMS project and the policy sector.

Attitudes towards the project OFRMS

In Figure 15.4, the evaluated project attitudes of the participating stakeholders have been plotted on a two-dimensional scheme. These evaluations are based on the in-depth interviews. The overarching impression that arises from the interviews is predominantly one of reserved judgment.

The views from the stakeholders cross the spectrum from particularly negative views to positive views. For instance, the negative attitude of IG2 led her to voice concerns about the effectiveness and appropriateness of the plan, as well as dissatisfaction with the level of involvement her organization had had until now. In contrast, the involved civil servants viewed both content and process very positively. Next to these civil servants the project had two other ardent supporters of the content: the expert responsible for the design of the proposed measure and one citizen. The majority of those interviewed were however more neutral and awaited further development before forming definite opinions. Two citizens felt the information provided to them was not enough to form a definite opinion, one civil servant felt that since he was not a "real" stakeholder (he did not himself live in the area), it was inappropriate to form a personal opinion.

Most respondents (of the in-depth interviews) who had participated in the OFRMS thought that it was generally legitimate. Civil servants believed the OFRMS had high project legitimacy, since resistance has so far been absent.

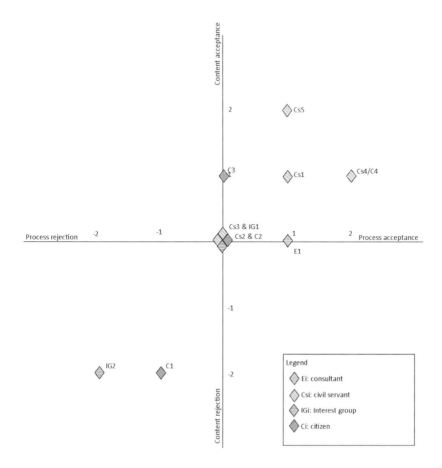

Figure 15.4   Estimated attitudes of participating actors towards OFRMS (based on in-depth interviews)

Among citizens and interest group representatives there was a general perception that although the current state of the flood management was deplorable, most citizens would find it a good thing that more attention was given to flood management. Yet one interest group representative nuanced this perception by indicating that attitudes toward the project could vary within the community from skeptical to something needing to be done.

In contrast to the perceptions of the interviewed participating actors, half of the non-participating citizens (respondents to the structured interviews) were unaware of the OFRMS, and only one respondent had been active in the project by attending a citizen meeting. Next to being unaware, respondents said they were not involved because they either did not have a personal stake or enough resources (time and knowledge) and because they expected the government to be unresponsive to them.

Attitudes towards content and process among those non-participating citizens who were aware of the project were very mixed with a substantial group feeling unqualified to make a judgment about the content, but the necessity of the project was widely recognized. To support a project, respondents said they needed to be able to trust the experts and expect positive side-effects. Strangely, although respondents aware of the OFRMS claimed they found the process acceptable, they simultaneously expressed little confidence that the process would lead to good decisions.

The image arises of a project in which judgment is reserved until more becomes known. The necessity for flood management measures is widely recognized, but due to the current lack of detail of the plans developed in the OFRMS, societal actors remain uncertain whether the proposed flood management measure is the correct thing to do. Most respondents seem to accept the process, but wild enthusiasm is absent. The reserved judgment of both participating and non-participating actors indicates that the project's legitimacy was not secured at the time of the study. The lack of resistance thus is due to the reserved judgments, rather than an indication of true project legitimacy.

Attitudes towards the Policy Sector

On basis of the in-depth interviews, the attitudes of actors participating in the OFRMS towards the Oxford flood management sector "were estimated (except those of Cs2 and E1). Figure 15.5 shows these estimated attitudes. The interest group representatives and one citizen (C1) questioned the approach taken to flood management, which they found not holistic enough. This citizen also complained about the current state of the flood management sector. One interest group representative (IG2) and one citizen (C1) were also dissatisfied with the processes. They were critical of the current financing structure of projects, which they believed promoted large invasive projects over maintenance and small scale improvements. On the other hand, the other interest group representative (IG1) was equally critical of the content, but stressed that participation was done and the processes were strongly evidence based.

Two citizens (C2 and C3) were more positive about the policy sector: Through STM-1 they felt empowered and listened to, because they saw their input taken up in the design of flood management plans. They were also positive, because they understood and accepted the constraints of the flood managers with regard to procedures etc. Though the citizens felt much was still wrong with how flood management (mal)functioned in the Oxford area, they were pleased with the progress that had been made in the last few years.

Civil servants were positive about the processes in the policy sector, which is what they expected them to be. The Environment Agency's area manager (Cs1)

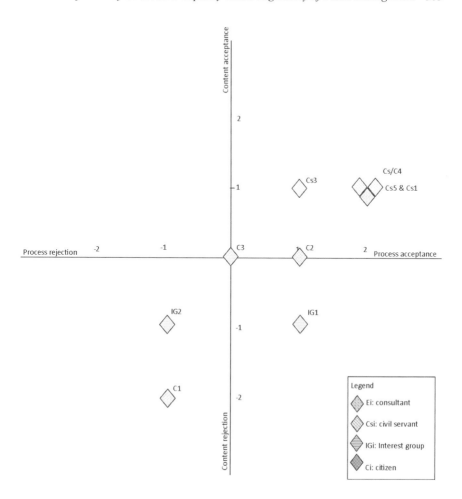

Figure 15.5 Estimated attitudes of actors participating in OFRMS towards the Oxford flood management sector (based on in-depth interviews)

was especially positive about the funding scheme, which he claimed made flood management very transparent. Content-wise the civil servants acknowledged the necessity of flood management, and claimed that progress had been made towards improving the flood management system.

Figure 15.6 shows that among non-participating citizens, attitudes toward the policy sector varied substantially. Most respondents to the structured interviews (83 per cent) were negative about the policy sector's process. The respondents were divided on the policy sector's content with about half accepting the content, and half rejecting it. There was particularly low trust in the behavior of governmental actors, and it was felt by 72 per cent respondents that too few flood management

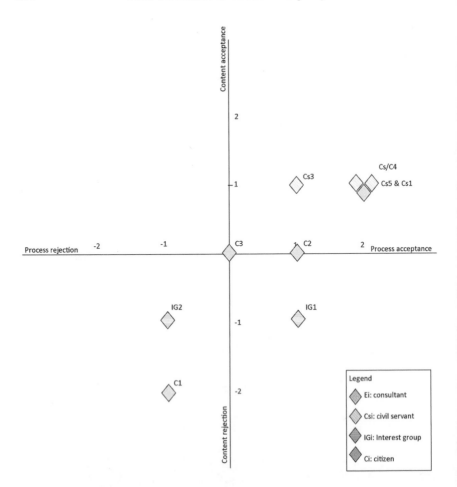

Figure 15.6   Attitudes of non-participating actors towards the flood management policy sector (based on structured interviews)

measures had been taken, while 94 per cent of the respondents thought that it was important or very important that such measures would be taken.

The image of the Oxford public contesting flood management processes and having mixed views on its content, is confirmed by the perceived legitimacy of these respondents. Approximately 1/3 of the respondents thought that most people were positive about the policy sectors content, 1/3 thought opinions varied strongly among the people, and 1/3 thought most had a negative attitude towards the flood management system. Meanwhile, participating actors had the perception that people in Oxford would be angry that their houses flooded, but be happy with the progress made and see the necessity of flood management for their area.

The results from the survey do not bode well for the legitimacy of the flood management sector in Oxford. Both support for the policy sector and perceived legitimacy score alarmingly low. With regard to these results it must be noted at this point that the survey was held shortly after the MP's expenses scandal became public in the UK. The alarming negative attitudes which speak from these results may well have been influenced by this scandal.

Connective Capacity of Flood Management Sector in Oxford

To assess how connective capacity influenced the legitimacy of the policy sector, this capacity needs to be assessed. This connective capacity is assessed through the connective strategies employed successfully in the policy sector. The connective strategies of two actors are focused on: the Environment Agency's strategies and those of the Oxford Flood Alliance's.

The Environment Agency employed six connective strategies. First, the Environment Agency explicitly took the OFRMS plans into account in the design of the STM-1. This means that only measures that were compatible with the proposed OFRMS were accepted for STM-1. On the other hand, the OFRMS itself included some short term measures as a result of the engagement process. The relationship between the two projects is made visible by the fact that the Environment Agency's project manager for the OFRMS is now taking up the follow-up project of STM-1 (STM-2).

Second, the Environment Agency used the different issues as constraints to the OFRMS project and gave room to the representatives of different interests to express their concerns. As a result, most stakeholders appear to favor a holistic approach to flood management and accepted that compromises between different issues needed to be made. This was particularly noticeable in the reactions of Oxford Flood Alliance members, who although negatively impacted, said they wanted flood management measures, but not at any cost. For instance, one citizen (C2) said:

> And even for villagers who want to be safe from flooding. Even they are going to be concerned about the amount of disruption and traffic and so on involved. Also these are quite environmentally sensitive areas. There are beautiful meadows here, that are actually a lovely place to walk, if you come back on this walking. It's lovely down here. You can see that there is wildlife and so on, we like, you know, and a lot of people are concerned about that. And again even people who have been flooded do not necessarily want that messed up.

As a third strategy, the Environment Agency placed much emphasis on informal consultation. The Environment Agency area manager arranged various meetings with stakeholders and even a site visit with the Oxford Preservation Trust. The area manager had also consulted with politicians at various governmental levels (MPs, county councilors, district councilors and city/parish councilors). In addition to providing further information, these meetings allowed the area manager to explain the limitations of the system to the politicians.

The Environment Agency also organized a site visit for some key stakeholders, to show them a comparable project which had been deemed a success by the Environment Agency considered. With this site visit, the Environment Agency hoped to alleviate concerns of these stakeholders. However, they were not completely successful in this, as one interest group representative (IG2), who had attended the visit, actually became more concerned as a result. She was not convinced that the implemented measure of the visited project would be appropriate in Oxford and was concerned the Environment Agency envisioned a comparable measure in Oxford.

Fourth, the area manager was very straightforward about the limitations of the Environment Agency. For instance, in a meeting with Oxford Flood Alliance, he responded to a question why no measures were taken upstream of Botley road, by saying:

> because I want to develop a plan I could implement somewhere in the next 15 years and with all the regulations for Port Meadow that would not be possible.

Fifth, the Environment Agency gave stakeholders access to the experts they consulted and allowed these experts to show their expertise. As a result, those stakeholders who met with the experts were more willing to accept that the proposed measures were effective and well-considered. The Environment Agency also made information on the OFRMS available through the consultation document and the SEA-report available on internet. This information was less well received than hoped: a detailed research report like the SEA, which was filled with scientific jargon, was not considered by Oxford Flood Alliance members. Moreover, the consultation document was seen as containing too little detail on the relevant issues for citizens and too much detail on "irrelevant issues". For instance, little information was provided on the possible side effects of the options during and after implementation in the consultation document. Yet all assessed options were listed, including the do-nothing option. This list of options was perceived as nonsensical and led to feelings of irritation.

The Oxford Flood Alliance had also developed four connective strategies worth considering here. First, the Oxford Flood Alliance focused on developing working relationships with civil servants. They found this to be more effective than trying to influence flood management through politicians. They found that informal sessions enabled more information to be presented to citizens by the civil servants without the need to commit to particular outcomes. For instance, throughout the STM1-project a positive working relationship developed between the Oxford Flood Alliance and the Environment Agency. The Environment Agency nurtured this working relationship by having regular informal meetings in which more information was shared than would normally be available to the public. The Oxford Flood Alliance nurtured this working relationship by refraining from publicly criticizing the Environment Agency. However, they were very aware that they had resources to put pressure on the governmental bodies if insufficient progress was made. These resources included, for instance, negative media attention and letter writing to non-responsive civil servants. Being active in this project gave these citizens a feeling of empowerment, both among those on the board of Oxford Flood Alliance and those supporting Oxford Flood Alliance. One supporting citizen said:

> And I think that [letter writing campaign] was actually very empowering for people, because we felt that it actually made a difference for us to write so many letters, because if they don't want us to do it, then if they're sensible they will do something about our problems. So I think that was a really good experience. (Interview C1)

Second, the Oxford Flood Alliance provided concrete suggestions, based on carefully collected documentation (for example, pictures made during floods, measurements taken by Oxford Flood Alliance members of water flows etc.). This strategy was successful in achieving the take up of the STM-1 project which the Oxford Flood Alliance had considerable input into.

Third, Oxford Flood Alliance members (but also other stakeholders) made use of personal connections they had, trying to wield their influence. For example the chair of a local flood action group is a retired archeologist from the city council and thus has connections to civil servants from the county and the city; a member of Oxford Flood Alliance is good friends with the local city councilor and another member of the Oxford Flood Alliance is married to a parish councilor. Although these contacts are not used heavily, they do allow an informal flow of information and influence through the network.

Fourth, Oxford Flood Alliance also organized site visits to areas they considered problematic. These site visits were attended by powerful supporters of the Oxford Flood Alliance and responsible governmental bodies. The site visits organized by the Oxford Flood Alliance functioned as events through which consensus on problem and solution identification could be developed. The site visits seemed to have indeed led to more consensus on the problems and to the development of some measures to address these problems.

A last connective strategy employed by stakeholders, besides the Environment Agency and Oxford Flood Alliance, was to consciously connect stakeholders with shared or compatible interest. Thus, informal connections existed between the county council and the city council on the archeological issues of the OFRMS, the nature conservation organization "Berkshire, Buckinghamshire and Oxfordshire Wildlife Trust" (BBOWT) and Oxford Preservation trust (OPT) for example. Until now these contacts have been very limited and have not therefore significantly influenced the web structure of the network where the Environment Agency in the center of this web.

These connective strategies have led to positive working relationships between most participating stakeholders and the Environment Agency. Also, these strategies seem to have resulted in a mobilization of proponents of the projects, in particular. Despite some connections between stakeholders, the stakeholder network in this policy sector has a distinct web structure, with the Environment Agency at the center of the network. This lack of connections between all actors might limit the connective capacity built through the above listed connective strategies. On the positive side however, no strong impediments seem present to make different connections that could alter this network structure and most stakeholders seem satisfied with the level of connective capacity as it is.

How Connective Capacity Influenced Legitimacy

So how has connective capacity of the policy sector "Flood management in Oxford" influenced the above presented attitudes towards the OFRMS and the STM-1 projects, and ultimately the policy sector in general?

It seems that especially the Environment Agency's efforts to connect with different stakeholders through informal meetings had a positive effect on the attitudes of most stakeholders. Such informal meetings and site visits gave stakeholders the feeling they were important to the Environment Agency and taken seriously. For instance, one citizen (C4), who was the chair of a local flood action group (not Oxford Flood Alliance) said:

> And this is [us] sitting down with the project manager, so not especially high powered and him explaining this lot [the questions we had]. [...] I mean it doesn't figure really. it's the environment agency possibly recognizing that [we] take slightly more professional or academic approach to this.

The site visit did not have the same positive effect on the attitude of all stakeholders, but this does not mean site visits cannot have a positive effect: the site visits organized by the Oxford Flood Alliance seem to have influenced the attitudes of Oxford Flood Alliance-members positively.

Second, the candor of the Environment Agency's area manager on the limitations of the OFRMS project had a positive effect on the project's legitimacy. Stakeholders could understand the limitations, as they faced these limitations in their own professional life as well and were more willing to accept the proposed measure as the most appropriate considering these limitations. For instance, C2 said:

> You just, there is no point in trying to propose a scheme that is potentially going to endanger those, because there is so much regulation, it would just never happen. And he is not going to, he has got a limited number of people, he has got a lot of work to get on with, he can't afford to have people spending lots and lots time dealing with trying to push through proposals that are meeting lots and

lots of opposition from other bits of government and so on. And I can understand that, because that's what my own working environment is like. I can completely relate to what he is trying to do.

However, it remains to be seen if "blaming the system" is a strategy that will not negatively influence the policy sector's legitimacy in the long term.

Third, the informal meetings provided access to experts and information. This contributed positively to attitudes of stakeholders as they gained the perception that the proposed measure had been well-considered. Also the use of specific experts helped in building trust in the measures as the expert working on it is trusted. For instance, one interest group representative (IG1) gained confidence in OFRMS because he trusted the consulted expert studying the possible effects of the measure on Port Meadow. He said:

> I wanted to know who they were getting to do the work[...], and they told me David Gowing [...]who I've engaged with [...] previously. So now that we knew David was doing that work we were quite content that it would be done thoroughly and adequately.

Fourth, the consultation document unfortunately influenced the attitudes towards OFRMS negatively. Since it did not contain the desired information, it only led to aggravation among the interviewed citizens rather than more understanding. The way the consultation document was set up raised the question among the interviewed citizens on how they could react sensibly to the document, again adding to a feeling of frustration.

Fifth, the success of the connective strategies the Oxford Flood Alliance employed led them to feel empowered and view the Environment Agency as responsive and willing to listen. Thus these strategies have positively influenced their attitudes towards the policy sector and both projects. The positive effect of these strategies lies chiefly in developing the perception that the Oxford Flood Alliance can be influential and that the policy sector is making progress through the developed projects. Finally, it is not clear how connecting actors with shared or compatible interests influenced the attitudes of participating actors. Also developing STM-1 and OFRMS in conjunction does not seem to have influenced their attitudes.

Thus, connective capacity seems to influence the attitudes of participating actors mostly positively. However, legitimacy is not only attributed by participating actors, but also by the impacted, non-participating actors. In contrast to the positive effects of connective capacity on the attitudes of participating actors, the attitudes of these non-participants seem not to have been influenced. Non-participants are mostly unaware of the projects and are dissatisfied with the current condition of the policy sector at large. The positive attitudes of participating actors seem not to have diffused through the broader community and thus the legitimacy of the flood management policy sector in Oxford seems under stress. Moreover it seems that opponents of the flood management sector, to date, have not been fully mobilized in the OFRMS-project. Until now, the fact that only proponents were mobilized has been positive for the project's continuance. However, the lack of active resistance seems to have quieted any concerns for support or legitimacy of the policy sector among Environment Agency civil servants. This poses a high risk for the later stages of the project when opponents may suddenly become mobilized and it might be more difficult to appease them at that stage.

Conclusion

In this chapter, it has been found that the connective capacity of the flood management sector in Oxford positively influenced the attitudes of participating actors towards the policy sector and the two imbedded projects. Several connective strategies of the Environment Agency especially seem to have influenced these attitudes positively. First, the Environment Agency did well being open, listening and taking stakeholders views seriously. We found that generally there was a more positive attitude towards the project as a result of engagement with the EA and secondly, the Environment Agency provided ample opportunities for stakeholders to access information and knowledgeable people. This information and contact with experts reassured stakeholders and provided a platform for answering their questions. Through these answers, stakeholders were better able to understand and therefore justify the proposed measures. Secondly, the openness of the Environment Agency about their limitations helped participating actors such as the Oxford Flood Alliance to understand these genuine limitations, again assisting stakeholders in justifying the proposed measures.

The connective strategies of the Oxford Flood Alliance also contributed to more positive attitudes of Oxford Flood Alliance members towards the projects and the policy sector. The active nature of the Oxford Flood Alliance and their development of connections with the Environment Agency contributed to Oxford Flood Alliance members feeling empowered. The take up of the Oxford Flood Alliance recommended STM-1 was pivotal in demonstrating the effectiveness of connective capacities in improving results and had a wider benefit on legitimacy as a whole. Through repeated engagement between Oxford Flood Alliance and Environment Agency a positive relationship developed, which resulted in a degree of understanding and sympathy towards them. As a result of this close working relationship, the Oxford Flood Alliance members were patient, accepting partial successes rather than feeling anger at a lack of full success. Thus, those connected show a distinct increase in acceptance of the Environment Agency's work and position, increasing legitimacy. However, these connections and the resulting positive attitudes haven't diffused to the wider community. Only those directly connected demonstrate these positive effects, raising the question how the attitudes of non-participants can be positively influenced or at least be taken into account in policy development.

Noteworthy, both project legitimacy and policy sector legitimacy were influenced by the connective strategies employed in the projects, but with a slightly different result. In reaction to these strategies, actors tended to postpone forming project attitudes for the OFRMS, and at the same time through participating, citizens gained the impression that the policy sector was making progress. This effect was absent for non-participating actors as they didn't experience these connecting strategies.

In short, this case study demonstrates that connective capacity can work to increase legitimacy by giving access to the means to overcome typical barriers for stakeholder engagement: that is, by answering stakeholder questions and providing opportunities to meet the project workers and managers allowing stakeholders to establish a degree of trust in them. However, as these positive effects of connective capacity do not seem to easily diffuse to the wider community, the importance of connections and direct engagement for legitimacy also presents a challenge where engaging with every stakeholder is just not feasible: How can legitimacy be diffused in such situations?

Bibliography

Beetham, D. 1991. *The Legitimation of Power.* Basingstoke: Macmillian Education.
British Geological Survey 2010. Groundwater and flooding in Oxford. Retrieved from http://www.bgs.ac.uk/research/groundwater/Oxford.html on: 14-07-2010.
Buijs, J. 2010. Understanding Connective Capacity of Program Management from a Self-Organization Perspective. *Emergence: Complexity and Organization*, 12(1), 29-38.
Charmaz, K. 2006. *Constructing Grounded Theory: A Practical Guide Through Qualitative Analysis.* Los Angeles: Sage Publications.
Connelly, S., Richardson, T. and Miles, T. 2006. Situated Legitimacy: Deliberative Arenas and the New Rural Governance. *Journal of Rural Studies*, 22, 267-77.
Connelly, S. 2011. Constructing Legitimacy in the New Community. *Urban Studies*, 48(5), 929-46.
Cuppen, M.E. Broekhans, B. and Enserink, B. 2011. Public participation in EIA and attitude formation. *Journal of Impact Assessment and Project Appraisal*, 30(2), 1-20.
Dahl, R. 1998. *On Democracy.* New Haven, CT: Yale University Press.
Eagly, A.H. and Chaiken, S. 1993. *The Psychology of Attitudes.* New York: Harcourt, Brace.
Easton, D. 1965. *A Systems Analysis of Political Life.* New York: John Wiley and Sons.
Engelen, E., Keulartz, J. and Leistra, G. 2008. European Nature Conservation Policy Making, From Substantive to Procedural Sources of Legitimacy, in

Legitimacy in European Nature Conservation Policy: Case Studies in Multilevel Governance (3-21), edited by J. Keulartz and G. Leistra. Heidelberg: Springer.

Environment Agency 2009. *Listening to you about Living with the Floodplain, Consultation for the Oxford Flood Risk Management Strategy*. Frimley: Environment Agency.

Environment Agency 2011. Oxford flood risk management strategy. Retrieved from http://www.environment-agency.gov.uk/homeandleisure/floods/127355.aspx on February 24, 2011.

Enserink, B. and Monnikhof, R.A.H. 2003. Impact Assessment and public participation: Facilitating co-design by information management – an example from the Netherlands. *Journal of Environmental Planning and Management*, 46(3), 315-44.

Fallon, R.H. 2005. Legitimacy and the constitution. *Harvard Law Review*, 118(6), 1787-853.

Fazio, R.H. and Zanna, M.P. 1981. Direct experience and attitude-behavior consistency, in *Advances in Experimental Social Psychology*, 14, edited by L. Berkowitz. New York: Academic Press, pp. 162-202.

Gilley, B. 2006. The meaning and measure of state legitimacy; results for 72 countries. *European Journal of Political Research*, 45(3), 499-525.

Grimes, M. 2006. Organizing Consent: The Role of Procedural Fairness in Political Trust and Compliance. *European Journal of Political Research*, 45, 285-315.

GWP 2000. Integrated Water Resource Management, Global Water Partnership TAC. Retrieved from http://www.gwptoolbox.org/images/stories/gwplibrary/background/tac_4_english.pdf on February 28, 2011.

Hanberger, A. 2003. Public policy and Legitimacy: A Historical policy analysis of the interplay between public policy and legitimacy. *Policy Sciences*, 36, 257-78.

Johnston, C.D. and Bartels, B.L. 2010. Sensationalism and Sobriety Differential Media Exposure and Attitudes Toward American Courts. *Public Opinion Quarterly*, 74(2), 260-85.

Lichtenthaler, U. and Lichtenthaler, E. 2009. A Capability-Based Framework for Open Innovation: Complementing Absorptive Capacity. *Journal of Management Studies*, 46(8), 1315-38.

Lipset, S.M. 1959. Some social requisites of democracy. *American Political Science Review*, 53(1), 69-105.

Mitchell, B. (ed.). 1990. *Integrated Water Management*. London: Belhaven Press.

Mitchell, B. 2005. Integrated Water Resource management, Institutional Arrangements, and Land-use Planning. *Environment and Planning A*, 37(8), 1335-52.

Monnikhof, R.A.H. and J. Edelenbos 2001. Into the Fog. Stakeholder input in participatory impact assessment. *Project Appraisal*, 19(1), 29-39.

Oxford City Council 2010a. *Statistics about Oxford*. Retrieved from http://www.oxford.gov.uk/PageRender/decC/Statistics_about_Oxford_occw.htm on July 14, 2010.

Oxford City Council 2010b. *Oxford Flood Area Partnership.* Retrieved from http://www.oxford.gov.uk/PageRender/decCD/Oxford_Area_Flood_Partnership_occw.htm, on 8 September, 2010.

Pardoe, J., Penning-Rowsell, E. and Tunstall, S. 2011. Regulation, negotiation and conflict resolution: Floodplain decisions in a post-PPS25 era. *Natural Hazards and Earth System* Sciences, 11, 2889-2902. DOI: 10.5194/nhess-11-2889-2011.

Partington, D. 2000. Building grounded Theories of Management Action. *British Journal of Management*, 11(2), 91-102. DOI: 10.1111/1467-8551.00153.

Penning-Rowsell, E., Viavattene, C., Pardoe, J., Chatterton, J., Parker, D. and Morris, J. 2010. *The Benefits of Flood and Coastal Risk Management: A Handbook of Assessment Techniques- 2010.* London: Flood Hazard Research Centre.

Scharpf, F.W. 1997. *Games Real Actors Play: Actor-Centered Institutionalism in Policy Research.* Boulder, CO: Westview Press.

Scharpf, F.W. 1998. *Interdependence and Democratic Legitimation.* Working Chapters 98/2, Cologne: Max Planck Institute for the Study of Societies, Retrieved from http://www.mpifg.de/pu/workpap/wp98-2/wp98-2.html, on February 14, 2011.

Scholten, G.A. 1975. Een Empirische Benadering van Legitimatie. *Beleid en Maatschappij*, 2(1), 17-29.

Serageldin, I. 1995. Water resources management: A new policy for a sustainable future. *International Journal of Water Resources Development*, 11(3), 221-32.

Taber, C.S. 2003. Information Processing and Public Opinion, in *Oxford Handbook of Political Psychology*, edited by D.O. Sears, L. Huddy and R. Jervis. New York: Oxford University Press.

Wallner, J. 2008. Legitimacy and Public Policy: Seeing Beyond Effectiveness, Efficiency and Performance. *The Policy Studies Journal*, 36(3), 421-43.

Watts, D.J. and Dodds, P.S. 2007. Influentials, Networks, and Public Opinion Formation. *Journal of Consumer Research*, 34(4), 441-58.

Weber, M. 1980. *Wirtschaft und Gesellschaft.* Tübingen: Mohr Siebeck.

Woltjer, J. 2002. The 'Public Support Machine': Notions of the Function of Participatory Planning by Dutch Infrastructure Planners.*Planning Practice and Research*, 17(4), 437-53.

Wu, F. and Huberman, B.A. 2004. *Social Structure and Opinion Formation.* Retrieved from arXiv:cond-mat/0407252v3 [cond-mat.other]: http://arxiv.org/abs/cond-mat/0407252.

Yin, J. 1999. Elite Opinion and Media Diffusion, Exploring Environmental Attitudes. *The Harvard International Journal of Press/Politics*, 4(3), 62-86.

Zanna, M.P. and J.K. Rempel 2010. Attitudes, a New Look at an Old Concept, in *Attitudes, Key Readings, their Structure, Function and Consequences*, edited by R.H. Fazio and R.E. Petty. New York: Psychology Press; Taylor and Francis (Reprinted from *The Social Psychology of Knowledge*, edited by D. Bar-Tal and A.W. Kruglanski, pp. 315-34, 1988).

Chapter 16

Great Lakes Water Governance: A Transboundary Inter-Regime Analysis

Cheryl de Boer and Gail Krantzberg

Introduction

This chapter emphasizes the importance of the nature of the relationship between society and institutions in the context of the Great Lakes governance regime. Since 1909, the International Joint Commission (IJC) has been in place to support binational management of transboundary waters between Canada and the Great Lakes.

There has however been significant development in the types of issues that society has been concerned with related to water management and governance in the Canada-US Great Lakes region since the IJC was formed. In the 1970s, the increasingly visible effects of industrial pollution supported a public outcry to improve the management of the health of the lakes. High-level agreements were signed, funds were dispersed, committees were developed and a number of goals were accomplished, leading to a revival in the overall status of the Great Lakes. At this time, the IJC, the Great Lakes community of experts, activists and stakeholders were highly engaged and supported by the developing regime. Since the 1970s and early 80s, there has been a slow decline in the perceived relevance and effectiveness of the Great Lakes water governance regime (particularly the IJC and some of its sub-groups) while the threats facing this globally significant fresh water resource are considered by experts to be immediate. The energy once exuded by the public and the governments towards enacting new and progressive ways of protecting and improving the lakes has slowly diminished. This chapter looks at the current governance context of the Great Lakes regime from a slightly different perspective which includes water related policy institutions as well as non-water specific related influences and the resulting conflicts and synergies that result: this is referred to as the inter-regime. The characteristics of this inter-regime are examined in terms of how they support the adaptive management of this ever changing and increasingly threatened resource. Clearly in such an interest and user heavy region, many interactions result between the various actors. We see connective capacity as being thus particularly necessary in reducing conflicting uses, policies and signals towards a more coherent and sustainability supporting governance regime. It is important for overcoming the traditionally separated mechanisms for improving water quality and quantity concerns. This chapter focuses on the various carriers of connective capacity and its focal points in terms of the government and societal spheres as they relate to the existing institutions.

Fluctuating Concerns in the Great Lakes Region

As consumerism and industrial production are on the rise, non-renewable and renewable natural resources are being used more frequently in order to satisfy human desires. Robert Hennigan (1970) at the Thirteenth Conference on Great Lakes Research expressed that there is a requirement for understanding and reform of the Great Lakes institutional ecosystem to establish an attainable and workable system for effective water management. Incorporation of the action elements of persuasion and education, legal action and economic incentives were noted as being particularly necessary for the success of this system. More than four decades later, this prophetic wisdom holds and speaks to the need to look at the water management issue as an integrated governance challenge and not a compilation of programs and policies applied piecemeal to appease the issues and worries of the day. Donahue (1988) refers to the current approach to resource management in North America as a band-aid solution method and says that the involved groups tend to be "ill-defined, experimental, and of limited authority and resources, unknown effectiveness, reluctant acceptance, and perpetual involvement in redefinition of goals and problems" (Donahue 1988: 120). Donahue also suggested that there is a need to advance beyond this and develop into a more appropriate vehicle for ecosystem based resource management and asserts that there "appears to be a compelling, yet inadequately articulated, sense of dissatisfaction, with present arrangements" (Donahue 1988: 120). Why then after over 20 years, has little been done to alter the current state of affairs if it is inadequate for proper basin and ecosystem management of the shared waters and why have the actions taken by those who have pointed out the inefficiencies in the system not brought about real change?

Putting the Pieces Together

A number of reasons can be seen to have contributed to the current state of affairs. Historically, governance of the various issues related to the health and management of the lakes was fulfilled in a fragmented and specialized manner. Actions were thus organized around these clear problems that needed to be solved. Once the issues are no longer so visibly and conceptually clear, the underlying strengths of the governance systems are brought to light. Without strong *connections* and *capacity* within the Great Lakes community, their ability to address not only more complicated water issues, but also issues that result out of more indirectly associated actions and policies (transportation, air quality management, economic development) becomes more transparent. The first chapter of this book highlights very effectively the various issues associated with the transition to a more integrated way of handling water; from government to governance. Our central question in this chapter is how the governance associated with the management of the Great Lakes has reduced its ability to improve its health and sustainability as a resource, particularly given the complex and intertwined nature of the issues that are currently being faced. The connective capacity of the regime is seen to be central in overcoming the disparate and sometimes conflicting interests that are impacting the governance of the Great Lakes.

According to Young (1989), the topic of regimes relates to the specialized arrangements including quite well-defined activities, resources or geographical areas which often involve subsets of international society. Though this is perhaps the more common thought of definition, Krasner (1983) much earlier defined regimes as they relate to the facilitation of a convergence of expectations. They are further posited as being constructed of institutions which possess norms, decision rules and procedures. We share this second view but see the convergence of expectations particularly as they relate to the desired management of the natural resource. In addition to this, we include all of the relevant government instruments as well as the informal and cultural institutions that influence the actions relevant to managing that resource. This choice is made due to our focus on the real implementation issues seen taking place as a result of regime influence. It is thus extremely important to study not only the recognized Great Lakes water governance regime contents but also any influences of other regimes such as agricultural development, economic development, transportation, et cetera since they have real-world consequences and influences (both direct and indirect). In our increasingly integrated global economy and environment, the actions taken to address any given problem will most certainly have impacts outside of the intended issue, sometimes referred to as institutional interplay (Underdahl and Young 2004). When the intended components of the recognized regime are combined with the non-deliberate effects of the implementation of policies and programs associated with other issue areas, we call this an *inter-regime*. This inter-regime is likely to develop with respect to any less easily defined issue area such as the overall management of an economically, culturally and environmentally significant resource as is the Great Lakes.

Despite the difficulty in making an exhaustive inventory and analysis of this inter-regime, its institutions and their relationships to society and their needs will be studied in order to assess the connection between the governance and sustainability of the Great Lakes. The contents as well as the structure/character of this inter-regime are important, such as the funding structures related to nature protection, social and cultural development. The "inter-regime" is here analyzed according to how it is able to foster sustainable water governance through the lens of the structural context and characteristics of the governance elements, which is further outlined in the following section. The framework presented is intended to highlight the main influences of the governance inter-regime (including the extent, coherence, flexibility, intensity, the various actors, levels, instruments, resources and issues) of the shared Canada-US waters on the sustainable governance capacity of the Great Lakes community.

In relation to the connective capacity of the inter-regime we see a number of interesting similarities between our framework and the ideas behind connective capacity. Generally, our framework aligns with connective capacity in that focus and value need to be associated with cooperation. Without giving cooperation the appropriate attention, the detrimental aspects of competition that can result from increased specialization will begin to erode against the improvements that have been made as a result of it. We choose here to look past the obvious benefits of a specialized/separated decision-making approach (as is briefly outlined in Chapter 1). Instead we focus on the system wide benefits that could be achieved through a more shared awareness of the common goals and desires across the inter-regime and how they interact towards the development of a governance system more inclined to support real improvements to sustainability as well as trust and confidence by the public and other stakeholders.

The governance inter-regime as conceptualized here should promote connective capacity from an institutional perspective and across regimes typically considered as separate.

Methodology

The data used for this analysis is taken from the Krantzberg et al. (2007) report on Great Lakes Governance. This elaborate piece of work was delivered based on an initial series of interviews with 25 different experts from government, academia, NGOs and industry familiar with the Laurentian Great Lakes, from Canada and the United States. The interviews (some by phone and others in person) took place in the winter of 2006 and centered on questions of governance, accountability, political will, the nature of the Great Lakes Water Quality Agreement, financing and other matters that interviewees chose to highlight. As background for the second stage of this research (a workshop held with other Great Lakes experts in the spring of 2007), the research team summarized the central tendencies and common themes of the interviews. The proceeding two-day workshop was held to develop a general understanding of the major issues seen relating to governance as experienced by 24 different stakeholders from Canada and the US who were also considered to be experts in Great Lakes governance related issues. Additionally, they were asked to comment on new models of governance and variations on the current governance structure. The responses incorporate the various aspects of importance in the inter-regime that are actively at play in the transboundary context. The conclusions of this chapter are thus drawn from the empirical data contained within the Krantzberg et al. (2007) report and the experiences of the authors from their participation in this exercise. Although this data is several years old, little has changed in the institutional structure and context of Great

Lakes governance and the issues brought forward are very much still relevant (see McLaughlin and Krantzberg 2011).

Development of a Water Governance Inter-Regime

At the turn of the 20th century, both nations formally recognized that a concerted binational effort would be needed for the preservation of the trans-boundary water systems. Hence, in 1909 both American and Canadian (British) Federal Governments signed the Boundary Waters Treaty Act (BWTA). The Treaty states that its purpose is to "provide the principles and mechanisms to help resolve disputes and to prevent future ones, primarily those concerning water quality and quantity along the boundary between Canada and the United States". The BWTA also provided for the formation of the International Joint Commission (IJC) whose role was to aid in the resolution of any disputes that may arise between the two countries in the governance of the shared waters. Six Commissioners, three of which are appointed from each of the Canadian and Federal governments, lead the IJC. These Commissioners are required to behave in a non-partisan manner that puts the interests of the lakes first and foremost. The IJC institutional support consists of more than 20 boards, made up of experts from the United States and Canada, to help it carry out its responsibilities. According to their inclusion in the BWTA and the Great Lakes Water Quality Agreement, their main responsibilities are related to authorizing uses while protecting competing interests in accordance with rules in the Treaty. One example as is shared on the IJC website (www.ijc. org) is that of the application procedure for dams or canals in these waters. The IJC must provide an assessment of such a project and if it is approved, the IJC can further set conditions to limit water levels and flows. This could be to protect shore properties and wetlands, the interests of farmers, shippers and others.

In the early 1960s, severe water quality deterioration forced the two governments to issue a reference for a study and recommendations from the IJC. A reference is the formal request (which must be agreed upon by both governments) by which the IJC is allowed to intervene in the decisions made regarding the management of the waters. Without an official reference, the IJC is limited to an information and communication role. This important reference resulted in the discovery that excessive phosphorus loads from anthropogenic sources were causing the severe eutrophication in Lake Erie and Lake Ontario. The 1964 reference led to the creation of the 1972 Great Lakes Water Quality Agreement (GLWQA), one of the most significant contributions of the IJC to Great Lakes revitalization (Krantzberg et al. 2006). The GLWQA's purpose is "to restore and maintain the chemical, physical and biological integrity of the waters of the Great Lakes Basin Ecosystem" (GLWQA 1987) and "set general and specific water quality objectives and mandated programs to meet them. However, it gave priority to point source pollution from industrial sources and sewage plants" (IJC 2005: 1). The GLWQA was successful in alleviating eutrophication (due to excessive nutrient inputs) and was revised in 1978 to better meet the emerging issues primarily related to persistent toxic substances. The second amendment in 1987 included the development of Remedial Action Plans for geographic Areas of Concerns (AOC's) in the Great Lakes as well as Lakewide Management Plans. Specific commitments for nonpoint source pollution, contaminated sediment, airborne toxic substances, pollution from groundwater and research and development priorities were also included (IJC 2005). The GLWQA has addressed developing concerns through a fragmented and issue specific targeted approach: new actions are reactive in relation to each new and emerging threat.

Ecosystem Melt-down and Institutional Build-up

In recent times, consensus has been reached by hundreds of Great Lakes scientists, that the Great Lakes ecosystem's health is in jeopardy and facing a tipping point. Actions are again urgently needed to restore system elements in critical near shore/ tributary zones where a chain reaction of adaptive responses to a suite of stresses are leading to catastrophic changes – referred to as ecosystem meltdown. Without at least partial restoration of these areas, the adverse symptoms being observed in the Great Lakes will intensify and to a large extent become irreversible. Concurrently, actions are needed to control or eliminate sources of stress that represent basin-wide threats to the biological, physical and chemical components of the Great Lakes that are essential to the stability and health of the ecosystem (Beeton et al. 2005).

Interviewees and workshop participants substantiated the lack of a coherent and coordinated vision that aligns North America's protection and management strategies for the Great Lakes. For example, industrial, energy production, private consumption and recreational uses have different and often discordant requirements for water quantity and quality. Further, "mature issues" that have already been in the public spotlight for some time such as water pollution due to sewage and industrial by-products continue to occur. New issues of concern are also continuing to arise, such as the presence and possible effects of pharmaceuticals and personal care products into the waste stream, air pollution and ongoing introduction of new exotic species.

From a water quantity perspective, pressures exist to divert water from the Great Lakes to areas both within and outside of the region. The Great Lakes Charter Annex (referred to as Annex 2001) was then signed by the Governors of the eight Great Lakes states and the Premiers of Ontario and Quebec to obtain a better understanding of and develop effective criteria for addressing the individual and cumulative effects of water withdrawals from the Great Lakes Basin ecosystem. This led to the signing of the Great Lakes—St. Lawrence River Basin Sustainable Water Resources Agreement (2005) which focused on collaborative approaches to water management across the Basin.

Taking this understanding of the general context of the Great Lakes regional issues, we now turn to explore the various governance related context (as suggested by our Great Lakes experts). The issues as described by the experts were categorized based on how they relate to the underlying sentiment of each of four regime characteristics: extent, coherence, flexibility and intensity. These four characteristics are derived from Contextual Interaction Theory (De Boer and Bressers 2011) and enable a broad look at the inter-regime in terms of content and structure. They were then further separated into what type of governance element they best related to: scales, actors, goals, instruments and resources. In this way, the various issues included in the data provide a general picture of the degree of fullness of each characteristic and provide some explanation of why this is the case.

An Inter-regime Analysis

In this section a perspective on water governance inter-regime analysis will be very briefly sketched as it is applied here to characterize the Canada-US transboundary water governance inter-regime. While "governance" includes all of the institutions, the policies and the actions, the governance inter-regime is regarded as the more structural context for the practical water management processes and actions. Concrete water management processes, for instance in a certain location, will always face case specific contexts that vary from one place to another. The structural context of the governance inter-regime applies however to a much larger set of water management processes, for instance to all of the different transboundary water resources along the Canada US border.

We make use of five elements of public governance that are helpful for analyzing this context. These elements are the scales, actors, goals, instruments and resources (Bressers and Kuks 2003). The roots of these elements have been developed by various authors and have been used to compare the sustainability of water governance regimes in six European national contexts and in Florida, Greece and Romania (Bressers and Kuks 2003, 2004, Kuks and Bressers 2003, Kampa 2007, Kampa and Bressers 2008, Vinke-de Kruijf et al. 2011).

Within the development of these elements, the concept of governance was elaborated as an enlarged concept of policy. Starting with a simple policy definition like "actors using means to an end", actors are seen to operate in multi-level and multi-actor networks. Goals result from multiple problem perceptions, which then often lead to having multiple instead of singular goals. The means available are both instruments and resources for their implementation and are characterized by multiple instruments that are joined together in strategic policy mixes. All parties involved use a wealth of formal and informal resources in interactive implementation. This multiple character highlights that the most important difference of the governance concept compared to the previous institutional descriptions is the acknowledgement of the impact the elements have together on each concrete water management process.

We have used this set of elements to examine the governance inter-regime, to uncover the crucial aspects that would enable more sustainable water governance. A number of similarities can be seen between the elements of governance developed here and the five different objects of fragmentation and integration as described in Chapter 1 (1. government layers and levels; 2. Sectors and domains, 3. Time orientation of the long and the short term; 4. Perceptions and actors frames; and 5. public and private spheres). Notably, 1., 4., and 5. show up in both models, however, we focus most closely on the institutional conception of connective capacity which includes within it the various instruments and individuals of importance to its overall function. The remaining two focal points (2. and 3.) are also considered important, however, they can more clearly be seen to show up in other aspects of our framework that links these external regime contexts to the interaction processes of actors (De Boer and Bressers 2011). Elements of public governance can be used to describe the aspects of the governance inter-regime that affect the ability of the goals to be achieved. When looking at the governance inter-regime as a whole, it is further helpful to assess how each of these elements contribute to four essential regime qualities as are expressed within Contextual Interaction Theory: extent, coherence, flexibility and intensity (De Boer and Bressers 2011).

Highlighting Gaps and Conflicts through Inter-regime Characteristics

Our analysis begins by identifying the aspects of the inter-regime in terms of how it influences water management practices in the Great Lakes not only through its direct contents, but also through its *extent* and *coherence*. Thus, the first two important qualities of our inter-regime that are related to integrated management are:

a. The *extent* of each of the elements of governance included in the inter-regime (scope of issues taken into account, completeness, comprehensiveness);
b. The *coherence* of each and between the elements of governance (the degree to which the various elements of the regime are strengthening rather than weakening each other; paying attention to separate issues only adds to complexity and fragmentation when it is not accompanied by thoughtful connections).

The development of governance inter-regimes can be seen to transition through different phases in regards to these elements. In the early stages, most simple governance regimes have little extent, ie. they begin with some piece of legislation, rule or law that attempts to reduce some negative impact on the resource. As more attention gets paid to the impact of different uses and activities, the extent of the regime increases by way of additional instruments to protect the resource (Knoepfel et al. 2001, 2007). As this happens, the number and breadth of instruments, actors, and influences increase and generally results in decreasing coherence since more complexity leads to fragmentation. In a more integrated inter-regime, these incoherencies are addressed through various attempts to either streamline or better coordinate the various pieces of the different regimes, which influence the resource. It is postured in Bressers and Kuks (2004) that as the regime moves from low extent and coherence, towards higher extent and coherence that the resulting regime (likely to resemble our definition of inter-regime) is more apt to ensure more sustainable management of the given resource. Lacking extent leaves important uses and users unregulated and lacking coherence leads to measures that hinder each other's effectiveness, which naturally can also be seen as a lack of connective capacity of the institutional structure.

As is recognized elsewhere in this book, water governance takes place in a complex and uncertain context. Connective capacity suggests that the answer lies somewhere in managing the levels of resistance and resilience in the system. In our framework and given the institutional focus, we place greatest importance in addressing the issues related to the structural needs of a dynamic governance inter-regime. In a more dynamic adaptive management perspective two additional criteria are relevant for understanding how the governance inter-regime supports the sustainable management of the resource (De Boer and Bressers 2011). Like with economic development, adaptive action in complex and dynamic circumstances requires many actors' creativity and effort. It is important that the governance inter-regime rewards initiatives from many stakeholders as long as they contribute to the common vision and also provides leeway for such initiatives.

The first quality added to the framework is the aspect of *intensity*. This is the degree to which the inter-regime elements urge changes in the status quo or in current developments. Secondly the *flexibility* of the inter-regime characterizes the degree to which the governance inter-regime elements support and facilitate adaptive actions and strategies (in as far as the integrated ambitions are served by this adaptiveness, not as a result of weak implementation). In terms of how these two characteristics relate to the likelihood of a more sustainable management of the resource, the relationship appears to have a point of optimality, which is related to the levels of the other regime characteristics and the specific characteristics of the context. For example, increased flexibility is likely to support the sustainable management of the resource when the cognitions and the motivations of the various implementers are in line with those of the policy developers and decision makers. Increasing the flexibility of an inter-regime beyond a certain point however is unlikely to further increase sustainability and even leads to a reduction due to a lack of clarity and responsibility for action or accountability. Accordingly, too little or too much intensity in an inter-regime under the non-corresponding conditions can lead to inappropriate levels of forced implementation which is generally conceptualized as not supporting the trust and social sustainability of the system. The four mentioned qualities of governance can be applied to all five elements of governance. This then creates a matrix of issues that are relevant for the degree to which the governance context guides and facilitates effective water management processes in practice.

Great Lakes Transboundary Inter-Regime Context

Extent

The extent of the inter-regime appears at first glance to be very high due to the numerous and extensive levels and scales, actors, problem perceptions and objectives, instruments and policy strategies included within it. Despite this, a number of issues related to the perception of the extent (ie. the scope of issues taken into account, completeness, comprehensiveness) were uncovered in the interviews and workshops. What is interesting is that most concerns about extent were generally related to the idea that there are so many policies and programs dealing with the Great Lakes that are relatively unclear, that it is too difficult to identify where the actual gaps are in terms of governance of the resource. A real lack of clarity was also stated as hindering the responsibilities and resources for implementation available, which could improve the governance. The inter-regime is also considered to be quite absent in its inclusion of the First Nations Communities, which could improve both the understanding of the scientific matters of the lake but also have more of a basis for sustainable management against short-term interests. The insufficient scientific information available and limited fact finding efforts reduce the ability to adequately define the issues that are part of the problem and hence the objectives are nearly impossible to describe in a manner where different groups or individuals can be made accountable. One key problem is that the instruments do not adequately require the polluters/ beneficiaries to pay and hence do not adequately govern the resource. Further, the resources are not available at the local group level to support the place-based action. This lack of resources and general lack of clarity reduce the ability of the inter-regime to support adaptive water management.

All in all, the contribution to sustainable management by a sufficient level of extent is quite uncertain. This is mainly due to a lack of clarity, though in relation to many other regimes around the world it is considered to be high, as it in itself, is not generally considered the limiting feature.

Coherence

As seen above, there are a large number of government levels, institutions, NGOs and the public involved in the governance inter-regime. This is an extremely important characteristic of this inter-regime. It has developed partially due to the understanding that it is a shared resource both binationally and locally and thus the more people that are involved, the less likely it is that one of those bodies will take from the resource in an unsustainable way. As was seen in the previous section however, this can have other than the intended results. For purposes of clarity, it is instructive to understand how these numerous instruments can work against the sustainable management of the resource based on their overall coherence.

The Canadian constitutional complexity in terms of water management has resulted in a mismatch of levels and scales when negotiating agreements. Additionally, there are no clear connections across the border regarding alignment of responsibilities for procedures, indicators, and the roles of fed/state/provincial levels. Logistically, there appear to be just too many levels and scales involved for effective negotiations to take place when all the parties who have a stake are involved since the issue itself is considered to be so large. Increasing decision-making at the local level over aspects important to the success of transboundary water governance has also reduced the faith in proper accountability and clear progress. The strong presence of a silo mentality is considered to even further contribute to the lack of coherence across the levels and scales.

A large number of the actors in the network have similar interests, although this is certainly not the case across the board. Comments were made that the connections between the Great Lakes regime and the Great Lakes Fishery Commission have not been taken advantage of despite their overlapping responsibilities in the Great Lakes. A general difficulty in bringing the actors together in consensual network relations is certainly a strain on the coherence of governance.

Some aspects of the Great Lakes regime goals are not perceived to be in line with other regimes (or the current conservative economic agenda). This level of incoherency reduces the ability of the agencies involved to implement the actions as has been agreed upon. Due to a lack of clarity, different actors use different definitions of the ecosystem approach as is outlined in the Great Lakes Water Quality Agreement and what is included within it. Thus the use of this term in defining the solution to the problem (or that the problem is a lack of ecosystemic management) in such an unclear way certainly adds to the incoherencies witnessed. The GLWQA and the surrounding inter-regime both work toward putting the interests of the lakes on the national agenda of each country. Policy strategies at the national levels in the US however, are not supposed to be heavily influenced through regional issues. This diminishes the ability for the EPA to develop specific policy related to the Great Lakes.

US and Canadian policy instruments and strategies differ and thus make joint agreements on measures more difficult (note that this is especially difficult where increased regulative detail is sought as opposed to focusing on a guiding vision, the achievement of results and the use flexibility to accomplish them). In addition, the manner of appointing the IJC is not delivering confidence in its impartiality. Concerns are strong that the recent politicizing of the IJC appointments has reduced the ability of the IJC to effectively act as an instrument to manage the lakes binationally. There are also constraints to integrating binational decisions into domestic law on both sides of the border.

The effects of incoherencies on the inter-regime are strong when looking from the perspective of by whom and how the inter-regime is implemented. As discussed above, the role of the IJC as an impartial binational organization is under question. This is in part due to the politicization of appointments by the national leaders. Whereas the general public had generally approved of previous appointees to the Commissioners roles, the last appointments were considered to have been made as a result of political favors. These new members were seen to have less connection to the various interests that had been prominent in decision-making and it was thus feared that they would no longer include these interests in the decisions taken by the IJC. In addition to this, the IJC is seen to have increased their position in the advocacy realm, which was viewed as having additionally limited their ability to be used as impartial scientific advice. Furthermore, the alterations made to the IJC as a result of the 1987 Protocol removed its resources that enabled the coordination function and data collection opportunities for reporting on progress. It was the belief of a number of experts that this was done in order to reduce the accountability of the two governments to meeting the goals of the GLWQA (this has not been verified but was seen to be regularly referred to). The responsibilities for reporting and data collection were transferred to an internal government group, which is by definition less likely to be openly accountable since the government is now responsible for reporting on itself, as opposed to an outside organization. Overlapping jurisdictions, poor institutional funding structure and having the responsible persons for implementation not in line with those able to provide resources for implementation are all part of the characteristics of the inter-regime that highlight the lack of coherency. The incoherencies continue further down the implementation trail. One example is that municipal governments have the responsibility to enact the GLWQA but are not given the resources to do so, and are requested to fit these actions into their agendas.

Flexibility

As has been discussed earlier and in many other texts relating to water management, it can be a highly complex and dynamic process situation in which success depends on quick and timely adaptive action. How then does flexibility appear to be of importance in the Great Lakes inter-regime? The word itself was used extensively in the discussions, being seen generally by the participants as something that is lacking in the overall inter-regime. In the sections below we illustrate the extent to which the problems in the inter-regime indeed relate to its degree of flexibility.

An inter-regime is more flexible when there is a decentralization of power that is supported by upper levels of government. This is closely related to empowering rather than controlling relations, and thus relies on trust. The high stakes that the two federal governments' hold for the control of these shared waters is certainly seen to inhibit the reform of the inter-regime towards supporting solutions that can come from local adaptive actions. The transfer of priority setting and assessment of governments' progress to an impartial third body such as the IJC would reduce such control, yet was mentioned as something that is unlikely to change. Thus, the lack of trust across levels and the desire to hold decision-making power at the upper levels reduces the flexibility of the inter-regime for local stakeholders and thus hinders their ability to act closely in relation to addressing local contextual issues.

Flexible inter-regimes can also be characterized in terms of actor relations in the policy network. The combination of giving leeway to each actor group to optimize its contribution to the whole program, while still viewing the program as a joint effort qualifies as flexibility. References to the prevalence of silo mentality within the inter-regime are relevant as this generally limits the opportunities to work symbiotically towards a common goal at the expense of sector based/ ministerial ambitions. This causes fragmentation of the policies (which was seen to be influential under coherence) and also restricts the leeway stakeholders have in compromising in order to optimize joint results. This results in sub-optimal results in overall governance and implementation when viewed from a Great Lakes perspective.

In terms of general problem perception and goal ambitions, flexibility implies that these are not only integrated into a sort of common denominator (like with coherence), but also that these mixtures are allowed to be different in emphasis according to the opportunities and needs of the context in the various concrete situations. This implies some acceptance of uncertainty and openness to emergent options, which relates to trust. With regards to this, there is a general perception among the stakeholders that the purposes and thus accountability need to be more goal and action oriented, as opposed to process control driven (hence more flexible).

The strategies and instruments are more flexible when means from different sources (like public policies and private property rights) are available and can be used in creative ways to achieve the desired goals. This aspect is difficult to assess, as there are indeed numerous varieties and types of instruments available as a result of the broad issue areas that are related to the Great Lakes. What makes it problematic is that in this context, this flexibility enables the incoherencies to be further exploited in ways that are perhaps more difficult to coordinate along shared understanding of the intent of the inter-regime. Thus, it could be said that this flexibility is quite high, but this does not necessarily contribute to the ability of the inter-regime to sustainably manage the resource.

Lastly the flexibility of the organization responsible for the implementation – the responsibilities and resources given by the policy program(s) – can be measured by the discretion available to pool resources like funds and people with those of others to serve integrated projects and to be held accountable on the basis of the balanced virtues of the achievements (as in an integrated project), rather than on the basis of separate performance criteria. References to this in the process of the interviews and workshop were limited and can perhaps be understood from two perspectives. Firstly, there are actually quite a few examples of opportunities for this within the scope of the Great Lakes. The Remedial Action Plans are based on meeting very integrated goals through a place-based community-oriented design. Also, the Great Lakes Sustainability Fund has a granting structure that is biased towards integrated projects with combined interests. Second, the lack of concrete goals at the inter-regime level makes this more easily attainable. The possible advantage thus of unclear goals for measurement is that it indeed reduces the stress put onto individual organizations to meet particular, independent and clearly defined goals.

Generally it can be said that flexibility is generally discouraged from the top level due to a strong history of using command and control methods to ensure that the implementing agencies are accountable to the interests of the government. This is as well the case from the lower levels due to a lack of trust in the overall regime. It is however clear that increased flexibility could support a more coherent and well-functioning overall regime if it were aided by a significant increase in the presence of trust and alignment of cognitions and motivations between the various levels of policy and implementation.

Intensity

The scale as well as the dynamic and change-oriented nature of the Great Lakes inter-regime requires energy to move forward and overcome current obstacles. With respect to the intensity actually present in the inter-regime, the participants raised a number of serious concerns. Political will to act in the bi-national interest was seen as very weak against the lobbying interests of specific interest groups and sectors related mostly to industrial and economic desires. The various institutions and instruments that are in place to prevent this are seen as not adequate to meet the sustainability goals of the inter-regime.

A conscious lack of effort, spent using science to develop policy based on strong influence of politics though concerns, is perceived to be greater from the Canadian side regarding being participative and a good partner and this is seen to reduce their desire to press contentious issues. The general strength and influence of international law is important in underpinning some of the perceived lack of intensity of the inter-regime. There is certainly no consensus with respect to the "binding" nature of the Great Lakes Water Quality Agreement as the political will of the day is seen to be what gives the various instruments real importance and chances for successful implementation. The funding connection between the IJC and the federal governments alters the ability of the IJC to be impartial and hence force difficult decisions in the direction where they are more politically safe. The responsibility for enforcement of the Agreement is unclear and so the lack of desire at the federal level to enforce environmental obligations and provide the necessary resources for implementation (perhaps as a result of incoherent problem definitions and objectives) causes this to significantly reduce the intensity of the inter-regime in protecting the lakes.

Overall, the intensity of the inter-regime towards a achieving common goal is scattered and thus weak. This is propagated by the rather high intensity of other regimes (such as economic development) which influence policy makers to put efforts elsewhere and the lack of appropriate instruments by which to determine progress and thus support at the local/grass roots level communities. Given the dwindling capacity that has taken place in the grass roots community over the past decades, these reductions in intensity at the inter-regime level are even more dangerous to the sustainability of the lakes. Botts and Muldoon (2005) express the concern that the governments of the Great Lakes are not sufficiently mobilized for coherent action and that there needs to be a revitalization of the binational sense of community amongst these neighbors for the future good of the Great Lakes. One example that is cited of the breakdown and distrust in the current decision and policy making structure is the withdrawal of the USEPA and Environment Canada from the institutional arrangements managed by the IJC in the 1990s.

Conclusions

As highlighted in this chapter, numerous agreements, protocols and action plans have been developed over the last few years to try and compensate for the lack of a concrete and current trans-boundary water governance structure. Where the political infrastructure is lacking, citizens groups and local governments have taken it upon themselves to protect their particular interests in their lakes and waters. All of the work and interest in the preservation of the shared waters have not provided an adequate transboundary water management system that is coherent, meaningful or sustainable. The continual addition of new actors, policies and programs without clear management and evaluation has eroded the possible gains in effectiveness and results and resulted in superfluous complexity. Although all of the characteristics discussed in this chapter are inter-related and are positioned as being important in supporting the sustainable management of the water resources, the coherence and flexibility characteristics stand out in their importance to the overall connective capacity of the inter-regime.

One pitfall of the federal governance of the Great Lakes is that the federal governments do not have the ability to (or have chosen not to) clearly inform stakeholders of their plan for ensuring that as many interests as possible are being considered in the water management structure. A neutral third party, such as the IJC, could have the ability to resolve issues that conflicting interest groups have concerning the Great Lakes basin ecosystems if only they were issued the responsibility and jurisdiction (in the ideal scenario) to do so. Having a truly non-partisan body responsible for communication as well as reporting increases the likelihood of more open communication across different sectors. If the process is led by the governments, which are given little trust by some sectors in terms of protecting their interests, it is less likely to be inclusive and thus truly connective.

The incremental policy formation which has been followed by the two governments, has developed from the decision making structure which was initiated when the number of stressors were understood to be limited, and is no longer appropriate for today's myriad of pressures on the system. It is a classic example of what is described in the regime theory mentioned of relatively simple regimes that experience several layers of add-on policies and programs without considering the resulting fragmentation. The GLWQA is essentially based on the idea of pollution control and elimination. Given the complexity of threats challenging the integrity of the Great Lakes basin ecosystem, the approach to Great Lake management is inadequate to create coherent governance. In order to address this, the IJC could for example take a broader view of the various goals and interests and thus understand and communicate more effectively the trade-offs that are necessary in managing a resource that is subjected to such great demands. The institutions involved in the governance inter-regime need to be able to support improved coherence and enable the right amount of flexibility to be used. The right level of flexibility is important to enable a strong governance presence while allowing local actors to provide innovative solutions to pressing issues.

Bibliography

Beaton, A. 2005. A Prescription for Great Lakes Protection and Restoration [Online]. Available at: www.greatlakes.net/sdstrategyteam/documents/ Prescription_for_Great_Lakes_3-28-05.doc [accessed: 6 January 2012].
Bressers, H.Th.A. and Kuks, S. 2003. What does "Governance" mean? From conception to elaboration, in *Achieving Sustainable Development: The Challenge of Governance Across Social Scales*, edited by H.Th.A. Bressers and W.A. Rosenbaum. Westport, CT: Praeger, 65-88.
Bressers, H.Th.A. and Lulofs, K. 2010. *Governance and Complexity in Water Management, Creating Cooperation through Boundary Spanning.* Northampton, MA. Edward Elgar.
Bressers, H.Th.A and Lulofs, K. 2009. Explaining the policy impact of the 1991 and 2000 firework blasts in the Netherlands by the core of five policy change models, in *European and North American Policy Change: Drivers and Dynamics*, edited by G. Capano and M. Howlett. New York: Routledge, 15-42.
Bressers, H.Th.A and Kuks, S. 2004. *Integrated Governance and Water Basin Management.* Dordrecht, Boston, London: Kluwer Academic Publishers.
Botts, L. and Muldoon, P. 2005. *Evolution of the Great Lakes Water Quality Agreement.* Michigan: Michigan State University Press.
De Boer, C. and Bressers, H.Th.A. 2011. *Complex and Dynamic Implementation Processes: The Renaturalization of the Dutch Regge River.* Enschede: University of Twente Press.
Donahue, M.J. 1988. Institutional arrangements for Great Lakes management, in *Perspectives on Ecosystem Management for the Great Lakes*, edited by L. Caldwell. Albany, NY: State University of New York Press. 115-40.
Great Lakes Water Quality Agreement as signed in 1972, revised in 1978 and amended by Protocol in 1987. International Joint Commission United States and Canada.

Great Lakes—St. Lawrence River Basin Sustainable Water Resources Agreement. 2005 [Online]. Available at: http://www.mnr.gov.on.ca/stdprodconsume/groups/lr/@mnr/@water/documents/document/200040.pdf [accessed: 6 January 2012].

Hennigan, R.D. 1970. *Effective Water Quality Management: Impossible Dream or Attainable Goal.* Paper to the 13th Conference on Great Lakes Research, International Association for Great Lakes Research, Ann Arbor Michigan, 31 March- 3 April.

International Joint Commission. 2005. A Guide to the Great Lakes Water Quality Agreement: Background for the 2006 Governmental Review.

Kampa, E. 2007. *Integrated Institutional Water Regimes: Realisation in Greece.* Berlin: Logos Verlag.

Kampa, E. and Bressers, H. 2008. Evolution of the Greek national regime for water resources. *Water Policy,* 10(5), 481-500.

Knoepfel, P., Kissling-Näf, I. and Varone, F. 2001. *Institutionelle Regime für natürliche Ressourcen.* Basel: Helbing & Lichtenhahn.

Knoepfel, P., Nahrath, S. and Varone, F. 2007. Institutional Regimes for Natural Resources: An Innovative Theoretical Framework for Sustainability, in *Environmental Policy Analyses: Learning from the Past for the Future: 25 Years of Research,* edited by P. Knoepfel. Berlin: Springer, 455-506.

Krantzberg, G., Bratzel, M. and McDonald, J. 2006. Contribution of the International Joint Commission to Great Lakes Renewal. *The Great Lakes Geographer,* 13, 2-37.

Krantzberg, G., Manno, J. and de Boer, C. 2007. *Great Lakes Governance, Report on an Expert Workshop of June 2007.* Joyce Foundation.

Krasner, S.D. 1982. Structural Causes and Regime Consequences: Regimes as Intervening Variables. *International Organization,* 36(2), 185-205.

Kuks, S. and Bressers, H.Th.A. 2003. Managing water resources in Florida and the Netherlands: The impact of national orientations on multiscale governance, in *Achieving Sustainable Development: The Challenge of Governance Across Social Scales,* edited by H.Th.A. Bressers and W.A. Rosenbaum. Westport, CT: Praeger, 109-34.

McLaughlin, C. and Krantzberg, G. 2011. An appraisal of policy implementation deficits in the Great Lakes. *Journal of Great Lakes Research,* 37, 390-6.

Ostrom, E. 1990. *Governing the Commons: The Evolution of Institutions for Collective Action.* New York: Cambridge University Press.

Ostrom, E. 1999. Institutional Rational Choice: An Assessment of the Institutional Analysis and Development Framework, in *Theories of the Policy Process* edited by P.A. Sabatier. Boulder, CO: Westview Press, 21-64.

True, J.L., Jones, B.D. and Baumgartner, F.R. 1999. Punctuated-equilibrium theory, in *Theories of the Policy Process* by P.A. Sabatier. Boulder, CO: Westview Press, 97-115.

Underdahl, A. and Young, O.R. 2004. *Regime Consequences: Methodological Challenges and Research Strategies.* Dordrecht: Kluwer Academic Publishers.

Vinke-de Kruijf, J. Kuks, S. and Augustijn, D. 2010. *Governing Change: Experiences from Two Water Sectors in a Transition Country*. Paper to the NIG Annual Working Conference: Rotterdam, NL, 25-26 November, 2010.

Wolf, A.T. 2005. Transboundary Water Conflicts and Cooperation, in *In Search of Sustainable Water Management*, edited by D.S. Kenney. Northampton, MA: Edward Elgar, 131-54.

Young, O.R. 1989. International cooperation: Building regimes for natural resources and *the environment*. Ithaca, NY: Cornell University Press.

Chapter 17

Conclusions: Towards a Synchronization Perspective of Connective Capacity in Water Governance

Jurian Edelenbos, Nanny Bressers and Peter Scholten

Introduction: Connective Capacity Unraveled

Water governance processes are excellent examples of complex, multilevel systems, heavily intertwined with other physical, social, political and economic subsystems (Schlager and Blomquist 2000). This book has discussed a variety of cases and ideas on water governance. The core idea throughout this discussion was the realization of connective capacity in water governance or lack thereof. In Chapter 1 we discussed the increasing fragmentation in water governance and beyond as an important driver for the desire to realize connective capacity. We have argued that the challenges in the water sector demand a governance approach which, in line with ideas such as integrated water resource management, aims at a form of integration and coordination between actors, domains, problems, solutions and ideas. Consequently, in this book we have been identifying possibilities for coordination and integration on many levels in water governance.

The issue of connective capacity has been studied in this book through a grid consisting of focal points and carriers of connective capacity. The main focus of this final chapter is to derive interesting insights and conclusions from the individual chapters. We use the grid of focal points and carriers to bring the different analyses, insights and conclusions together. As such, this chapter functions as a vehicle to interconnect the yet fragmented insights spread throughout the book.

This chapter is structured as follows. We start in the next paragraph with drawing crosscutting conclusions by explicitly looking at the three carriers of capacity: (1) at the level of individuals (agency), (2) at the level of instruments (approaches), and (3) at the level of institutions (arrangements). We analyze the capacity of these carriers through the discussion of the five focal points of this book, that is, interrelationships between governmental layers and levels, between sectors and domains, between time scales, between frames and perceptions, and between government and society spheres. Thus, connective capacity is generated through (a combination of) specific carriers, which we defined as agency, approaches and arrangements, and manifests itself in the integration between governmental layers and levels, between sectors and domains, between time scales, between frames and perceptions, and between government and society spheres.

We continue in the following section with more reflexive and general conclusions on how connective capacities in water governance processes can be developed and realized. In this we develop a perspective of synchronization of connective capacities in water governance processes. We argue that synchronization of connective capacity will enhance the chances that connections are being realized in complex, dynamic and compounded water governance projects and programs. In the final section, we conclude by formulating some final thoughts on connective capacity and synchronization in water governance.

Crosscutting Conclusions through the Lenses of Carriers of Connective Capacity

Diving into the Individuals (Agency)

In the realization of connective capacity, or rather the addressing and overcoming of fragmentation, individual actors such as leaders and managers play a vital role. This was confirmed by the contributions along the vertical line of individuals, or agency, in this book. In these chapters we encountered individuals such as political leaders, managers and boundary spanners, whose activities are all indications of a shared tendency in creating coordination within focal points. Although one of the basic messages of this book as a whole is that cooperation between large numbers of actors is important for reducing fragmentation, this process generally does not occur by itself. It needs explicit attention of specific people managing the interactions among actors with different perspectives, interests and values.

Leaders and leadership are required to address and stimulate cooperation processes. More specifically, what the chapters on agency argue is that a specific type of leadership is required. This leadership ought to focus on creating connectivity of people, organizations, issues and ideas. Leadership is not confined to one specific leader; rather multiple types of leaders, with their specialties and talents, are required to make a shared movement towards greater integration and coordination. This leadership can be found in different people. Scholten and Edelenbos (Chapter 2) focused on political leadership on regional (provincial) level in The Netherlands and found that a leadership style with a mixture of transformational, transactional and daring components resulted in connections across provincial boundaries and jurisdictions. Political leaders that both have clear ideas and visions about solving water issues and are willing to adjust their views to those of other actors succeed in realizing connections across government levels. A combination of entrepreneurial, visionary and adaptive management style will result in realizing meaningful cross-level connections. Scholten and Edelenbos argue that water governance practice sees many merges between these styles and provides room for each style to contribute to connective capacity.

Situational conditions and personal preferences determine the 'cocktail' of styles being implemented.

Bressers and Deelstra (Chapter 8) also stress the importance of leadership activities in water governance and found that enabling leadership in combination with a mixture of administrative and adaptive leadership will result in realizing connections between short and long term orientations within water governance processes. Some leaders have more characteristics of administrative leadership, which leads to an increased focus on short-term measures. Other leaders have more characteristics of adaptive leadership, which leads to an increased focus on long-term measures and plans. These diverging leadership styles, and the leaders who present characteristics of these styles, can be connected through leaders performing enabling leadership. The enabling leadership style mediates between short term and long-term interests and connects actors with different time orientations. Sometimes these leadership combinations are embodied in one leader, but more often it is spread among different leaders in the same project or program. Leadership then becomes part of interaction among different leaders, instead of the repertoire of a single actor. Through including a variety of leadership styles and activities the short term can be linked with the long term in water governance.

Warner (Chapter 5) found through studying the Grensmaas case in The Netherlands that leadership is a 'bricolage' of different leadership strategies (attention-seeking, linkages, relational management and arena strategies). Regarding interrelating frames and perceptions he found that rhetorical persuasion is important. Especially, through attractive framing and tailoring the message, conflicting domains and sectors like economy, environment and water safety are reconciled that facilitates support and ongoing interaction in water governance processes. However, Warner's contribution also shows that these discursive strategies only hold if people feel represented by the overarching frame. In practice, these frames often represent only a small group of actors. New appealing frames have then to be developed to address other actors as well. Framing and other connective strategies can be seen as continuous processes that change throughout the course and time of water governance processes.

Verduijn (Chapter 11) explores framing strategies further by studying the Dutch Second Delta Commission in its role as a policy entrepreneur. He concludes that, especially in the agenda setting stage of water governance processes, a strong coherent mono-dimensional frame, stressing the urgency of water safety, is important to manage perceptions and creating awareness in government and society. To support its main frame of perception, the commission [seen as an 'agent'] used strong storylines on decline (crises, threat by climate change) and control (water safety), and rhetoric that stressed appealing historical values, identity and collectiveness. But the strong story line ('working together with water') also offered opportunities and room for different actors to relate to other focal points in order to generate enough support and legitimacy for action. In this case connectivity was facilitated through the existence of this strong story, rather than the presence and inclusion of varying perspectives and frames, as was argued by Dewulf et al. (Chapter 12, see next paragraph).

Edelenbos, Van Meerkerk and Klijn (Chapter 14) developed a specific form of leadership that they coined *complexity sensitive management*, which is focused on connecting different spatial functions in the development of the project, connecting various interests and viewpoints in water governance networks, adaptivity to demands and wishes of stakeholders and creating time and space for anchoring results from governance processes to grass-roots organizations. People performing this kind of boundary spanning strategy have a greater chance to really develop legitimacy in water governance processes. Governmental, societal and private spheres are connected in a legitimate way. Water managers that embrace complexity succeed in developing trust among stakeholders from different spheres (public, private, governmental) which result in higher perceived legitimacy of processes and (see for example, Edelenbos 2010).

All contributions emphasize that connective capacity is achieved through a variety of styles, activities and strategies. There is not one best way when it comes to leadership styles. Moreover, leadership is not only performed by political leaders and public managers, but can be done by all kind of stakeholders in the water governance process. There is a variety of administrative, political and civic leaders (see also 't Hart and Uhr 2002) that form an action arena in which leadership takes shape. Leadership could involve a citizen activating other actors to be against or for a water governance project or a private entrepreneur who develops brilliant ideas that become the driving force for specific water governance innovations (see Chapter 5 by Warner). The contributions all show that leadership is characterized by multiple ownership, rather than the classical – and often 'heroic' – view that leadership belongs to one strong and decisive person. Leadership becomes a product of interactions instead of a single action of one person. Leadership in complex water governance occurs within and out of interactions and events (see also Uhl-Bien et al. 2007).

The agency of specific individuals such as boundary spanners, who have the capability to cross various boundaries and actively establish connections between them, can be of great value in these processes (for example, Williams 2002). Several contributions stress the importance of framing strategies that can play an important role in bringing different sectors together. Boundary spanners in the water sector recognize they are well advised to find strategies that target both the actors' *goals* and the *relationship* with other actors in their network. This requires both empathy (what do others want?) and acumen to locate policy opportunities (see Chapter 2 by Scholten and Edelenbos). The power of communication and persuasion features heavily in this approach. This brings the persuasive style next to the already often-stressed importance of facilitative styles of boundary spanning and network management in water governance processes (Klijn et al. 2010) and calls for combinatory styles as they are developed in the chapters of Scholten and Edelenbos (Chapter 2) and Edelenbos, Van Meerkerk and Klijn (Chapter 14).

Boundary spanning activities are not easy to do; it requires certain capacities (resources and competences) of people (Williams 2002). Moreover, it requires a specific personality, style and motivation, in which people accept and embrace high levels of dynamics and unpredictability. Leaders accept that things might happen not as planned, even see the inescapability of it and see opportunities to use these unforeseen happenings in their favor to realize connection between scales, levels, and domains in water governance.

At the same time there seem to be limits to boundary spanning. There is a thin line between spanning and blurring boundaries between the private and public sectors, which has implications for traditional ways of vertical accountability. The spanning of organizational boundaries and the development of horizontal relations in water governance networks brings tensions to existing accountability procedures in representative democracy. Water governance networks offer "…new ways of connecting public policy-making to citizens and stakeholders, overcoming the constraints and limitations of representative democracy and party politics" (Klijn and Skelcher 2007: 588). However, representative democracy provides the democratic foundation of hierarchical-instrumental policy making, which often conflicts with the horizontal processes in water governance networks (Klijn and Skelcher 2007). Leadership operating in water governance networks has to deal with this tension; they have to deal with institutions, which are based on traditional foundations of representative democracy on the one hand and the fragmented and complex reality of governance networks with all kind of actors (citizens, NGOs, companies, etcetera) on the other hand.

Diving into the Instruments (Approaches)

In this book a variety of possible instruments for creating connective capacity in water governance practices has been distinguished. These instruments ranged from serious water and climate gaming (Chapter 6 by Zhou et al.), stakeholder involvement methods and tools (Chapter 15 by Cuppen and Pardoe), transition arenas (Chapter 9 by Van Eijndhoven et al.), bridging instruments for knowledge frames (Chapter 12 by Dewulf et al.), to broader policy measures (Chapter 3 by Vinke-De Kruijf et al.). Where the individuals carrier in essence revolved around many similar individuals (leaders/managers) the instruments carrier turns out to be more diverse. Despite this diversity there is an important similarity between the discussed instruments. All approaches concern instruments to strengthen communication and multi-actor interaction in water governance processes. These can be characterized by a top-down steering approach, such as the policy interventions in Romania, but they can also have a focus on creating bottom-up debate, such as the stakeholder involvement in the UK and the serious game.

Vinke-de Kruijf, Kuks and Augustijn (Chapter 3) discuss recent regime changes in the water sector in Romania. The transition from a communist state centered towards a pluralistic and decentralized political system, part of the EU, caused fragmentation and incoherence in water governance. The creating regional associations with coherence between resources and instruments led to the evolvement of policy networks. Within these networks, cooperation structures and processes in the water services sector and the flood risk management sector could develop. In a transition country as Romania, undergoing many changes from a former communist country towards a new EU-member state, Vinke-De Kruijf, Kuks and Augustijn argue that bottom-up processes alone cannot overcome fragmentation, and that top-down interventions are also required to create coherence between governmental levels.

Zhou, Bekebrede, Mayer, Warmerdam and Knepflé (Chapter 6) stress that new gaming techniques (serious water gaming) can be used as a socio-technical interface to assist in developing a reflexive environment for decision-making. The usage of serious gaming in cross-sector issues, such as climate change and its effects on water management and spatial planning, is fruitful for overcoming possible cross-sector tensions. In this virtual environment, different stakeholders from water management and spatial planning sectors learn that they are mutually dependent in realizing their goals. The relatively informal interaction created in the game leads to increased awareness of each other's positions, interests and possibilities. Moreover, they become aware and gain a better understanding and experience of the need for skills required for cross-sector cooperation.

Van Eijndhoven, Frantzeskaki and Loorbach (Chapter 9) analyze the instrument of envisioning in transition arenas from the transition management approach. The arena functions as a temporary informal network in which change agents identify and reframe persistent water problems, develop a long term vision and a shared agenda for moving in the direction of this vision. Interactions in this transition arena lead to reframing of the fragmented problem perceptions and joint visions and future solutions and measures in water governance processes. Transition arenas can be useful instruments for engaging actors in interaction and connecting different time scales and orientations of different actors through this interaction.

Addressing the complex and varied challenges for water and climate policy requires contributions from a wide range of often-disconnected knowledge frames and networks, argue Dewulf, Brugnach, Termeer and Ingram (Chapter 12). When frame differences remain unrecognized or unaddressed in these processes, dialogues of the deaf, intractable controversies and stagnations are likely to occur. Dewulf et al. stress the need for bridging knowledge frames and networks in order to realize coherence in the debate on climate adaptation and water governance. Connecting different ways of knowing requires intertwining of contents (knowledge frames) and relations (knowledge networks). These bridging knowledge frames and networks need three interplaying assets: (1) a process through which actors can develop boundary experiences; (2) a temporary organization structure that functions as a place for regular meetings, and (3) a joint content (boundary object) that provides a shared point of reference. These three assets together can be seen as boundary 'configurations' that form an interrelating and recurring cycle that enhances the development of connective capacity. These boundary configurations are contingent, that is, they are formed to the specific situational nature of the climate and water issue. Each issue needs a specific configuration of boundary organization (structure), boundary object (substance) and boundary experience (process, relational capacity) to really establish knowledge frames and networks.

Cuppen and Pardoe (Chapter 15) analyze the Oxford Flood Risk Management Strategy in the UK and stress the importance of the development of stakeholder platforms in enhancing legitimacy of water governance processes. These platforms focus on regular informal meetings with stakeholders and site visits that gave stakeholders the feeling that they were treated and taken seriously. This connective management approach enhanced the legitimacy of the flood risk management strategy. Through connectivity between governmental and societal spheres, a more positive approach of participants in stakeholder involvement processes towards water decisions can be created. Especially openness and interestedness towards the participants helps here, together with access to information and an honest and open approach about the process' limitations. This stakeholder involvement leads to more legitimate outcomes and results.

All contributions discussing the carrier of instruments, stress the role and place of learning processes regarding the development of connections between actors, ideas, plans and so on. They all stress, in different ways and by different forms, the meaning of informal spaces of interaction. These spaces stimulate cooperation, bring heterogeneous actors closer together, and develop processes in which these parties learn about each other's standpoints and build a shared storyline.

However, these informal spaces are also very fragile. Van Eijndhoven et al. indicate that these spaces (transition arenas) also bear the risk of becoming disconnected with their environment. Short term and long term can be connected in intermediate steps, definable in arenas by those who are open to them and able to think outside the realm of solely short term or solely long term. However, when these freethinkers become lone frontrunners, disconnected from their own organization, support base or working environment, the connection between short term and long term is still not made for the issue as a whole in formal decision-making processes and procedures. This increased interaction likewise has to be consolidated in real implementation projects afterwards. The time connections reached in transitions must not solely exist between participants (for example, arena members or leaders of a program) but also between these representatives and their wider background. Leaders can perform this task by consulting with their organization on various intra-organizational levels. Transition arena members can do this by communicating with their organizations but also with the organizations they see as targets for realizing future change. Cuppen and Pardoe also stress this fragility as they discuss that the effect of connectivity reached in a stakeholder platform is only limited to those involved in that platform. It does not automatically spread to the wider community. These are the drawbacks of selective activation and participation in platforms, transition arenas and serious gaming. This can lead to lost connections regarding public, private and societal spheres (Cuppen and Pardoe), short-term, mid-term and long-term orientations (Van Eijndhoven et al.) or sectors and domains (Zhou et al). In order to last and become embedded, connections need to be constantly reassessed and reconsidered at all times in water governance processes.

Diving into the Institutions (Arrangements)

Water governance processes do not take place in an institutional vacuum. The previous section has indicated the importance of institutional embedding and democratic anchorage of these processes. Regarding the connective carrier of institutions, the different contributions present a picture of diversity of insights.

Keskitalo, Juhola and Westerhoff (Chapter 4) argued that situational and country-specific institutional conditions are highly important for the creation of cross-level climate adaptation policies. Through studying climate adaptation policies in the UK, Finland, Sweden and Italy, they found to what extent the governmental structures of different countries influence the development of adaptation policy. The national political systems of the countries constitute the context for how the different government levels are related to one another and whether they reinforce each other or not. Climate policies can get isolated in many ways as a result of poor multi-level connections. These policies can get 'lost in translation' as they originate from the local government but are not facilitated by national policies, or as they are formed on national governmental level, but are not followed up and implemented on local governmental level. Keskitalo et al. draw an important conclusion that vertical linkages between scales and governmental levels do not merely happen in a top down fashion in the way government steering is regularly conducted, but that sub-national actors can also influence the policy process on higher levels of governance from the bottom up. They underline not only the importance of formal institutional structure of national governmental systems, but also of informal rules and administrative practices that may differ between states and impact how and on what levels certain issues are handled. Hence, a well-functioning multi-level governance institutional system and process will enhance development and diffusion of adaptation policies.

The interplay of agency and structure is also stressed in the contribution of Bettini, Rijke, Farrelly and Brown (Chapter 7). They focused on the Australian water scarcity issue and argue that the combination of formal rules and regulations and the informal 'rules-in-use' create an institutional setting which forms the architecture for the governance of water. They stress the importance of flexible institutional settings for solving water issues. This facilitates the interconnectivity between town planning and water supply provision that originates in informal interaction settings and is built through repeated interaction over time in which informal rules between actors are shaped. Water governance is only transformed if collective reflection of existing formal rules and consensual development and acceptance of new rules take place that will break down walls between sectors and build up new relationships. Informal network formation is identified as an important element in overcoming institutional fragmentation between sectors and levels. However, these networks need to be powerful and persuasive enough to change formal institutional settings and to diffuse new ideas and policies. These informal networks need subsequently to be followed up by formal spaces in order to consolidate. In this way the importance of boundary spanning to formal spaces is also stressed, as already dealt with in this concluding chapter.

Van Leeuwen and Van Buuren (Chapter 10) studied the role of the Steering Group in the Southwestern delta of The Netherlands as an institutional arrangement in realizing connections between short and long time orientations. This delta consists of many different local and regional projects with their own narrow boundaries and time horizons. The short-term developments in these projects sometimes conflict with the long-term ambitions. In order to realize the long-term ambitions one has to transcend the project boundaries. The steering group succeeded in bringing people from different projects together and developed an appealing and convincing frame (within the context of the so-called "implementation strategy") in which various developments and investments are meaningfully connected to each other as part of a transition path towards a sustainable future. The institutional arrangement of the steering committee functions because this arrangement is vertically and horizontally inclusive as it unites relevant authorities and project organizations from the various governance scales and levels as well as from the various functional domains (water safety, ecology, etcetera). The program manager of the steering group showed sensitivity to the complexity and compounded nature of the water issue and always looked to find ways to look beyond single organizational boundaries and to span actors' frames to incorporate the broader picture and connect levels, domains and time orientations.

Diverging frames often relate to differing values. Van Ast, Bouma and Bal (Chapter 13) stressed the importance of the institutional background by discussing value systems about water in a comparative case study between The Netherlands and India. Values can have roots in centuries old histories, providing a significant degree of meaning to water related decisions. The discussion on values of water relates to other focal points of this book as well. For example, values concern both the physical system of water as well as the social system, leading to crossovers between sectors and domains and potentially also layers and levels and government and society. Here we see the importance of frames as a connector, as also stressed by the contributions of Dewulf et al., Warner, and Verduijn.

De Boer and Krantzberg (Chapter 16) dealt with inter-regime cooperation between Canada and the United States and started with a similar view as Van Leeuwen en Van Buuren by looking at specific institutional arrangements. De Boer and Krantzberg looked at various arrangements, but highlighted the International Joint Commission (IJC) in its work on realizing transboundary cooperation between countries regarding the Great Lakes. The difficulties in bi-national cooperation and government-society integration are shown by De Boer and Krantzberg. They demonstrate that the inter-regime between Canada and the United States failed to develop transboundary cooperation and to include local stakeholders. However, arrangements such as the IJC did not have enough resources (responsibility, jurisdiction) and skills (network management, boundary spanning competences) to establish the likelihood of more open communication across different sectors and spheres. This led local stakeholders to develop their own initiatives, separate of the formal structures. The neutral inter-regime party could play a vital role in mediating between these interest groups, as the local stakeholders also differ on issues. Despite the involvement of local stakeholders, the lack of connectivity between them and the lack of connectivity realized through the inter-regime, led to increasing fragmentation. Despite sharing a physical environment, the USA and Canada were not able to create a truly shared inter-regime body to guard this physical environment.

Fragmentation and Connectivity in Water Governance

Fragmentation in Water Governance is Here to Stay

In the introduction we already argued that water governance projects are characterized by fragmentation, due to the process of specialization not only within the field of water (water quality such as freshwater waste water, water quantity such as droughts and water safety), but also in relation to other fields and sectors like spatial planning, nature development, water services, economic development, ecology, etcetera. Water governance projects have a complex and compounded nature, meaning that these projects are inherently and highly interconnected with other fields and sectors. For example fresh water touches upon the issue of agriculture and economic and social development.

In the previous section we have discussed the capacities of three different carriers of connective capacity in water governance processes. As various contributions in this book show, water professionals started to consider interdependencies and dynamics of both nature and ecosystems and develop capacities to connect different time lines, sectors, scales, etcetera. However, we can also distract from the contributions that fragmentation is a persistent problem in water governance. Despite the efforts of scholars practicing different water paradigms, the issues that prevail for water governance (for example, institutional fragmentation, lack of coordination) remain unresolved due to: (a) the rigidity of existing paradigms within communities of practices and the relative closed nature of water-expert communities in relation to other policy domains, and (b) due to the increasing interconnectivity of water problems (droughts, quality of water, water safety) relating to climate change on the one hand and spatial planning functions (agriculture, urban development, etcetera.) on the other hand. In order words, water governance is under constant pressure of fragmenting forces. Cuppen and Pardoe, for example, show with their Oxford Flood Management case that even when the Environment Agency's puts in effort to connect with engaged local stakeholders (the Oxford Flood Alliance) this at the same time means that other citizens or the wider public are not actively involved. Each boundary judgment to involve certain actors means at the same time that other people are selected out of the water governance process. Trustworthy relationships are built for some in these government-citizen interactions, but lose ground for people that are not in the participation process. Regarding the legitimacy of water governance processes, this raises a new question on how attitudes of non-participants can be positively influenced and taken into account in policy development. Warner arrives at the same insight as he indicates for the Grensmaas project in The Netherlands that the formation of the project consortium, which involved private parties (gravel excavators and construction companies), public agencies (regional and national) and civil–society organizations (environmental groups), led to an alienation of citizens which resulted in a counter attack by this group of stakeholders.

De Boer and Krantzberg show by studying the transboundary cooperation efforts between Canada and the United States regarding the Great Lakes that an institutional arrangement as the International Joint Commission leads to even further institutional fragmentation as this commission is not perceived as truly non-partisan with no real authority and communicative power. As a result stakeholders develop their own go-alone strategies leading to more diversity, more complexity and more conflict.

Van Eijndhoven et al. argue in their chapter that transition arenas are capable to connect sectors and time lines in their safe spaces beyond formal institutions and procedures, but have the risk of losing legitimacy and meaning to those that are not in the transition arena. The selective participation on personal basis and not as delegates or representatives of their institutions leads to fragmentation in decision-making and implementation phases once the transition arenas cease to exist. Van Eijndhoven et al. call this the paradox of connectivity: by connecting interest and actors from spatial planning and the water domain, the urban innovation projects that are realized through communication and negotiation in the transition arena are the frontrunners that sometimes remain disconnected from the urban practice. As a result, the concept of urban water dissolves.

From these insights and examples we can conclude that fragmentation is and will be an inevitable characteristic of water governance. Because water governance is complex and compounded of nature, each boundary judgment for developing, activating and realizing a connection through agency, approach or arrangement will lead to new fragmentation on a different level, time orientation, frame, domain or sphere. The contributions in this book demonstrated that water governance processes are interconnected with processes of economic and social development in a variety of ways. Water governance processes are simultaneously taking place on multiple levels of local action, regional development, national policy making and global rulemaking. Fragmentation is a persistent side-product of complexity and society's tendency toward specialization. Therefore, fragmentation has to be viewed as 'a fact of life' in water governance, a persistent phenomenon that cannot be solved once and for all, by any single connective capacity or combination of capacities.

However, this does not mean that we have to come to terms with fragmentation. There are many negative effects of fragmentation, such as conflicting policies, non-cooperation between parties, deadlocks in governance processes and illegitimate, ineffective and splintered water policies that are poorly embedded in wider environmental, infrastructural, ecological and urban policy developments. Fragmentation is therefore something to work on, even within the awareness that absolute reduction or the creating of tailor-made solutions is impossible. Even if there are no stable, fixed and clear-cut answers, this volume has taught us that connective capacity can give temporary alleviation of fragmentation problems.

Insights from the Chapters on Connective Capacity

Some contributions stressed that certain leadership styles can result in interconnectivity. The contributions by Scholten and Edelenbos (Chapter 2), Bressers and Deelstra (Chapter 8) and Edelenbos, Van Meerkerk and Klijn (Chapter 14) regarding agency and leadership have shown us that leadership styles that accept complexity and uncertainty in water governance processes, that is, a complexity embracing style of water management, will lead to more connectivity towards levels, sectors, time lines and public, private and societal spheres. However, Warner (Chapter 5) makes an important note that boundary spanners and complexity leaders are not only adept at breaking down boundaries, but they are also adept at enforcing boundaries to protect themselves from too much complexity and dynamics. Boundary spanning can be understood as a continuous process of connecting and disconnecting and of bridging and buffering (Meznar and Nigh 1995).

In this concluding chapter we do not want to suggest that realizing connections is the ultimate goal in water governance. There are limits to organizing connections; they depend on time and energy. Moreover, due to bounded rationality it is impossible to organize and handle all connections at the same time. Furthermore, connections often mean that explorative communication takes place which can go at the expense of progress, reaching (intermediary) results (exploitation) and going more in-depth in certain single issues. Connections often depend on individuals such as leaders and therefore inevitably face cognitive and social constraints. We have already indicated at the beginning of this section that a connection at one level often means a disconnection at another level. A redefinition of boundaries will not make boundaries disappear, but will create a new fragmentation. Schlager and Blomquist (2000: 15-16) argue that boundaries are multiple, overlapping and often contested. Coordination and integration means drawing new boundaries and creating new contestations over who is in charge or what has to be integrated or coordinated.

However, we found empirical proof that addressing fragmentation by classical measures alone, such as developing integrated policy, more unity in organizational structures and more powerful and decisive decision-making and implementation, will not lead to coherence and interconnectivity but will often cause new fragmentation and disconnection. For example, strong and decisive leadership is often stressed in literature originating from a classical and everlasting desire of 'getting renewed control over' and 'being in charge again' (Teisman and Edelenbos 2011). Many of these measures are rather simplistic answers, desires and reactions to existing and still growing plurality and complexity in water governance practices due to globalization, individualization and the forming of a network society. The strive for simple answers by one organization, person, procedure or policy that has to counter fragmentation and bring all splintered and fragmented pieces together in one puzzle is understandable, but turns out to be insufficient. This one puzzle, seen as the one best solution, does not exist in a plural and complex water governance system. Ideas of a single and simple structure or mechanism are based on the desire of stability and order. We argue that complex water governance practices can only be countered by complex, dynamic and situational responses that change and adapt continuously. Each of the governors and public managers can claim control and centrality, but in practice they will not be able to shirk from the complexity and dynamics in water governance. The features of complexity and dynamics imply a continuous coordination and integration effort for which no simple, stable and ever-lasting fix suffices.

A Synchronization Perspective on Connectivity Capacity

The most important conclusion from our volume is that the development and enhancement of connective capacity in water governance need continuous and dynamic processes of coupling and re-coupling. This insight corresponds with the perspective of synchronization that already has been explored in the field of water governance by Edelenbos and Teisman (2011). This view on connective capacity enhances the chances and opportunities of coherence and interconnectivity in water governance.

Synchronization can be understood as the occurrence of confluent circumstances, of two or more meaningful converging events or activities (see Jung 1950, 1989, Jaworksi 1998). Based on the insights that are provided in the chapters in this book, we can further deepen this perspective of synchronization on connective capacity in water governance.

The synchronization perspective corresponds strongly with the notion that agency and leadership is not devoted to one person or organization. Contrary to the classical view on leadership (for example, Bryson and Crosby 1992), in which one person or organization is in control and in charge and is held sole responsible for connecting different sectors, scales and time frames to one another, we emphasize from our study that leadership is a result of a complex interaction and coordination process among many people with different leadership styles and competences (for example, Uhl-Bien et al. 2007, Teisman et al. 2009). Edelenbos, Van Meerkerk and Klijn (Chapter 14) found that a complexity sensitive and embracing style in which people are constantly looking for interlinking actors, agendas and ambitions has better chances to reach legitimized outcomes from water governance processes. Also Bressers and Deelstra (Chapter 8) stress that the intermingling of different management styles of various managing actors will enhance interconnections between short and long-term orientations in water governance. And finally, Scholten and Edelenbos (Chapter 2) argued that interconnections are best developed through a leadership effort that combines both a focus on the process dynamics of decision-making and a focus on the specific content of the proposal, whereby the content can be shaped through continuous processes of mutual adjustment of the different parties on different levels.

Synchronization would also imply that one institutional structure in capturing coherence and interconnectivity is not sufficient, and therefore institutional diversity (Ostrom 2005, Sabatier 1986) is needed in which boundaries constantly change and new meaningful interconnections between boundaries have to be developed (Williams 2002). These insights have been found, for instance, in the contribution of Bettini, Rijke, Farrelly and Brown (Chapter 7), in which they stress that a constant interplay between rules in use (agency) and formal rules (institutional setting) has to be realized in order to facilitate sector and level connectivity. Van Leeuwen en Van Buuren (Chapter 10) argue in similar vein, the continuous interaction between institutional arrangements and agency via program management activities in order to connect short, middle and long-term orientations in water governance. Therefore we would argue that from a synchronization perspective, integration, coherence and interconnectivity are no longer primarily based on redefining boundaries from a fragmented system towards a more compounded end state system. It is much more about the art of constantly defining and redefining boundaries and continuously crossing these (new defined) boundaries (for example, Adger et al. 2005, Teisman and Edelenbos 2011). Synchronization implies a continuous interplay between on the one hand *exploiting* (employ) developed and defined institutional structures, arrangements and settings in order reach meaningful outcomes in water governance networks, and on the other hand *exploring* (investigate) and redefining these structures and settings once they are not perceived as functional and legitimate anymore.

Bettini et al. (Chapter 7) also stress in their contribution that exploration of new institutional settings take place in informal settings and free spaces. The importance of these spaces is also stressed in the contributions of Van Eijndhoven et al. (transition arenas), Zhou et al. (serious gaming) and Cuppen and Pardoe (stakeholder platforms). In these informal spaces new ways of working and thinking are explored and developed. This stresses the element of self-organization in water governance. Literature from public administration (for example, Teisman et al. 2009), policy sciences (for example, Rhodes 1997) and adaptive water management (for example, Ostrom 2005) argues that self-steering and self-organization are crucial for effective processes of integration, coherence and connectivity. The concept of self-organization captures processes that evolve out of events, actions and interactions and form an institutional structure. In self-organization processes, people, whatever position they have in the system, adjust to demands or changing circumstances (Cilliers 1998, Heylighen 2002). Self-organization is guided by the reflexive capacity of actors that are able to receive, encode, transform and store information and use this to (re)consider their actions (Teisman et al. 2009: 9). This reflexivity is created in free spaces that are shaped and processed beyond and between formal organizational structures. The receptivity of participants in these networks undergoes a set of iterative phases (awareness, association, alignment, acquisition, application) towards an organizational form in which they influence each other and strengthen each other, through their own specific qualities (Bressers 2011, Jeffrey and Seaton 2004).

Thus, a synchronization perspective considers the creation of reflexive spaces that are developed bottom up and that go beyond formal existing structures. These spaces are of great importance in developing capacity to respond adequately to the complex and dynamic nature of water governance processes.

This brings us at another important aspect in a synchronization view on connective capacity in water governance: boundlessness. Synchronicity starts from the assumption that (water) governance systems are not clearly organized, not stable and above all not clearly demarcated. There is no ideal scale and boundary for who and what should be involved to address wicked and complex water problems (Adger et al. 2005). Where organizational integration opts for an ideal scale and (organizational) structure, synchronicity accepts the empirical observation of the multi-level structure of complex processes and issues (Young 2002). This point is also stressed in the contribution of Keskitalo, Juhola and Westerhoff (Chapter 4). They argue that climate adaptation and water governance are shaped in interplay between the local, regional and (trans)national level. They found that interaction does not merely happen in a top down fashion, but that sub-national actors can also be influential on higher levels of governance from the bottom up. The national institutional system determines how different governance levels are related and whether they reinforce each other. Adaptation policies are the result of multi-level governance processes, which take shape differently in various settings, as Keskitalo et al. (Chapter 4) found in studying countries as Finland, United Kingdom, Italy and Sweden. Vinke-de Kruijf et al. (Chapter 3) also stress the importance of multi-level interaction, and they point out in studying transitions in the water services sector and flood risk management sector of Romania that combinations of top-down interventions by national government and European Union and bottom-up initiatives from local and regional governments are needed to realize robust changes and coherence in these two sectors. Top-down intervention can even help bottom-up initiatives, as national authorities encouraged local authorities (owners of infrastructure) to organize themselves at regional level and to delegate their water services to a certified regional operator (service providers).

In the debate about water management many authors stress the importance of cross-scale and multi-level interactions (Young 2002, Adger et al. 2005, Olsson et al. 2007). A synchronization view focuses on how to interrelate actions, events and processes in surrounding subsystems. It is about developing an institutional rich environment (Imperial 1999), in which roles and actions overlap. Patchworks of multi-level structures and processes are formed that are up to the necessary tasks and challenges (Ostrom 2005).

A synchronization view on connective capacity in water governance does not opt for a 'strong' or unitary organizational structure to shape this multi-level interaction. On the contrary, one looks for diverse and loose couplings between organizations on different levels and at different scales. These couplings are featured by flexible organizational structures, informal interaction processes and bonding substance. We can find this exact argument in the contribution of Dewulf et al. (Chapter 12). In their study of the climate debate they argue that a development of connecting networks and connecting frames is crucial in order to prevent dialogues of the deaf. Also Verduijn (Chapter 11) stresses the importance of discursive strategies to create a meaningful dialogue in water governance. The result of the study of Dewulf et al. (Chapter 12) is that connective networks and frames are realized when boundary organization (structure), boundary object (substance) and boundary experiences (process, relations) come together in a boundary configuration. From these findings we can conclude that connectivity therefore emerges from a process of synchronization in which actors with mutually accepted substance are working together in temporary coalitions and exchange information, knowledge and experiences and are in this way able to synchronize a variety of actions on a certain place and time without being part of one fixed hierarchical structure.

The concept 'loose coupling' (Jung 1950, Jaworski 1996) explicates the ability to form coalitions of stakeholders across boundaries in temporary institutional settings with reflexive attitudes and extensive and redundant interaction and communication processes among various actors. Connectivity appears to emerge more easily on and beyond the boundaries of subsystems than in the core of one of the constituting subsystems, and can be achieved at the borders of existing subsystems rather than at their core (Teisman and Edelenbos 2011). This is in line with the literature on boundary spanning (c.f. Williams 2002), also discussed in several chapters of this book, for instance Warner (Chapter 5), and Edelenbos, Van Meerkerk and Klijn (Chapter 14). However, boundary spanning is more than just interrelating actors, agendas and ambitions in informal spaces and temporary institutional arrangements. It is also about developing and implementing connections outside these new boundaries towards existing formal power structures and decision-making procedures as it is also stressed by Scholten and Edelenbos (Chapter 2). Difficulties in formalizing this support we saw in the chapter by De Boer and Krantzberg (Chapter 16), Bettini et al. (Chapter 7) and Cuppen and Pardoe (Chapter 15) demonstrated how, despite support of participating stakeholders, this did not automatically spread to non-involved stakeholders outside the informal spaces. Connectivity *across* networks is related to the integration *within* a network or single organization (Tushman and Scalan 1978). A strong or good functioning connectivity across networks can be hampered with a poor connectivity within a single organization. Tushman and Scanlan (1978) denominate boundary spanning as "a two part process" that is composed of obtaining information from outside units and disseminating this information to internal users. It is about continuously thinking and acting 'inside-out' as well as 'outside-in', and to constantly reassess the connections made from these two viewpoints.

To Conclude: Stay Reflexive and Adaptive in Water Governance

In this chapter we have brought all insights from the different contributing chapters together. In discussing the contributions we found that a new perspective on integration and connectivity in water governance was needed in order to fully grasp and give full meaning to the results and insights coming from the individual chapters. From the various contributions to this book we found that fragmentation is a persistent phenomenon in water governance (as in other domains), that cannot be solved and ruled out once and for all. Fragmentation also has a function in the sense that specialization and therefore deeper (and specialized) understanding of specific aspects can be reached. The consequence, however, is that coherence and interconnectivity is lost in water governance. Connective capacity in water governance is needed to really face the complex, compounded and dynamic character of water governance processes. However, connectivity is as much part of the problem as it is the solution, as breaking down boundaries at the same time means creating new boundaries that again can hamper connective capacity in water governance.

Connective capacity in water governance is thus about being aware of the problems with existing boundaries in water governance, but at the same time remaining reflexive for its potentials and opportunities, but more importantly also the pitfalls of these spanning activities and structures. This means water governance has to stay adaptive at all times and in every circumstance. It requires people, organizations and institutions that are willing and capable in adapting and not resisting to complexity. Exactly this is led us to propose a new perspective on connective capacity in water governance processes: to develop the capacity to constantly (re)assess the values and problems of connections, and then reconsider the connections, and change these again to new insights, new situations and new developments.

Connective capacity is not the result of a deliberate and planned action by one individual or organization, but the result of interplay among different actors that leads to often unplanned and coincidental interconnection and coherence. Plural, complex and dynamic water governance processes ask for a synchronization view in which coherence arises spontaneously during the process. The complex nature of water governance systems needs to be faced by complex connective capacity attempts over and over again.

Bibliography

Adger W.N., Brown, K. and Tompkins, E.L. 2005. The political economy of cross-scale networks in resource co-management. *Ecology and Society*, 10(2), 9 [online]. URL: http://www.ecologyandsociety.org/vol10/iss2/art9/.

Bressers, N. 2011, *Co-Creating Innovation: A Systemic Learning Evaluation of Knowledge and Innovation Programmes*. PhD Thesis, Rotterdam: Erasmus University Rotterdam.

Bryson, J. and Crosby, B. 1992. *Leadership for the Common Good: Tackling Public Problems in a Shared-power World*. San Francisco, CA: Jossey-Bass.

Edelenbos, J. 2010. *Water as Connective Current/water als spanningsvolle verbinding*, inaugurele rede. Den Haag: Boom/Lemma.

Hart, P 't and Uhr, J. 2002, *Public Leadership: Perspectives and Practices*. Canberra: ANU E Press.

Heylighen, F. 2002. *The Science of Self-organization and Adaptivity*. Available at: http://www.eolss.net.

Imperial, M.T. 1999. Analyzing institutional arrangements for ecosystem-based management: Lessons from the Rhode Island Salt Ponds SAM Plan. *Coastal Management*, 27(31), 31-56.

Jaworski, J. 1996. *Synchronicity: The Inner Path of Leadership*. San Francisco, CA: Berrett-Koehler Publishers.

Jeffrey, P. and Seaton, R.A.F. 2004. A Conceptual Model of 'Receptivity' Applied to the Design and Deployment of Water Policy Mechanisms', *Journal of Integrative Environmental Sciences*, 1(3), 277-300.

Jung, C.G. 1989. *Synchroniciteit*. Rotterdam: Uitgeverij Lemniscaat.

Klijn, E.H., Steijn, B. and Edelenbos, J. 2010. The Impact of Network Management on Outcomes in Governance Networks, *Public Administration*, 88(4), 1063-82.

Klijn, E-H. and Skelcher, C. 2007, Democracy and Network Governance: Compatible or Not? Four Conjectures and their Implications, *Public Administration*, 85(3), 587-608.

Mesnar, M.B. and Nigh, D. 1995. Buffer or Bridge? Environmental and Organizational Determinants of Public Activities in American Firms, *The Academy of Management Journal*, 38(4), 975-96.

Olsson, P., Folke, C., Galaz, V., Hahn, T. and Schultz, L. 2007. Enhancing the fit through adaptive co-management: Creating and maintaining bridging functions for matching scales in the Kristianstads Vattenrike Biosphere Reserve, Sweden. *Ecology and Society*, 12(1), URL: http://www.ecologyandsociety.org/vol12/iss1/art28/.

Ostrom, E. 2005. *Understanding Institutional Diversity*. Princeton, NJ: Princeton University Press.

Rhodes, R.A.W. 1997. *Understanding Government*. Buckingham and Philadelphia: Open University Press.

Sabatier, P.A. 1986. Top-down and bottom-up approaches to implementation research: A critical analysis and suggested synthesis. *Journal of Public Policy*, 6, 21-48.

Schlager, E. and Blomquist, W. 2000. Local communities, policy prescriptions, and watershed management in Arizona, and Colorado, in *Constituting the Commons: Crafting Sustainable Commons in the New Millennium*. Eighth Conference of the International Association for the Study of Common Property, 31 May-4 June, Bloomington, IN.

Teisman, G.R. and Edelenbos, J. 2011. Towards a perspective of system synchronization in water governance: A synthesis of empirical lessons and complexity theories, *International Review of Administrative Sciences*, 77(1), 101-18.

Teisman, G.R., Van Buuren, A. and Gerrits, L. (eds). 2009. *Managing Complex Governance Systems*. New York: Routledge.

Tushman, M.L. and Scanlan, T.J. 1981. Boundary spanning individuals: Their role in information transfer and their antecedents. *Academy of Management Journal*, 24(2), 289-305.

Uhl-Bien, M., Marion, R. and McKelvey, B. 2007. Complexity leadership theory: Shifting leadership from the industrial age to the knowledge era. *Leadership Quarterly*, 18(4), 298-318.

Williams, P. 2002. The competent boundary spanner. *Public Administration*, 80(1), 103-24.

Young, O.R. 2002. *The Institutional Dimensions of Environmental Change: Fit Interplay and Scale*. Cambridge, MA: MIT Press.

Index